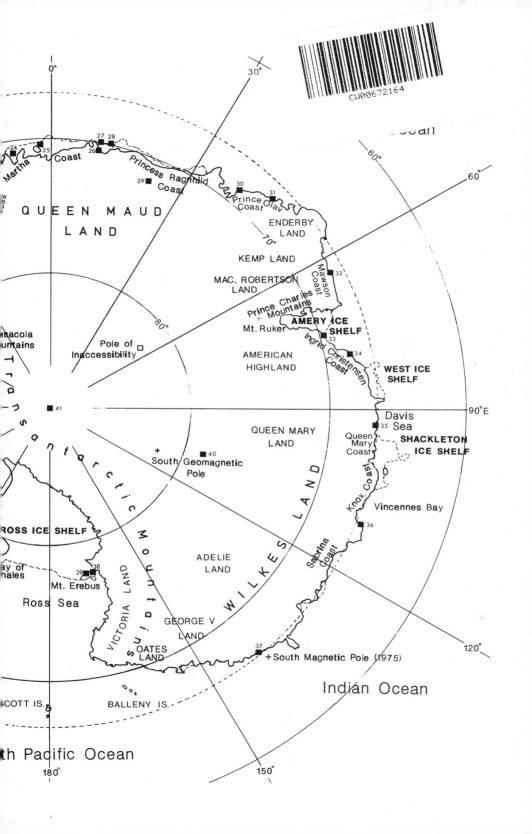

The Polar Regions

Polar Research Series

edited by Bernard Stonehouse

The Polar Regions

A Political Geography

Sanjay Chaturvedi

Scott Polar Research Institute,
University of Cambridge, UK

Published in association with the

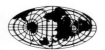

Scott Polar Research Institute
University of Cambridge

by

JOHN WILEY & SONS
Chichester · New York · Brisbane · Toronto · Singapore

Published in 1996 by John Wiley & Sons Ltd,
                      Baffins Lane, Chichester,
                      West Sussex PO19 1UD, England

                      National   01243 779777
                      International (+44) 1243 779777

Other Wiley Editorial Offices

John Wiley & Sons, Inc., 605 Third Avenue,
New York, NY 10158-0012, USA

Jacaranda Wiley Ltd, 33 Part Road, Milton,
Queensland 4064, Australia

John Wiley & Sons (Canada) Ltd, 22 Worcester Road,
Rexdale, Ontario M9W 1L1, Canada

John Wiley & Sons (SEA) Pte Ltd, 2 Clementi Loop #02–01,
Jin Xing Distripark, Singapore 0512

Library of Congress Cataloging-in-Publication Data

Chaturvedi, Sanjay.
    The polar regions : a political geography / Sanjay Chaturvedi.
       p.   cm. — (Polar research series)
    Includes bibliographical references and index.
    ISBN 0-471-94898-5
    1. Polar regions.   I. Title.   II. Series.
    G587.C48   1996
    919.8—dc20   95–44829
                                                          CIP

British Library Cataloguing in Publication Data

A catalogue record for this book is available from the British Library

ISBN 0-471-94898-5

Typeset in 10/12pt Times from author's disk by Dorwyn Ltd, Rowlands Castle, Hants
Printed and bound in Great Britain by Biddles Ltd, Guildford and King's Lynn

This book is printed on acid-free paper responsibly manufactured from sustainable
forestation, for which at least two trees are planted for each one used for paper production.

To my parents

Contents

List of figures

Preface

Global importance of polar regions

According to conventional wisdom, the Arctic and the Antarctic are "poles apart" because of their relative physical isolation, harsh natural attributes and apparent separation from both the wider international community and each other. However, the past decade has witnessed a dramatic transformation in the amount of attention focused upon the polar regions, especially in the policy priority accorded to environmental protection. It becomes increasingly evident that polar regions play a vital role in shaping climate and influencing the global environment. Early signs of change that could be of vital global significance may be detected in these unique natural laboratories. A vivid example is the discovery of the ozone hole in the stratosphere over Antarctica. Another example is the Arctic haze phenomenon, which has also been linked to anthropogenic sources of pollution. Thus, in the 21st century, Arctic and Antarctic research will be valued for both its intrinsic polar merits and its contribution to an understanding of global problems.

This book proposes that the "poles apart", *sui generis* theme is outdated and should not be allowed to obscure either the manner in which the polar scene today both reflects and influences international relations in general or the fact that existing polar controversies are merely Arctic and Antarctic manifestations of the linkages as well as contradictions between economic growth and the imperatives of environmental conservation, sometimes so casually covered under the term "sustainable development". It studies the two polar regions together, as "social science laboratories", testing some of the assumptions of the new geopolitics and evaluating its promise and prospects there.

The new geopolitics

Throughout the first three-quarters of the present century, there was general acceptance of the proposition that confrontation was endemic in an essentially Darwinist international situation. Geopolitical thinking and theorizing of this period often manifested tendencies to separate space and substance and to speak of the effects of the use of space as existing independently of objects. What it so obviously ignored was the elements – the people, materials, resources and even history – which make up territorial units. In this power-politics-driven and excessively state-centred geopolitical discourse, and the policy-making influenced by it, territory and territorial control always necessarily implied more power and capability.

After World War II, when geopolitics seemed to be frozen into the Cold War psychosis, new thinking began to move geopolitics in a somewhat more idealistic direction. The result has been a radical change in the nature and purpose of geopolitics from concern with the power of the state to a more positive concern for peace and a more equitable and sustainable management of the space and natural resources of the planet; that is, there has been a move towards eco-geopolitics. The new geopolitics reclaims the tradition of geopolitics from the strategic community and military planners and challenges the imperialist legacy of political geography. The humanist proposition on which it rests is that ideologies, organizations and systems must never be regarded as autonomous and independent of human beings themselves. The arrogance of having conquered nature should also be tempered now by an acknowledgement of the finite capacity of the natural environment to endure and assimilate human-induced changes.

A central aim of the new thinking in geopolitics, to which this book fully subscribes, is thus to address the question of securing a peaceful, socially just and environmentally sustainable order at local, regional and global levels through patient negotiations and consensus, rather than by domination or use of force. The thrust of eco-geopolitics is peace, since it replaces the obsession with national security with the concept of comprehensive civil security and stresses that in the long run an *ecologically sustainable* and *equitable* development and management of space and resources, rather than their acquisition and physical control, hold the key to national power and comprehensive universal security. Peace then becomes not absolute in the sense of a mere absence of war or a complete non-existence of conflict attendant upon incompatible interests or the prevalence of perfect celestial harmony. Instead, peace is taken to be relative – a condition signified by the achievement of positive results in the domain of conflict anticipation, conflict management and conflict resolution.

Traditionally, security has been defined in an extremely narrow sense of security from "others", and the defence of the state has been viewed as the first responsibility of governments. Territorial control, then, becomes one of the methods of achieving security both at home and abroad. Taking illustrations from both polar regions, this book argues that this is a negative view of security and, that if the concept of security is broadened to include non-military, especially ecological, issues, the narrowness of vision and the intellectual and practical limitations of geostrategic analysis can easily be identified.

The polar regions and the new polar order(s)

The Antarctic Treaty was first negotiated at a time when a series of treaties had already agreed not to do things that nobody wanted to do anyway or not to do things that still could not be done technically. The Antarctic Treaty had elements of both premises because of the nature of the place and the diversity of national interests involved. Therefore, the attempt to use this treaty as a pioneering move towards disarmament, by banning nuclear weapons from the continent, was regarded by the major powers as costing them little. But, whatever the motivation, the precedent was important as an early experiment in new geopolitics during the Cold War.

Over the last two decades, however, the nature of debate about the Antarctic has changed in fundamental ways. What had initially been perceived and cast in terms of physical and scientific access on strict conditions has, as a consequence of the Law of the Sea debate and as part of the environmental protocol negotiation considerations, been substantially broadened in scope. The protection of Antarctica in the ecological sense has come to the fore in an enlarged debate about exploitation of mineral and marine resources. Questions about the geographical division of responsibilities arising from the age of imperial exploration, and the needs of the fragile populations of sea mammals and birds that inhabit the Antarctic shoreline, have also assumed increasing importance. The future of the Antarctic regime raises questions concerning the adequacy of the internal mechanisms of the present-day Antarctic Treaty System (ATS) to respond successfully to the increasingly diverse and, in certain realms, even conflicting uses of Antarctica; questions about the relationship of the ATS with the UN and the NGOs; about the requirement for membership with respect to the capabilities of the developing countries; about the effectiveness of the resource management systems set in place by the Seals and Marine Living Resources Conventions; about the nature and likely effectiveness of the recent Protocol on Environmental Protection; about the regulation of a fast-growing tourism industry; about the need for a Secretariat to deal with Antarctic "local government" needs; and about the nature of potential disputes that could well be defused in advance by coming to an early agreement.

Unlike the Antarctic, no international regime has been created so far for the Arctic, which some people have described as "the last unmanaged frontier". However, technological developments, combined with energy and resource extraction potential, mounting environmental concerns and the organization of indigenous peoples in pursuit of their land rights, self-government and social justice have brought the Arctic from the typical Cold War situation of a hegemonic conflict to quite a different situation of emerging choices for international cooperation and conflict resolution. A new geopolitical order is in the making as the Arctic nations strive to establish agreements to regulate their joint efforts in science, economic development and environmental protection.

The present study shows that the significance of the geopolitical context can change rapidly with advances in science and technology, political innovation and regime formation, the formation or dissolution of alliances, the integration or disintegration of states and also on account of an increasing awareness that the physical environment is composed of delicately interlocked ecosystems that are sensitive to human interventions. Accordingly, issues relating to both conflict and cooperation in the polar regions are approached and dealt with here not in terms of geographically predetermined conditions but rather as choices emerging from political, economic, technological, ecological and social–cultural changes and the resultant perceptions of both the policy-makers and the peoples concerned.

The organization of the book

The first chapter elucidates the nature and promise of the new geopolitics. It finds that there is no single theme, but rather a number of strands, and establishes the relevance of some of them for the polar regions. Chapter 2 defines the two polar regions and explores the complexity of the various facets of their environments. It underlines the importance of the Arctic and the Antarctic as ecological regions in both regional and global terms. Chapter 3 takes a critical look at the imperial past of the polar regions and pinpoints the legacies of conflict and territorial aggrandizement bequeathed by the old geopolitics. Chapter 4 examines at some length the implications for the Circumpolar North of Cold War discourse and practices, illustrating how its political geography was transformed into a militarized geography.

Chapter 5 brings out the contrast between the highly militarized, conflict-ridden Arctic and the non-militarized, peaceful Antarctic throughout the Cold War and accounts for the political success of the ATS in this respect. Chapters 6 and 7 are concerned with the developments that promise to liberate the political geography of the Arctic from excessively state-centric concerns on the one hand and from Cold War geostrategy on the other. Chapter 6 is about grassroots political geography: the relationship of Arctic indigenous peoples with the land and their physical environment; indigenous demands for control over land, water and related resources and the political movement towards self-determination. The promise and prospects of various initiatives for international cooperation as well as the relevance of the Antarctic experiment for resolving pending boundary disputes in the Arctic are scrutinized in Chapter 7.

Chapters 8 and 9 examine issues that have suggested themselves in the course of the study and locate them within the distinctive geopolitical settings of the Antarctic and the Arctic. Broadly speaking, the subject under discussion here relates to the linkages and contradictions between the demands of growth-oriented modernization and the imperatives of environmental conservation – often compressed and simplified under the concept of sustainable development. Chapter 8 assesses the strengths and limitations of the Protocol on Environmental Protection to the Antarctic Treaty, points out the changing nature and directions of Antarctic science, discusses the management needs of the fast-growing tourist industry and performs an environmental audit of the ATS. Chapter 9 approaches the notion of sustainable development in the Arctic from various angles – stressing the relevance of indigenous perspectives and insights in illuminating the fundamental meaning of the concept – and examines the various options and obstacles on the way.

The concluding chapter briefly summarizes the issues tackled in the study, comments on continuity and change in polar geopolitics and discusses the prospects for the new geopolitics in both the polar regions in the 1990s and beyond.

Acknowledgements

During research for this book, I have incurred a number of debts. I wish to thank above all the Trustees of the Leverhulme Trust, who generously provided a grant over two years (1993–5) for research on "The Future of the Antarctic Treaty System and Its Relevance for the Arctic" at the Scott Polar Research Institute (SPRI), University of Cambridge, England, of which this book is the major outcome. I am deeply beholden to Dr Peter Wadhams, under whose able and inspiring directorship the project was carried out. I would also like to thank the Vice Chancellor of the Panjab University, Professor T.N. Kapoor, and the members of the Syndicate for releasing me from my duties at Chandigarh in order to enable me to carry out this research. The foundations of this book were originally laid at SPRI during 1991–2, when I was awarded the Nehru Centenary British Fellowship by the Foreign and Commonwealth Office (FCO), London. I am grateful to the FCO and the British Council for their consistent support and encouragement. No less is my gratitude to the managers of the Brian Roberts Fund at SPRI for their generous financial support on various occasions.

It is an honour and a privilege to have served on the research staff of SPRI, where friends and colleagues were always willing to provide encouragement and support. Dr John Heap, Director, SPRI, was most generous with his profound insights on the Antarctic. Dr Bernard Stonehouse, in his capacity as the editor of the Polar Research Series, perused various drafts of the manuscript and offered valuable suggestions for its revision. Dr Terrence Armstrong was most kind in allowing me to draw upon his formidable knowledge of the Arctic regions. Dr Peter Clarkson, Executive Secretary, SCAR, was always willing to share both his ideas and documents. Mr William Mills, ably assisted by a highly motivated library staff, spared no efforts to help with the best polar collection in the world. Mr Bob Headland not only allowed access to the archival material but also supplied the up-date on Antarctic Treaty/SCAR membership for this book. Mr Harry King, Dr Charles Swithinbank, Dr Beau Riffenburg, Mr Peter Speak, Dr Graham Poole, Mr Steigerwald Hans-Peter, and Mrs Maria Pia Casarini-Wadhams all contributed through stimulating discussions. While N. McEnore and Anne Jackson meticulously prepared the maps, Mrs Irene Burns and the office staff spared no efforts in further ensuring that my stay at SPRI was pleasant and productive.

During my stay in Cambridge I had the privilege of a By-Fellowship at Churchill College (1992), Associateship of Clare Hall (1993) and Associate Membership of St. Edmunds College (1994). I express my gratitude to the Masters and Fellows of these distinguished colleges for providing me with the most congenial academic environment that any author could hope for.

Some eminent scholars made outstanding contributions to my research with insightful comments on areas within their expertise. There is no way to sufficiently thank Professor Madan Mohan Puri, Director, Centre for the Study of Geopolitics, Panjab University, Chandigarh, for his role in bringing this project to fruition. His encouragement and confidence in my work at a very early stage was a turning point for me personally. He read through the manuscript and offered valuable suggestions. I am also much indebted to Dr Klaus Dodds for an expansive review of the manuscript, enlightened criticisms and invaluable comments. I am intellectually indebted to Professor Ladis K.D. Kristof, Dr Geoffrey Parker, Dr David Taylor, Professor Peter J. Beck, Professor Martin Ira Glassner, Professor Franklyn Griffiths, Professor Oran R. Young, Dr Donald R. Rothwell, Dr Willy Østreng, Dr Jean Hubert, Dr Jyrki Käkönen, Dr Olav Stokke, Professor E.M. Borgese, Dr Krishan Saigal, Academician Vladimir M. Kotlyakov, Professor Grigory A. Agranat, and Dr Lyse Lyck.

My thanks are also due to Rosemary Graham, University of Cambridge, for her outstanding contribution in the preparation of the manuscript at different stages. Her editorial skills, passion for perfection and attention to details have greatly benefited the book. My thanks are also due to friends in the United Kingdom who provided intellectual and moral support while this project was completed – Satinder Jaswal, Sukhdev Mann, Jean Churchman, Ingrid Marn and Rachel Massey. To my Godparents, Mr and Mrs Mohinder Singh Jaswal, my gratitude is both personal and eternal.

I also wish to thank the individuals and organizations that made it possible for me to visit both the polar regions and gather useful information and experience for the book. During the 1994 Antarctic summer, Quark Expeditions took me as a lecturer on-board *Alla Tarasova*. My warmest appreciation goes to Dr Bernard Stonehouse for proposing my name for this assignment and to Mr Greg Mortimer and Mrs Margaret Werner for making it so rewarding and enjoyable. I am also grateful to Dr Christopher Stephens, Chairman, Indigenous Development International, McDonald Institute, University of Cambridge, for not only sharing with me his knowledge of Arctic indigenous issues but also sponsoring a visit to the Canadian North. Mr Jack Stagg, Assistant Deputy Minister, Policy and Strategic Direction, Department of Indian and Northern Affairs (DIAND) Canada, kindly agreed to sponsor my travel and stay in Whitehorse. I remain grateful to him and to the officials at the DIAND regional office, Whitehorse, for helping me with invaluable information and documentation for the book. Thanks are also due to Mr Terry Fenge at the Canadian Arctic Resource Committee, Ottawa, for extremely useful discussions and information.

I would like to thank Dr Iain Stevenson, Mrs Claire Walker and the staff at John Wiley & Sons, Chichester, for their encouragement, advice and support in finalizing the publication of this book. Thanks also go to Mrs Indu Bal for reading the page proofs. Finally, I am grateful to my wife, Veena, and my sons, Pranshu and Pranjal, who were magnificently tolerant – yet again – of what the process of book creation does to family sociability.

I am of course entirely responsible for the contents of the book. Any errors of fact and judgement are unintended, but mine alone.

List of abbreviations and acronyms

AEPS	Arctic Environmental Protection Strategy
AMAP	Arctic Monitoring and Assessment Programme
ANCSA	Alaska Native Claims Settlement Act
ANILCA	Alaskan National Interest Lands Conservation Act
ANRC	Alaska Native Review Commission
ASMA	Antarctic Specially Managed Area
ASOC	Antarctic and Southern Ocean Coalition
ASPA	Antarctic Specially Protected Area
ATCM	Antarctic Treaty Consultative Meeting
ATCP	Antarctic Treaty Consultative Party
ATP	Antarctic Treaty Party
ATS	Antarctic Treaty System
BIOMASS	Biological Investigation of Marine Antarctic Systems and Stocks
CAFF	Conservation of Arctic Flora and Fauna
CCAMLR	Convention on the Conservation of Antarctic Marine Living Resources
CEC	Commission of the European Community
CEP	Committee for Environmental Protection
CHM	Common Heritage of Mankind
COMNAP	Council of Managers of National Antarctic Programs
COPE	Committee for Original Peoples' Entitlement
CPD	Committee on the Present Danger
CRAMRA	Convention on the Regulation of Antarctic Mineral Resource Activities
CYI	Council for Yukon Indians
EEC	European Economic Communities
EEZ	Exclusive Economic Zone
EIA	Environmental Impact Assessment
EU	European Union
FAO	Food and Agriculture Organization
GIFUK	Greenland-Iceland-Faeroes-United Kingdom

GNP	Gross National Product
HBC	Hudson Bay Company
IAATO	International Association of Antarctica Tour Operators
IASC	International Arctic Science Committee
ICBMs	Intercontinental Ballistic Missiles
ICC	Inuit Circumpolar Conference
ICSU	International Council of Scientific Unions
IGY	International Geophysical Year
IOC	Inter-governmental Oceanographic Commission
IUCN	International Union for the Conservation of Nature and Natural Resources
IWC	International Whaling Commission
MUPA	Multiple Use Planning Area
NAMCO	North Atlantic Marine Mammal Commission
NATO	North Atlantic Treaty Organization
NGO	Non-governmental organization
NSR	Northern Sea Route
NWT	Northwest Territories
OPEC	Organization of Petroleum Exporting Countries
RW	Radioactive Waste
SALT	Strategic Arms Limitation Talks
SCAR	Scientific Committee on Antarctic Research
SCOR	Scientific Committee on Oceanic Research
SDI	Strategic Defence Initiative
SLBMs	Submarine-Launched Ballistic Missiles
SLOC	Sea Lines of Communications
SPA	Specially Protected Area
SPS	Specially Protected Species
SRA	Specially Reserved Area
SSBNs	Nuclear-Powered Ballistic Missile-Firing Submarines
SSSI	Site of Special Scientific Interest
UNCLOS	United Nations Convention on the Law of the Sea
UNEP	United Nations Environment Programme
UFA	Umbrella Final Agreement
WWF	World Wildlife Fund

1

The new geopolitics

In the aftermath of the Cold War, international politics is in flux (Hogan 1992). Doubts persist about the prospects of a safe future for humanity as a whole. In the past, discourses on national security have been obsessed with threats of military aggression across borders and equally convinced about the military capability of meeting such threats. Clearly these now represent only one among many dangers that pose a risk to human life or inhibit the development of humanity's full potential in harmony with nature (see Brown *et al.* 1994). More immediate threats include ecological catastrophes, such as destruction of the ozone layer that protects us from carcinogenic ultraviolet radiation (Roan 1990), climate shifts and harvest failures (Brown 1994). Finite resources are being used up rapidly, topsoil is increasingly being eroded (Scoging 1991), forests are being destroyed for fuel and profit (Durning 1994), the oceans seem no longer capable of performing the dual function of food producer and waste receptacle (Weber 1994), pollution is generated at a rate that far exceeds nature's capacity to render it harmless and many species are likely to become extinct. The human population may soon exceed a sustainable level, if it has not already done so, and many of its vital cultures are disappearing.

Can such realities be explained by traditional geopolitics that, as Simon Dalby (1990a: 40) puts it, "treated the States as autonomous spatially defined entities struggling with other similar entities in attempts to enlarge their power by increasing their control of the territory"? For that matter, can the Cold War geopolitical discourse of mutual suspicion, rivalry, ceaseless pursuit of power politics and deterrence provide any real capability or security for a humanity threatened by environmental degradation in an increasingly interdependent (Janelle 1991: 79–81) world?

Emphasis throughout this study is on a critical geopolitical perspective in understanding contemporary polar realities. Without claiming to offer a comprehensive account of either geopolitics or "critical" geopolitics, I identify the key assumptions and themes of what has loosely come to be termed as the "new" – in contrast to the "old" – geopolitics. My argument is that the essence of a new geopolitics, both in theory and in practice, lies in the acknowledgement of both a new geography and a new politics. As politics becomes more civil-society-oriented, transcending narrow state-centric concerns, and as geography becomes more humanized (Kristof 1992) and ecocentric, the interaction between the two should create sufficient momentum to achieve a paradigm shift in geopolitics. The "newness" of this geopolitics lies essentially in the willingness and ability of politics to take cognizance of, and accordingly respond to, the ecological dimensions of geography: i.e. the finite capacity of the natural environment to endure and assimilate human-induced changes. In this chapter not much is said about the "old" geopolitics; Chapter 3 examines at length the manner in which the old geopolitics of territorial domination and expansionism has affected both the Arctic and the Antarctic in the past.

New geopolitics: major themes and challenges

What kind of geopolitics is new? Despite frequent use, the precise meaning of the term "new geopolitics" remains unsettled (O'Loughlin 1994: 174–5). The new thinking in geopolitics is marked by a number of special features including: a holistic and developmental approach; the investigation of possible and potential future worlds with non-domination as the governing principle, while accepting the transitory nature of all geopolitical phenomena (Parker 1985: 165–6); a belief in geographical "possibilism" rather than geographical determinism; a belief in the freedom of the human will to make decisions among the possible choices (Starr 1993: 1–9); a diachronic view of geopolitics as an active process of constituting the world order rather than an accounting of permanent geographical constraints (Agnew and Corbridge 1988: 266–85); the changing thrust and nature of competition in the new economic world order from the military–political sphere to the economic (Corbridge and Agnew 1991); an alternative geopolitical discourse that challenges the conventional attempts to "master space by disempowering communities" and that articulates a geographical vision of the world in which "the market is at once tamed, decentralized and 'disestablished' and where empowered global citizens are able to challenge opposing elements of the present dynamic globalization" (Agnew and Corbridge 1995: 227); a view of geography as only one of many possible conditioning factors in international relations and as such having a "facilitating" rather than a pure effect (O'Loughlin and Luc 1993: 12); a geopolitics helping foster a "new world era of accommodation", one that "conceives of the political earth as a unified system evolving in developmental stages" (Cohen 1994: 16) as well as an "ecopolitical discourse" with a strong emphasis on environmental security (Dalby 1992a, 1992b).

Indeed, new thinking in geopolitics, despite the variation in focus and emphasis, promises to extend the scope of political geography far beyond conventional state-centric preoccupations to incorporate examination of questions relating to ecological and economic security in the context of emerging global civil society. Before we examine these themes, particularly the ones with special bearing on the polar regions, it is important to acknowledge the contribution of the emerging school of "critical geopolitics" in seeking to challenge the assumptions and conceptual infrastructure that have historically defined the study of geopolitics. Through its engagement with contemporary theoretical developments, including postcolonialism, geopolitical economy and critical development theory, critical geopolitics has come to emphasize the

> importance of constructing theoretically informed critiques of the spatializing practices of power; undertaking critical investigations of the power of orthodox geopolitical writing; investigating how geographical reasoning in foreign policy in-sights (enframes in a geography of images), in-cites (enmeshes in a geography of texts), and therefore, in-sites (stabilizes, positions, locates) places in global politics, and examining how this reasoning can be challenged, subverted, and resisted. (O'Tuathail and Dalby 1994: 514)

In other words, by questioning how geographical discourse and systems of power conspire together to construct and project maps of global politics (with "friendly centres" and "threatening peripheries", "core identities" and "marginalized sites", "tame regions" and "wilderness zones"), critical writers are creating the necessary intellectual spaces for the articulation of a new geopolitics.

Geopolitical discourse and geopolitical reasoning

In the words of O'Tuathail (1994: 527): "Critical geopolitics . . . is a question not an answer, an approach not a theory, which opens up the messy problematic of geography/global politics to rigorous problematization and investigation." It is of crucial importance to explore how geopolitical reasoning is integrated into a political discourse to sustain, augment and justify social and political practices of dominance in international as well as national politics (see Dalby 1988, 1990a, 1990b, 1991). In a general sense, a discourse constitutes the limits within which a set of ideas and practices is considered to be natural: that is, it determines what questions are considered relevant or even intelligible (Barnes and Duncan 1992: 8). Discourses, therefore, are practices of significance, providing a framework for understanding the world. In this book the term "discourse" is understood as a set of rules or perspectives for the acquisition and organization of knowledge, with its own dominant metaphors that facilitate further knowledge and insights but simultaneously limit it. The dominant discourse not only provides the interpretative context within which "facts" are assigned significance but also determines which facts are to be interpreted.

The texts of geopolitical discourse, it should be noted, are not free-floating, innocent contributions to an "objective" knowledge but are rooted in "power/knowledge", serving the interests of particular groups in society and helping to sustain and legitimate certain perspectives and interpretations. As O'Tuathail and Agnew (1992: 195) put it: "The study of geopolitics in discursive terms, therefore, is the study of the socio-cultural resources and rules by which geographies of international politics get written." Accordingly,

> The challenge for the student of geopolitics is to understand how geographical knowledge is transformed into the reductive geopolitical reasoning of intellectuals of statecraft [a whole community of state bureaucrats, leaders, foreign-policy experts and advisers who comment upon, influence and conduct the activities of statecraft]. How are places reduced to security commodities [as the Arctic was for example during the Cold War], to geographical abstractions which need to be "domesticated", controlled, invaded or bombed rather than understood in their complex reality? (Ibid.)

Although a critical historiography of geopolitics is a necessary step on the way to a new geopolitics, it is only a first step. The scope of critical geopolitics needs to be broadened to include the non-Western world, as Dodds (1993) has done in his study of South American geopolitics and Antarctica. It is equally important to go below nation-state level and explore how formal geopolitical reasoning has been used to marginalize certain minority groups, especially indigenous peoples. Chapter 6 has more to say on this theme.

The responsibility falls on a critical geopolitics to construct alternative discourse(s) directed at reconceptualizing the notions of sovereignty and security in an increasingly interdependent world, while examining the question of an ecologically sustainable present as well as future at local, regional and global levels in an emerging global society.

Needless to say, perhaps, the success of such alternative discourses on the ground (they may have to compete and even coexist with the hegemonic security discourse) will depend to a large extent upon radical changes in the perceptions, policies and practices of those who speak and act on behalf of modern nation-states. At the same time, a formal geopolitical reasoning, that talks not of the dividing but of the unifying themes, is also required. However, while focusing on the "new" in geopolitics, it will be important not to exaggerate the discontinuities in the old geopolitics. In other words, we will have to watch for both continuities and departures from the past.

4

Globalization and the nation-state

According to Parker (1994: 174), the fundamental difference between the old and the new is that "while the old geopolitics was concerned primarily with the nation-state and the promotion of its interests, the attention of new geopolitics is directed towards those issues which are of wider concern to humanity as a whole". A critical reassessment of political geography and geopolitics has come from a new generation of geographers since the late 1970s. For example, in France, Lacoste (1976, editorial) lamented in *Hérodote* that previously geography had been far too much the handmaiden of the state for such purposes as political domination and war-making.

One can, therefore, argue that whereas the old geopolitics focused on the segments which make up the global totality, the new geopolitics focuses on the totality itself. This observation instantly raises a question pertinent for this study. What role and relevance do the polar regions have in the global totality, now that their geopolitical isolation is being increasingly eroded? At the same time, the fact cannot be ignored that nation-states have not disappeared, nor are they likely to in the foreseeable future, as key component parts of the world's geopolitical space. The starting-point of the new geopolitics thus remains the nation-states. However, the nation-states are under the tremendous pressure of the complex dynamics of "regionalism" and "globalism", driven by forces such as weaponry of mass destruction, technological innovation, environmental decay, growing international investment and trade, and a global market economy. Fissures in their rigid geopolitical space, then, are too obvious to be ignored, together with their diminishing functional importance. Yet, as Falk (1994: 2–3) puts it, "almost any generalization about regionalism seems suspect, and must be qualified".

The new geopolitics, like this study, faces a series of complex questions as attention is drawn beyond the nation-state and focused between the state level and global totality. One finds yet another level, consisting of groups and clusters of states located within particular geographical areas. What kind of geopolitical entities are the regional clusters of this sort – with the European Union constituting the most significant example of this type of development, sharing certain commonalities such as proximity, interactive and discursive "distinctiveness" – going to become in future? Will they eventually create genuinely transnational structures, equipped with the necessary will and capability to bypass the hegemonic interests both within the nation-states and in the world at large, thereby serving the interests of the "region" concerned? Or will they simply "replicate many of the spatial characteristics of the nation-state at the transnational level" and eventually become some kind of "Regional States" (Falk 1994: 13; Parker 1994: 176)? What will be the implications of "regional cooperation" for the resource-supplying peripheries within the nation-states that are now going to be integrated into a new regional order? What about the people and perspectives at the grassroots level, the ones long marginalized by the dominant centres of power in the name of "national interests"? As the new geopolitics reaches both *below* and *beyond* the nation-state level, will dominance be replaced by non-dominance as the fundamental governing principle of both national and international politics? Will the emergence of a region ensure ecologically sustainable and socially equitable development for civil society as a whole? Or will it imply further exploitation of natural resources, now in the name of "regional interests" rather than "national interests"?

"Regionalization" and "globalization" processes may not yet appear to be of marked relevance for the Antarctic and the institutions established so far for its multinational governance. However, now that the forces of regionalization have reached northern Europe, with Sweden and Finland joining the EU, the questions raised above have profound implications for the Arctic. We will return to this theme in Chapter 7.

Rethinking environment and security

Once we accept ecologically sustainable development and the management of space and resources as one of the primary concerns of the new geopolitics, in contrast to the obsession of the "old" geopolitics with spatial control and domination, the traditional distinctions between land power and sea power become blurred. Once it is acknowledged that nearly 80% of sea pollution comes from land-based sources and that coastal zones are replacing the conventional boundaries between land and sea, one requires new perspectives as well as vocabularies to explain and deal with this new situation. It is highly questionable whether the simple possession of a coastline or the character of its harbour would today give a coastal state any power or capability, as Mahan had assumed, unless backed up by sound coastal-zone and port-management policies. The foremost issue-areas that need to be addressed, on the way to realizing the objectives of eco-geopolitics, relate to security, sovereignty and development.

Widely used, or rather misused, by the practitioners of statecraft to invent justifications or rationalizations in support of many policy actions, the term "security" has been closely associated with the themes of sovereignty and political community understood in territorial terms (Buzan 1991). Cast in the narrow perspective of the modern nation-state, the drama of security has focused on the construction of identities "under threat" – who or what identity is being threatened by whom or what – and on prescribing the ways and means of providing protection against such threats to social order.

Security, especially during the past half-century, has been primarily and exclusively the concern of states and their strategic communities and

6

military alliances. Backed up by the realist understanding of international politics (which supplied the justification for most state policies of "national security" and excessive reliance on military power as the *sine qua non* for statehood) and the notions of "sovereignty" in international law that grant complete control over what goes on inside a state to the government of that state, such an understanding of security has tended to focus on states as unitary, homogenous actors, playing down the multitude of internal factors and justifying internal repression, the abuse of human rights and the maintenance of order in terms of the political status quo in many states (Chomsky 1992: 20–1). Consequently, perceptions and policies based upon such notions of security have failed miserably in dealing with situations of rapid social change and in recognizing the need to develop new forms of political community and transnational institutional organizations to deal with global environmental problems.

Realization is growing that the definition of security called for is multi-aspected and multidimensional, in which socio-economic and environmental components share a place with political and military ones (Prins 1990; Käkönen 1992; The Commission on Global Governance 1995: 77–84). Security must be defined in terms of the rights and entitlements of individuals and communities – which presupposes respect for human rights, concern for psychological and spiritual values and access to the means of social and economic development (see Langlais 1995). Cultural survival is also an issue for many ethnic groups and aboriginal peoples.

Since many problems, especially those of an environmental nature, are truly global in scale, no nation – however powerful it may believe itself to be or however fiercely it may seek to exercise its sovereignty – can hope to come to terms with such problems in isolation (Mische 1989). Global problems, be they political, economic, social or environmental, provide for few sanctuaries, thereby overcoming what has often been taken to be one of the critical distinctions between domestic and international political theory (see Hurrell 1995).

The political community today can no longer be considered as unquestionably "secured" within state boundaries (Walker and Mendlowitz 1990). And security in turn can no longer be clearly understood in terms of spatial strategies of distancing and boundary-making as the key protection of a geographically demarcated political community. This is more so in the case of environmental themes, where it needs to be emphasized that ecological regions do not necessarily coincide with territorial boundaries. Linking environmental themes to the traditional language of national and international security may not be a useful way forward, since the word "security" has a geostrategic–military ring to it. Obviously, an altogether new set of vocabulary is needed to explain and communicate the emerging political challenges of environmental degradation. Ecological metaphors of context, diversity, interconnection, adaptability and mutualism might be much more useful for explaining comprehensive–universal security than the current physics terminology of force, centralized control commands and containment (Dalby 1992a: 515).

There are valid reasons for believing that the environmental crisis is inseparably linked to the development crisis and can be resolved only through a radical change in our understanding of the relationship between human economic activity and the ecosystems and our perception of the nature of human progress. The following beliefs are so deeply embedded in contemporary mainstream development thought and policy as to be considered almost a modern theology: (i) sustained growth is both feasible and desirable for human progress; (ii) integration of the global economy holds the key to growth and is beneficial to all but a few narrow vested interests; and (iii) international assistance and foreign investments are vital for alleviating poverty and protecting the environment. Even the World Commission on Environment and Development (1987: ix), entrusted with the task of proposing "long-term environmental strategies for achieving sustainable development by the year 2000 and beyond", could not escape the contradictions that continue to undermine the efforts to reconcile the perceived imperative of economic growth with the finite nature of the earth's ecosystem. Many of the conclusions of *Our Common Future* reaffirmed the commitment of conventional development thinking to economic growth: "If large parts of the developing world are to avert economic, social, and environmental catastrophes, it is essential that global economic growth be revitalized" (Ibid.: 89). In a way this contradicted its own assumption that growth and overconsumption are root causes of the problem.

According to the Commission, "Sustainable Development is development that meets the needs of the present without compromising the ability of future generations to meet their own needs" (1987: 43). While this definition provides a criterion for sustainable development itself, it does not define needs, does not require that needs be efficiently met – which would demand in return yet another value-based criterion for efficiency – and leaves open the possibility that the present generation could live beyond its needs so long as future generations' needs are met (Norgaard 1994: 17). In short, it makes no attempt to indicate how sustainable development is achieved and thus leaves the whole issue more or less open to different interpretations (Richardson 1994).

It is indeed unfortunate that most development thinkers, policy-makers and institutions have so far failed to come to terms with the reality that economic growth and progress, as conventionally understood and measured, rely upon increasing the flow of physical materials – such as petroleum, minerals, biomass and water – through our economic system. And it is upon nature that we depend for the supply of these materials and for absorbing the resulting waste. However, we have now reached the critical point, beyond which further advances in human well-being must be achieved without further increasing the economic system's physical throughput. Further economic progress, including the elimination of the deprivation from which more than one billion people suffer, will depend on reallocating the ecological space that human beings have already appropriated. Realization of intergenerational equity, elimination of wasteful consumption and rational use of physical resources will remain at best hypothetical unless economic activity is brought into balance with the limits of the ecosystem in an orderly way. Otherwise nature might do it for us in a far more brutal way.

The current efforts of policy-makers to deal with sustainability by fine-tuning existing policies and institutions – while proceeding with growth-oriented modernization projects – are not only inadequate and misguided but also chiefly responsible for making the concept of sustainable development ecopolitically suspect. The appeal of economic growth for governments is multifaceted: it clearly serves as a crucial bulwark for the maintenance of the political status quo, reduces the political pressure on the ruling élite to reallocate national income to combat social deprivation and offers the prospect of more for everyone with sacrifice for none. The concept of sustainable development is simply empty if it is not taken to mean in reality a radical transformation of thought, policies and institutions, while allowing peoples and organizations at the grassroots level to regain control of the remaining ecological resources to meet basic domestic needs. So defined, the notion of people-centred, civil-society-based sustainable development poses a serious challenge to growth-centred mainstream development thought and policy.

New geopolitics cannot afford to neglect the ongoing debate about sustainable development, not only because the issues involved relate to land and to the human communities that are bound to the land in one way or another but because they show that divergent perspectives on sustainable development carry "important implications for the way power is understood between groups of people, as well as for the environment itself" (Redclift 1992: 33). No less important in considering the geopolitical dimension of sustainability are the questions about: (i) the relationship between knowledge and power, reflected in popular resistance to the dominant world views of the environment and resources, and (ii) who has rights to what resources, what manner of claim on these resources these rights bestow and what management prerogatives flow from these rights (Usher 1984: 390–1). We will return to the theme in Chapter 9.

Summary: towards a normative geopolitics?

Unprecedented opportunities should arise for the further development of a normative geopolitics that continues on the one hand to challenge the hegemonic security discourses with their underlying national biases and on the other to provide theoretical explanations for both the process of change and the consequences of this change. They depend, however, on the realization of the following transitions to:

- a non-partisan geopolitical thinking that looks at the world as a whole and not just in terms of "East–West" competition or "North–South" divisions.
- an integrated single political–economic logic in a geographic perspective to explain contemporary global developments.
- the realization, especially on the part of state actors, that in the transformed global economic reality the ability to persuade is more important to national capability than the ability to command others by military means and especially the willingness to use supranational structures to address critical issues of international management that are simply beyond the capability of individual state actors.
- an integrated science of the biosphere which can provide the information on which effective environmental management must be based; a holistic science, which goes beyond the traditional fragmented disciplinary approach and which also takes into account the relevant socio-economic considerations and indigenous knowledge and wisdom.
- economic development which is sustainable and equitable; the transition to a new ecological economics, which supports and underpins sustainable resource management and environmental improvement, taking the human economic system as embedded in the earth's natural ecosystem.
- the development and application of technology for the service of environmental management and improvement.
- an "open civil society" that looks after the interests of minorities and takes into account the minority opinion.

Environmental change alone may bring about a paradigm shift in geopolitics, but it is clear that a shift in values is at the root of the issue rather than simply a shift in the play of interests. The conventional understanding with regard to "scale of analysis" in political geography, in terms of local, regional and global levels of analysis, may not work that well in the case of environmental change. The traditional, state-centred geopolitics was too narrow and parochial in its conceptualization of both geography and politics, in its understanding of the processes by which environmental problems are generated, in its appreciation of the political forces that impact on environmental issues and in its treatment of the normative dimension. At the same time, it failed to acquire and adopt a proper understanding of the increasingly global context of political interaction in terms of relationships between local issues addressed in a global context and global issues addressed in a local context. This novelty, with its emphasis on encouraging new forms of global and local cooperation and promoting new forms of social justice, provides both an opportunity and a challenge to the new geopolitics in the search for ecologically sustainable and socially equitable development and management of space and resources. We now move on to an account of the environment in the polar regions, in the context of which the issues raised above will be approached and analysed.

Suggested reading

Agnew, J. and S. Corbridge 1995. *Mastering Space: Hegemony, Territory and International Political Economy*. London, New York: Routledge.

Dalby, S. 1990. *Creating the Second Cold War: The Discourse of Politics*. London: Pinter Publishers.

Glassner, M. I. 1993. *Political Geography*. New York: John Wiley & Sons.

O'Loughlin, J. (ed.) 1994. *Dictionary of Geopolitics*. Westport: Greenwood Press.

Parker, G. 1985. *Western Geopolitical Thought in the Twentieth Century*. London: Croom Helm.

Taylor, P. J. 1993. *Political Geography: World Economy, Nation-State and Locality*. London: Longman.

2

Environment at the poles

To describe the environment of the two polar regions fully in a single chapter is an impossible task, especially when the environment is taken to include, in its broadest possible sense, obvious physical attributes, less visible but vital ecosystems, potential as well as exploited resources and subjective human settings. By necessity then, this chapter is much like an impressionist painting. Only the broadest strokes can be applied to the canvas, with the intention of drawing the geopolitical context in which to approach, later on in the study, the issues related to the sustainable development and management of the polar regions.

Delimiting the polar regions

Boundaries tend to depend upon the subject under investigation and technical convenience. For example, favouring straight-line boundaries that are mappable, such as meridians and parallels of latitude, some geographers would take the Arctic and Antarctic Circles as polar boundaries. There is, however, a strong case for rejecting the Arctic Circle, and its Antarctic counterpart, because of their artificial nature and irrelevance to: atmospheric and hydrospheric circulation, faunal distribution, climate change, the tree line or the limits of permafrost and to general isotherm patterns (Dunbar 1992: 110). Adopting flexible boundaries, e.g. zones with overlapping ecological and geopolitical attributes, could be much more useful and illuminating for the purposes of the present study.

The southern polar region

For the southern polar region – including continental Antarctica, the Antarctic Peninsula, several groups of islands close by and a band of ocean partly invested with sea ice – the most generally accepted boundary from an ecological standpoint is the Antarctic Convergence (Sugden 1982; Stonehouse 1989; Glassner 1993), so named because early interpretations of the temperature and salinity suggested a sinking of the northward-moving Antarctic surface water below the less dense southward-moving Subantarctic water. More recent studies, however, have shown that there may be divergent or convergent fields of motion, together with many sharp discontinuities in temperature and salinity. An alternative name thus is the "polar frontal zone", which implies neither convergence nor divergence (Baker 1975: 9). Although this zone is a mobile one, with eddies and loops that span an area up to 150 km wide, it has a fairly constant mean position from year to year, appearing at an average latitude of about 50°S (Laws 1985).

Narrow subpolar zones, the Subarctic and the Subantarctic, separate polar from temperate regions in the two hemispheres (Stonehouse 1989: 2–15). The most commonly accepted Subantarctic boundary is the Subtropical Convergence, a less clearly defined belt of water, circling the earth in lower latitudes, mostly between 36° and 40°, and marking the zone where Subantarctic water sinks below warmer temperate water masses. The Subantarctic region lies between the Antarctic and Subtropical Convergences in the southern Atlantic, Indian and Pacific Oceans and contains 11 scattered groups of islands, collectively called the Subantarctic Islands. New Zealand's South Island and the southernmost tip of South America also fall within this zone. Due to the latitudinal variation among these islands, from 54°S in the case of Macquarie Island to 37°S in the case of Iles Amsterdam, there is a wide range of climates, soil conditions and ecology.

The northern polar region

One useful definition for the Arctic region, from an ecological angle, is the natural tree line, the northern limit of the boreal forests, corresponding well to the line of the 10°C July isotherm. Despite the problem in deciding where trees give way to tundra vegetation, on a broad scale one can identify a relatively sharp zone between the two (Sugden 1982: 17). It is easily documented by aerial photography, is an area of significant environmental change, is a boundary for the very strong surface winds to the north which severely affect animal life, is important in terms of animal distribution, coincides approximately (as pointed out above) with a mean July temperature isotherm of 10°C and thus is also of climatic significance, and is an important boundary in human terms, especially in North America, where it separates quite clearly the Arctic Inuit peoples from forest Indians (Ibid.: 18).

The following states qualify as Arctic states: Russia, with nearly half of the Arctic land area and coastline; the United States, which in Alaska has the area to the east of the Bering Strait; Canada, with its important northern territories and the Northwest Passage; Denmark, on account of Greenland; Finland; Sweden; and Norway, with its mainland territory bordering on the Arctic in the Barents Sea, and its control of the Svalbard Archipelago, Bear Island and Jan Mayen Island, leaving that country in a unique position at the maritime gateway to the Soviet Arctic ports, the Northeast Passage and the central Arctic Ocean. Various Arctic-rim states, however, have different traditions in defining the Arctic (see CAFF 1993: 22–4).

It is the wide circumpolar belt of coniferous forest south of the tree line that defines the Subarctic lands, a zone characterized by short warm summers and long, often severely cold winters and permafrost. In geopolitical terms, the boundary between the Arctic and the Subarctic is hard to pinpoint, because the Subarctic is where the "present frontier of settlement and development is found, throughout the Circumpolar North" (Armstrong *et al.* 1978: 2). Moreover, historically speaking, as the next chapter will show, the reasons for outside interest in the Arctic region – including the extraction of raw materials, provision of living space, expansion of transport systems, use as strategic space, colonization of indigenous homelands and the situations flowing from them – have made this boundary arbitrary and extremely porous.

The physical settings

The most obvious geographical/geopolitical contrast between Antarctica and the Arctic is that whereas the former is an island continent of disputed ownership, separated by the Southern Ocean from the temperate islands and continents to the north (Map A), the latter is an ocean basin almost completely surrounded by lands under sovereignty (Map B).

In contrast to the Arctic, the most noticeable feature of Antarctica is its unique isolation. Even its closest neighbours (Argentina and Chile) are countries of the middle latitudes. The distance from Antarctica to Africa is 2100 miles, to New Zealand 1200 miles, to Australia 1550 miles and to Tierra del Fuego about 620 miles. To reach Antarctica it is necessary to voyage across seas exposed to the fiercest winds in the world. Between 55° and 65°, no land intervenes in the west-to-east circulation of sea and air.

The Antarctic continent is divided into two distinct geological regions – East and West Antarctica – by the "Transantarctic Mountains", which stretch over 3000 miles. East, or Greater, Antarctica is mountainous, most of its mountains lying deeply buried under the ice. It includes the South

Pole, where the ice is nearly 9000 ft thick. West, or Lesser, Antarctica is a cluster of high volcanic islands, deeply dissected by channels and contiguous with the Peninsula (Stonehouse 1989: 19). Only about 2% of the continent is exposed; the rest lies under an ice mantle that in places is over 4000 m thick.

In winter, Antarctica more than doubles its size, as pack ice stretches up to 700 miles from the coast. On the Greenwich meridian, Antarctica is 2250 miles across in summer and 3400 miles in winter. Antarctic sea ice also has a more uniform thickness than Arctic sea ice, as the divergent forces of Antarctic winds and currents tend to disperse the pack, minimize the formation of pressure ridges and make the ice pack generally more navigable by icebreakers. First-year Antarctic sea ice averaging less than 1 m thick probably comprises at least 80% of the total Antarctic sea-ice area in winter (Wadhams 1991: 4–13).

The Arctic Ocean is a nearly land-locked deep ocean basin subdivided by a series of undersea ridges. Unusually broad continental shelves underlie 30% of its area, particularly on the Eurasian side of the basin, where they commonly extend more than 900 km offshore. The Barents–Kara Shelf, bordering the Eurasia Basin, is one of the world's broadest (Kristoffersen 1990: 365). There is only one deep connection with the rest of the World Ocean, through the Fram Strait between Greenland and Spitsbergen. It forms a subsystem of the world's ocean transport system with vital interconnections. For example, the organic chemicals dumped into the seas off South Africa appear in the Arctic. Similarly, as Dunbar (1992: 104–6) points out, the traces of the heavy metals sent down a Soviet Arctic river eventually make their way to the Indian Ocean. Furthermore, since the Arctic Ocean is nearly land-locked, it receives a great variety of materials from the surrounding land areas, including both anthropogenic and naturally occurring contaminants. About 10% of the world's rivers discharge into it, although it represents only 1.5% of the world's ocean volume, with the largest runoff into the Kara and Laptev Seas (Aagaard 1993: 1). The net flow into the Arctic Ocean is through the Bering Strait and out of it through the Canadian Archipelago.

Dynamics of polar ecosystems

The implications for political geography of taking into account the presence of dynamic ecosystems in a given physical setting can be far-reaching: a geographical setting can no longer be treated as a passive stage on which the drama of humankind is being enacted. Radically different political responses are called for, in contrast to those obtained from the traditional, state-centred geopolitics. Since ecosystems cannot be controlled or dominated in the pursuit of power politics, an attempt should be made to understand, conserve and manage them. There are no better places on our planet than the two polar regions to illustrate these points.

In an ecological perspective, individual plants and animals are found together in communities and are intimately linked with abiotic components (solar heat, minerals and water) to form ecosystems (C. Young 1989: 29). The search for the factors that may link these communities now recognizes the merits of comparing Antarctic and Arctic ecosystems (see special issue of *Ambio* 1989). The following sections briefly illustrate the complexity and variability of polar ecosystems, underlining their susceptibility to human impact.

Antarctic ecosystems

Since about 98% of the land area within 60°S is covered with snow and ice, this surface provides the substrate for the largest of the diverse Antarctic ecosystems (Laws 1984, 1985; Stonehouse 1989), exceeded in area only by the entire Southern Ocean ecosystem. Ecosystem development here is restricted to a sparse microbial community, rarely permitting even the growth of snow algae. Whereas local impacts on these ecosystems may well arise from any of a wide range of chemical and physical agents, the potential risk from the external agents is much higher.

The ice-free habitat of terrestrial ecosystems is confined to less than 2% of the Antarctic surface area, marked by low plant diversity. This area is predominantly the coastal land at lower latitudes, with the important exception of the Dry Valleys of southern Victoria Land at latitude 75°S and numerous inland nunataks (exposed mountain peaks). On the continent, the microflora that dominate are algae, lichens and mosses, becoming increasingly rare at higher latitudes before fading out in the driest zones (Walton 1987: 88).

The Southern Ocean ecosystem, comprising myriad interconnected systems such as sea ice, marginal ice, open oceans and benthos, is said to be the largest readily defined ecosystem on earth (Foster 1984; Berkman 1992), characterized by remarkable physical and biogeographical diversity. It is krill (*Euphausia superba*) – the principal herbivorous invertebrate in the Southern Ocean, feeding on phytoplanktonic algae – that transfers much of the biomass produced by phytoplankton to the fishes, birds, seals and mammals. For the survival and well-being of as many as 38 species of sea birds, including penguins, six species of seals and numerous species of whales south of the Convergence (Stonehouse 1989: 153–7), krill continues to be critical.

The Arctic ecosystems

Despite the fact that the Arctic Ocean proper is one of the least biologically productive of the world's oceans, it has a variety of subenvironments

17

where productivity is high and upon which indigenous populations depend. Marine productivity is enhanced especially in the seas where water from the Atlantic and the Pacific mixes with Arctic Ocean waters.

Although the Arctic Ocean food chain has been called simple, it too begins with phytoplankton. Among the more important contributors, at least in spring, are over 300 species of algae that live in and on sea ice, especially its lowest parts (Horner 1989: 123–46). Ice algae, together with other phytoplankton, are the basic food for species further up the food chain. The Arctic Ocean has no "direct equivalent in the south, except in the much smaller gyres of the Weddell and Ross Seas where the pack ice circulates" (Stonehouse 1989: 158).

While few would disagree that "despite their relative simplicity, polar ecosystems are both complex and variable enough to be puzzling" (Stonehouse 1991: 154), consensus is lacking over whether or not they are "fragile". Crucial in the whole debate, however, is the question of how much is – or remains to be – known about polar ecology. The nature and complexity of a given natural environment, therefore, depends not only upon its physical attributes and ecological dynamics but also upon its human geography and the way in which that environment is perceived.

The human settings

One major difference between the Arctic and the Antarctic is that the former has indigenous inhabitants. It is this humanized landscape (Berger 1988: 40–1; 1989), which has evolved over thousands of years, that gives the northern polar region a complexion and complexity not found in its southern counterpart. There are several indigenous communities living in seven Arctic-rim countries – the United States, Canada, Denmark/Greenland, Norway, Sweden, Finland and Russia (Map C). Iceland has no indigenous population.

The term "Alaska natives" encompasses the Yupiik, Inupiat, Aleut, Athabaskan, Tlingit, Haida and Tsimshian peoples (Oswalt 1990: 12–39). Together they constitute just over 15% of the population of the state of Alaska, or more than 85 000 people out of approximately 550 000 statewide (Korsmo 1994: 81). They speak 20 different languages. Fifty-six per cent of the Alaska natives are concentrated in non-urban areas, including more than 200 small villages with populations smaller than 2500. However, the state's most populous city, Anchorage, is home to more than 14 000 native people. Aleuts inhabit the Pribilof Islands in the Bering Sea and the Aleutian Chain. Alaska natives have a variety of occupations and lifestyles, from subsistence hunting and fishing to state and corporate office.

Over half of Canada's land surface lies north of 60°N but is inhabited by fewer than one-third of 1% of Canada's people. In this huge landmass,

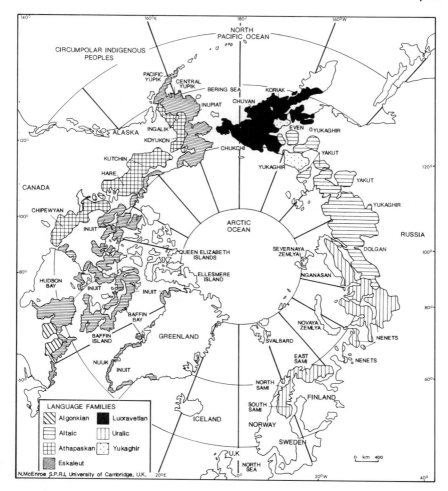

Map (C) Circumpolar indigenous peoples

indigenous peoples (roughly 52 000) constitute a larger portion of the population than in the rest of Canada, ranging from an Inuit population of 80–5% in Nunavut (around 22 000), to a mixed Indian/Métis/Inuvialuit population in the Mackenzie Valley part of the Northwest Territories, constituting about 50% of the total of that area, to an Indian minority (roughly 5000, together with people of mixed native ancestry) in the Yukon that make up about a quarter of the overall population. Eight bands of Cree, with a combined population approaching 9000, reside in the James Bay region of northern Quebec. Several thousand Naskapi, Montagnais and members of other indigenous American tribes spread across the region from northern Quebec to Labrador.

Greenland, Kalaallit Nunaat (the "Greenlanders' Land"), the world's largest island with an area of 2 175 000 sq km, is the homeland of about 45 000 Inuit out of a total population of 55 385 as of 1 January 1992 (Greenland Home Rule Authority 1992: 6). The majority Inuit population comprises three distinct linguistic groups: Kalaait along the west coast, Inughuit (popularly known as Polar Eskimos and well known as the world's most northerly indigenous inhabitants) in the far north around Thule, and Iit on the east coast. Permanent human habitation is only possible along the ice-free coastal areas, which cover 341 700 sq km or one-sixth of the total area. The rest of the country is covered by the immense inland ice, in some places rising to well over 3000 m.

The Sami, or Lapps, are the indigenous people of the area in northernmost Europe known as Lapland. The area they inhabit comprises a crescent-shaped zone extending from the eastern edge of the Kola Peninsula in the Russian northwest and running along the northern periphery of Fennoscandia to the vicinity of Dalarna in Sweden and Røros in Norway. Because artificial borders were imposed upon them, the Sami have been parcelled into four separate countries: Norway, Sweden, Finland and Russia. There are approximately 60 000 Sami in all, of whom 40 000 are in Norway, 15 000 in Sweden, 4000 in Finland and 1500–2000 in Russia, living mostly on the Kola Peninsula east of Finland (Beach 1994: 152). Despite a broad range of traditional subsistence lifestyles and adopted modern livelihoods, the Sami are best known for their reindeer herding. Whether herders or non-herders, they regard the reindeer as a basic guardian of their culture, language and identity.

In comparison with their circumpolar counterparts (roughly 230 000 in 1989), Russia's indigenous peoples are far more numerous (totalling over one million), and live in a vast territory covering about 45% of the former USSR and 58% of the new Russian state. This territory encompasses almost all of Siberia and stretches along the coastline of the Arctic Ocean from the White Sea in the west to the Bering Strait in the east, including Kamchatka and the island of Sakhalin. There are 26 officially recognized "Small Peoples of the Soviet North and Far East", whose combined population in 1989 was about 240 120 (Dahl 1990: 13). In the same year the population of the two much larger indigenous peoples, the Komi and the Yakut, who have their own autonomous republics, was 344 500 and 382 000 respectively. Finally, several indigenous groups are not recognized at all, and their situation is most precarious. The indigenous peoples of the Russian North are reindeer nomads, hunters, trappers and fishermen.

The Antarctic "indigenous" population, on the other hand, is unique and, with one exception (Beltramino 1993), not so well documented. The Antarctic landscape is dotted with scientific stations, the small settlements visited mostly by men, from both the northern and the southern hemisphere, in connection with scientific activity and logistic support. The residence period is normally one year at the permanent stations established on land or ice (with wintering-over personnel numbering little more than a thousand) and varies from a few days to several months during the summer season at stations in the field or at sea (with summer personnel numbering more than 12 000, which includes more than 6000 tourists and visitors per annum).

From 1977 onwards, there have been couples and families at the Argentine Esperanza station, and from 1984 at Villa Las Estrellas, established by Chile. This particular aspect of Antarctic demography is far more geopolitical than the number of civilians present in Antarctica at any given time might suggest. The Antarctic is thus politicized at least in this respect (Chaturvedi 1983). Furthermore, even though invisible on the icy continent, the maps of seven claimants (Argentina, Australia, Chile, France, Norway, New Zealand and the UK) do carry the imprints of their respective "national territories" or "dependencies" (see Map D). We will return to these invisible, but none the less consequential, boundaries in the next chapter.

The polar regions in global change

The polar environment plays a key role in the operation of certain global systems, such as the atmosphere, lithosphere, hydrosphere and biosphere. One good example is the role of the polar heat sinks in influencing global atmospheric circulation. Polar seas play an important role in the exchange of CO_2 between ocean and atmosphere, since they may be large sinks for the CO_2. In addition, it is the contrast between the cold conditions of these regions and the heat of the equatorial areas, combined with the rotation of the earth, which shapes the circulation patterns of the atmosphere. These patterns in turn exercise a major controlling influence on global climate (Maxwell and Barrie 1989).

A number of phenomena and processes characteristic of the Antarctic region have an important role to play in global change (see Weller *et al.* 1991). The Antarctic region, with a high negative-radiation budget, acts as one of the earth's "refrigerators". Any change in the budget will have global consequences for atmospheric and oceanic circulation. A detailed record of past global climate and atmospheric chemistry extending over hundreds of millennia is preserved within the Antarctic ice sheet and in the sediments of the Southern Ocean. The dynamics and thermodynamics of Antarctic sea-ice cover are also intricately linked with the ocean–atmosphere exchange of heat, water and gas (Weller 1993: 3). Antarctic sea ice is thus a major element in the global climate system, and a sensitive indicator of the effects of global change on physical and biological systems.

In the event of global climate change due to increasing greenhouse gases in the atmosphere, the polar regions are expected to experience the greatest warming. Resultant changes in the altitude of sea ice are likely to have world-wide climatic implications. Changes above the level of high natural variability are best recorded in the polar regions. At the same time, plant communities existing under polar conditions are known to be sensitive to temperature change, and hence are reliable indicators of climate change.

The Antarctic ice sheet contains enough water to raise the global sea-level world-wide by some 60 m. Any greenhouse climate warming which makes even a small change to this volume of ice is likely to have a significant impact on sea-level. If, as is predicted, a major climate warming takes place over the next century, the boundary conditions acting at the Antarctic ice sheet are likely to change. These in turn are likely to lead to: increased snow accumulation associated with the warmer atmosphere and less sea ice; increased surface melting in summer associated with higher air temperature; and increased melting of ice shelves from below associated with the penetration of warmer ocean water and/or changed patterns of ocean circulation (Weller 1989: 13).

Very little change is likely to occur in the Antarctic, as no significant warming of the Southern Ocean is expected in the next hundred years. On the other hand, the ice cover of the Arctic is expected almost to disappear in summer (Morel 1992: 15). In order to be certain, the interactions between the ice sheet and the bounding ocean and atmosphere need to be quantified by empirical studies and theoretical models of the physical processes involved. The problem of sea-level rise, however, cannot be solved by the study of a single continent (Ibid.); it has to be addressed on a global scale, taking into account not only the polar regions but also the circulation of the world oceans. This illustrates global ecological interdependence and the need to approach the climate problem by means of a world-wide, interdisciplinary research effort to which regional scientific programmes would make their contributions.

Another recent, and dramatic, example of global ecological interdependence is the Antarctic ozone hole (Gardiner 1992: 17). The ozone layer protects not only human beings but also the communities of plants and animals, embedded in ecosystems, from solar ultraviolet radiation. It is now well established that ozone depletion is caused by man-made chemicals, the CFCs and some related chemicals – halons. It is equally clear that the Antarctic is particularly vulnerable to the effects of the chlorine discharged from CFCs, released mostly in the heavily populated northern hemisphere.

The depletion of Antarctic ozone is far from being fully understood (Weller 1993: 24). Important questions remain about the seasonal character of the depletion, its "spread" to other latitudes, the detailed chemistry and microphysics of the phenomenon and the likely effect of ozone depletion on Antarctic organisms. One area of concern is the consequences of increased levels of ultraviolet radiation (UV-B in particular) for the phytoplankton that constitutes the base of the food web in aquatic eco-systems. Studies have revealed that increased levels of UV exposure could result in reduced primary production and in altered community structure. The UV-induced changes could also affect the entire Southern Ocean eco-system by weakening the base of the food web and altering trophodynamic relationships (Weller 1989: 17).

One major difference between the Antarctic and Arctic is the much more confused circulation of stratospheric winds in the Arctic. In the Antarctic the stratospheric winds, blowing around in closed loops, and the chemical processes giving rise to ozone depletion, last for several weeks without a break and thereby succeed in destroying most of the centre of the ozone layer. In the Arctic, it is now known that all the conditions for ozone depletion can be found, yet they never quite manage to produce a deep ozone hole. As the temperatures are cooling during the Arctic winter, the winds which blow not in circles but quite erratically over the Arctic carry the air away and bring in fresh warmer air. Furthermore, there is an early breakdown of circulation over the Arctic which carries the ozone-hole-producing formation away. Nevertheless, if we continue putting more chlorine into the atmosphere, the risk will increase that the circulation in one particular year will persist long enough for ozone depletion over the Arctic to become substantial.

Yet another example of how fast pollutants travel in the global eco-system is the problem of Arctic haze. Until about two decades ago, it was assumed that, given the extreme distances from the centres of human activity, only very long-lived components such as CO_2 or certain nuclear debris would be able to reach the highest latitudes. However, assumption about the relative isolation of the polar environments from natural and anthropogenic activities in lower latitudes has now been replaced by the knowledge that "on all time scales of events – from individual volcanic or nuclear explosions to recurring ice ages – trace substances are transported via complicated pathways to the poles and deposited to some extent in the very stable cryospheric archives" (Heintzenberg 1989: 50). Nevertheless, our understanding of the airborne or deposited distribution of pollutants in the polar regions is still limited.

Evaluating resources

The environment is not, in itself, a resource. Resources are those products and properties of the physical environment which human beings are technically capable of utilizing and which provide desired goods and services (Rees 1991: 7). Thus there is no such thing as a "natural" resource. The identification of resources varies from time to time and place to place as a function of technology and social structure. Both the changing definition and the utilization of resources are also consequences of images. Specific preferences illustrate how perceptions define resources.

Antarctic resources

In recent years, increasing pressure on global resources – both real and imagined – combined with the development of technology has turned international attention to the Antarctic, thought to be fabulously rich in mineral, marine and other resources (see Map D; Wassermann 1978; Zumberge 1979; Chaturvedi 1985b). Even if the requisite polar technology becomes available, could these resources be exploited economically and in an environmentally acceptable fashion? How does the relatively recent gold-mine image of the Antarctic correspond to what is known and, more pertinently, what is not known about this polar region?

Minerals on land

Some 200 million years ago Antarctica was contiguous with South America, Africa, Australia and India in a single landmass known as Gondwanaland. A continental reconstruction for the Proterozoic Era (2500 to 590 million years ago) suggests that the province of stratiform zinc, lead, copper and silver deposits in central Australia may continue into Terre Adélie. The Yilgarn gold, nickel, uranium and copper province of Western Australia may continue into Wilkes Land. The Indian manganese and iron province would continue into the 70° to 10°E sector. The West Antarctic magmatic arc, on account of its apparent continuity with the Andes, may have large metal deposits similar to those of the central Andes: copper, antimony, tin, molybdenum, silver, tungsten, zinc, lead, iron and gold.

However, these continental comparisons are highly simplistic. The continents that do not appear in the Gondwana reconstruction (North America, Europe and Asia) are also well endowed with mineral resources and contain two-thirds of the world's known metal reserves. The Gondwana analogy, therefore, states the obvious: the Antarctic crust is probably as mineralized as that of the other continents.

Antarctic geology, however, is still in its infancy (Zumberge 1979: 10; Parsons 1987: 67–97; Larminie 1991: 83–4). Much more rigorous and sophisticated technology is required for mineral prospecting in the Antarctic and is obviously far beyond the financial resources of the current programmes of pure research on the continent. To date, however, the only known mineral deposit of any size is the low-grade iron formation in the Prince Charles Mountains, Mac. Robertson Land, and on Mount Ruker. Similarly, the widespread Permian coal-bearing formations of the

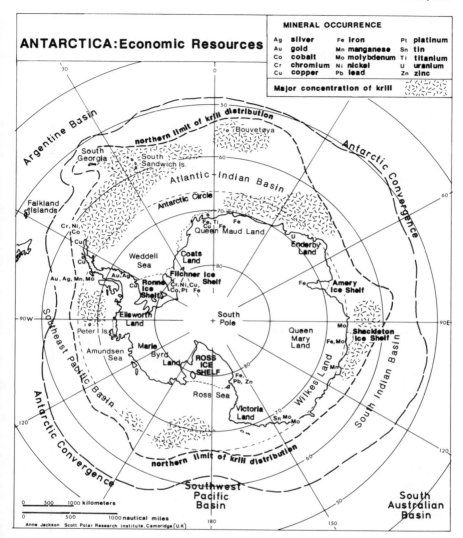

Map (D) Antarctica: economic resources

Transantarctic and Prince Charles Mountains are commonly cited as a potential deposit, but it is most unlikely that Antarctic coal, any more than Antarctic iron, could compete with thousands of millions of tonnes of more accessible and higher-grade coal resources which remain untapped in other parts of the world. On the present evidence, the Dufek Massif (on an ice sheet some 550 km inland) would, without doubt, be the prime target if mineral exploitation were ever to be undertaken in Antarctica.

25

Typical Antarctic conditions seriously question the relevance and utility of the otherwise powerful tool of geochemical exploration. Given that soil is very rare, the only sampling medium generally available in Antarctica is the rocks themselves. The special problem of hard-rock mining in the Antarctic is largely one of remote location and the lack of certain basic amenities. Antarctic mines would have to be self-sufficient to an unprecedented degree. The total lack of indigenous energy resources, an indigenous population, a power-generation and distribution infrastructure and internal communication within the continent further underlines the challenge. The possibility that Antarctic coal and other minerals would be found conveniently close to each other is also unlikely.

Prospects for oil and gas

The global oil crisis in the early 1970s coincided with the well-publicized prospects of finding oil and gas in the continental shelf of Antarctica. Speculation was rife (especially after small amounts of ethane and methane were reported in the Ross Sea continental shelf by the *Glomar Challenger* in 1973) that there might be another Gulf around the continent of Antarctica (Auburn 1978: 31). The world-wide repercussions of the oil crisis and their stated implications gave the rumours (as well as the widely cited figures of 45 billion barrels of oil and 115 trillion cubic feet of natural gas in the continental shelves of West Antarctica) considerable political weight.

For a petroleum geologist, the one and only encouraging factor at present is the known existence of large sedimentary basins on the continental shelves of Antarctica (see Behrendt 1983). On present evidence, the Ross Sea sector of the continental margin of Antarctica is the most promising sector. It is considered to be the least difficult area to exploit because the relatively mild sea-ice conditions make it more accessible.

The Antarctic continental shelf with its great depth (averaging 500 m, approximately eight times the world average), rugged topography and landward gradient poses an immense challenge to those contemplating exploitation of its oil and gas reserves. Yet another factor to deter petroleum exploration is the broad band of sea ice surrounding the Antarctic continent for most of the year. Sea ice covers virtually all the continental shelf for much of the year, with large areas of the Weddell Sea, Bellingshausen Sea, and eastern Ross Sea under perennial ice cover. In terms of physical as well as behavioural characteristics, the Antarctic ice pack differs from its Arctic counterpart. Arctic sea ice, being generally confined to the land-locked Arctic Basin, favours the formation of pressure ridges and multiyear sea ice (see Wadhams 1991). As most of the ice cover is first-year ice, Antarctic sea ice is relatively uniform in thickness, ranging from 1 to 3 m and averaging 1.5 m. However, fast ice, permanently attached to the coast, may be several metres thick.

In addition to the sea ice, ice shelves make up large portions of the Antarctic continental margin. The three largest ice shelves – the Ross, Ronne–Filchner and Amery – receive about 53% of the total ice drained from the continent, although they cover only about 10% of the coastline. The massive ice shelves, responsible for most of the large tabular icebergs in the Antarctic (some icebergs are also derived from ice tongues, outlet glaciers and tidewater glaciers), have a thickness of about 200–250 m near the calving margin, and tabular icebergs with drafts up to 330 m have been reported. However, side-scan sonar records show abundant iceberg furrow and gouge marks to depths of about 400–500 m. The drift and motion of these icebergs is unpredictable – several icebergs have exceeded a speed of 2 knots.

In addition to the extreme cold, Antarctic and Subantarctic storms pose formidable hazards to those contemplating oil-exploration activities or even the collection of geophysical data on the Antarctic margin. Antarctic conditions thus make all other sites for possible drilling, including the Arctic's Beaufort Sea, appear quite benign and far less challenging. Weather forecasting at present is entirely inadequate for such conditions and the season for drilling uniquely brief. From the time the sea ice breaks up to allow a drillship to get on station to the time it must leave or risk being trapped in for the winter may be less than 90 days.

The technology for exploratory drilling in Antarctic waters seems to be available (Westermeyer 1982: 319; Keys 1984: 127–8). Drillships can now operate in water more than 1000 m deep, and, if threatened by storms or icebergs, they are able to disengage from a wellhead quickly after sealing it. Wellheads can be sunk below (or in valleys of) the sea bottom to escape collision with icebergs. Blowout preventers are now more reliable. However, many more technical developments are needed if exploration is to advance to a stage of exploitation.

Even if we accept that the technology for oil exploration as well as exploitation is just round the corner, we cannot afford to overlook the environmental considerations. What would be the consequences of a major oil spill for the Antarctic ecosystems? In the case of the *Extoc I* blowout in the Bay of Mexico (June 1979), 35 million barrels of oil escaped over a period of nine months before it was brought under control, making it the largest oil spill in history. In the unyielding environment of the Antarctic, spills or blowouts occurring in late summer or autumn might not be controlled until the next summer. There could be tragic and cumulative impacts on the marine and terrestrial ecosystems, ice, beaches and soils, including protected areas. Opinions vary on the severity and the extent of damage that may be caused by such an accident, but everyone is agreed that we just do not know enough to be in a position to act.

Furthermore, even if the environmental concerns are successfully dealt with, the economic questions of cost/benefit in the extraction of oil from the Antarctic would be yet another formidable hurdle. The costs of oil production in Antarctica, at the current reckoning, are expected to be so enormous that only a very large oil field will seem worth developing – one yielding, say, more than a quarter million barrels a day (Dugger 1978: 337). In fact, by the time other petroleum resources are exhausted, oil and gas might no longer be used as fuels but might still be essential for the chemical industry.

Icebergs

The 27 million cubic kilometres of ice in the Antarctic cap represent about 70% of the usable fresh water on earth. Countries with fresh-water deficiencies have thought of Antarctic icebergs as a potential fresh-water resource. Taking only 10% of the estimated annual iceberg yield would provide some 120 billion cubic metres of usable fresh water a year, enough to irrigate 15–25 million acres of land (UN, Report of the Secretary General 1984: 102–3).

Many questions remain unanswered (Agrawal 1977: 11; Schwerdtfeger 1986; Rothwell and Kaye 1994). Who owns the icebergs? Are they free for the taking? What would be the effects of iceberg towing on the weather? What are the implications of taking water from desert to desert? What will be the impact of melting ice on the marine ecology where a beached iceberg radically alters water temperature and salinity? For the time being, the prospect of cheap and unlimited water from Antarctic icebergs seems to be dormant, if not dead, but the concept of iceberg utilization is not (Wadhams 1990: 203–15). A world in which water will become an increasingly important resource cannot for ever ignore the estimated 5000 icebergs calved from Antarctic glaciers and ice shelves every year (Quigg 1983: 82–4).

Marine resources

Biologically speaking, the richest, southernmost waters of the Indian Ocean, the Atlantic and the Pacific harbour the world's last great undeveloped fishery. Despite the reckless harvesting of marine mammals in Antarctic waters over a period of two centuries (see Brown 1963; Everson 1978), the idea of the southern seas as a rich source of food is comparatively recent. Two circumstances have added to the possibility of Antarctic waters attracting increasing international attention. First is the fact that exploitation of conventional fish may have reached or exceeded its limit. In recent years there has been a steady increase in the total world fish catch (including shellfish) to a plateau, reached in the early 1970s, of around 70 million metric tons. Although much of the increase in the past has been due to anchoveta fishery, if that component is excluded the underlying trend is still upward.

Secondly, this increasing pressure on established fishery resources has meant that in recent years there has been a tendency for those nations with a distant-water fishing capability to look further afield. The recent trend by coastal states of establishing 200-nautical mile exclusive economic zones (EEZs) has meant that the southern seas, an area of limited international control, have attracted a great deal of attention. After the formalization of the EEZ by the United Nations Conference on the Law of the Sea (UN-CLOS), the alternative fishing grounds around Antarctica have acquired high priority. These developments have occurred in parallel with the growing perception that food supplies generally may become increasingly scarce.

South of the Antarctic Convergence there are crabs and lobster, squid and octopus and fin fish, in unknown quantities (see Kock 1992: 166–201). Of the 20 000 kinds of fish in the world's oceans, only about a hundred have been found in the southern seas. Of these perhaps 20 species have potential for commercial exploitation, especially various kinds of Antarctic cod and icefish which are already being harvested. A catch of 299 metric tons of crabs *Paralomis spinosissima* and *P. formosa* was reported from the South Georgia Island area during the 1992–3 season (ATCM 1994a: 115).

Antarctic fin fish are also attracting interest. In fact, there are early indications that some Antarctic fishing nations may already be switching their focus from krill to fin fish. The latter may be able to sustain a fishery of a million tons. Nearly 300 000 tons were reported to have been caught in 1977. Countries such as Germany, Japan and Argentina are believed to be evaluating the possibility of exploiting Antarctic fin fish. In addition, the coasts of Antarctica are rich in seaweeds, including many already in use in other parts of the world as food or for the production of algae products. The benthic marine algae of Antarctica represent a potential resource.

However, it is krill – a small, shrimplike crustacean of exceptional nutritional value – that has become the focus of attention today. In all, six species of krill are found in the Southern Ocean, of which *E. superba* is the largest, most abundant and alone in being of commercial interest. The standing biomass of krill may range between 44.5 million and 7.5 billion tons. Potential yield estimates range from 25 million to 2.25 billion metric tons annually. The major international effort to learn more about the southern seas and their fauna is known as BIOMASS – Biological Investigations of Marine Antarctic Systems and Stocks (see El-Sayed 1988). A preliminary estimate of the standing stock of krill based on the First International BIOMASS Experiment (FIBEX) data was 650 million metric tons.

Krill fishing has been in progress since the early 1960s, when the Soviet Union sent the first krill fishing ship to Antarctica. In the mid-1980s, nearly 87% of the total landings were made by Soviet vessels, about 6% by Japanese; the rest were from Poland, the German Democratic Republic

29

and other countries. In recent years, the countries that have engaged in krill fishing – experimentally or commercially – include Chile, Germany, Japan, Poland, the Republic of Korea, Russia and Ukraine. The total resulting catches rose from 22 343 tons in 1973–4 to 477 025 tons in 1979–80. In 1981, however, the catch fell slightly to 448 000 tons, rising again to 529 505 tons in 1981–2 (UN, Report of the Secretary General 1984: 105–8). Recent experiments by marine geologists from Germany, Japan and Poland have shown that there is no difficulty in echo-locating krill swarms; impressive catch rates have been achieved thereby.

In the 1992–3 season the total krill catch in the area south of the Antarctic Convergence – the area covered by the 1982 Convention on the Conservation of Antarctic Marine Living Resources (CCAMLR) – on the basis of figures submitted by the major fishing countries (Japan, Russia, Poland and Chile) is 81 394 metric tons (CCAMLR 1993: 2–3). This figure is substantially less than the total reported catch of 302 961 tonnes for the 1991–2 season. The most recent decline is due to a reduction in fishing by the Russian and Ukrainian fleets, which took only 9000 tonnes, compared to the previous season's catches of about 300 000 tonnes (ATCM 1994a: 115).

Arctic resources

The Arctic region, in sharp contrast to the Antarctic, "is destined to become a major source of raw materials of critical importance to advanced industrial societies both in the Arctic Rim States and in other Northern Hemisphere States like Japan and Korea" (Osherenko and Young 1989: 45). In the case of hydrocarbons alone, responsible estimates of potentially recoverable reserves in the region range between 100 and 200 billion barrels of crude oil and up to 2000–3000 trillion cubic feet of natural gas (Conant 1992: 180). This alone should be sufficient to act as the catalyst for prospectors, despite the harsh natural conditions that substantially add to the costs of production, and delivery over long distances to southern markets.

The striking trend towards industrialization of the Arctic during the 1970s and 1980s, focusing primarily on energy resources but extending also to other raw materials, may well be seen in retrospect as a part of the great "scarcity" debate that raged in the late 1960s and early 1970s. It reflected the prevailing fears among the advanced Western countries, that Third World and socialist-country mineral producers could gain a monopoly over the supply of key minerals and thereby hold the former to ransom. Dependence on imports would then leave them vulnerable to price rises, such as those imposed by OPEC, or trade embargoes. Such fears were largely unfounded, but they did contribute at that time to the "great energy rush" to the Arctic, while in the case of Antarctica they conjured up a "goldmine" image.

Fuel and oil resources

The exploitation of hydrocarbons has fuelled the industrialization of the Arctic (Osherenko and Young 1989: 47–8). Major occurrences are known in both the American and the Russian territories, with smaller discoveries and promising sites elsewhere. The Prudhoe Bay field, located on Alaska's North Slope and discovered only in 1968, originally contained an estimated 9–10 billion barrels of recoverable oil and 26 trillion cubic feet of recoverable natural gas. North Slope is the largest discovery to date in the US. According to one rather conservative estimate, the recoverable reserves of oil in the North American Arctic run to 50 or more billion barrels (Ibid.: 47). The recoverable reserves of natural gas here amount to over 300 trillion cubic feet, though none of this gas is currently exploited commercially due to the lack of a transportation system. It provides two million barrels of oil per day and some 25% of the total domestic production comes via the Trans-Alaska Pipeline system from Prudhoe Bay (Conant 1992: 188).

The Russian Arctic contains more known mineral resources than any other Arctic region (Ibid.: 180). Siberia contains 80% of the country's potential oil reserves, and 90% of its gas and coal reserves are believed to be located there (Wilson 1987: 96). West Siberia is the major source of Russia's (and the former USSR's) oil and gas, accounting for 64% of the oil output of the former Soviet republics and 71% of the natural gas output in 1991 (Sagers and Kryukov 1993: 127). Encompassing the largest structural–sedimentary basin in the world, it is one of the world's premier locations of hydrocarbon deposits. At peak production (for oil) in 1988, the region yielded 415.1 million tons (mmt) of crude oil and 510.8 billion cubic metres (BCM) of natural gas (Ibid.). Even larger natural gas fields are located above the Arctic Circle, close to the Russian Arctic sea coast.

By 1992, as a result of 300 000 km of seismic exploration in the Barents Sea, and 50 000 km of seismic exploration in the Kara Sea, some 60–70 promising geological structures had been discovered. Subsequently, nine fields have been discovered in the Barents, Pechora and Kara Seas (see Moe 1992: 57–68). In the Pechora Sea the fields are: Priyazlomnoye (oil); Pomorskoye (gas and condensate, some oil); Severo-Gulyayevskoye (oil and consdensate); in the Barents Sea: Murmanskoye (gas); Shtokmanovskoye (gas and condensate); Severokildinskoye (gas and some oil); Ludlovskoye (gas and condensate); and in the Kara Sea: Rusanovskoye (gas and condensate) and Leningradskoye (gas and condensate). The total recoverable reserves of these fields (recoverable in the sense of fulfilling geological and technical conditions for production, and not in the sense of "commercially recoverable", are calculated at 12 000 BCM of natural gas and 400 million tons of oil, according to official statistics (cited in Ibid.: 58; Moe 1994: 132). Even if it is premature to say how much of this can be produced, the region is beyond doubt important in a long-term Russian resource perspective (Butler 1990). Figures for natural gas reveal a resource base several times the size of what has been discovered on the whole Norwegian shelf. Norway stands out as the country richest in natural gas in Western Europe (Ibid.).

In comparison to the hydrocarbons, other fossil-fuel resources in the Arctic are quite small. The Russian Far East's vast reserves of both hard and brown coal have thus far not been exploited at high enough levels to make the region self-sufficient in coal-based energy consumption. The gigantic but geographically remote reserves of the Tunguska and Lena coal basins seem destined to remain poorly explored well into the next century. On the other hand, coking coal production in the more accessible South Yakutian Basin could undergo significant expansion if a long-proposed new integrated iron-and-steel facility were to be built in the Far East region (ZumBrunnen 1990: 85–90). The Russians mine coal in the Pechora Basin, producing 30 million tonnes a year, and Norway, together with the former Soviet Union, has been extracting about one million metric tons from three coal mines in Svalbard (Armstrong 1992: 126). The US Arctic has been estimated to contain about as much coal as the rest of the country combined (*Arctic Research of the United States*, Spring 1993: 11). However, the production of this coal will be limited until the energy needs of Alaska grow substantially or the Pacific-rim countries provide sufficient impetus for further coal production. Some other Arctic coal deposits are known, but few are worked because of the relatively low unit value of the commodity (Armstrong 1992: 126).

Though not as formidable as in the Antarctic, factors such as low temperatures, sea ice and remoteness increase drastically the cost of most operations in the Arctic too. Sea ice is considered to be the most important consideration for engineering in the Beaufort, Chukchi and northern reaches of the Bering Seas as well as in Siberian waters. One of the major difficulties in opening up the Arctic has been ensuring adequate logistical support. Pipelines in the Arctic face problems unknown elsewhere. The great seasonal temperature variations, permafrost (both onshore and offshore) and other environmental impacts have already resulted in some of the most complex and costly civil engineering ventures in history (see Williams 1989).

Resource exploitation in the Arctic has already been quite intensive at a few specific locations such as Prudhoe Bay (Alaska) and Noril'sk (Siberia). Ever-expanding technologies have been having an impact on the ecology through such activities as the use of modernized transport vehicles, drilling for oil and gas, and mining and fishing. Contaminants released by ships add to the risk of affecting marine life through collision and noise. Worst affected by the ice-breakers are perhaps the distribution and migration patterns of mammals (seals, walrus, polar bears), affecting in turn the indigenous peoples whose subsistence depends on them. Oil spilt in the higher latitudes degrades at slower rates than oil spilt in warmer waters in that it can be trapped between ice and water for quite some time. The implications for marine ecosystems need not be laboured (see Brinken and Pyzhin 1993).

Mineral resources

Siberia's pre-eminence is once again obvious, but Russia's dependence on its northern territory is greater than that of the other Arctic-rim states. Nickel, cobalt and platinum-group metals are all combined in an unusually rich concentration of deposits in the Noril'sk area of northern Siberia, giving rise to one of the world's largest cities within the Arctic Circle and stimulating the development of an unusual icebreaker-supported year-round transport route through the Arctic Ocean (Shabad 1987: 82). The huge Noril'sk operation had brought the Soviet Union to the front rank of world producers of these metals. There is also a much smaller mining enterprise, in the Tuva Autonomous Republic of southern Siberia, where cobalt, in association with nickel, is derived from arsenide ores.

As in the case of tin (mined at Pevek and Deputatskiy), Siberia for long had a virtual monopoly in gold mining, with the focus gradually shifting from the Transbaykal region to the Aldan district in the 1920s, the Kolyma district in the 1930s and the Chukchi Peninsula of northeastern Siberia in the 1960s. The Polyarnyy lode mine and concentrator opened in 1969 on the Arctic Ocean coast. In Magadan Oblast' proper, the Karamken complex began production in 1978 and the Dukat complex in 1980 (see Kaser 1983). This output, second to that of the world's largest gold producer, South Africa, has always been a great help to the government in power in terms of adjusting the balance of payments – selling gold in the West when additional convertible currency was needed.

The northern Republic of Yakutia (now called Sakha) presently produces over 99% of all Russian diamonds (Zhuravlyov 1993), the country's second source of hard-currency receipts after energy carriers. As the world's leading diamond producer, in 1991 alone Yakutia sent to Moscow 12 million carats of jewellery diamonds, which is nearly 25% of the total world output of precious stones. In the same year, a diamond-bearing unique vertical intrusion, known as a kimberlite pipe, was drilled at Lac de Gras in the central mainland Northwest Territories in Canada, about 200 km north of Yellowknife. This news triggered the largest land-staking rush in Canada: 52 million acres (Hummel 1994: 13). Preliminary work to date indicates the presence of a cluster of 62 pipes with gem diamond concentrations and valuations comparable to those for diamond mines in Africa (Canadian Government 1993a: 1). A diamond deposit – said to be one of the world's largest – has also been discovered in the Finnmark region of Norway and in Finnish Samiland (Pearce 1994).

The Red Dog lead–zinc–silver mine, north of the Arctic Circle, is one of the largest zinc-producing mines in the world, generating 60% of the US zinc output. The in-ground value is estimated to be $11 billion at 1983 prices (*Arctic Research of the United States*, Spring 1993: 12).

In Greenland, deposits have been discovered at Narsaq alone which according to one estimate could "theoretically supply enough uranium for perhaps fifty years of Danish power consumption" (Taagholt 1993: 6). Other mineral deposits are: gold (deposits in East Greenland, due to low quality, have no commerical interest today, but newly discovered deposits in southwest Greenland, of much higher quality, are now undergoing detailed study); platinum (found with gold deposits in East Greenland); chromium (southwest Greenland); silver; lead; zinc; and rare earths such as niobium which could perhaps be used in the production of superconductors. Some big oil companies, in collaboration with the Danish/Greenlandic company Nunaoil, are carrying out seismic surveys of the continental shelf in both East and West Greenland to identify potential sources of oil and natural gas (Ibid.). The north Greenland area, although interesting in terms of both oil and mineral potential, is too inaccessible given current prices and technology (Poole *et al.* 1992: 192).

The offshore hard minerals most mined in the Arctic are sand and gravel, especially in the eastern Chukchi Sea and Beaufort Sea, for use as aggregate by the petroleum industry for the construction of onshore facilities and temporary artificial islands. A single production island could consume in excess of 20 million cubic metres of sand and gravel (Hale 1990: 561). Dredging activities for sand and gravel on the Arctic shelves, though likely to keep pace with nearby offshore construction projects, are not likely to become widespread in the Arctic in the foreseeable future. Dredges capable of operating through ice could be designed and built, but the production capacity would be much smaller than in the ice-free season.

No deep-sea mineral deposits have yet been identified in the Arctic Ocean Basin (Ibid.: 564). If they were to be found, however, the absence of appropriate mining technologies, coupled with weak metal markets and the difficulties of working in the Arctic, would preclude their development in the foreseeable future.

Marine resources

The fringing seas of the Arctic Ocean are rich in a variety of marine species. The boundaries of the areas for which statistical records are published do not coincide with those of the Arctic, but, using a generous interpretation of Arctic and Subarctic, one may say that the seas in these two zones yield about 14% of the world catch of salt-water fish – in absolute terms, 3.3 million metric tons from the North Atlantic sector and 7 million tonnes from the North Pacific sector (1983 figures, *Yearbook of*

Fisheries Statistics: FAO). In 1988, nearly 40% of the Soviet Union's approximately 10.5 million tons, or 12% of the world's harvest, of ocean products came from the Russian Far East. It has been suggested that this region's output of fish and marine products will increase by 28% by the year 2000.

Arctic and Bering Sea waters support some the most productive fisheries in the world. The Bering Sea supplies nearly 5% of the world's fishery products. An estimated 4 million metric tons of 43 commercial species are caught every year by fishermen from the United States, Russia, Japan and other nations. Together with the Gulf of Alaska, the Bering Sea has been estimated to contain 36 billion pounds of cod, sole, flounder, perch, mackerel and pollock alone (Canfield 1993: 258). Since the passing of the Magnuson Fishery Conservation and Management Act in 1976, American groundfish operations in Alaska have developed into an industry with an annual product value estimated at $2.2 billion. In 1989, Alaska pollock, with a landing of 1.1 million metric tons, was the most important US fish in quantity, accounting for 28% of US commercial landings. No wonder Alaska leads all the American states in both total volume and the total value of fish landed. In 1990, the Alaskan fishing industry produced 46% of all US seafood, with an estimated wholesale value of $3 billion (Ibid.).

In recent years, as in the case of US east-coast fisheries, those off the coast of Alaska have been increasingly the focus of intense exploitation of stocks with poorly understood population levels and structures. As a result, dramatic and unexplained fluctuations have occurred in the catch of groundfish and shellfish and in the stocks of marine mammals. There is concern that the walleye pollock population may crash, as others have in the past (*Arctic Research of the United States*, Spring 1993: 12).

Waters off Greenland are rich, especially in cod and shrimp, and the Greenlandic economy has an almost critical dependence on their sustainable development. More so, because the last remaining mining activity, at Marmorilik, ended in 1990, and the prospects for tourism are not currently so bright. During 1989 and 1990 the total catch rose to levels in excess of 50 000 tons. Today shrimp fishing and processing is the dominant industry in Greenland, accounting for over three-quarters of the total value of her exports of fish and fish products (see Poole 1994).

The Barents Sea, with its ecosystem stretching southwards along the Norwegian coast and westwards into the Norwegian Sea, is among the most promising and productive ocean areas in the world today. While fish quotas have been cut back drastically elsewhere due to a sharp decline in fish stocks, the stocks in the Barents Sea are on the increase (Hoel 1994: 115–16). Whereas groundfish and pelagic fisheries have traditionally been important in Barents Sea fisheries, economically the most important species is cod. The annual total allowable catch is of the order of 700 000 metric tons (Ibid.). Other important groundfish fisheries in the area – providing food for marine mammals, hence central to the ecosystem – are haddock, redfish and saithe. There is also a substantial shrimp fishery and a whaling and sealing industry.

Tourism in the polar regions

A rapidly growing consumer of resources in both the polar regions is tourism. Although not a direct consumer, tourism is a resource-dependent enterprise, its "capital assets" being natural landscapes and their biota together with elements of historic and cultural heritage. The effects of tourism on the polar ecosystems are presently poorly understood. There is now a growing awareness both inside and outside the tourist industry that further growth and long-term profitability must be realized in the context of conservation and the sustainable use of natural resources. Regulation of tourism in the Arctic and Antarctic poses problems of its own and needs innovative forward-looking approaches involving, for example, governments, non-governmental organizations, the tourism industry and the individual tourists. In the case of the Arctic, the concerns of the indigenous peoples are also of vital importance. Chapters 8 and 9 of this study have much more to say on these issues.

Summary and conclusions

The chapter has attempted to bring out the complexity of the "natural" environment in the polar regions, in terms of its ecological dimensions, subjective geopolitical settings and discursive "representations". The bipolar contrast has established beyond doubt the significance of the Arctic and the Antarctic as exceptionally important ecological regions on our planet. Lack of scientific knowledge and understanding of the polar environments creates impressions that are mostly at odds with reality. The resultant (mis)perceptions in turn colour attitudes to exploration, development and conservation, often leading to futile controversies and unnecessary conflicts. As a result, opportunities to learn about the nature and evolution of polar environments are either lost or mismanaged.

No combination of circumstances – supply, demand, discovery, technology – that would make the extraction of hard minerals economically attractive in the Antarctic can be foreseen until well into the 21st century. Nevertheless, expectations of future wealth give a great deal of importance even to these hard minerals, frozen deep beneath thousands of feet of Antarctic ice, leading to a discursive transformation of the Antarctic from being "empty" to "central" in the dominant discourse of the international political economy. These expectations have not been confined to those currently active in Antarctica. As we shall see in Chapter 4, they have also started galvanizing the so-called "outsiders".

The Circumpolar North, on the other hand, is already well integrated into the international political economy and far more deeply impacted by the forces of economic globalization and political fragmentation. Even though significant differences are to be noted among the Arctic-rim states in terms of resource endowments, economic production, material and physical flows, interactions and movements, on the whole the Arctic areas appear to be increasingly embraced by the discourse and practices of the world market economy. We will return to this theme in Chapter 9.

Both the polar regions, however, challenge the traditional geopolitical discourse of spatial domination and illustrate in more than one way that geography has to be much more than physical geography: a human geography sensitive to the rhythms of ecology in its treatment of space and resources on the one hand and aware of converging, or diverging, subjective human perspectives on the other. In an increasingly interdependent world, in both the economic and the ecological senses of the term, the idea of international cooperation is not just an ideal but an imperative.

Suggested reading

Sturges, W.T. (ed.) 1991. *Pollution of the Arctic Atmosphere*. London: Elsevier Science Publishers.

Sugden, D.E. 1982. *Arctic and Antarctic: A Modern Geographical Synthesis*. Oxford: Basil Blackwell.

The State of the Arctic Environment Reports 1991 Rovaniemi: Arctic Centre, University of Lapland.

Weller, G. *et al.* (eds) 1991. Volumes I and II. *International Conference on the Role of the Polar Regions in Global Change*. Proceedings of a Conference, 11–15 June 1990. University of Alaska, Fairbanks: Geophysical Institute, and Center for Global Change and Arctic System Research, University of Alaska.

3

Colonization and demarcation: a bipolar geohistory

To understand the contemporary geopolitical realities of the polar regions we have to refer to their history. Only by focusing on the geography behind both the history and the politics of the Arctic and Antarctica can we understand not only what happened in the past, but also *why* it happened. Since the history of the geographical exploration of the polar regions has been well recorded (see Christie 1951; Bertrand 1971; Cameron 1974; Headland 1989; Fogg and Smith 1990; Imbert 1992; Baughman 1994; Holland 1994; Vaughan 1994), I intend limiting this chapter to a very broad discussion – in both a spatial–geographical and a temporal–historical sense – of the imperial past of the Arctic and Antarctica.

If geography is concerned with the study of places as they have been, and continue to be, transformed by human intervention (Livingstone 1992: 347), then the key questions for this chapter become: What has been the impact of the socio-economic and intellectual environments of the imperial era on the polar regions? How were the geographies of the two polar regions perceived and put to human use (or "abuse") in the imperial context? What was the motivation behind, and the consequences of, those practices for the physical – in the case of the Arctic, also human – geography of the polar regions? What kind of legacies have those practices left?

My argument is that penetration of both the polar regions by the imperial–colonial forces needs to be seen as an extension of a similar but much larger process emanating, at least to begin with, from Europe, and unfolding differently in various parts of the world. This perspective demands an examination of the "sites" involved in the process. The use of the word "site" in the plural is intended to suggest to the reader the distinction as well as the interconnection between the site affected by the imperial process (a geographical place such as the Arctic or Antarctica with its natural–geographic attributes) and the site (the geographical, cultural, political and theoretical viewpoint, with its ideological–geographical representations of the polar regions) from which that process emanates. Indeed, "there will be many Geographies of a place depending on where it is viewed from" (Taylor 1993b: 194).

This chapter is divided into four major parts. Part one outlines the "broader context" against which issues pertaining to the territorial annexation, colonization and demarcation of the two polar regions are tackled. Part two deals specifically with the colonization of the Arctic homelands and its implications for indigenous peoples. Part three discusses the successful solution to the Svalbard (Spitsbergen) question. Part four examines the claims and counterclaims of territorial sovereignty asserted in Antarctica from about the turn of the present century. This chapter has no intention whatsoever of undermining the scientific motivations for, or achievements of, polar exploration, which remain noteworthy in their own right and have been well recorded (Fogg 1992; Levere 1993).

Imperial geography and geopolitics

The origin and history of the concept of sovereignty and its various manifestations in the polar regions are closely related to the nature and evolution of the nation-state, particularly the development of centralized authority in early modern Europe. The absolutist state replaced the system of feudal domination, and the acquisition of new territory – whether by conquest in Europe or colonization of the "new world" – became a means of extending the royal domain and the emergence of the sovereign state the necessary instrument of Europe's colonial expansion (Camilleri and Falk 1992: 14–15).

Throughout the period of colonial expansion between the 16th and 19th centuries, states did not, however, adhere to any one doctrine of territorial acquisition (Triggs 1986: 4). Territorial expansion was justified on grounds ranging from elaborate religious ceremonies to 14th-century papal bulls. In practice, states found it necessary to substantiate their claims to title by "actual settlement and administration" coupled with at least the intention of excluding others, by force if necessary. By the end of the 19th century, state practice recognized that only by establishing an effective presence could a state protect its newly asserted territorial claims. Such was the intention behind the agreement at the African Conference of Berlin in 1885. The question then would become how the notion of *effective* occupation would operate in a relatively remote and inhospitable environment such as the polar regions.

If International Law, in the imperial context, tried to grapple with the issue of "effective occupation", then Geography too as an academic discipline emerged in the late 19th century as a tool of imperialism (Taylor 1993a: 105; but see the qualifications made by Heffernan 1994). For the countries engaged in the contest for territories and colonies in the non-European world, the pressing need for topographical surveys, charts of coastlines and potential port facilities, evaluation of natural resources, reports on indigenous peoples and a spectrum of other information ensured a central role for geographers and the organizations that sponsored them (Bassin 1994: 112–13). However, "the distant and little known lands that were to be appropriated and colonized had not only to be explored in terms of their coastlines and mountain ranges but had to be located conceptually within the imperial consciousness" (Dodds 1996, forthcoming). The relatively less problematic pursuit of practical geographical information about landscapes thus had to be supplemented by a far more complex task of "representations of space", involving "all of the concepts, naming practices, and geographical codes used to talk about and understand" those landscapes (Agnew and Corbridge 1995: 7).

When Social Darwinism appeared in the 19th century, the nature of the global terrestrial unity came to be conceived in mainly biological terms (Parker 1985: 10–11). Accordingly, states, considered as living beings, were taken as being subject to the laws of nature, experiencing growth and decay, feeling an insatiable hunger for yet more territory. Some extreme protagonists of the organic theory took these metaphors literally, considering that the state was indeed a living entity (see Hepple 1992).

These aspects of 19th-century Europe combined to produce a "politically committed" geopolitical thinking, the most outstanding spokesman of which was Friedrich Ratzel (1844–1904). Ratzel identified the state as a biological organism, constantly growing, and with this growth went an increased need for territory from which to derive its sustenance. Ratzel termed this territory the *Lebensraum* and maintained that the state had to expand physically as its population grew or risk exhaustion of its sustenance base and decline (Bassin 1987a: 127). To gain power through territorial expansion therefore remained the central goal of national action. Ratzel generalized these ideas into a series of what he called the seven laws of state growth (Glassner 1993: 224), leaving no doubt that he interpreted the contemporary contest among the European powers in Africa and Asia in terms of a quest for *Lebensraum* (Bassin 1987b: 127; Kost 1989: 371).

Rudolf Kjellén (1864–1922), who coined the term *Geopolitik* in an article on the boundaries of Sweden in 1899 (Holdar 1992: 307), was also a product of this social and intellectual period. Inspired by German idealist philosophy, Social Darwinism and the *Zeitgeist* of imperialism, he broke with the then dominant view of the state as an exclusively legal entity, viewing it instead as a power in foreign affairs and using an organic analogy to describe its existence. *Geopolitik* was the first category of Kjellén's

41

system of Political Science. He defined it as the study of the state as "a geographical organism or a phenomenon in space". The state was in constant competition for power with others. The maximum gain of power became the "central motive" of state action and of politics (Kost 1989: 371).

Alfred Thayer Mahan (1840–1914), who has been described as a "geopolitical strategist", viewed geographical factors primarily in terms of their impact on the power capabilities of states (Seager 1977: 1). His cherished and passionately promoted dream was an enduring Anglo-American alliance as the key to mastery of the world. Mahan held that command of the seas generated the economic strength and prosperity of a people and thus constituted the decisive factor in political relations among states. Accordingly, future world power must rest on control of the seas; mere land powers, however large, were destined to decline and decay (Sloan 1988: 87–95, 97–101). Countries could – and Mahan was convinced that the USA should – expand their political power by way of the seas.

A contemporary of Mahan and Kjellén, Sir Halford J. Mackinder (1861–1947), while greatly emphasizing land power, wanted his geopolitical thinking to be an aid to statecraft (see Parker 1982), helping to enlighten the policy-maker who was otherwise ignorant of the geographical realities of the world (Parker 1985: 18–19; Glassner 1993: 226–7). Underlining the impending revolutionary developments of his age that technology had initiated in the early 20th century, Mackinder declared that, with man's exploration of the globe now complete, the world had become "a closed political system". Advances in transport technology rendered the idea of world domination, for the first time, a viable political proposition. The polar regions were to be no exception.

The creation of a naturalized geopolitics in the early part of the 20th century implicitly recognized the importance of Social Darwinism and the fin-de-siècle. In their different ways, the geopolitical writings of Mackinder and Ratzel acknowledged that "geopolitics was now determined by the natural character of states that could be understood scientifically akin to the new biological processes that marked the period" (Agnew and Corbridge 1995: 56). The implications of such a discursive and intellectual shift were several-fold – the state was reconceptualized as an organism with specific biological needs, and the importance of natural boundaries and economic nationalism was recognized. As we shall note, the polar regions were not immune from such a transformation. Territorial claims in the Antarctic were intellectually justified on the basis of appeals of using natural features (such as geological continuity in the case of South American territorial claims) to designate the natural area of a state, for instance. Naturalized geopolitical discourse was an important intervention in the creation of a "closed world" in the first part of the present century.

The "discovery" and colonization of the Arctic homelands

For reasons of relative proximity, and in most cases geographical contiguity, the Arctic was penetrated by the imperial impulse and the vigorous assertion of nation-state authority long before Antarctica fell under the claims of European and the postcolonial states of the southern hemisphere.

The Russian colonization of northern Eurasia: from the Urals to the Pacific

By the middle of the 16th century the colonial expansion of European states was well under way. Muscovite Russia, by this time one of the most formidable states in Europe, joined the wave of European expansionism. Using similar means of conquest and colonization, it annexed the largest continuous territory of any empire – the whole of northern Eurasia, which came to be called Siberia. This was achieved almost entirely by Russians, or by those in Russian service, more by a process of infiltration than by military action (Armstrong 1965: 9). Nevertheless, the whole process had a great impact on the life and fate of the indigenous population because this vast mass of land, despite the severity of its climate, was not "empty". By about 3500 BC several Neolithic cultures existed which, however sparsely distributed, extended over the whole of northern Eurasia, as far as the shores of the Arctic Ocean.

Russian territorial expansionism has always been characterized by one striking feature: expansion into immediately contiguous territories. With the single exception of Russia's ultimately abortive occupation of Alaska, the product of this process – not dependent upon fleets of sailing-ships plying long distances across the oceans – was an empire based on a single unbroken landmass of continental proportions, a circumstance that served to differentiate it in an unmistakable fashion from the maritime empires of Western Europe. The routes used by the incoming Russians were the waterways, which could be travelled by boat in summer or by sledge in winter. The east–west layout of the tributaries of the northward-flowing rivers of Siberia was to prove most convenient. Moreover, "there was never at any time a direct threat to Russian power in northern Eurasia by another country capable of taking and occupying large parts of the territory" (Armstrong *et al.* 1978: 25).

By 1620 the annexation of western Siberia, despite considerable resistance by the indigenous peoples, was complete and the Muscovite colonial regime firmly in place. About 1.25 million square miles of land had been added to Muscovy and a network of fortified towns laid down to extend the Tsar's government to the indigenous peoples.

In its colonial pursuit, essentially mercantile in nature (see Bassin 1988), the Russian state exploited the indigenous peoples as producers of wealth:

fur provided enormous riches throughout the 16th and 17th centuries (Forsyth 1992: 39–41). This wave of commercial exploitation led, however, to the influx into Siberia of not only Russian soldiers, officials and trappers but also a variety of craftsmen, priests and merchants. Since importing grain into Siberia from European Russia was exorbitant in cost and very time-consuming due to the distances involved, the government decided to make Russian settlements beyond the Urals self-supporting in agricultural produce. Thus began a movement of peasants from Russia into Siberia which later became a mass migration.

As the Russians continued their take-over of northern Eurasia during the 18th century, the life of the indigenous peoples was gradually, but irrevocably, altered without regard for their wishes or rights. In its encroachment on native peoples and their land, Russian colonialism showed similarities to that in other parts of the Arctic (Ibid.: 43). Traditional tribal organizations underwent profound changes during this period, as did many ancient social institutions. The ethnographic map of Siberia also altered as the 20th century approached. Those areas occupied by tundra Nentsy, Chukchi, Evenks and Evens grew noticeably, while Entsy, Yukagirs, Koryaks, Itel'mens and Eskimos lost much of their territory (Vakhtin 1994: 37). Demographically, as Forsyth recorded (1992: 115, 190–200), the number of Russians living in Siberia increased from some 300 000 at the beginning of the 18th century to perhaps 900 000 at the end of the century, and then to about 2.7 million by the middle of the 19th century. This figure had almost doubled by 1900, reaching eight million by 1911. Consequently, the relative population of indigenous peoples fell. By 1911 they represented only 11.5% of the inhabitants of Siberia. The two most important geopolitical landmarks in this process were the creation of a continuous land route from the Urals to Irkutsk and beyond (beginning in 1763) and the construction of the Trans-Siberian Railway (beginning in 1891). The practice of sending exiles and political prisoners to Siberia also contributed to the waves of immigration (Armstrong 1965: 81–7; Wood 1989: 12–15).

The Far East, the "tattered edge of Siberia", was the last part to be reached by Russian colonists (Lantzeff and Pierce 1973: 195–219). Kamchatka was annexed by a party under the Cossack Atlasov in 1697. Chukotka, the peninsula facing the Bering Strait, was the last part to be subdued, owing to the warlike disposition of the Chukchi (Armstrong 1965: 25–26). It was not until the 19th century, however, that Russian settlements and treaties truly consolidated Russia's hold on its Pacific periphery (Hausladen 1990: 8–11).

Although the Russian conquest of the Asiatic North was practically over by the end of the 17th century, there remains another, less successful stage: the extension of the eastwards movement across the North Pacific to North America. This phase of colonization began in the wake of Vitus Bering's second voyage (1733–43), when hunter–trappers, hearing of the abundance of sea otters in the region, rushed to exploit this new and easy source of wealth, first in the uninhabited Komandorskiye Islands and then in the Aleutians.

At around this time Russian imperial expansion towards the northeast encountered, for the first time, competition from other European powers, particularly Britain. In the wake of the loss of the American colonies, British interest in the region manifested itself in the voyages of Cook in 1776 and of others later – Meares, Portlock, Vancouver. This clash had its origin in competition for markets, since both sold fur in China. In 1786 the Russians claimed the American coast north of latitude 55° 21'N, and the offlying islands (the Aleutians and the Kurils), on the basis of Bering's discoveries, which antedated Cook's. This eastward push of Russia's empire and the fur trade converted the passage from Kamchatka to Alaska into a busy sea lane. In 1799 the Russian American Company was granted a monopoly over all commercial enterprise and the right to govern Russian America. Learning from Britain's success with the East India Company and the Hudson's Bay Company, the Russians preferred commercial penetration to a direct claim of sovereignty. The Russian American Company's activities extended at their peak as far south as Fort Ross in California. However, by the mid-19th century the company ceased to be profitable, and Russian America turned into a fiasco because of the enormous problems of communication and supply (Armstrong *et al.* 1978: 125). In 1867, the Russian colonies in Alaska were sold to the United States for $7 200 000. The purchase failed to evoke much popular support in America, as many felt that the transaction had no commercial value. Income from salmon fishery and gold mining would soon prove the critics wrong. It goes without saying that the indigenous communities had no role in the deal. They were not even aware of it (Hall 1987: 151).

From the 17th to the 19th centuries, administration of the indigenous peoples was carried out by governors, acting through local chiefs and elders. "In practice, the tribes were thrown upon the mercy of the Siberian administration which, even compared to that of European Russia, was notorious for its embezzlement of state property and violence" (Vakhtin 1994: 37).

At the time of the Bolshevik revolution, the indigenous peoples possessed various rights and privileges but only in theory. The new rulers chose to be driven by pragmatic geopolitical reasoning, rather than by ideological considerations, and decided to retain the status quo with regard to the centre–periphery relationship *vis-à-vis* Siberia and the Far East. By 1923 the dominance of the Soviet authorities was well established in most parts of the North, to the extent, as Mark Bassin has noted, that "Russia" was being increasingly characterized by a new generic term – *mestorazvitiye*. The Urals and the High Arctic were no longer considered geographical divides, rather

Russia was now depicted as a single geopolitical, geo-ecological and geocultural entity whose boundaries refused to acknowledge the divides posed by geology or morphology (Bassin 1994).

The former indigenous administrative structures had been dismantled and the "Statute of the Indigenous Peoples" abrogated. In April 1924, the Presidium of the Central Executive Committee voted to establish the "Committee for Assisting the Peoples of the Far North", better known as the "Committee of the North", but the committee could not achieve much due to lack of funding and the growing political power of totalitarian communism (see Vakhtin 1994: 42).

Throughout the 1930s, the Russian North was subjected to large-scale exploitation of natural resources by the Russian Communist Party regime (see Taracouzio 1938: 141–251). For example, in Yakutia alone, as many as 20 000 hunters were after fur in 1937, killing annually up to 1.5 million squirrels, 250 000 ermine and 35 000 Arctic fox, which were worth around 16 000 000 roubles to the Soviet Russian state for foreign trade (Forsyth 1992: 298). The "imperatives of 'building socialism' made it inevitable that more and more Russian intrusion into native territories would take place, and that the lives of the native peoples would become increasingly subordinated to the industrial development of the Soviet Russian state" (Ibid.). While before 1917 the interest of imperial officialdom in the Arctic was "spasmodic", under the Soviets the situation changed drastically as described by Taracouzio (1938: 140)

> By having given the task of Arctic exploration into the hands of a communist state, and subjected the actual process of this exploration to rigid planning; by having preserved the emphasis on the materialistic aspect of the problem, and resorted to the propaganda so essential for a Marxist, the Soviets have made the history of their Arctic exploration a convincing proof that by Sovietization of the Arctic they mean Soviet mastery over it in the fullest sense of the term, and that physical conquest is only one aspect of this process. The other two . . . are its economic development and its social-cultural reconstruction.

By the time of World War II, the basic infrastructure for the future exploitation and development of the region was well in place. As Lantzeff and Pierce (1973: 230) point out: "If the Russians had not penetrated and appropriated the region, other peoples would have done so . . . plundering of natural resources by the seventeenth- and eighteenth-century Russians was nothing unique, but merely an expression of attitudes which prevailed everywhere until now, when ideas of conservation are beginning to gain acceptance."

Colonization of the Canadian North

It was on 20 July 1871 that "one of the largest transfers of territory in all of recorded history was being effected" (Zaslow 1971: 1). In return for a cash and land settlement with the Hudson's Bay Company, the Canadian government added to its dominion Rupert's Land and what was then called the "North-Western Territory". The latter at that time included parts of the country as far south as the 49th parallel. It was only after 1912 that the name "Northwest Territories" was given to those parts of Canada lying beyond the 60th parallel. Throughout the 1870s, the Canadian authorities were making treaties with, or rather imposing treaties on, the prairie Indians to extinguish their title to land. Well within a decade the frontiers were firmly established. Thereafter, the opening of the Canadian North would be a gradual advance of frontiers and frontier experience from the rear of the province of Canada to the prairie northwest, then gradually northward along several fronts to the northern coasts of Canada and the islands beyond.

For 200 years prior to the transfers, following the grant of its charter by Charles II in 1670, the Hudson's Bay Company (HBC) had been almost the absolute lord and proprietor of Rupert's Land – all the land draining into Hudson's Bay – named after the king's cousin, Prince Rupert, first governor of the company. From the very beginning, the company faced serious competition from French fur traders operating from Montreal (Hill 1967: 4–7). The rivalry with the French continued until the surrender of New France in 1763.

By then the fur trade had become the dominant economic, social and political force in New France and Rupert's Land. By the time the HBC and the North West Company amalgamated in 1821, the fur traders had made their way as far as the mouth of the Mackenzie River. In the process the indigenous peoples became firmly involved in the fur-trade economy and dependent for their living on the outsiders. The Inuit communities had also been affected by whaling, which reached its peak between 1820 and 1840 (Bone 1992: 54).

From 1821 to 1870, the HBC was at the zenith of its power and prestige. However, the Canadians had begun to resent the company's dominion over most of the territories into which they themselves wanted to expand. Even the imperial authorities in London could not escape the conclusion that the time had arrived for the company to surrender at least its control of territories to Canada. The need to colonize the fertile parts of those territories was being acutely felt in view of the possibility that American immigrants might turn them into another Oregon. Throughout the 17th and the 18th centuries, no real desire for colonization had manifested itself in the fur trade. All this was to change, however, in the second half of the 19th century, as a result of growing Anglo-American friction on the one hand and the substantial political presence of the United States in the American High Arctic on the other.

In 1867 Canada achieved Dominion status within the British empire. The same year, following secret negotiations, from which perhaps the British were excluded, America purchased Alaska from Russia. This was the first major blow to the dream, nurtured since the 1850s, of a "Great Britannic Empire of the North", rivalling the United States (Levere 1993: 244).

In 1871, Rupert's Land and other holdings of the HBC were transferred to Ottawa. A decade later, the British government transferred to Canada the rest of the Arctic possessions and the Arctic Archipelago (including the islands not yet discovered). The Dominion of Canada was suddenly transformed into one of the world's largest states. Zaslow (1971: 2) argues that it was precisely the "empty" undeveloped quality of the country northwest of Canada – home to some 15 000 nomadic aborigines and a small number of transient white men, engaged in prospecting, fur trading, fishing and whaling or the saving of souls – that was the major geopolitical attraction for Canadians. *"Expansion became a national duty for Canada, a commitment with destiny"* [emphasis supplied].

Whereas the Dominion government was mindful of the urgency of bringing under its "effective occupation" the remote northerly parts of the new territories, an Order in Council of 23 September 1882 recommended "that no steps be taken with the view of legislating for the good governance of the country until some influx of population or other circumstances shall occur to make such provision more imperative than it would at present seem to be" (cited in Smith 1966: 204; Levere 1993: 341). The indigenous populations of Inuit and Indians clearly were assumed to be in no need of good governance from the south. Coincidentally, it was at this very time that the Conference on Africa (in Berlin), already referred to, was imposing the requirement of effective possession as a condition for full sovereignty.

In 1888, a Senate committee on the Resources of the Great Mackenzie Basin investigated the question, which led to the publication of a "highly enthusiastic report on the potential for agriculture, fisheries, forestry, mining and petroleum, setting the precedent for the optimistic and promotional tone that has continued to this day to pervade the government pronouncements on northern resources" (Armstrong *et al.* 1978: 79). While the report was followed by an enlarged programme of governmental surveys, the national priority at that time was to populate the southern agricultural prairies, establish their institutions and integrate their economy and society into those of Canada as a whole (Fisher 1977).

The North had to mark time until 1897, when the Klondike gold rush transformed the southern Yukon (see Coates and Morrison 1988: 77–116). The indigenous peoples lost control of their traditionally occupied land, became involved in the gold economy and were exposed to "new" diseases. For the Canadian government, the "circumstances" so desperately needed for asserting and consolidating sovereignty over its new acquisitions had finally arrived. Ottawa lost no time in dispatching detachments of North-West Mounted Police to the Yukon to impose Canadian law and order on the fast-burgeoning population of the area. According to Morrison (1985: 2) "The Canadian government wanted to make the northern frontier become and remain 'Canadian' so that Ottawa's absolute sovereignty would be unquestioned" (Ibid.).

However, after a brief encounter with gold, the Yukon was left with a deep recession and a shrunken economy, a fate common to all those places in the Arctic that, at one time or the other, were subjected to boom-and-bust cycles of reckless economic growth. The gold rush had also affected the indigenous peoples far beyond the Yukon River valley. Subsequent economic growth, assisted by technological improvements in the transportation systems in the upper Mackenzie region, foreshadowed further exploitation. The federal government sought to remove native title to the land through a treaty: by 1899, signatures had been sought, with the assistance of the Mounted Police and missionaries, for a hastily drafted and vaguely formulated "Treaty 8". As a result, the upper Mackenzie River valley, from Edmonton in the south to Great Slave Lake in the north, and from the middle of northern British Columbia to the east end of Lake Athabasca, was opened up for exploitation. More treaties were to follow the northward expansion of Canada. While one major purpose of these treaties was to help the indigenous communities live in a world dominated by white civilization, reserves created to provide permanent shelters for nomadic or semi-nomadic peoples were expected to be useful for enforcing state authority.

As Zaslow (1971: 283–4) has concluded in his analysis of the northward expansion of Canada during the years 1870–1914, Canadian governments favoured authoritarian and centralizing methods. The greatest failures involved the treatment of native peoples and the mismanagement of resources.

In 1914, on the instructions of the Department of the Interior, a compilation of all available information on the resources of northern and northwestern Canada (Chambers 1914) was published. Provocatively entitled *The Unexploited West*, the study divided the vast region under review into five district territorial units and provided a comprehensive list of "facts" about the climate, the soil, the timber, the rivers, the lakes, the minerals, the fish and the game "obtained at the risk of life and limb by fur trader, explorer, missionary, geologist and sportsman", which it claimed "now have a practical value". Even a casual perusal of the study is enough to reveal the then predominantly exploitative attitude to nature and its resources.

During and immediately after World War I, there was a general lapse in activity in the North. When it resumed, it was strengthened by a new-found confidence based on Canada's wartime achievements and reinforced by reports from Stefansson (the Canadian explorer) and others that the natural-resource base was even greater than previously believed. Another reason was the flat denial of Canadian sovereignty over Ellesmere Island by the Danish explorer Knud Rasmussen and the endorsement of this denial by the Danish government. Canada launched a strong protest and undertook measures to demonstrate effective occupation of the island through regular ship patrols of the Eastern Arctic and by the establishment of a number of permanent police posts and post offices. Denmark let the issue of Ellesmere Island drop and, at least tacitly, accepted Canadian sovereignty. The Canadian government, however, was convinced that consistent northward economic expansion was the best way of achieving two complementary objectives – the economic development of the North and the consolidation of state authority over the area. In other words, colonization and demarcation were to go hand in hand, and so they did for many decades to come. Consequently, by the late 1960s "the agricultural, forestry, hydro, and mining frontiers had been pushed to their economic and nearly to their physical limits" (Zaslow 1988: 367). On the question of ecology, "governments and public had simply taken the environment as a given to be used freely by authorized persons or corporations in their own interests" (Ibid.: 370).

The Nordic approach to the colonization of Sami homelands

The Sami, according to some scholars, have inhabited the far north of Norway, Sweden, Finland and Russia's Kola Peninsula for the last 8000 years. Before 1600, the Sami lived in their homelands, unrestricted by nation-state boundaries, until the gentry, the king and the Church pushed their claims northwards (Zorgdrager 1984: 13–14; Beach 1994: 170–1). The Sami were exposed to products like wool and flour and the bartering system. For centuries, Vaughan points out (1994: 268), "the subjection of the native Arctic peoples of Eurasia to Norwegians, Swedes and Russians was characterized by the levying of tributes in furs and other northern products. The first people on record to fall victim to this form of exploitation were the Sami."

With the consolidation of state authority to the south, certain "traders", called *birkarlar*, received royal sanction and support for their trading activities. They were granted judicial competence over specific areas claimed by a king. In return, they would pay a certain percentage of the goods to royal authorities. The *birkarlar* divided the territory of the Sami into *Lappmarks*. However, once the riches from Samiland generated more activity, and the licensed "third-party" traders were found to be dishonest in their dealings with the Crown, the powers of the day decided to assume more direct control of both territory and taxation. Most notable in this respect were the kings of the Wasa ruling house of Sweden (1523–1654), who introduced direct taxation by appointing Lapp bailiffs in the civil service, whereas *birkarlar* were now only allowed to trade with the Sami (Zorgdrager 1984: 14).

In the early 17th century, King Charles sent his Lapp bailiffs to the north. The "discoveries" that followed led to certain central sites being chosen for churches all over the area claimed by Sweden. The motives behind this project were: to involve the entire Sami population in tending the state reindeer; to turn the Sami into sedentary cattle raisers by "ordaining that every family should live on the lake assigned to it" and forbidding free movement; to centralize markets; to regulate legislation; to enhance and enforce Crown authority by building churches and Christianizing the inhabitants; and to alter and raise taxes, demanding that the Sami should pay taxes not in fur but mainly in dried fish and reindeer. This meant that in a relatively short period (from 15 to 20 years) "the Sami turned from a hunting people into a nomadic pastoral people" (Ibid.: 16–17). The introduction of reindeer herding, and the concomitant nomadic way of life, forced the Sami outside their traditional hunting and fishing territories.

Shortly after 1630, at a time when such commodities were needed to finance the wars which Sweden was waging on the European mainland, silver and copper ore were discovered in Sami territory in the north of Sweden. Besides causing border conflict with Denmark, the exploitation of the ore led to the abuse of the Sami as a labour force under harsh conditions. Those who chose to resist were severely punished.

In contrast, for the Sami in Norway the 17th century was probably a relatively quiet period. The Danish kings showed reasonable concern for preserving the Sami's territorial and fiscal privileges against the obtrusive Swedish bailiffs and the Russians. Only when the Swedes exerted renewed pressure in the early 18th century and started to build churches in disputed border areas did the Danish–Norwegians begin to take an interest in the Christianization of the Sami in the interior (Finnmark). One of the by-products of the great Nordic war (1700–21) was the decision to create a definite national border in the interior to the extreme north.

The traditional territories, the old *Lappbys*, of the different Sami groups were now partitioned. Since Sami had migrated for centuries without hindrance across what had now become the border between Norway and Sweden (which then included Finland), a codicil was added to the border treaty of 1751 to ensure the immunity of transborder traffic. Termed the Sami Magna Carta, it grants the old *Lappbys* a central position. Its implementation has been regulated by bilateral commissions, the last one (which is still in force) from 1972. As a result, Swedish Sami access to Norwegian grazing grounds is now greatly restricted (Beach 1994: 172). While some penetration across the border is permitted to some *samebys* (the approximately 50 defined social and territorial herding units of Sweden, before 1971 called *Lappbys*), the time spent in Norway as well as the degree of penetration permitted are tightly controlled.

In 1751 the Swedish government also defined the border of the *Lappmark*, dividing the Swedish coastlands on the Gulf of Bothnia, the territory of the Swedish farming population, from the forest and mountain areas, the *Lappmarks*, to the west. The colonization of these *Lappmarks* by Swedish farmers was again greatly encouraged. Beach (1994: 174) has defined this phase as one of "policing Sami–settler relations", characterized by the spread of farming and escalating conflicts between farmers and herders. Legislation was increasingly devoted to the strict regulation and inspection of herding in order to smooth herder–settler relations. Yet another kind of geographical reductionism was thus introduced: "Anything (such as a commitment to farming and a permanent house) which might cause the herder to leave nomadic life or neglect his reindeer – allowing them to spread unattended and cause damage – was frowned upon by the authorities" (Ibid.).

In 1809 Sweden had to cede the Grand Duchy of Finland to Russia. Russia did not wish to acknowledge the codicil of 1751 and, after years of discussion, closed the Finnish–Norwegian border in 1852. The Finnish Sami, who could no longer go to the Norwegian coast in the summer, were seriously affected. However, the worst off were the Sami from the Norwegian province of Finnmark, especially the community of Kautokeino. They lost nearly all their winter pastures, which lay in Finnish forest areas.

The old geopolitics of territorial expansionism and domination, with the difference of course that it was being practised not *externally* but *internally*, revealed itself in the policies adopted by the states *vis-à-vis* indigenous peoples in the second half of the 19th century. Norwegian policy at that time, as Bjorklund (1990) has shown, was deeply influenced by the prevailing Social Darwinistic ideas of cultural evolution.

A report from the Norwegian Ministry of Finance in 1848 stated that all lands which were not recorded as being privately owned were in fact state property (Brantenberg 1991: 72). Whereas a farmer's cultivation of land was seen as providing evidence of his title to it, the land in Finnmark belonged explicitly to the state, because originally it was only inhabited by a nomadic people, the Lapps, who had no permanent dwellings. This was why "Finnmark from Time Immemorial had been regarded as a Colony" (Ibid.).

The state Land Act of 1902 (Section 1c 7.7) laid down that state land for private ownership was to be reserved for Norwegian citizens and those who could speak, read and write the Norwegian language and use it in everyday life. In order to survive economically, as landowning peasants, Sami had to demonstrate competence in Norwegian language and culture. The only way they could be culturally redeemed and brought back to civilization was by making "them" (the Sami) look and feel like "us" (the Norwegians). The official view in Sweden, Finland and Norway, examined in greater detail in Chapter 6, has for a long time been that the Sami are without any land rights also because they never made any treaties concerning their aboriginal land rights (see Korsmo 1993).

The Danish approach to the colonization of Greenland

The Greenlandic Inuit, or Kalaallit as they call themselves, belong to a Mongoloid people who reached northwest Greenland in several waves after migrating from northeastern Siberia, across the Bering Strait via the North American continent and the Canadian Arctic Archipelago, about 4000 years ago. During a millennium-long era of constant migrations, the Inuit created what is universally known as one of the most highly developed and ingeniously adapted hunting cultures the world has ever seen (Gad 1970: 8–25).

European settlement in Greenland began c. AD 985, when the Norseman Erik the Red sailed from Iceland and established two colonies in the south and southwest. For almost 500 years, the Norse settlement subsisted on farming and on products from cattle, sheep and goats. In the latter part of the 15th century the last Greenlandic Norsemen mysteriously vanished. Speculations about their demise vary from disease and starvation to conflict with the *Skraelings*, who may have been competing directly with the Norsemen for scarce resources (Ibid.: 26–88; Armstrong *et al.* 1978: 170; Nuttall 1994: 4). Alternatively, there may have been a change in the climate, combined with the collapse of supplies from overseas in the wake of the plague. Under such circumstances no agricultural community could survive in Greenland. The Inuit, however, thrived.

In 1721, Denmark sent a Lutheran missionary to Greenland, with a twofold royal mandate: first to establish contact with the Norsemen of Greenland and convert them from Catholicism to the Lutheran faith; secondly to reassert the Danish–Norwegian claim to Greenland. For almost a century an armada of European whalers had been exploiting the resources of the Davis Strait: Dutch, English and Scottish whalers had plundered the abundant stocks of the Greenland right whale, which by then had been brought to the point of virtual extinction in the waters around Spitsbergen. Even though the hunting gear and methods of the Inuit of West Greenland, as well as their economy and world view, had been greatly affected by the foreign whalers, no attempt had been made to seize their land. This was soon to change. Even though the whole project eventually foundered because of the vastness of the country and the severity of the climate, the King of Denmark sent reinforcements to the mission in 1773. As one trade post after the other was established along the Greenlandic coast, the aboriginal socio-cultural structure was exposed to unprecedented pressures, and the people became more dependent upon income from trade and other activities.

In 1782, the Danish government issued detailed instructions to the Royal Greenland Trade Company which were to form the basis for Danish involvement in Greenland for two centuries (Vaughan 1994: 130–6), with the intention of making Greenland a fully fledged Danish colony. By this time, the Inuit population along the west coast had established permanent contact with Danes and other Europeans. The Royal Greenland Trading Company was controlled and owned by the state. Its entire structure was based on the trader, the official effectively in charge of each colony and trading post. In essence a non-profit-making organization, the Company's explicit aim was not the exploitation of the people but to achieve a balance in trade. The cost of maintaining missionaries and all other expenses had to be met from the sale of Greenlandic products. Present in all major Inuit settlements on the west coast, the Danish state was completely intolerant of any other European nations' attempts to establish close contact with the Kalaallit. East Greenland, given the harshness of its climate, was still inaccessible. However, on the west coast there was a progressive northward expansion and the establishment of colonies which were later to grow into large towns.

What distinguished the Danish colonial attitude to Greenland from that of other imperial powers was that it was isolationist and paternal and aimed to protect Inuit hunting culture. However, its "inherent weakness was that it isolated the Greenlanders from the world for which they were being prepared, and there was no timetable to guide and test progress" (Armstrong *et al.* 1978: 172).

By the time the 18th century drew to a close, the fortunes of the Inuit, traders and missionaries were inextricably bound up with the hunting way of life. Even though the Royal Greenland Trading Company took steps to ensure that Inuit remained self-reliant and that all their needs were being met from hunting, it could not stop them from entering into a trading economy which was based on whale blubber and sealskins. Dependence on European goods proved hard to avoid.

In the early part of the 19th century, due to the gradual warming of Greenland's southern coastal waters, and the subsequent migration of seals to colder waters along the west coast, the subsistence economy of many settlements was severely disrupted. Several species of fish, most notably cod, appeared in the now warmer waters of the south and forced a transition from hunting to fishing. What began as a modest cod fishery in 1911, expanded rapidly over the next two to three decades. This also meant significant social and cultural changes for the Inuit (Nuttall 1994: 6). Despite the fact that fishing had traditionally been regarded by the Inuit as a lowly pursuit in comparison to hunting sea mammals, many were now compelled to change their attitude. Traditional hunting camps were abandoned as people moved to other areas in search of good fishing grounds or to larger settlements in search of employment. The resulting social breakdown of Inuit communities did much to undermine the well-intentioned efforts of the Danish administration.

During the main colonial period (1721–1940), Danish administration was extended over all Greenland. Whereas responsibility for the Inuit in the

Angmagssalik area of East Greenland was assumed by Denmark in 1894, a decade after their discovery, it was not until 1921 that Danish jurisdiction was extended to the far northern Inuit in the Thule area. In 1933, a long controversy with Norway over the sovereignty of northeast Greenland was finally settled in Denmark's favour by the International Court of Justice. Danish sovereignty over the whole island was then beyond question. Colonial status was abolished in 1953 and Greenland became an integral part of the kingdom of Denmark, thus giving the Greenland Inuit equal status to Danes. What Home Rule has come to mean in practice to the Greenlandic Inuit will be discussed in Chapter 6.

Politicking over Svalbard: an exception in the Arctic

Svalbard is a group of islands lying approximately midway between northern Norway and the North Pole, between 74° and 81°N latitude and 10° and 35°E longitude. Spitsbergen (previously known as West Spitsbergen) is the largest of these islands. They contain abundant reserves of coal and other minerals, including potentially significant quantities of oil and gas. The island group has no indigenous population.

Following the discovery of large schools of whales in the local fjords by the Dutch explorer William Barents in 1596 and the British exploring expedition under Henry Hudson in 1607, there were sharp clashes between English and Dutch whalers (Mathisen 1954: 9). As a result, the Muscovy Company, "the company of English Merchants for discovery of new trades" (Vaughan 1994: 58), persuaded the king of England to annex the islands so that the company could carry out its whaling undisturbed. After applying in vain to Christian IV of Denmark for the right to purchase sovereignty over Greenland, James I confirmed in a Royal Decree of April 1614 the sole right of the Muscovy Company to carry out whaling from Svalbard, including the right of its men to defend themselves and maintain the sovereignty of England over the country. This was followed by the formal act of occupying certain parts of Svalbard. Occupation, however, was contested by England's rivals, and, despite an attempt at reconciliation with the Dutch in 1618, the Muscovy Company was compelled to limit its whaling monopoly to a relatively small stretch of coast.

In the first half of the 17th century the Dutch, who were by then the leading seafarers and traders of Western Europe, had effectively challenged English supremacy in Svalbard whaling. As the century drew to a close, it was rare for the English whalers, who were also adversely affected by unfavourable domestic conditions, to visit Svalbard, and the English king's claim to sovereignty could not be sustained, whereas the Dutch whaling industry grew dramatically. As the 18th century advanced, stocks of whales were so seriously reduced in the waters off Svalbard that the whaling ships were forced to find other areas of operation. Only Denmark–Norway maintained interest in the archipelago as well as claims to sovereignty.

Initially, Denmark–Norway's claim was based on the belief that the archipelago was part of the old Norwegian dependency of Greenland and on the Norwegian claim to sovereignty over the "Northern Sea", i.e. the ocean between Norway, Iceland and Greenland. The prevailing impression was that a continuous belt of land stretched from the southern coast of Greenland eastwards as far as northern Russia and that Svalbard formed a southern promontory of this landmass. Christian IV's claim therefore extended as far as the borders of Russia. It recognized neither the English occupation of Svalbard nor did Christian entertain the Dutch demand for the right to undertake whaling. He tried to assert and sustain the sovereignty of the Norwegian Crown over the archipelago both by a show of force and by diplomatic manoeuvring and at least succeeded in enforcing his demand that whaling at Svalbard be undertaken only by those who procured a pass issued by himself.

After fjord whaling died out in the middle of the 17th century, the question of sovereignty over the islands was no longer of such importance, other than to Norway–Denmark, although Norwegian sovereignty was not expressly manifested. A common understanding seemed to have developed that whaling and sealing off the islands were to be open to all. Moreover, since the islands were uninhabited, the rights and duties generally associated with the exercise of sovereignty did not apply in the case of Svalbard.

In the second half of the 19th century, Arctic sealing had become an industry of considerable importance for the population of northern Norway. In 1867 some families in the Norwegian town of Tromsø appealed to the king for a state grant to enable them to settle in Svalbard. The application was turned down. The scientist and explorer Adolf Erik Nordenskiöld had found during his expedition in 1864 coprolite deposits on West Spitsbergen which were later investigated for their commercial potential. It was thought that the settlers could make a living by mining these deposits in addition to their hunting. Furthermore, effective occupation of an area was seen to be a necessary condition for its acquisition. Professor Nordenskiöld urged the king to place under his protection a settlement which he intended setting up to support scientific research, choosing the colonists from among the population of northern Norway. However, there were those among the Swedish cabinet ministers who thought that Svalbard ought to become a part of Sweden, given the contributions made by Swedes to scientific research.

The government in Oslo showed little enthusiasm for Nordenskiöld's project. Over the years Norwegians had caught walrus, seals and white whales, and hunted polar bears and reindeer there, but these engagements did not warrant any change in the political status of the islands. It was, moreover, likely that the acquisition of Svalbard would involve expense and result in disputes with foreign powers. But, if Svalbard had to be occupied by any one state, then – for reasons of national interest and prestige – that state would have to be Norway. Norway must, however, reserve the right to abandon its occupation of Svalbard at any time, should it entail any disadvantages (Mathisen 1954: 8).

Despite reservations on the part of the Norwegian government, it was decided at a Cabinet Council in Stockholm to make an application to the interested powers. Before the king committed himself to the occupation of the islands by Norway, he wanted to ensure that no power had any objection. The diplomatic note was so phrased as to give the impression that the islands had never been considered as belonging to any power in the past. The Danish government immediately responded to the Swedish–Norwegian colonization project, stating that it had no objections if no other power did. The French and the German governments accepted the plan on the condition that the commonly accepted practices in fishing and shipping in those territories would continue to hold good. The British response was that provided the Joint Kingdoms would guarantee British fishermen the same rights of access as they had previously enjoyed, they would not oppose the plan. In Russia, however, the plan was received somewhat differently. In Russian business circles, a campaign was launched on the grounds that the islands actually belonged to Russia and that it would be a great setback for her to lose this territory.

By 1871–2, there was an understanding between Sweden–Norway and Russia to treat the islands of the archipelago as *terra nullius*, or no man's land, which "had up to that time been the de facto situation" (Singh and Saguirian 1993: 57–8). In 1906, newly independent Norway reaffirmed its commitment to *terra nullius* status for Svalbard. Soon there was keen competition for space and resources on the archipelago. As a result, the *terra nullius* conception of the archipelago came under stress. What was needed now was a system of laws and administration for a large, resource-rich area in an Arctic environment with no indigenous population, "while at the same time preserving the area as an 'open' territory. No model existed" (Ibid.).

As early as 1909, Norway took the initiative of organizing a conference of all the powers interested in Spitsbergen. However, Russia, supported by Sweden, insisted on preliminary negotiations among the three most interested parties before the conference. Norway consented because of its concern about the presence of a private American mining company in Spitsbergen. By holding *pourparlers* among the three northern powers, Norway could postpone inviting the United States to the full conference. What eventually emerged from the *pourparlers* was an agreement in principle, stating that the archipelago was to remain *terra nullius*, and not to be annexed by any state, while remaining open to citizens of all states. The islands were to be administered by an international commission, to be called the Spitsbergen Commission, composed of a Norwegian, a Swedish and a Russian member, chosen by their respective governments. The commission was authorized to occupy real estate and to levy taxes to support the administration of the area. Land was for ever to remain public property, and rights of occupancy were only to be allowed for the purposes of exploiting natural resources.

The immediate US response was that "it could not adhere to any convention without prior recognition of the indisputable validity of the claims of American citizens as recorded in the State Department" (Ibid.: 60–1). While accepting the principle of *terra nullius* for the archipelago, it insisted upon the recognition of the right of Americans to own the land. Among other "interested powers" – the states whose nationals either historically or actually frequented the islands for the purposes of resource exploitation – Germany expressed certain reservations about the provisions for land use and the proposed international jurisdiction over the archipelago, Belgium chose to remain silent, the French more or less agreed, the Danish government wondered how the administration plan would be funded, the government of the Netherlands insisted upon compulsory arbitration for disputes arising from the interpretation and application of the convention and the British government simply reported that it could not accept the "Projet de Convention". Obviously, agreement among the major actors was conspicuous by its absence.

However, pressure to renew diplomatic negotiations soon built up. Between 1912 and 1914, new mining claimants arrived in Svalbard. Russian claimants also surfaced. The Spitsbergen question thus had high priority on the Norwegian foreign-policy agenda, also because of the involvement of Norwegians in practically all events occurring on the archipelago. In 1914, on Norwegian initiative, a meeting of all interested parties was convened: Belgium, Denmark, Germany, Great Britain, the Netherlands, Russia, Sweden and the United States. Whereas consensus prevailed over the *terra nullius* principle, there was sharp disagreement about the administration of the islands. Even though World War I did not affect the archipelago, the negotiations – the last involving the three powers most directly concerned – could not proceed further.

In early 1919, at the Paris peace conference, Norway requested that the Spitsbergen question be taken up and the islands allocated to Norway. On 7 July 1919, a Spitsbergen Commission was duly formed and a treaty was drafted by which the contracting parties recognized the sovereignty of Norway over the archipelago, subject to certain limitations, including equal rights of access to resources for nationals of the signatory powers, and providing for the demilitarized status of the islands. As Singh and Saguirian (1993: 66–7) point out: "In effect, representatives of Great Britain, France, the United States and Italy, who made up the conference's Spitsbergen

Commission, acted as de facto surrogates for the interested countries not represented at the peace conference." The factors favouring diplomatic bargaining included: (i) the negotiations taking place in the overwhelming presence of the victorious powers, (ii) the use of procedures unique to the peace conference, (iii) the gradual acquiescence of Sweden to the practicality of a Norwegian Spitsbergen, (iv) the absence of Germany from the commission's deliberations, and (v) the uncertain geopolitical equation between the Western powers and Russia in 1919 (including Russia's absence from the peace conference). Finally, in February 1920, the Spitsbergen Treaty was signed by the representatives of Denmark, France, Great Britain, Italy, Japan, the Netherlands, Norway, Sweden and the United States (for the text see Østreng 1977: 101–5).

The Treaty, while recognizing the "full and absolute" sovereignty of Norway over the archipelago, gave nationals of the signatory powers equal rights to exploit living and non-living resources (Articles I and II). The Treaty conferred upon Norway all the obligations of sovereignty but few benefits. The Treaty provisions imposed significant restrictions on Norwegian sovereignty on the one hand and provided the actors concerned with fairly straightforward choices and benefits. However, it is important to bear in mind that the major concerns in 1919 included property rights and rights of exploitation for fishing, whaling, hunting and coal mining. What motivated most states to sign the Treaty was the perceived benefit from possible future commercial ventures. An exception *par exellence* had been made in the colonial–imperial chapter of Arctic history. Even though Russia protested about the conclusion of the agreement without her participation, she would eventually adhere to the Treaty in 1935. The decision made good practical sense to the Russian government during the early 1930s, when gaining international recognition for the new Soviet government topped the agenda in Moscow. So the Soviets traded support for the Spitsbergen Treaty for diplomatic recognition of the Soviet government by Norway.

Imperial "assault" on the Antarctic

Throughout the 18th century, in practically all the voyages to southern regions, designs for colonization played a part. This was despite the fact that theoretical geographers were still grappling with *Terra Australis Incognita* and were not yet sure of its actual size or shape. There were greatly exaggerated expectations of discovering in the southern lands enormous wealth and a large number of inhabitants to serve the colonial masters. These lands were thus considered feasible and fit areas for colonization till Captain Cook's reports of the area poured in after 1772. If it was all ice and frozen waste then why should anyone, nation or private entrepreneur, expend effort or invest capital in such futile ventures? And yet a curious mix of rivalry among the major powers of the pre-industrial world and the commercial activity of sealing and whaling caused men to go to the southern regions and explore the "empty space". The discursive transformation of the Antarctic was thus initiated, greatly encouraged by the potential for increasing knowledge and imperial power as geographical societies and whaling expeditions proliferated.

The Seven Years' War (1756–63) had so exhausted the great powers and overstrained their taxable capacity and social fabric that most leaders rejected the idea of venturing abroad and advocated introspection and domestic reforms instead. Yet France, smarting from the defeat of 1763, was taking immediate measures to strengthen its position for the future and seemed determined to occupy unsettled territories and key points on sea routes in order to forestall similar British colonial initiatives (Kennedy 1989: 149–50).

Louis Antoine, Comte de Bougainville, a distinguished military commander in Canada, was ordered in 1763 to proceed to the Falklands and establish a French colony there. So he landed at Port Louis, East Falkland Island, in January 1764 and took formal possession of the whole group for King Louis XV. The same year, the French government recognized the Spanish claim to these islands and agreed to transfer to Spain Bougainville's settlement at Port Louis in return for financial compensation. The British promptly reacted by sending (1764–6) Captain Byron to take possession of the Falklands so that any ambiguity about its status was settled once and for all. On 23 January 1765, this British naval expedition took formal possession of the whole group of islands for King George III. Yet another government-supported British naval expedition (1765–7) followed and established a settlement at Port Egmont, Falkland Islands, and on discovering the French settlers at Port Louis ordered them to leave within six months. Instead, negotiations between France and Spain followed in Madrid, and upon payment by Spain of financial compensation to Bougainville, the French settlement at Port Louis was formally transferred to the Spanish authorities on 1 April 1767.

In June 1770, a Spanish expedition with 1600 troops forcibly expelled British settlers and the garrison from Port Egmont, bringing Britain and Spain to the verge of war. After prolonged negotiations an agreement was concluded on 22 January 1771, by which the British garrison was reinstated without affecting in any way the question of sovereignty, which has been a matter of dispute ever since (Headland 1989: 73).

If dispatching Bougainville to take over the Falklands was something of a reflex decision, the French government expedition of 1772, under the command of a young, high-born Breton named Yves-Joseph de Kerguelen-Trémarec, was a more determined and calculated affair. Kerguelen reported that he had taken possession of "South France" in the name of the

King of France, an exercise repeated subsequently at various spots on the island (Bush 1982b: 475). To the disappointment of Kerguelen and his entourage, however, the so-called "South France" turned out to be a barren island (actually an archipelago), without any vegetation whatsoever and an incalculable expanse of ocean to the south of it. The same island today goes by the name of Iles Kerguelen, also described as the "Land of Desolation".

The same year, a French expedition sailed under the command of Captain Marion du Fresne, and discovered Prince Edward and Marion Islands. A bottle confirming the act of taking possession was placed upon a pyramid of rocks on Crozet Island nearby (Ibid.).

There still persisted a general belief that the southern continent was attached to some known lands. If it was habitable, the English wanted it. And if there were still more habitable islands on its fringe, they wanted those too. One of the most enthusiastic supporters of such a venture was the irascible Alexander Dalrymple, the first hydrographer to the Admiralty. He happened to have come upon the otherwise forgotten records of the Spanish discoveries in the South Pacific and had become a passionate propagandist for the exploded theory of *Terra Australis*.

The Admiralty promptly appointed the 40-year-old James Cook to command the *Endeavour* on its mission to Tahiti in August 1768. The official instructions of this voyage (Bush 1988: 221) establish beyond doubt that the actual motive behind the voyage of James Cook was to search for that mysterious and supposedly promising, bountiful continent and thus pave the way for its colonization by the British. However, the illustrious mariner did not achieve anything spectacular, except that he shattered the silly dream the far south had been in the minds of men of the time.

During his second voyage (1772–5), Cook "landed in three different places, displayed our Colours and took possession of the Country in his Majesty's name under a discharge of small arms", thinking that South Georgia was part of a large southern landmass, and he discovered the South Sandwich Islands (Ibid.: 221–2). For nearly 40 years after this voyage Europe was preoccupied with the Napoleonic Wars, and after the Battle of Waterloo (1815) commercial and political attention was directed more towards the Arctic and the Northwest Passage than to the Antarctic.

Sealing period (1780 to 1892)

Since the early 12th century, the Dutch, French and Scandinavians had hunted seals, walrus and even whales up to the edge of the Arctic Circle. By the middle of the 18th century, this monopoly had passed to the vessels sailing from British and New England [American] ports. The blubber was of vital importance at a time when mineral oils were almost unknown and the candle was the universal means of providing light at night. The caulking of ships, the manufacture of paints and the preservation of ropes, sails and timbers, not to mention the lubrication of clocks and other up-and-coming devices, equally depended upon the supply of animal fats in sufficient quantities. The whaling industry – and subsequently the elephant seal oil industry – received a major impetus in 1736, when whale-oil lamps first lit London streets (Headland 1989: 69).

Following publication of the reports of the voyages of Cook and Kerguelen, until the beginning of this century the majority of those visiting the Antarctic were sealers from Britain, Cape Colony, France, New South Wales, New Zealand, Tasmania or the United States (New England states). They can be credited with the discovery of many of the peri-Antarctic islands, the first landings on Antarctica (1821) and first wintering over in Antarctic regions.

In 1800, there were as many as 17 ships, mainly British and American, around the island of South Georgia. Between them, in less than four months, they slaughtered 122 000 animals. One vessel alone, the *Aspasia*, under the command of Edmund Fanning, secured in its hold over 57 000 pelts. Fanning (1924: 218) reported that there were 16 other British and United States sealing vessels working at South Georgia during the 1800–1 season. James Weddell, visiting the island in 1822, estimated that not fewer than 1 200 000 seals had been taken from South Georgia during the preceding years and concluded bluntly: "these animals are now almost extinct". However, the data for this period are imperfect; for example, whereas 62 sealing vessels are recorded as sailing for the South Shetland Islands in 1820, there is evidence to suggest that at least 91 sealing vessels operated there during the subsequent austral summer (Headland 1989: 41).

Sealing during this period was undoubtedly a highly profitable business and rivalry between British and American sealers was keen. The sealers always kept the discovery of new sealing grounds secret, with the result that no definitive accounts of the magnitude and extent of seal catches in the southern waters are available. The extermination of the fur seals of the South Sandwich Islands, for instance, if they ever existed, is an unrecorded chapter in Antarctic history. The early sealing industry declined as the populations of fur seals and elephant seals were reduced to such a level that they were no longer profitable; the former were hunted to near-extinction. (Significantly enough, prevailing scientific knowledge anticipated no depletion of fishery stocks, as nature was thought to be too generous in this respect.)

With the final turning away, in 1843, of Sir James Clark Ross from the icy outline of the Antarctic continent, there began what has been termed "the age of averted interest". For almost half a century, from 1843 to 1893, but for the visit of an occasional sealing vessel, the waters of the Antarctic remained almost as undisturbed as they had been before Captain Cook first showed the way to the far south.

The Sixth International Geographical Congress (London, 1895) declared: "The exploration of Antarctica is the greatest piece of geographical exploration still to be undertaken" and urged scientific societies throughout the world to promote expeditions to that area before the century came to a close. Attention was drawn in particular to "the fact that the continent remained largely beyond the measurements, classifications and naming practices of European science" (Dodds 1996, forthcoming). As John Murray, a leading Scottish authority, lamented in 1899, "I always feel a little shame that civilised man, living on his little planet – a very small globe – should, in this nineteenth century of the Christian era, not yet have fully explored the whole of this little area; it seems a reproach upon the enterprise, civilization, and condition of knowledge of the human race" (quoted in Ibid.). In 1901, Sir Clements Markham, President of the Royal Geographical Society, London, urged that the *assault* on Antarctica should not only be international but also well coordinated (see Baughman 1994: 50–2). This marked, so to speak, the dawn of what has come to be known as the "Heroic Age" in the Antarctic.

Whaling period (1919 to 1942)

One major impetus to this upsurge of enthusiasm for further probing of the southern regions was economic in origin. There had been reckless, brutal harvesting of the fur seals, but the whales inhabiting these waters and the surrounding seas were quite untouched. Figures on the magnitude of whaling activity in the southern regions in the last quarter of the 19th century are hard to come by. It is generally agreed, however, that it was extensive and attractive enough as a commercial proposition to draw public attention and whaling ships to the southern waters. Thus motivations of science and commerce combined to promote and sustain practically all the expeditions of the so-called "Heroic Age". Enderby Brothers, the largest English whaling firm, gave its ship captains the freedom to undertake exploratory cruises while on sealing voyages. As a consequence, a number of important discoveries were made. Charles Enderby was an original Fellow of the Royal Geographical Society, which had been founded in 1830 (Bertrand 1971: 3).

The second major exploitation of Antarctic resources thus began in 1904 with the establishment of the modern whaling industry. Thereafter, until World War II, the majority of vessels operating in the Southern Ocean belonged to the Norwegian whaling fleets and to scientific investigations associated with the industry. At various times shore stations operated on the Falkland Islands, South Shetland Islands, South Orkney Islands, South Georgia, Iles Kerguelen, Macquarie Island and Campbell Island; floating factories (as distinct from factory ships) were to be found moored at these and several other stations. The pelagic whaling fleet operated throughout the Southern Ocean from 1925 until recent times, reaching a maximum of 41 factory ships in Antarctic regions in the 1930–1 season.

The partitioning of Antarctica

The prevailing imperialist–colonialist attitudes and policies did result in some of the venturing nations staking claims on the frozen and formidable continent from the beginning of the present century. Significantly, these claims were initially fashioned by considerations of prestige and politics, and rivalry among the pre-industrial powers, as well as the commercial interests of sealing and whaling. Scientific experimentation and exploration for resources were to be added subsequently to the motives for the territorial annexation of Antarctica.

In 1908, Great Britain set out to consolidate earlier territorial claims by setting up her Falkland Island Dependencies. British royal letters patent of 21 July of that year (Bush 1988: 251–2) made Britain the first country publicly to claim (very specifically) territorial sovereignty in Antarctica:

> Whereas the group of islands known as South Georgia, the South Orkneys, the South Shetlands, and the Sandwich Islands, and the territory known as Graham's Land, situated in the South Atlantic Ocean to the south of the 50th parallel of south latitude, and lying between the 20th and 80th degrees of west longitude, are part of our Dominions.

The assertion that the territories listed "are part of our Dominions" shows that the United Kingdom was basing its claims on earlier activities and not on these letters patent alone. It was thus reflecting the attitude of claimant states in general. As Bush (Ibid.) has shown, with the exception of the South Sandwich Islands, which were discovered by Captain Cook in January 1775, although he did not land there or formally take possession, the British title to the named territories had previously been officially asserted by diplomatic note or otherwise.

So great was the hunger for more territory and resources, and so intense the urge to deny them to others, that despite the obvious lack of geographical knowledge "Graham Land" was mentioned in the letters patent. The limits within which "anything that might be called Graham Land could possibly lie" were defined to the north, east and west, but the southern extent was deliberately left open.

These undefined lands in the southern hemisphere were to be administered, on behalf of the Crown, by the Governor of the Falklands. Whether these included at that time any part of the South American continent has been a matter of some controversy (Ibid.: 254). Argentina was to assert in 1947 that since the 50th parallel undoubtedly cuts across the South American continent, the letters patent of 1908 did consider "Patagonia as belonging to [the] British" (Ibid.). On the other hand, the British position

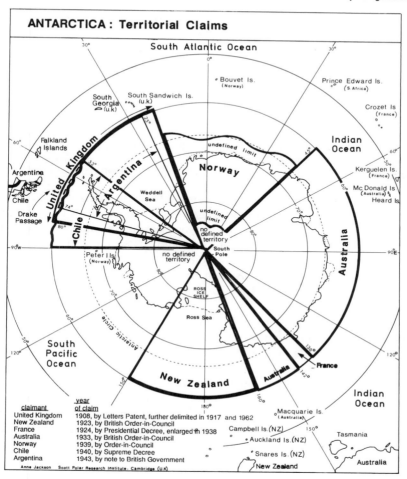

Map (E) Antarctica: territorial claims

has been that these geographical coordinates were "merely a general description of where the named places lie" and therefore the Argentine allegation was baseless. Argentina has also asserted that the 1908 letters patent, as well as the ones that followed in 1917, have no validity because they were mere unilateral statements and "it can not be considered that mere administrative acts of an internal nature can be a substitute for real acts which must be carried out on the terrain itself in order to acquire effective possession" (Ibid.). According to Headland (1989: 241), "although, for administrative convenience, these territories were constituted Dependencies of the Falkland Islands, the British title to them is separate and in no way derived from the title to the Falkland Islands. Neither part of

South America nor the Falkland Islands were included in the territories specified, although the opposite has been argued on the basis that the sector specified incorporated them". Be that as it may, the claim stood unchanged and unchallenged until 1917, when new letters patent modified the limits of the Dependency to produce an Antarctic sector, such that it would include

> . . . all islands and territories whatsoever between the 20th degree of West longitude and the 50th degree of West longitude which are situated south of the 50th Parallel of South latitude; and all islands and territories whatsoever between the 50th degree of West longitude and the 80th degree of West longitude which are situated south of the 58th parallel of South latitude. (Bush 1988: 265)

It is to be noted that the northern coordinates were changed in the letters patent of 1917, as all territories alleged to be under British sovereignty were now placed within fixed geographic coordinates and were not just named territories. Not content with this, and since their claim had not at that time provoked any protest or rejection from any quarter, including their Antarctic competitors, Britain formally claimed, by an Order in Council of July 1923, the Ross Ice Shelf and its surrounding coasts as "British Settlement" (Ibid.: 44), and placed it under the administration of the Governor-General of New Zealand.

In addition to the islands adjacent to the coast and to the Ross Ice Barrier, the sector defined by the Order in Council included the Balleny Islands and Scott Island, discovered respectively by John Balleny, a sealer, in 1839, and the *Morning*, which was on her way to relieve Scott's first expedition of 1902–3. The western boundary of the Ross Dependency had already been decided in February 1921, during a conference at the Colonial Office, on the understanding that the Australian and New Zealand governments were to have separate spheres of control, which might conveniently be divided by the meridian 160°E.

The 1926 Imperial Conference appointed a Committee to look into the question of British policy in the Antarctic:

> His Majesty's Government have . . . come to the conclusion that it is desirable that the whole of the Antarctic should ultimately be included within the British empire, and that, while the time has not yet arrived that a claim to all the continental territories should be put forward publicly, a definite and consistent policy should be followed of extending and asserting a British control with the object of making it complete. (Bush 1982b: 104)

The details of the Committee's report (see Ibid.: 100–7) need not detain us here. What is worth pointing out, however, is that at the time of the Imperial Conference, which indeed was the high point of British imperial ambitions in Antarctica, Norway and Argentina were preparing seriously to contest British dominance and soon the attention of the United States would also be drawn to the Antarctic. As a result, the grounds upon which the British claims were based would be strongly challenged. We may note in passing that, in the case of the three rising powers, at the time of the Imperial Conference Germany was prostrate in the wake of its decisive defeat, Russia had collapsed in revolution and the United States, even though clearly the most powerful nation in the world, had preferred to retreat from the centre of the diplomatic stage. Antarctic affairs during the 1920s and beyond, rather like international affairs in general, still seemed to focus upon the actions of Britain and her allies, namely Australia and New Zealand, or France. All this, however, was to change in the following decade. The Committee, probably mindful of the challenges in the making, advocated a gradual and cautious process of bringing the Antarctic regions under British sovereignty (Ibid.: 101–2).

The Committee formulated a three-stage process for asserting British sovereignty over Antarctica which was to become a blueprint for future British action: (1) public intimation of the Summary of Proceedings at the Imperial Conference, particularly for the areas discovered by the British mentioned above, and such discovery should be regarded as having conferred an "inchoate" British title; (2) formal local taking possession by an officer authorized for such purposes; (3) issue of letters patent annexing the area and making provision for its government (Bush 1982b: 102). In respect of the third requirement, also the most difficult, it was pointed out that in the polar regions control "need not be continuous" (since this would be impossible) provided that it attains such effectiveness as is reasonably possible along the coasts of the area which are the subject of a claim, whether those coasts consist of land or frozen sea. The best way of establishing such local control for the area, it was thought, would be through periodic visits by ships dispatched by, or with the support of, the government, whose officers would be commissioned to exercise authority in the name of the government.

In view of the Committee's recommendations, a comprehensive strategy was soon worked out for the annexation of the areas identified as having "inchoate" British title, and the BANZAR expedition (1929–31) was launched under the leadership of Sir Douglas Mawson, who was convinced of the need for unified control of Antarctica under a British Inter-Imperial administration for the purposes of exploiting its resources, the Antarctic pelagic whales in particular (Swan 1961: 215; Beck 1983: 76). On the basis of the proclamations of sovereignty that followed, an Order in Council of 7 February 1933 (Ibid.: 142–3) placed under the authority of the Commonwealth of Australia "all the islands and territories other than the Adélie Land which are situated south of the 60th degree of South latitude and lying between the 160th degree of East longitude and the 45th degree of East longitude".

The idea behind the claims was, apparently, to enable the British government to regulate and control the whaling activities in these Antarctic and Subantarctic regions (Beck 1983; 1984: 74–5). Britain was rightly concerned about the overexploitation of whales and the destruction of a highly profitable industry. But "in closing the commons, Britain began a process that had troublesome consequences" (Quigg 1983). The British did, in fact, collect cess for the use of South Shetland ports by Norwegian whaling vessels. In the broader context, however, as Beck (1986: 29) aptly puts it,

> . . . the adoption of a policy of Antarctic imperialism coloured British government attitudes towards the southern continent during the post-1920 period . . . By 1933 the British Empire laid claim to some two-thirds of Antarctica, even if the initial British desire to control the whole continent was in the process of qualification as a result of an appreciation of international realities . . .

Anticipating an Australian claim (supposedly prompted by Britain), France formally annexed on 21 November 1924, by Presidential Decree, "the islands of Saint Paul and Amsterdam, the Kerguelen and Crozet archipelagos and Adélie Land" (Bush 1982b: 494). The decree was repealed in 1955 upon the establishment of French Southern and Antarctic Lands as a separate French overseas territory. The French Antarctic area comprises a relatively small wedge sandwiched between the slices of the Antarctic territory claimed by Australia. In defining its claims to Adélie Land as a sector extending to the South Pole, France followed the British practice of laying claim to the area between the discovered and "occupied" coast and the Pole. The French action, therefore, caused considerable unhappiness but the United Kingdom, Australia and New Zealand chose not to raise any objection and kept quiet.

There were probably also pragmatic reasons for the French claim. Coal deposits were found on the Iles Kerguelen, frequented by many American sealing and whaling vessels. The French government was also sensitive to the fact that commercial interests in Australia had been pressing the British Colonial Office to assert maximum British control effectively in the Antarctic region. Mainland Antarctica at that time had virtually nothing to offer, obliging France to focus her activity on the islands she had claimed. Thus, a sealing and whaling station, established by a Franco-Norwegian expedition in November 1908 at Port Jeanne d'Arc on Kerguelen Island, was occupied and superintended intermittently until 1911 and again from 1921 to 1929. Unsuccessful attempts were made to keep and graze sheep flocks on the islands. In 1947, France even granted a concession for the harvesting of elephant seals there.

Norway was the next country to stake its claim, on 14 January 1939, to "that portion of the shore of the Antarctic continent which stretches from the boundary of the Falkland Islands Dependency in the west (Coats Land boundary) to the boundary of the Australian Antarctic Dependency in the east (45° east Longitude) with the territory lying inside this shore and washing it" (Bush 1988: 147). In 1957 the territory's constitutional status was changed: it became a dependency of Norway and was called Dronning

Maud Land. It had been officially stated that the "object of bringing these islands in the Southern Ocean under Norwegian sovereignty was to give the Norwegian whaling industry in that region points of support and to guard it against possible encroachment" (Ibid.: 144).

Perhaps no less compelling for Norway as a reason to take immediate action were the Nazi German incursions in the area and the gathering clouds of World War II in Europe. The Nazis decided to acquire a foothold in Antarctica and adopted the ruse of taking to whaling. German whaling interests in the Falkland Islands Dependencies had been manifested as early as February 1911 when an enquiry from a "German whaling company" about obtaining a whaling licence for South Georgia and the South Shetland Islands was addressed to the British Foreign Office (Barthelmess 1993: 127). The response was negative as a month earlier the Colonial Office had received a report recommending that no further licences be granted, since whale catches in Antarctic waters claimed by Britain had risen from 95 to over 6000 in just about six seasons. Thereafter it was not until the 1930s that the German interest in Antarctic whaling revived.

As a result of the introduction of pelagic whaling in the second half of the 1920s and the discovery of new Antarctic whaling grounds, the industry experienced an unprecedented boom. In the single season of 1928–9 the output was 1 047 000 barrels of oil valued at £5 513 000 (Darnley 1930: ix). German industrial circles could hardly ignore developments in the Norwegian stock index for whaling shares, which averaged 20–5% above those for other industries (Barthelmess 1993: 129). This resulted, in November 1926, in the setting up of a whaling planning committee in Hamburg that proposed German participation in Antarctic pelagic whaling. But in 1929 a development plan for German pelagic whaling was resisted by the Hamburg Chamber of Commerce. In the world-wide economic depression of the 1930s, Germany was suffering from an extreme shortage of fats and oils. As much as 45% of the fat supply had to be imported, mainly from Norway. When, early in 1935, Norway demanded an oil price 50% higher than in December 1934, the German government was compelled to change its stance on whaling.

German interest in southern whaling intensified competition within the industry and was responsible for a further claim to part of Antarctica (see Dey-Nuttall 1994). The decision of the Third Reich, under Hitler, to dispatch the *Deutsche Antarktische Expedition* with the *Neu Schwabenland* on 17 December 1938 was seen by other whaling nations as an attempt to gain a foothold in Antarctica that would consolidate German participation in whaling. Hitler's political interest in the polar regions was perhaps as significant as the economic motivation. As Christof Friedrich (1980: 35) pointed out: "Spurred on not only by his early, Nordic Aryan romantic interest in the polar regions, but by the growing urgency of Germany's isolation and encirclement, Hitler set in motion the preparations for

69

renewed polar expeditions. Of particular incentive was the fact that vast areas of these icy tracts remained unclaimed by any nation." The brief of the expedition was to conduct aerial reconnaissance and mapping. Alfred Ritscher, leader of the expedition, wrote that the

> enterprise derived from a directive from Hermann Goering, as Commissioner for the Four-Year Plan, to continue earlier German research work (E.V. Dry-galski, Wilhelm Filchner) . . . at the same time obtain a stake so that Germany might in future be assured of participation in whaling, undisturbed through the claims of other great powers. (quoted in Sullivan 1957: 124)

We may note in passing that German interest in the Antarctic more or less coincided with the heyday of the German school of *Geopolitik* (see Brunn and Mingst 1985; Klein 1985; Parker 1985: 51–4; Bassin 1987a: 115–34; Bassin 1987b; Kost 1989: 369–85). German geopolitical theories of pan-regions did not include the polar regions in their racial and political calcula-tions. It remains speculation as to whether German geopolitical thinkers voiced support for Hitler's polar adventures. As it happens, Hitler did not challenge the Norwegian claim to Queen Maud Land. He was preoccupied with other territorial annexations and before long had occupied Norway itself. When the Third Reich went down in ruins, the negatives of the expedition's 11 600 aerial photos were apparently destroyed. "Neu Sch-wabenland" remained only a chilly haven for the Hitler legend, kept alive by German publications (Friedrich 1980) which circulated rumours that Hitler and Eva Braun had landed by U-boat at a "New Berchtesgaden" built there by the 1938–9 expedition!

The Norwegian claim was asserted well before the Germans could reach Queen Maud Land and was based on the discovery and exploration carried out in the Antarctic by the Norwegians in the past. The claim was traced back to 14 December 1911, when Amundsen had raised Norway's flag at the South Pole and named the polar plateau "Haakon VII's Plateau", and was further supported by the Norwegian expeditions of the 1920s and 1930s. The Norwegian area lay exactly between that of the British and that of the Australians. In order to provide shore bases for its whalers operating in these areas, Norway had proclaimed its sovereignty over Bouvet Island and Peter I Island in 1928 and 1930 (see Bush 1988: 123–37).

The Norwegian claim promptly brought a sharp reaction from quite unex-pected quarters. The Soviet Union declared that it "would reserve its opin-ion as to the national status of the territories discovered by the Russian citizens" (Bush 1988: 152–3). The reference here was to the "discovery" of Antarctica by Bellingshausen in 1820. The Soviet Union/Russia has never recognized the legal validity of any of the territorial claims to Antarctica (Chaturvedi 1985b), but it has reserved for itself "all rights based on the discoveries and explorations of Russian navigators and scientists, including the right to present corresponding claims in the Antarctic" (UN 1984: 95).

Curiously enough, Soviet/Russian legal commentators have contested the validity of effective occupation as a legitimate requirement under international law on the grounds that: (1) ever since the Berlin Conference of 1885, it had been used by the imperialist states as a convenient tool for exercising unlawful control over territory; and (2) in the case of the polar regions, given the harsh environmental and climatic factors, it is both impractical and unjustifiable to impose demands of effectiveness (Joyner 1991: 288–90).

Norway did not specifically invoke the "sector" policy favoured by other Antarctic claimants, and it must be assumed that its claim does not extend to the South Pole, as all the others do. Norway deliberately refrained from doing so because the practice of making pie-shaped claims is disadvantageous to Norway in the Arctic, where it was originally applied.

We may pause briefly to take note of the sector principle in a bipolar context. The essence of this principle seems to lie more in pragmatic–geopolitical considerations than in theoretical–legal arguments. The fascination with the sector theory could be interpreted as an example of a kind of geopolitical urge to write over/fill those blank empty spaces in both polar regions. It was initiated by a Canadian, Senator P. Poirier, in 1907, as the basis for Canadian sovereignty over Arctic "land and islands" (Franckx 1993: 79–81). Since the senator talked about territory while reacting to an increased foreign presence on Canadian territory, it has been argued by some that his sector theory was "only intended to apply to land and not to water" (Ibid.: 80). Others, on the other hand, have maintained that waters lying inside the Canadian Archipelago are also subject to Canadian sovereignty. Notwithstanding the vagaries of Canadian policy concerning the geographical scope of the sector principle, the geopolitical reasoning appears to be that it makes good sense to draw two lines, extending from either end of the main landmass, that run due north until they converge at the geographic North Pole. Everything inside this wedge, one might argue, should fall within Canadian jurisdiction. Depending upon the political advantages or disadvantages that would accrue from its adoption, countries have either opposed the sector principle or merely tolerated it. On the Arctic rim both Canada and Russia, bordering the two great sea passages dotted with numerous islands, have found it most convenient to assert this principle, supposedly based on the concepts of continuity and contiguity, for obvious geopolitical and legal advantages.

Applying the sector principle to the Antarctic is much more difficult, however (Quigg 1983: 115–16). In the first place, large parts of the Antarctic, especially in the South Pacific, face no country from which meridians can be drawn. South America and Africa are themselves triangular, with their apex towards the south. Moreover, if every country were to choose to assert an Antarctic claim just by drawing lines of meridian to the Pole, dozens of claims could follow – including those by Uruguay, Brazil and

Peru, which continue to take this "theory of projections" seriously. And how could northern hemisphere countries make claims at the opposite Pole on the basis of a sector principle?

Given the obvious shortcomings of applying the sector principle to Antarctica, certain adaptations were called for. The triangular sectors reaching the Pole had their bases measured not by the boundaries of the claimant country but by the stretch of Antarctic coast explored by that claimant country. This resembled the policy of convenience adopted by the colonial powers in Africa and the 13 colonies in America to validate the sector principle by continuity or "hinterland" while claiming inland areas over which effective control had not been established. This proved useful in rationalizing such anachronisms as France's Adélie Land being opposite Tasmania or Australia's claim being far larger than it would be if meridian lines were dropped from Brisbane and Perth. "Although the Ross Dependency is opposite New Zealand, its boundaries were not drawn in strict conformity to the sector principle, and Britain's claim, of course, bears only remote relation to its Falkland Islands possession" (Ibid.).

It needs to be noted at this stage that an expanding pool of cartographic and geographical knowledge in the second half of the 20th century was gradually transforming the Antarctic "from a smooth and undifferentiated space into a differentiated and striated landscape" on sheet maps, especially those of the claimant states (Dodds 1996, forthcoming). As the British designs to have an "Antarctic empire" were frustrated by various counterclaims of territorial sovereignty, especially those of Argentina and Chile, the need for accurate geographical knowledge about the region for "the simple political expedient of strengthening existing territorial claims and resource evaluations" was acutely felt by the officials in London. The Falkland Islands Dependencies Surveyors (FIDS) and Colonial Officials attached to the FIDAS expeditions in the 1950s thus strove for an accurate cartographic representation of "British Antarctic territory" and employed modern technologies associated with aerial photography and aviation in the pursuit of "knowing", "naming" and "mastering" the Antarctic environment. As Dodds puts it:

> The naming of particular places in Antarctica was an important prelude to inserting those places on maps and in polar narratives. Claims to knowledge were often compromised by the nature of the landscapes themselves and the need for on the ground observations.

> The FIDAS surveyors performed more than simply the well-appreciated service of providing physical information about the Antarctic, they actually helped sustain a continuing imperial administrative fiction. FIDAS employees, along side their Falkland Islands Dependency Survey colleagues enabled imperialist dreams in the face of accelerating decolonization of Africa, the Middle East and South Asia. Yet the will to knowledge was frequently compromised by the polar environment itself, a fact rarely appreciated by officials in London. (Ibid.)

European imperial–colonial motives and strategies in the Antarctic, however, came under challenge from a number of post-colonial states. In the case of the United States, the appeal of naturalized geopolitical discourse was of course most keenly felt on the so-called American "frontier". Territorial colonization and expansion went hand in hand with arguments of "racial fitness" and national superiority (Agnew and Corbridge 1995: 57). American attitudes to the last great polar frontier, however, were coloured by ambivalence – on the one hand United States citizens were active participants in Antarctic exploration and had undertaken some claimant action (one only has to recall the widely used description "Little America"). On the other hand, the US refused to accept existing territorial claims well before the 1959 Washington Conference. In the case of our South American examples, the logic of naturalism was to be effectively employed in the official legitimization of territorial claims by Argentina and Chile. There are no clearer examples of the discursive and political power of naturalization than in their arguments that the natural boundaries of those states extend towards the Antarctic on the basis of geological and geographical continuity and proximity.

Antarctica and the United States

Among the non-claimant nations, the position of the United States is unique and has been widely discussed (Auburn 1982: 61–77; Quigg 1983: 126–33; Shapley 1985: 20–68; Beck 1986: 36–9). It has been most active in Antarctica, particularly after the 1930s. The country has without doubt at least as good a basis for a claim as any other nation. On numerous occasions, it has also been under considerable external as well as internal pressure to stake a claim, but it has neither made a formal claim to Antarctic territories, nor has it recognized the claims of other countries. Much more irksome and unsettling, at least from the viewpoint of the claimant states, has been the United States' policy of "sitting on the fence": reserving its own rights in this matter, which probably includes the option of asserting a territorial claim sometime in future if compelled by circumstances. Under periodic review, the US has maintained this public position since 1934.

The United States has had four official attitudes this century to the issue of claims. They can broadly be identified thus: the period up to 1924, when it seemed to lack a formulated policy; from 1924 to the mid-1930s, when it came close to denying the possibility of claims to Antarctica by any country; from the mid-1930s to the beginning of the International Geophysical Year (IGY) in 1957–8 when, against the backdrop of the Cold War and the competing presence of the rival superpowers in the Antarctic, it encouraged its nationals to claim territory on its behalf; lastly, from the IGY to the present, when it has wholeheartedly supported the moratorium on claims and the bases of claims under the Antarctic Treaty of 1961. The United States has probably derived much more geopolitical advantage from its denial of the territorial claims of others than it could possibly have gained from staking one itself.

The issue first arose in 1924, when the Secretary of State, Charles Evan Hughes, in reply to an official inquiry by Norway, stated: "It is the opinion of this Department that the discovery of lands unknown to civilisation, even when coupled with the formal taking of possession, does not support a valid claim of sovereignty unless the discovery is followed by an actual settlement of the discovered country" (Bush 1988: 432). For very many years after that, US Antarctic policy was to be based more or less on Hughes's dictum. This was despite the fact that a largely ignored study by the navy in the same year (1924) showed lively interest in Antarctic sovereignty, "particularly in view of the possibility of the discovery of fuel and other mineral resources" (quoted in Quigg 1983: 127).

Credit for bringing about a change in US policy, from the least active to the most active in the Antarctic region, goes to the Antarctic veteran Richard Byrd. At the time of his first expedition (January 1929), Byrd enquired of the State Department whether he should or should not claim for the US the Antarctic regions hitherto unclaimed. To his disappointment, no clear answer was forthcoming. So Byrd and his team acted on their own, and staked claims, particularly in what is today Marie Byrd Land.

However, these American claims were never formalized or taken up by the US government. As the war loomed in Europe, President Roosevelt ordered in 1938 a complete re-examination of America's policy. Lincoln Ellsworth, who was leaving on another expedition, was secretly given some quite remarkable instructions. Signed by the Secretary of State, Cordell Hull, they confirmed the appropriateness of his asserting claims as an American citizen in the name of the United States (Bush 1988: 438). At the same time, he was not to "indicate or imply advance knowledge or approval of the Government of the United States but . . . he should leave it for his government to adopt its own course of action" (Ibid.).

Ellsworth followed the instructions with enthusiasm and claimed a 300-mile area, now known as the American Highland, in the interior of the Australian claim. Meanwhile, the requested study prepared by the Department of State was delivered to the president in early January 1939. Suggesting modifications to the Hughes Doctrine (Ibid.: 440–1), the study recommended that the United States seriously consider making a claim, but it failed to make a convincing case. The problem before the State Department was that "effective occupation" was no longer an "impossibility", as Hughes had assumed. Moreover, the study was unable to resolve the dilemma that retention of the Hughes Doctrine would make it difficult for the United States to make a valid claim, while to drop it would make non-recognition of existing claims even more difficult. Nevertheless, a letter from Cordell Hull to Roosevelt (February 1939) indicates that the State Department was thinking about a claim that would include not only Marie Byrd Land but also the so-called "American Highland" in the Australian zone and part or all of the Antarctic Peninsula (Quigg 1983: 132). After World War II had started, the United States made it plain to the Western allies that it intended to overfly Antarctica wherever and whenever it pleased, in order to keep track of the Germans and any other unfriendly outsiders (Bush 1982b: 513–14).

Realizing the implications of delay in establishing the US presence in the Antarctic, President Roosevelt pushed through Congress an appropriation of $340 000 in mid-1939. The objective was to create the United States Antarctic Service and to launch the first official Antarctic expedition in a century. It happened to be the Byrd expedition, and its aim was to "make an investigation and survey of the natural resources of the land and sea areas of the Antarctic regions" (Bush 1988: 446).

Admiral Byrd was handed the formal instructions by Roosevelt which included a rather contradictory declaration:

> The United States has never recognised any claims to sovereignty over territory in the Antarctic regions asserted by any foreign state. No member of the United States Antarctic Service shall take any action or make any statements tending to compromise this position.

> Members of the Service may take any appropriate steps such as dropping written claims from airplanes, depositing such writings in cairns *et cetera*, which might assist in supporting a sovereignty claim by the United States Government. (Ibid.: 445)

Earlier, Roosevelt had sent Byrd a personal letter, dated 12 July 1939, underlining the need to prove that human beings could permanently occupy a portion of the continent winter and summer, and that it was well worth a small appropriation to maintain such permanent bases because of their growing value for four purposes: national defence of the western hemisphere, radio, meteorology and minerals. Each of these four was said to be of approximately equal importance (Quigg 1983: 131). Shortly thereafter, the President wrote another personal letter (Ibid.: 132), addressed this time to Under Secretary Sumner Welles, in which he maintained, as his "own personal view", that

> . . . we should give some study to a new form of sovereignty, i.e., a claim to sovereignty for the whole sector lying south of the Americas, on behalf of and in trust for, the American Republics as a whole. Under this the United States, being the only Republic which has taken the initiative in exploring and possibly settling the area, would act not only in behalf of its own exclusive sovereignty, but would include all the other Republics – and in the future if the American sector proved valuable in any shape, manner, or form its sovereignty could be managed by an inter-American Republic governing body.

It looks as if the president, in making this suggestion that came to naught, was influenced by the approaching war in Europe, just a few weeks away. American interest in the Antarctic, like that of the other Antarctic-oriented actors, was overshadowed by the war, and no clear, rational American policy for Antarctica emerged.

South American geopolitics and Antarctica

It has been convincingly argued that one major, though frequently over-looked, source of Antarctic tensions in the past has been the geopolitical – or, rather, geostrategic – thinking that has flourished in the last quarter-century in South America (see Child 1988, 1990b; Beck 1990a). Indeed, the impact of traditional geopolitical thinking on the Antarctic-related percep-tions and policies of South American countries has been substantial. The intellectual (Social Darwinistic) roots of South American geopolitics can be traced back to the early 20th century, to a Chilean text that cited the ideas of Ratzel (cited in Hepple, 1992: 137) and an Argentine text that made use of Mahan's theories of sea power (Dodds 1993: 365). Thereafter, largely due to the efforts of Argentine and Brazilian military writers, the field expanded rapidly, and after World War II an extensive geopolitical literature was published and popularized in South America. Obviously, the decline in and subsequent revival of geopolitics in North America and Europe was never experienced in South America (Hepple 1986a). Nor did the legacies of *Geopolitik* and Nazism inhibit the South Americans from either writing on geopolitics or translating the works of Ratzel and Haushofer into Spanish and Portuguese and citing them extensively.

Until the widespread democratization of South America in the 1980s, perhaps the best-known example of a geopolitician in uniform has been the former professor of geopolitics at the Chilean War Academy and president of Chile: Augusto Pinochet. Throughout the period of authoritarian rule, be-tween the 1960s and the early 1980s, the military governments fully and actively supported those writing on geopolitical issues. The military regimes not only extended political and financial support to military academies and re-search institutions, they also injected geopolitical ideas into the national educa-tional system of various Southern Cone nations. In the campaign to make society "geopolitically conscious", national newspapers such as *El Mercurio* in Chile and *La Nación* in Argentina also played a part by providing regular geopolitical commentaries on regional and international developments.

Throughout this period, geopolitical reasoning was used to construct a discourse through which to articulate dangers, both "internal" and "exter-nal", to the state. And in the case of Antarctica and Amazonia, geopolitics and cartography were also used to appropriate and colonize "empty spaces" (Dodds 1993: 367). The appeal of naturalized geopolitical discourse was an important element in the intellectual and physical colonization of those places. Like all organisms, so argued General Pinochet, organisms required space and resources to ensure their healthy growth. As Jack Child has perceptively noted, South American geopolitical discourse consistently interpreted the Antarctic and the surrounding oceans as a frozen *Lebensraum* (see Child 1988).

For example, in the case of Argentina, well within 20 years of its first manifestation of interest in the Antarctic by way of dispatching naval expeditions to the region in the early 1900s, and the subsequent establishment of a meteorological base in the South Orkneys in 1904, the "Argentine Antarctic Sector" had been incorporated into Argentine sovereign territory, and schoolchildren were taught that Argentina consisted of three parts: mainland, insular and Antarctic Argentina (Dodds 1993). In this context, the writings of Argentine geopolitical writers assumed critical importance as an input into the state education system and as an aid to designing official maps that were used to perpetuate the notions of Argentine Antarctic territory. Most Argentine geopolitical literature revolves around two themes: first, providing counterarguments and counter-rationale to the British (and other South American states') narratives and claims to the Antarctic; and secondly, promoting similar tales of heroic voyages and "serious" scientific study (Ibid.: 368). Curiously (or not so curiously perhaps, given the symbiotic but subtle relationship between Antarctic science and politics), Argentine geopolitical writers devote a considerable amount of effort to highlighting the achievements of their scientists in Antarctica.

Argentina and Chile started asserting their rights in the Antarctic before the end of World War II. Chile staked its claim to a sector between 53° and 90°W longitude, basing it theoretically on the colonial rights of the captaincy-general of Chile to "Southern Territories". Chile holds that the Spanish kings granted concessions to the conquerors, in this case Pedro de Valdivia and Pedro Sancho de Hoz. Valdivia came to have under his command "all the territories of the Governorship of *Terra Australis*, the northern boundaries of which were constituted by the southern bank of the straits of Magellan", in the period that followed until the end of Spanish rule. So "Chile was born to independence in possession of territory which included the natural prolongation of the country to the pole". The father of the Chilean nation, O'Higgins, accordingly declared: "the sovereignty of the nation to which he gave independence included the Antarctic lands" (see Bush 1982b: 346–67; also De La Barra 1955: 9–29).

The government of Chile issued its decree, "on well founded antecedents since independence", on 6 November 1940 (Bush 1982b: 311):

All lands, islands, islets, reefs of rocks, glaciers (pack-ice), already known, or to be discovered, and their respective territorial waters, in the sector between longitudes 53 and 90 West, constitute the Chilean Antarctic or Chilean Antarctic territory.

This had an immediate impact abroad (see Ibid.: 313–22). The British government of Winston Churchill, on 25 February 1941, protested on the grounds that the sector so defined included that part of "His Majesty's possessions known as the Falkland Island Dependencies of which the boundaries were defined by the letters patent of the 28th March, 1917" (Ibid.: 322). Shortly after the issue of the decree, the British ambassador in Santiago would point out to the Chilean government that its decree encroached on British-claimed territory. The United Kingdom brought Prime Minister Churchill's note to Chile's attention again in November 1944, but Chile found time to respond to the note only in late January 1946.

The reaction of the United States to the Chilean decree was in keeping with its previous stand that it recognized no sovereignty claim in the Antarctic. Argentina too declared its reservations about the decree. Some negotiations between Chile and Argentina had taken place between 1906 and 1908 but without result. The 1907 proposal of a treaty to divide "the islands and continents of the 'American Antarctica' between the two nations", for the reason that Britain was claiming all such territories, and therefore Chile and Argentina would have to make a common stand against British hegemony, had also fallen through. The decree encouraged the two countries to hold discussions in March 1941, but all that emerged was that (i) a South American Antarctic existed, and (ii) the only countries with exclusive rights of sovereignty over it were Chile and Argentina (Hayton 1956: 586).

All these protests, however, made no difference to Chile, which went ahead and established the Chilean Antarctic Commission by a decree of 27 March 1942 (Bush 1982b: 323–5). On 21 January 1947, it chose to explain and expound its claim in Antarctica on four counts: historical, geographical, legal, and diplomatic and administrative (Ibid.: 348–67).

Chile's geographical contiguity has been advanced in further support of the claim of geographical continuity: Graham's Peninsula constitutes a prolongation of American continental territory; the geological structure of these two territories, it is contended, is strictly symmetrical. The Antarctic thereby becomes the Chilean Polar Dominion, exposed directly to the preponderant influence on its climate by means of the sea and air currents that the southern continent sends towards Chile. So much so, that the Chilean polar sector is the "natural prolongation of our continental territory" (Ibid.: 354).

Actual Chilean activity in the Antarctic began in 1947, when Chile established a permanent base at Greenwich Island in the South Shetlands, off the Antarctic coast. The Chilean President, González Videla, visited Antarctica to inaugurate the new O'Higgins Station (the first visit by a head of state to Antarctica).

Argentine Antarctic activity began in 1903 when the Argentine ship *Uruguay* penetrated Antarctic waters and ultimately rescued the Nordenskjöld party of the Swedish South Polar Expedition at Snow Hill Island, where they had wintered after their ship, the *Antarctic*, had been crushed in the ice. Until 1939 Argentina's concern with the Antarctic was more or less limited to the annual relief of the Laurie Island station. In July 1939 a permanent interdepartmental National Antarctic Commission was established (Bush 1982a: 594–5) as a direct result of Norway's delineation of its claim made earlier that year, and its subsequent invitation to Argentina to the Bergen International Exhibition of Polar Exploration.

The Argentine Commission sent expeditions in 1942 and 1943 to the Palmer Peninsula area and to the South Shetlands. With the election of Juan Perón in February 1946, and the establishment of a constitutional government, the Antarctic became one of the major areas of Argentine political, military and diplomatic activity. Argentina inaugurated a major Antarctic expeditionary programme, establishing a number of small stations on the Palmer Peninsula. In the same year, 1946, the Antarctic Commission was reactivated, and an intensive publicity campaign was launched to make Argentina "Antarctic-conscious". From that date on, Argentina resolved to pursue a relatively rigorous policy of exploration and the establishment of bases to support its contention of effective occupancy. In 1951 the Instituto Antártico Argentino was created and placed under the Ministry of the Army; Antarctic matters were thus centralized within the Argentine government.

The Argentine claim is primarily based on: (i) the succession of original Spanish "rights"; (ii) geographical proximity; (iii) geological affinity based on the presumed geological continuation of the Andes through the island chains into the nearby Antarctic region; and (iv) effective occupation, including the maintenance of the Laurie Island station since 1904. For many years Argentina did not issue a formal claim statement, even though consistently taking the position that "Antarctica Argentina" had been an integral part of its metropolitan territory since the very foundation of the Republic. Nevertheless, as early as 1904, Argentina took possession of the South Orkneys, and in 1946 delimited its claim. On 28 February 1957, a decree was passed by the government of Argentina to re-establish the national territory of Tierra del Fuego, the Antarctic and islands of the South Atlantic.

The national territory comprised the eastern part of Isla Grande and other islands of the archipelago of Tierra del Fuego, Isla de los Estados and Isla Año Nuevo, in accordance with the boundaries fixed by the Treaty of 23 July 1881, the Islas Malvinas (Falkland Islands), the islands of South Georgia, the South Sandwich Islands and the Argentine Antarctic sector contained within the meridians 25°W and 74°W and the parallel 60°S (Bush 1982b: 26–7). The capital of the territory was declared to be the town of

Ushuaia, in which the local government and principal federal offices were to be located.

The closest Antarctic neighbours, Argentina and Chile, with almost similar grounds for their claims to the Antarctic Peninsula, thus had shown persistently keen and manifest interest in the frozen region since World War II. Quite often they came to blows with each other over the region, even though they maintained a common front against their rival Great Britain in the race for the South Pole. Both Argentina and Chile firmly believe that their own claim is the better one. Repeated efforts to delineate a boundary between the two claims have come to naught. Negotiations having failed in early 1948, they issued a joint declaration:

> Until such time as the [boundary] line of common neighborliness is covenanted . . . in the antarctic territories of Chile and of the Republic of Argentina . . . both governments will act in common accord in the protection and juridical defence of their rights in the South American Antarctic Sector, included between the meridians of 25° and 90° Longitude West of Greenwich, in which territories it is conceded that Chile and the Argentine Republic have indisputable rights of sovereignty. (Quoted in Hayton 1956: 591)

Yet, before the year was out there was conflict between them! When the boundary treaty of 1881 between the two came into dispute, they entered into another in 1922 which provided, interestingly enough, for obligatory arbitration by the British Crown.

Argentine and Chilean ambitions in the Antarctic have been challenged by other South American states and their geopolitical writers. The most interesting challenge has come from Brazilian writer Therezinha de Castro, who with her compatriot P. Azambuja has attempted to use a sectoral map and the frontage theory, thereby undermining the British, Chilean and Argentine claims (Hepple 1986b). The frontage theory suggests that South American Antarctic claims should ". . . be defined by the two meridians which form the frontage's limit. The actual sectors vary according to whether the meridians are drawn from either mainland, insular or maritime boundaries, and inevitably there is a little consensus on the limits . . ." (Child 1990a: 295). In other words, the choice of drawing the claims from offshore islands or the mainland becomes crucial in determining the size of a country's claim. Whereas Argentina's claim is substantially reduced, Ecuador, Chile and Brazil benefit from their choice of distant offshore islands. From the British point of view, "the omission of the Falklands and the South Sandwich and Georgia Islands is particularly surprising but 'necessary' to marginalize and exclude the British presence in the region" (Dodds 1993: 371).

The geopolitical reasoning behind the frontage theory is well expressed in Castro's contention that "Antarctica is fated to be constituted as a cornerstone of our destiny, thanks to its importance as a base of warning, interception and departure in whatever emergency might occur to affect the defence of the South Atlantic" (quoted Ibid.). Furthermore, Brazil, with the longest Atlantic coastline, has to be sea-oriented both for reasons of economic expansion and for the defence of the South Atlantic. The frontage theory appears to have opened up the Antarctic to countries which till recent times had no interest in it: Ecuador, Peru and Uruguay. Moreover, such geopolitical arguments, with the help of frequent and often unqualified references to "defence" and "security" in the South Atlantic, have provided a pretext for the involvement of Brazil in the Antarctic. The latter, along with India and China, acceded to the ATS in 1983, and as a consequence de Castro's geostrategic arguments have diminished in saliency.

Summary and conclusions

The polar regions have been perceived differently at different times in history, and the human perceptions of, and attitudes to, these regions have also changed from one historical period to another. The construction and representation of the polar environment has varied accordingly. Despite marked variations in policy attitudes and preferences, depending upon the Pole in question and the national interests at stake, both the polar regions have been deeply affected by the sovereignty discourse, the geography of imperialism and the geopolitics of state power. Both have been subjected to a predominantly state-centred and power-political geopolitics that was based on the premise that territory and territorial control necessarily implied more power and security and that for its own sake. Such an attitude to space and its resource endowments explains why both the Arctic and Antarctica have been subject to territorial claims of sovereignty and experienced reckless exploitation of their natural resources. In the process, the ecological unity of the polar environment has been tampered with and, more often than not, destroyed, with serious consequences for delicately interlocked ecosystems and wildlife.

What, then, are the polar legacies, both visible and not so visible, of the age of imperial exploration and "discovery"? Whereas the most visible ones are the territorial boundaries across the polar landscapes at both ends of the globe, which in some cases continue to generate conflict, the least visible in the case of the Arctic are the entrenched north–south orientations of the Arctic-rim states that are at odds with the circumpolar ecological unity of the Arctic. Given that the present century has had its share of the imperial–colonial past, it will be illuminating to observe both the continuities and the departures from the past as the study proceeds.

Suggested reading

Armstrong, T. 1965. *Russian Settlement in the North*. Cambridge: Cambridge University Press.

Forsyth, J. 1992. *A History of the Peoples of Siberia: Russia's North Asian Colony 1581–1990*. Cambridge: Cambridge University Press.

Headland, R.K. 1989. *Chronological List of Antarctic Expeditions and Related Historical Events*. Cambridge: Cambridge University Press.

Holland, C. 1994. *Arctic Exploration and Development c. 500 B.C. to 1915: An Encyclopedia*. New York and London: Garland Publishing, Inc.

Østreng, W. 1977. *Politics in High Latitudes: The Svalbard Archipelago*. London: C. Hurst & Company. (Translated from Norwegian to English by R.I. Christophersen)

Riffenburgh, B. 1993. *The Myth of the Explorer*. London: Belhaven Press.

Sahurie, E.J. 1992. *The International Law of Antarctica*. Dordrecht: Nijhoff Publishers; New Haven: New Haven Press.

Vaughan, R. 1994. *The Arctic: A History*. Dover: Alan Sutton.

4

The Arctic and the Cold War

Once subjected to the hegemonic conflict between the two superpowers, hooked on to the Cold War geopolitical discourse and entangled in its containment militarism, the Arctic experienced unprecedented militarization and nuclearization. Its physical as well as human geography came to be dominated by a militarized geography, characterized by confrontation, the arms race, divided security and conflict lines. Accordingly, various features of its physical environment – land, air, waters, ocean basin, the continental margin, bays, inlets, rivers, peninsulas, mountains, etc. – were perceived as strategically significant, in the sense of being "likely to be involved in a major way in an armed conflict between the great powers" (Jalonen 1988: 157). Suddenly, Arctic resources became a military liability. At the same time, there occurred a serious distortion of perceptions and dislocation of priorities in the Arctic-rim states, exposing the indigenous societies and economies to hitherto unknown impacts.

This chapter raises the question of whether it was Arctic geography *per se* or its perceptions that induced militarization of the area during the Cold War. What exactly is the role that geography plays, in general, in inviting cooperation or generating conflict? Was it due to certain "inherent" geographical properties that the Circumpolar North witnessed such extensive militarization for nearly four decades (Skogan 1992: 258), in sharp contrast to the south polar region? In other words, was the Arctic doomed to be militarized on account of its geographical characteristics – location, topography, configuration of its land and waters and the distribution of resources?

This chapter aims to trace in some detail the transformation of the Arctic into a frontal zone in the East–West conflict and to examine the socio-economic, cultural and politico-geographic impact of the conflict on Arctic societies. It begins by analysing the nature of Cold War geopolitical discourse and the geostrategy flowing from it that led in the first place to what Østreng (1992b: 14) calls the "formation of a fully integrated, multidimensional security policy line where the boundaries between military and non-military issues nearly disappeared". The implications of this narrow, excessively state-centred and highly militaristic view of security are examined for (a) cooperative interactions at a multinational level, and (b) their effect on the indigenous peoples of the Arctic.

Cold War geopolitics: practice and discourse

The causes, nature and consequences of Arctic involvement in the Cold War need to be examined in the broader regional/global context of one of the greatest power struggles of this century. I try to show here that Cold War geopolitics is about both practice and discourse.

Given the extensive spatial reach of the Cold War, its multiple, multilevel and multifaceted spin-off effects, powerful ideological appeal and extraordinary length, it is not surprising that opinions are divided over its origins and causes. The Cold War, in fact, meant many things to many people (see Chomsky 1992: 9–19; Gaddis 1992: 22–3). Geopolitically speaking, the Cold War meant to the USA and its allies a crusade against the "evil" communist heartland, whose territorial and ideological expansion into the Eurasian rimlands, including the High North, had to be contained at all costs. This was, essentially, the American world view to start with. Eventually, the United States sought to make it hegemonic and the guiding geopolitical principle for Western policy-makers throughout the Cold War.

Such, then, were the circumstances in which the broad contours of the post-war geopolitical world views of the two superpowers were first defined, later embalmed in Cold War psychosis and eventually imposed upon the allies on both sides of the resulting Iron Curtain. The virtual division of Europe was further consolidated by the Berlin crisis of 1948, but the crisis did not lead to military conflict. "This was to typify the Cold War for its whole life. Europe became the main East–West front, with the greatest build-up of armaments ever facing one another, but without the massive arsenal ever being fired in anger: deterrence, not war, was the game" (Taylor 1993: 54).

A detailed analysis of the dominant geopolitical discourse of the post-World War period has been made by Dalby (1990a), who points to a group of high-profile foreign-policy experts in the USA of the mid-1970s who attempted to render their particular set of security discourses hegemonic. In the writings of the Washington-based Committee on the Present Danger (CPD), he identifies a series of "Security Discourses", namely Sovietology, the realist literature in international relations, nuclear strategy and geopolitics, in order to construct an ideology of a Soviet Union as dangerous "other" (Dalby 1988: 415; 1990b).

These discourses promoted: (a) a highly determinist interpretation of Russian history to rule out the possibility of peaceful coexistence with the Soviet regime; (b) the subordination of the political objectives of development, environment and justice to power politics; and (c) reduction of political matters to a zero-sum game between the superpowers, thereby undermining "the concerns and aspirations of the peoples whose territory becomes a section of cartographic space in which each superpower's 'projected power' seeks spatially to contain that of the other" (Ibid.: 423).

According to yet another illuminating perspective (Agnew and Corbridge 1995), the Cold War geopolitical discourse was intensely "ideological" in the sense that it "centred much more explicitly around competing conceptions of how best to organize the international political economy" (Ibid.: 65). Furthermore, it had the following characteristics:

> . . . a central systemic–ideological conflict over political–economic organization; "three worlds" of development in which American and Soviet spheres of influence vied for expansion into a "Third World" of former colonies and "nonaligned" states; a homogenization of global space into "friendly" and "threatening" blocks in which universal models of capitalism–liberal democracy and communism reigned free of geographical contingency; and the naturalization of the ideological conflict by such notable concepts as containment, domino effects and hegemonic stability. (Ibid.)

It was typical of the Cold War discourse that singular attributes of a particular place were subordinated to its perceived position in the abstract spaces of the Cold War. "It was 'friendly' or 'threatening', 'ours' or 'theirs'. This homogenization of global space made knowing the details of local geography unimportant or 'trivial'. All one needed to know was: whose side are they on?" (Ibid.: 72). Moreover, such geopolitical discourses are not confined to the élite geopolitical texts; they are also interpreted in terms of the popular culture through the media. The proliferation and perpetuation of enemy images across a wide spectrum of society is thus ensured. Sharp (1993: 496) has shown how the Self–Other dualism of the USA–USSR determined the form of all media articles about the Soviet Union in the period 1980–90, so that "a description of events in, or characteristics of, the USSR (totalitarianism, expansionism and so on) automatically implies that the opposite applies to the US (in this case: democracy, freedom . . .). The Soviet Union becomes a negative space into which *The Reader's Digest* projects all those values which are antithetical to its own ('American') values" (Ibid.).

In the prevailing Cold War climate, marked by fear and suspicion, both sides were gripped by a totalitarian image of the other side. The totalitarian thesis was used by both superpowers to mobilize support for Cold War policies and to justify the economic costs of military build-ups (Dalby

1990a: 67). Such a view did not favour critical and objective discussion of international relations in the post-war period, and the power-politics-dominated understanding of interest became immensely important in the post-war political discourse. National interests, viewed as intimately related to security, were understood in the sense of preventing the potential adversary from invading one's space – perceived strictly in the territorial sense. This in turn implied physical protection and political alignments on a regional and, especially in the US case, a global scale.

The US policy of containment and deterrence has had two faces that have alternated in dominating American foreign policy in the post-war years. George Kennan was inspired by the traditional conception of good versus evil, which he incorporated into his geopolitical thinking. He concluded that Stalin's challenging heartland had to be contained (Barnet 1992: 117), arguing that the crusade against expansionist Moscow had to be concentrated on the most important geographical and strategic areas. This thinking dominated the American perception in the late forties, fifties, and again in the early seventies when Nixon and Kissinger were in power. Just as the Nazis used the pseudo-theory of Haushofer's *Geopolitik*, so too American strategists "looked to classic theories [of Spykman and Mackinder] for their justification of an already formed global view" (O'Loughlin and Heske 1991: 44). No less important was the use of geographical and geopolitical vocabulary (heartland, rimland, pivot area, land power versus sea power, etc.) in crude geopolitical reductionism of the complex identity of places.

Paul Nitze, who succeeded Kennan as head of the Policy Planning Staff in January 1950, and was the author of what is widely recognized to be the basic US Cold War document, NSC 68 (April 1950), emphasized the military threat and called for a considerable and costly defensive strength. Together with an emphasis on conventional defence, he also advocated nuclear build-up and war-making on the grounds that "the Cold War is in fact a real war in which the survival of the free world is at stake"; "the assault on the free institutions is world-wide"; and "the idea that Germany or Japan or other important areas can exist as islands of neutrality in a divided world is unreal, given the Kremlin design for world domination" (quoted in Chomsky 1992: 10, 11).

These and similar arguments, however, were abandoned in Kissinger's geopolitics, which undermined the rationale of the policy of containment and instead highlighted the US role as the power balancer in a more complicated global scheme (Sloan 1988). As a result of the Strategic Arms Limitation Talks (SALT) process, and arms control in general, political attention shifted to the technical arcanum of nuclear weapon systems rather than the geopolitical context of their potential usage in global rivalries.

It was not until the late 1970s that the geopolitical context and geostrategic arguments for US nuclear–military policy were revived, in the extensive writings of Colin Gray. This is perhaps the most interesting example in recent times of the hijacking of geopolitical concepts and the grafting on to them of geostrategic prescriptions. The idea behind Gray's selective reassessment of past geopolitical literature seems to have been, as Dalby (1990a: 106) puts it, to bring back the geopolitical premises of foreign policy that were "no longer accepted by the *détente* advocates and arms controllers".

Gray's central argument is that the essence of international politics is power – defined and understood in terms of territorial control. The ultimate test of power is the ability to wage and win a war in a world where the most fundamental factor in foreign policy is geography because it is the most permanent factor. The leitmotif of geopolitics, Gray feels (1977: 14), is the struggle of land power against sea power, and the major geographical configurations on the globe continue to pose unresolved problems of nuclear strategy for the West.

Consequently, the Western democracies were left with few choices because of the *inherently expansionist* nature of the Soviet Union, its historical experience and rigid internal controls (Gray 1976: 114–27). The oceanic alliance of the West had, therefore, to intervene in the rimlands to check this expansion, which required an enormous nuclear arsenal to stave off any threat of military intervention. According to Gray's grandiose "Theory of Victory" (Gray 1979), when deterrence collapses, triggering off a major conflict, plans must be in place for the conduct of that conflict.

Within half a decade of the publication of the *Geopolitics of Superpower* (Gray 1988), the "world's last large colonial empire" (Glassner 1993: 303) vanished in a bewildering whirlpool of internal contradictions and centrifugal tendencies. The question remains: can the disintegration of the USSR be explained by our discussion of Cold War geopolitics, especially geostrategy in the guise of geopolitics?

The lack of an answer (see Steel 1992) is also due to the narrow focus, intellectual poverty and political bias of the Cold War variety of geopolitics that nourishes state-centred geostrategic discourse about security. It provides a spatial reasoning and rationale for the "hegemonic conflict" (Østreng 1992b: 14) that arises between rival political systems – in both an ideological and a material sense – and develops cumulatively, as it did during the Cold War, "so that conflict in one area spills over to other areas". It is a powerful ideological weapon in the hands of those promoting the vested interests of military–industrial complexes, fabricating threats of all kinds. The distinction between military and non-military issues virtually evaporates. Choices for cooperation are inhibited and seriously retard an objective assessment of mutually beneficial possibilities that may lie beyond the realm of real or imaginary "otherness". If I do not share your conception of "otherness", then I am not your friend and thus, invariably, am siding with the enemy.

The Arctic in the Cold War psychosis

It is to the Arctic part of the Cold War geostrategic game that we now turn. The containment era of the Cold War coincided with the beginning of a period in which the political significance of the Arctic changed drastically, narrowing down simultaneously the policy-makers' options for cooperation in non-military realms.

In sharp contrast to the past, when most strategists considered the Poles a "wrong place for any large military operations" (Balchen 1956: 30), from then on, the Arctic was perceived as a key geostrategic deployment area in any global conflict. This change in perception was due, primarily, to expansion of the geographical scope of the US policy of containment and to the new ways of looking at the world such as "the view of the airman" (see Sloan 1988: 127–50). Long-range polar flights, advances in missile technology, new radar systems and other modern technical achievements such as *USS Nautilus* travelling under the Arctic icecap in 1957 were crucial for transforming the Arctic into a major strategic arena during the Cold War (see Hobbs 1986: 85–96; Osherenko and Young 1989: 18–28; Heininen 1994: 158). Accordingly, Arctic-specific geography acquired a new geostrategic perspective: for example, the shortest route between three continents – Asia, Europe and North America – is over the Arctic Ocean, and most of the core industrial regions in Europe, Russia, North America or Japan lie well within 7000 km of the North Pole. Indeed, with the adoption of the new Polar Projection, the northern coasts of Alaska and Canada acquired unprecedented geopolitical and geostrategic significance, especially as they were now recognized as being closer to Russia than to Washington or Ottawa. It was hard to escape the fact that the USA and Russia were immediate neighbours in the Arctic, just 57 miles apart at the Bering Strait.

Geographical proximity came to be perceived not so much for the opportunities it might offer for cooperation as for its probable geostrategic advantage or disadvantage during conflict. National security was understood, by and large, in terms of spatial strategies of distancing, defending the national boundaries on land, water and air, and forging strategic alliances to maintain the balance of power. The following examples none the less indicate the manner in which both the geography and geopolitics of the Arctic region were overtaken and overwhelmed by Cold War-related geostrategic considerations.

A militarized geography

Formerly an icy waste, the Arctic Ocean now assumed immense strategic significance in the context of controlling the air space and the ocean beneath it. The importance of the Ocean as an actual or potential deployment area for strategic ballistic-missile-firing submarines (SSBNs) increased greatly after the under-ice passage by the nuclear-powered *USS Nautilus* in 1957 (Larsen 1989: 170). The protective cover the Arctic pack ice provided against air and satellite surveillance of submarine operations, as well as the nuisance value of its ambient noise and currents, which interfered with underwater electronic (sonar), acoustical (sound) or magnetic anomaly detection, further augmented its importance. Moreover, it was thought that the constantly moving pack ice provided ideal opportunities for the SSBNs to surface and fire their missiles (Østreng 1982a: 30–3).

In the North Atlantic there was extensive naval deployment in the area where Soviet naval units were operating. In the event of war, the advance of the Soviet Northern and Baltic Fleets into the Atlantic was to be checked by Norway in the Barents and the Norwegian Seas and by Denmark at the Baltic approaches. The Atlantic area flanked by Greenland in the west and the Scandinavian peninsula in the east acquired strategic significance because it was seen to provide a vital passage between the two antagonists. Furthermore, the sea routes to Siberia from Europe and the all-important supply lines between the USA and Europe could be controlled from this area.

The Barents Sea was seen by both sides as the most strategic in the entire Arctic region. Its importance to the USSR arose from the obvious handicap of critical dependence on straits or narrow sea areas while proceeding from home territory into the high seas and vice versa. Haunted by memories of how such choke-points had been closed in wartime, the Kremlin had perceived a vital stake in the sole exception to the geohistorical handicap: the passage between Svalbard and northern Norway. Whereas the geographical advantage of this passage lies in its considerable width (it is 345 nautical miles wider than the others), and in being almost ice-free throughout the year, its geopolitical attraction lay in the fact that its northern limit, Svalbard, remained partly demilitarized, while its southern side, mainland Norway, had chosen not to allow military bases and nuclear installations on its territory (Østreng 1992a: 29). The Norwegian Sea, in conjunction with the Barents Sea, was therefore regarded by the Soviets as the one natural and highly strategic passage area for civilian and military communications to and from the Kola Peninsula and the coast of northern Siberia (with the exception of the Denmark Strait, which in any case remained tightly packed with ice in severe winters).

The Faeroes, Shetland and the Orkneys assumed importance as warning and base areas between Iceland and Scotland. Their shallow waters offered the additional advantage of enabling the passage of enemy vessels to be blocked with conventional types of mines, for which the requisite technology was now available. The Norwegian fjords and harbours were strategically significant in controlling the exits from the base areas in the Kola

Peninsula, while equipment for use by NATO forces could very usefully be stored on Norwegian territory.

Iceland, by virtue of its location south of the Arctic Circle, at the entrance to the Atlantic from the Arctic Ocean, became a "natural" advance base for NATO's naval defence of the North Atlantic (Lee 1986: 191). General surveillance of Soviet naval activity and early warning in case of war were to be carried out from the Keflavik base, in conjunction with similar warning installations in the Faeroes, in Norway and in Great Britain. With the arrival of submarine-launched ballistic missiles (SLBMs) in the sixties, and the subsequent emergence of a scenario in which Soviet submarines equipped with missiles would have to approach the oceans via the North Atlantic, the relatively narrow waters between Greenland, Iceland and Great Britain further augmented Iceland's strategically crucial position (Gunnarsson 1988: 75–8). Were NATO to adopt a more forward defence in the North Atlantic, Iceland would be an excellent base from which to mount attacks on Soviet installations in the Kola Peninsula.

Extending as far south as New York, and in a geographical/geopolitical sense regarded as belonging to the North American continent, Greenland's role in the Cold War strategy was considered to be sufficiently significant to cause the USA to enter into a treaty with Greenland as early as 1941 (Petersen 1993). However, the strategic significance of Greenland responded to the changes in geostrategic doctrines, which themselves were affected by the leaps of technology curves. By about 1950, for instance, Greenland's World War II role as a "stepping-stone" between America and Europe for limited-range aircraft was changing. An extended range and the introduction of air-fuelling made Thule vital to the Strategic Air Command (SAC) as a support base. By the 1960s, Thule's importance for early warning of missile attacks on the United States was further consolidated as the hub in the Ballistic Missile Early Warning System (BMEWS). The advances in radar technology in the 1980s led to a major upgrading of the Thule radar, and there was much speculation about its possible connection with the Strategic Defence Initiative (SDI) programme (Ibid. 1993: 32). Given that the potential operation area for an attack submarine, its missiles capable of reaching every corner of the NATO countries, is the area around Greenland, the country's strategic position became unparalleled (Taagholt 1993: 3).

From the USSR's point of view, its northwestern and adjacent areas were seen as the key to its defence. The Kola and White Sea coasts were ideal base areas for the Soviet strategic submarine (SSBN) forces, with the adjacent Arctic waters offering optimal operational concealment and launch stations. No wonder, therefore, that the majority of Soviet SSBNs – 60% of the total force – were stationed there. Of these, all the most modern vessels (*Delta* I, II and III and the *Typhoon* class), built since 1971, use the Barents Sea, the Kara Sea and the Arctic Ocean itself for operational hiding as well as launching. The greatest threat to the NATO allies was perceived to be the Northern Fleet of the USSR (Tol 1988: 134–5), which was widely acknowledged to be a strong, balanced, modern force.

The Norwegian Sea was perceived by the Kremlin as an important launch area for Western seaborne nuclear-attack forces (carrier-borne aviation in the 1950s and SLBMs after that), thereby marking the area as vital for Soviet defensive strategic anti-submarine warfare. The significance of this strategy – and thereby of the Norwegian Sea – declined somewhat following the shift in Soviet naval strategy in favour of defence of Arctic SSBN Ocean Bastions. Since the deployment of the long-range Trident missile in 1980, the perceived threat posed by the remaining Western SLBMs with launch stations north of the Greenland–Iceland–Faeroes–United Kingdom (GIFUK) gap kept the Northern Fleet on alert.

Svalbard, as already noted, remained something of an exception throughout the Cold War. The Soviet Union kept a watch on the activities of other nations in Svalbard so as to ensure that it was never used as a base for controlling the sea passage between northern Norway and West Spitsbergen or for conducting hostilities against northwest Russia.

Strategies and counterstrategies

A great deal has been written on the subject over the past four decades (see, for example, Ries 1988; Grove 1989; McGwire 1989; Cox 1992; Miller 1992). Much of what was written in the form of strategic studies during the Cold War, however, has become more or less irrelevant in its aftermath.

In the 1950s the Arctic was perceived by both sides as a natural route for any nuclear attack using strategic bombers (Jalonen 1988: 157). This brought to the forefront the strategic nuclear perspective that required control of forward bases on the territory of other friendly states, so that the adversary's territory came well within weapon range (Tamnes 1991: 91).

The United States thus had the option of using both Arctic airspace and forward bases. It preferred to make use of the former, since bases located on the territory of other states could be lost, due to political circumstances, at any time. The Soviet Union did not have such an option and therefore turned its attention to the Arctic itself. However, because the ICBMs trace great circles while using polar routes, various launch and attack points on the Arctic icescape became vitally important for both. Geography thus imposed almost equal constraints on the superpowers' choice of strategy.

By 1956 the development of intercontinental bombers and early-warning systems had accorded a new offensive and defensive significance to the Arctic. The introduction of the B-52 meant that in the planning of the US Strategic Air Command, representing the dominant strategic force in the

Arctic in the 1940s and 1950s, the importance of the forward military bases declined (Jalonen 1988: 158). The early years of the 1960s witnessed a decline in the significance of strategic bombers due to the development of ICBMs and submarines. It was around this time that Thule became an important support base for the Strategic Air Command.

The most important strategic development of the late 1960s and early 1970s was that the sea-based deterrence of the Northern Fleet was augmented by Soviet *Yankee*-class submarines equipped with short-range missiles. In order to reach targets in the United States these submarines would have to sail through the GIUK gap between Greenland, Iceland and the United Kingdom, and then take up positions off the east coast of the USA. Such a possibility galvanized the USA into drawing up a counterstrategy that would allow interception of Soviet submarines in transit during war. This compelled the Soviets to ensure that their own retaliatory capability, together with the credibility of the balance of terror, was not eroded. The much-needed strategic breakthrough for the Soviets came in 1972 with the deployment of the first *Delta*-class submarine, equipped with SSN-8 missiles which had a range of 4300 nautical miles and were capable of striking any targets in Europe, North America and China from a launch position in Arctic waters. By stationing its *Delta* and later *Typhoon* submarines north of the GIUK gap, as well as under the polar ice, the Soviet Union was in a position to pre-empt Western countermeasures that could have punctured its strategic combat potential (Ellingsen 1988: 162).

The second Cold War, in the early 1980s, was characterized both by a much more aggressive containment policy and by a renaissance of geopolitics as the guiding principle of US strategy (O'Tuathail 1994a: 216–17). In sharp contrast to the preceding period of *détente*, 1967–79, attempts to negotiate broke down and a serious impasse was obvious in American–Soviet relations. As Sharp (1993: 495) points out, "in American geopolitics the division between east and west was so ingrained in the structure of world-scale political narratives that it no longer needed explanation. To a majority of the population it had become a matter of 'common sense' that the USA and USSR were polar opposites."

Under these circumstances the Arctic was pushed into its new and highly vigorous phase of militarization. The aggressive maritime thrust of Mahanism was brought back and rejuvenated, with emphasis on the build-up of a still more powerful naval capability. This coincided with a new awareness of the traditional geopolitical conception of the United States as a sea power that required naval superiority. The role of the Navy as a flexible and effective instrument in protecting the global interests of the United States was brought to the forefront of strategic planning. The northern areas had remained a maritime theatre for the entire post-war period, but it was during the early eighties that US maritime interests reached a new peak (see Jalonen 1988: 163–4).

The Arctic came to be affected increasingly by High North features in US nuclear strategy, driven by the vision of a solid Hemisphere Defence or strategic defence, and backed up by the much-publicized new, forward Maritime Strategy with its vigorous thrust of deterrence (Miller 1988). As a result of further Soviet build-up in its vicinity, the Nordic region, particularly Norway, assumed unprecedented geostrategic significance in US calculations. Some of the objectives of the new Maritime Strategy were to emphasize early forward operations in the Norwegian Sea so as to forestall Soviet advances from the north and thereby also protect NATO's Atlantic sea lines of communication, put pressure on Soviet strategic submarines and deny the Soviet "blue-water" Navy access to open seas (Tunander 1989: 65–9; Tamnes 1991: 296). By early 1986, the Maritime Strategy had been fully embraced by the US Navy. Thus the Arctic was gradually transformed "from a *military vacuum* prior to World War II, to a *military flank* in the 1950–70 period, and a *military front* in the 1980s" (Østreng 1992a: 30).

The most interesting feature of these strategies and counterstrategies appears to be that they were formulated in response to hypothetical situations, in anticipation of possibilities that never materialized. Regardless of whether there actually were plans for an armed conflict or whether they were even necessary, the mere fact that threats were being perceived as real and technically possible made them tenable political issues. These political issues with their underlying "enemy images" also helped to keep in business huge military–industrial complexes whose very survival and profits depended upon further perpetuation of threat perceptions – described at great length and with remarkable sophistication in so-called "strategic studies". Furthermore, they provided "an efficient mechanism of population control" as well as "easy formulas to justify criminal action abroad and entrenchment of privilege and state power at home" (see Chomsky 1994: 1–4).

Reduced choices

Forced to live in the shadow of a conflict between the two imperial systems, the others, the small states on the Arctic rim – incidently all on the side of the United States, at least in principle – were left with very few choices, while being obliged to accept US perceptions of the Soviet threat to their national security. They responded with national variations, which essentially reflected the combination of their perceived core security problems and the individually specific circumstances of geographic location and national politics, but it was hard for them to escape the pressures of the Cold War. Let us now examine briefly the Cold War predicament of the small Arctic states and their responses.

The most immediate neighbours of the Soviet Union – the Scandinavian countries and Finland – found themselves in a precarious position that demanded geopolitical prudence and flexible strategic responses: the need to balance geographical proximity to Mackinder's heartland and the geostrategic doctrines and politico–military interests of the United States on the one hand with their individual national security concerns on the other posed a challenge to all the Nordic countries.

Finland, in comparison to the coastal states of the Arctic Ocean, was not an active contributor to the security–political equation of the Arctic. Finnish objectives manifested themselves instead in political and strategic assessments on the one hand, and political viewpoints, recommendations and initiatives on the other, with the aim of influencing the behaviour of other powers and securing a policy which would correspond to Finnish security interests.

The Finnish perceptions of threat during the Cold War were in a category of their own, even though resembling in some ways those of another neutral country, Sweden. In the Finnish perception of the geostrategic importance of the Nordic region as a whole, as articulated in the report of the Third Parliamentary Defence Committee in 1981 (Ruhala 1988: 119), the arms race between the two superpowers was principally connected to the "central balance" and did not pose a direct threat to the Nordic countries *per se*. Even though there was no denying that by the 1980s the Nordic region evoked and invited more strategic interest than before, in the Finnish view there was little reason to believe that the situation would change in the foreseeable future.

Finnish foreign policy therefore did not recognize the usefulness of the Nordic balance – a concept underlining the conviction among the Nordic countries that they would somehow be able on their own to strike a balance between the two rival blocks. It emphasized instead the need to maintain stable conditions in the North. Finland did not want to be dependent on balancing and counterbalancing (for example) the nuclear and base policies of Scandinavian NATO members which it found itself unable to influence any way but which could adversely affect its international position (i.e. Finnish–Soviet relations). Finnish security policy took the form of political *détente* and arms-control initiatives based on a policy of neutrality. The overall objective was to counter the perceived threats with political responses so as to ensure that strategic stability, defensive political objectives and relatively low tension continued to characterize the Arctic and Nordic regions in spite of the military build-up that was dominating the Arctic landscape (Ibid.: 127–8).

Denmark's involvement in the Arctic game of the Cold War arose from the fact that Greenland, the world's largest island, happens to be an integral part of the Danish realm. Danish Arctic policy, quite reactive in nature (Petersen 1988: 39), was dominated by that country's membership of

NATO and driven by its willingness to be guided by the United States' perceptions and policies with regard to the defence of Greenland. Thus, the defence of Greenland became closely integrated in the defence of the North American continent, although its importance fluctuated with shifting American interests in the global strategic–nuclear contest with the Soviet Union. What provided this policy with a sort of rationale and strength was the firm belief among Danish politicians that Greenland played a central role not only in the defence of the western hemisphere but of the whole NATO area, and that this role was important both to the security of the Alliance, including Denmark, and the stability of the strategic balance. There was also an awareness of major US interests in Greenland and of the serious implications of questioning them.

Sweden's self-image, over the centuries, has been more that of a Baltic state than an Arctic power (Huldt 1988: 317). This Baltic tilt, as well as the broader geopolitical orientation towards Central Europe, can also explain to some extent the rather delayed realization in Sweden of the implications of the steady militarization of its northern neighbourhood. As Huldt points out, Sweden has had a "geo-historical predisposition to look south and east rather than west and north in strategic matters" (Ibid.: 318). However, with the so-called "Nordic balance" coming under tremendous strain during the 1980s following the massive Soviet build-up in the North, especially in the Kola Peninsula/Murmansk base complex area, the Swedish Defence Committee, in its report published in 1985, felt obliged to respond to a tendency to a gradual increase in the strategic significance of the North European and North Atlantic area.

Canada's unique situation during the Cold War was marked in the first place by the fact that, after the Soviet Union, it was the geographically most exposed continental country within the circumpolar basin, yet only in a limited sense could it be called an Arctic neighbour of the USSR (Cox 1988: 16). Unlike the Scandinavian countries, therefore, it was neither exposed to specific pressures from Moscow in matters relating to territorial sovereignty, security or even trade, nor did it have any security problems with its immediate neighbour, the United States.

At the same time, the "special relationship" in defence-related matters under the common NATO umbrella was uneasy on account of the difference in the American and the Canadian perceptions of the importance of the Arctic (see Young 1987). Much more problematic, however, were differences over the question of the Northwest Passage, where Canadian–American interests conflicted despite a considerable amount of agreement and complementarity in defence-related matters. The American world view and its underlying self-image as a maritime power made the United States oppose setting up a precedent in the Arctic which might eventually be applied to other international straits around the world and restrict the deployment of its naval forces. The Canadian argument was that the

Northwest Passage does not fall into the category of established routes of transit and that certain characteristics make Canada's Arctic Archipelago unique: an indigenous population used its frozen waters for the greater part of the year, as if they were land.

Moreover, the Canadians remained anxious that, whether they liked it or not, the defence of the US strategic deterrent had to remain a priority in Canadian security policy; at the same time they were attracted to the resource potential of the Arctic (Lenarcic and Retford 1989: 171–2). The task facing both countries was to "build on largely common interests in defence and move forward essentially convergent interests in energy, without prejudicing the fundamental and conflicting interests of either state in the jurisdictional realm" (Kirton 1984: 315). This complex linkage between the sovereignty and security dimensions of its Arctic involvement placed Canada in a difficult situation towards the end of the 1980s (Dosman 1989: 2–3).

Notwithstanding the ups and downs of the 1970s in Iceland's relationship with the United States, the two agreed in 1985 to construct two radar sites in Iceland to monitor Soviet naval activities. The US base at Keflavik remained most unpopular, often causing political debate within the country, so Iceland could use the threat of forbidding the base and withdrawing from NATO as an effective bargaining card in obtaining United States agreement to the extension of Iceland's fishery zones as well as to Iceland's desire to be a *de facto* nuclear-free zone (Osherenko and Young 1989: 33).

However, it has convincingly been argued that it was a perceived threat from the USSR to the independence of small nations that drove Iceland – a country with no armed forces and in which public opinion was generally apathetic about geostrategic matters – to abandon its long-preferred state of unarmed non-alignment and join NATO, despite heated domestic debate and substantial disagreement about the issue (Lee 1986: 198). Consequently, the Alliance had to accept that Iceland would provide facilities similar to those available during World War II only in the event of an emergency and only by mutual agreement; the Republic would not raise any armed forces, nor would it permit troops on its territory in peacetime.

Frozen disputes and lost opportunities

The acute sense of insecurity on the part of Arctic-rim states during the Cold War and the resultant international tensions were further heightened both by the search for oil and gas, and by the lack of defined boundaries in the Arctic. Economic zones, territorial claims and questions of sovereignty caused friction between neighbouring countries and among NATO allies. In fact, the Cold War did not displace the more traditional conflicts between the Arctic States (Osherenko and Young 1989: 157–84; Käkönen 1994: 3).

The European Cold War was waged on many fronts and took a heavy toll in resources and human lives. But, with the exception of the Cuban missile crisis of 1962, it was kept within bounds that were acceptable to both the major adversaries. Each superpower justified its intervention as directed towards the containment (military but also psychological) of the other, and both sought to preserve their respective spheres of influence. The Arctic states did not suffer direct military intervention, but they could not escape the side-effects of a conflict in which the two imperial systems were bent upon establishing hegemonies within their respective areas. Moreover, the Cold War created a structure of thought and behaviour which made collaboration between the two antagonistic blocks, in any normal sense of civilized intercourse between national states, extremely difficult.

Accordingly, the meanings of both peace and national security were reduced to their respective bare minimum of absence of conflict and geo-strategic deterrence. The potential and promise of cooperative action at the multinational level were confined by and large to the military arena and alliances, barring the period of *détente* during the 1970s, when some convergence of national interests could be observed beyond the local-issue areas. For most of the Cold War period the Arctic states saw their perceived interests as having little in common and thus felt only marginally motivated to cooperate in non-military realms such as science and environmental protection. The following examples show how a hegemonic conflict affects the prospects for international cooperation.

Up to 1970, the only two categories of Arctic-related activity that qualified as international, in the sense that several states engaged in the same type of activity are collectively "either affected by or have an interest in the others' involvement" (Østreng 1992a: 31), were science and the military. The relationship between science and the militarized politics of the Arctic during the Cold War was very direct and intimate. Keenness for cooperation among scientists from all over the Circumpolar North notwithstanding, Cold War considerations placed tight restrictions on such activities: there was no easy, uncompromised exchange of scientific knowledge between the East and the West. The few foreign scientists who conducted field studies in the far north of Canada during the 1950s and 1960s, for instance, were subject to security restrictions in their work. Similar restrictions were in place in Alaska and Greenland. The Soviet government totally excluded foreign researchers from its northernmost onshore and offshore regions. The Northern Sea Route was in practice closed to Western transport throughout this entire period. Long before the 1982 Law of the Sea Convention was signed, foreign scientists wishing to do research within the country's 200-mile zone had to apply for permission. Furthermore, Soviet scientists were officially prohibited from participating in international organizations for Arctic research.

Moreover, science that could help military operations to overcome the limitations of harsh Arctic conditions received top priority in matters of research and funding, and since the military is neither much bound to market conditions nor particularly affected by social priorities in general, the Arctic witnessed long-term capital-intensive research projects in certain specific fields like ice behaviour and meteorology, couched and conducted in the secrecy typical of military operations. As Østreng (1992a: 32–3) puts it, "the desire of researchers for scientific co-operation ran aground on the reef of politics. Scientists were mobilized for military purposes and were therefore unable to realize their own wishes for co-operation in basic research."

It was not until the early 1970s, with the onset of *détente*, that the Western states inclined seriously towards the idea of cooperating scientifically with the USSR. For example, in 1970 the United States invited several nations to participate in "The Arctic Ice Dynamics Joint Experiment (Aidjex), with the objective of studying the thermal balances and the relationship between ice cover and atmosphere" (*Aidjex Bulletin* 1971 (11): 11–12). However, only two countries, Canada and Japan, accepted the invitation. The Soviets declined because, among other reasons, they probably felt that "the economic and scientific reasons for investigating the Arctic Ocean are intertwined with military ones, which have elicited great interest on the part of the US Navy" (Ibid.).

The polar bear regime: an outstanding exception

As early as 1954, the International Union for Conservation of Nature and Natural Resources (IUCN) had recommended certain measures for the protection of polar bears in the Arctic. Whereas the estimates of the total population of polar bears ranged from 5000 to 10 000, the mean figures of annual kills from 1963 to 1968 came to about 350 in Alaska, 500 in Canada, and 150 in Greenland. In 1968, some 1250 polar bears were reported to have been killed. In 1969–70, the figures for Svalbard alone rose to more than 400, and at least 100 were killed illegally in Alaska in the name of adventure sports (Curry-Lindahl 1975: 239). This was despite a unanimous recommendation, passed at the Alaska meeting of Canada, Denmark, Norway, the USSR and the USA in 1965, that the bears be considered an international resource and that each nation should do its best to protect them until an agreement could be reached (Cooley 1969). However, there were still no restrictions on the hunting of polar bears from Norwegian ships. This practice was, however, considerably restricted, and better protection provided for females with cubs, as a result of two more meetings of the polar bear specialists, convened under the auspices of the IUCN in 1968 and 1970. But the shooting of bears from the decks of ships and from oversnow vehicles was still allowed. In 1973, as a result of the persistent efforts of the IUCN, a fourth meeting on polar bears was convened by the government of Norway in Oslo in November 1973 and an *Agreement on the Conservation of Polar Bears* was concluded by the United States, Canada, Denmark, the USSR and Norway (text in *Polar Record* 1975, 17(108): 327–30).

Under the Agreement, the signatories resolved, *inter alia*, to coordinate polar bear research (Article VII), to safeguard the habitats of the polar bears (Article II), and, save for conservation, and scientific purposes or traditional hunting by the local people, to bar the taking (which includes hunting, killing and capturing) of polar bears (Article III). The Agreement calls upon "each Contracting Party to take appropriate action to protect the ecosystems of which polar bears are a part, with special attention to habitat components such as denning and feeding sites and migration patterns, and shall manage polar bear populations in accordance with sound conservation practices based on the best available scientific data" (Article II). The implementation of this Agreement, however, for reasons discussed in Chapter 9, has so far not been encouraging.

Otherwise, the Soviets continued to respond either entirely negatively or at best half-heartedly to most of the initiatives for cooperation that came from the West during the 1970s. The ice of mutual suspicion started melting only in the 1980s, especially after 1 October 1987, the day Mikhail Gorbachev delivered his historic speech in Murmansk.

Socio-economic consequences and intimidated natives

The Cold War confronted the indigenous populations throughout the Circumpolar North, causing great harm to their environment, culture, health and human rights. As Mary Simon (1992: 56) puts it, "militarization tends to undermine the self-determination of indigenous peoples. In many instances, it imposes costly and undesired policies, priorities, and activities within the boundaries of their territories, usually leading to a significant loss of control by native peoples over their lands and waters." People from Alaska had no dealings with those from the Chukotskiy Peninsula, just across the Bering Strait. Even those with close family ties on the other side of the strait were not allowed to visit each other (Armstrong *et al.* 1978: 262).

The indigenous peoples were found to be quite resourceful and enterprising for the purposes of "bolstering" defences. In 1958, 1050 Inuit, ranging in age from 18 to 45 years, were recruited as scouts to "fill the chinks in the vast Alaskan coast defence network". They were also to be assigned the dangerous task of picking up radioactive debris to substantiate Soviet nuclear blasts in Siberia. Yet their repeated appeals to the authorities to let them use some of the gas from plentiful naval petroleum reserves created by the government in the area were ignored (*The Polar Times*, December 1959: 8).

The enormous socio-economic impact of the Cold War on the peoples and resources of the Arctic has been analysed by a Danish scholar (Lyck 1993: 8–14), who maintains:

> The military presence and activities first of all brought the then modern world to the Arctic. It was done via heavy capital inflows in form of construction of bases, aeroplanes, vessels and weapons and in the capital was embodied totally new technologies in the Arctic. (Ibid.: 9)

Local communities' dependence on the military installations, in terms of employment and the level of services, was to grow with the passage of time (Andersen and Taagholt 1994: 243–4). Militarization provided an additional stimulus for resource extraction and the setting up of megaprojects. The demographic transformation of some parts of the Arctic landscape, from areas of extremely low population into areas where – after the establishment of military bases and the arrival of numerous "foreigners" – the indigenous majorities became minorities in their homelands, was obvious.

Ecological neglect

In the Cold War game ecological concerns were conspicuous by their total absence or relative neglect in the national priorities and calculations of the Arctic states. By the mid-1970s, it was clear that dramatic environmental changes were taking place in some parts of the Arctic. Radioactive fall-out from nuclear explosions in Siberia and Alaska was causing atmospheric contamination, with serious consequences for the relatively simple Arctic ecosystems and short food chains. Prospecting for oil and gas in Alaska and Canada had led rapidly to deliberate and mindless destruction of the tundra. For example, the part of Alaska between the Brooks Range and the north coast, that was a virgin landscape as late as 1963, by the end of the decade had started showing signs of degeneration due to erosion ditches, the tracks of motor vehicles and other irreparable damage caused by human activities (Curry-Lindahl 1975: 238). Around the same time, the polar bears in the Canadian Arctic were found to be carrying a high concentration of DDT, just like the DDT-contaminated penguins in the Antarctic, at the end of the food chain, showing how chemical poisoning was affecting the whole world.

The most dramatic, indeed shocking, example during this period is the disposal of radioactive waste in the Arctic seas (Gizewski 1993–4: 18–21; Keller 1994a: 16–18). As the Cold War progressed, the nuclear arms race and the development of nuclear power raised the problem of how to handle large quantities of radioactive waste (RW). In the highly charged atmosphere of the Cold War, this problem was not given priority and the simplest solution was to dispose of RW directly in the sea – a practice followed by most countries with developed nuclear industries. The rationale was simple. Safely isolated in deep water, far away from the environment of humans, the waste would slowly undergo radioactive decay and eventually be rendered harmless. Any leaks, it must have been reasoned, would be diluted into near-nothingness by the seemingly limitless waters of the world's oceans.

The Arctic seas came to be treated, especially by the Soviet Union, as ideal dumping sites in national back yards where the nuclear waste could be disposed of, out of sight and at minimum political cost (see Map F). The scientific evidence that was being collected, garnered or perhaps even manipulated to demonstrate the harmless nature of such activities, deliberately played down the elements of uncertainty – which in fact far outnumbered the ones to the contrary. The harsh reality today is that there is an extensive, potentially explosive, solid and nuclear fuel waste lying in the shallow waters of the Arctic, the disastrous effects of which are bound one day to have serious implications for marine ecosystems and human health.

In a recent report submitted by the Government Commission on Matters Related to Radioactive Waste Disposal at Sea (created by Decree No. 613 of the President of the Russian Federation, 24 October 1992), headed by Dr Aleksey V. Yablokov, and entitled "Facts and Problems Related to Radioactive Waste Disposal in Seas Adjacent to the Territory of the Russian Federation" (Yablokov 1993), there is a confession that the Russian Navy is still dumping minor amounts of radioactive waste because it lacks processing and storage plants.

It is equally true that others (the USA, Great Britain, Belgium, Germany, Korea, Italy, the Netherlands, New Zealand, France, Switzerland, Sweden) have also disposed of their radioactive waste at sea between 1946 (when the United States became the first to carry out RW disposal at sea in the northeastern Pacific Ocean at a distance of about 80 km from the California coast) and 1982 (the last officially recorded disposal of RW at sea, not counting dumpings by the Soviet Union and Russia). The most blatant violations of international law, however, are on the Soviet/Russian account to date. According to the Yablokov report, the Soviet Union dumped 2.5 million curies of radioactive waste, including 18 nuclear reactors from submarines and an icebreaker. Sixteen of these power plants were cast into the shallow waters of the Kara Sea, six of them heavy with radioactive fuel, turning this Arctic site near major northern fisheries into the world's largest known nuclear dump (*The New York Times*, 27 April 1993). This is almost exactly twice the total of 1.24 million curies of

ANTHROPOGENIC ACTIVITY IN THE RUSSIAN ARCTIC

LEGEND

▲ – oil
Au – gold
Fe – iron

mineral resources
■ – coal
Al – aluminum
An – potassium

△ – gas
Ni – nickel
Cu – copper

⊙ – thermal power stations
⊛ – nuclear power station
⊙⊛ – main industrial centers
– oil and gas pipelines
✳ – centers of concentration of prehistoric archaeological monuments

––––– – the northern boundary of open ground agriculture
········ – the southern boundary of permafrost
········ – the boundary of 10°C (July) isotherm of tundra zone
–·–·– – the Northern Sea Route
⌇ – areas of farm lands with animal breeding and vegetable production

‖‖‖ – acid atmospheric precipitation (measured by snow cover)
○ – underground nuclear explosions for "peaceful" (industrial) purposes
× – areas of nuclear contamination (nuclear explosions, accidents, technological emissions)

Scale 1:20 000 000 Compiled by Dr. Alexander S. Shestakov, Inst. of Geography, Moscow, Russia radioactive refuse dumped into the oceans by a dozen-odd nuclear states from 1946 to 1982, according to the IAEA. A curie is the amount of radiation given off by one gram of radium and in any nuclear material is equal to the disintegration of 37 billion atoms per second.

The debate about the potential health risks of the newly disclosed oceanic dumping and what, if anything, should be done about it, is likely to grow as the legacies of the Cold War are brought to the attention of the general public and become serious political issues. Yet the fact of the matter, which also emerges quite clearly from this debate, is that at present the most unsettling thing about the whole issue is the element of uncertainty. As the Yablokov report (1993: 14) points out, "as yet, even an approximate estimate of the amount of radioactive contamination that could have have entered the ecosystems of the Barents and Kara Seas has not been made", nor is there any "information on radionuclides that have entered the marine environment due to accidents or disasters". However, radionuclide contamination of the Barents and Kara Seas needs immediate international action. "Failure to make such a demonstration of intent could easily be interpreted as indifference, or worse, as a tacit acknowledgement that the materials disposed of so far have resulted in minimal injury, and that further sea disposal would be both cheap and without political disadvantage" (Ash 1994: 47).

Summary and conclusions

The Cold War period is typical of the way in which such situations can transform the political geography of an area into a military geography. They reduce drastically the choices for genuine international cooperation in non-military realms and lead to the formation of an extremely narrow and excessively state-centred view of security. Consequently a geographical setting is perceived and treated as an inanimate, passive platform on which geostrategic moves and countermoves are made with very little reference to ecological considerations. While geopolitical concepts are hijacked by strategic communities for the purposes of defending their territory against real or imaginary threats from beyond their national borders, it is often overlooked that ecological problems simply do not recognize artificial boundaries and that the imperatives of environmental security demand transnational approaches and multinational efforts in domains that include the production and exchange of scientific knowledge.

It is debatable whether the "operational options" are offered by the region's "own particular characteristics" *per se*. The physical–geographical setting offers a context for all kinds of human behaviour but not the options, be they geopolitical or geostrategic. The latter are functions of politics, not of geography. It is suggested that Arctic geography, with its universal as well as state-specific factors, should be treated as providing at best a context – facilitating and/or constraining – for the choices that the policy-makers evolved or confronted during the Cold War. The key to understanding conflict or cooperation seems to lie in the attitudes and perceptions of the actors, which of course have a spatial dimension in that they are influenced by certain geographical facts and phenomena. Decisions related to conflict and/or cooperation do not flow from the geographical realities *per se*, nor are they taken after looking at maps. More often than not, it is the other way round: it is after the costs and benefits of the related considerations have been weighed and analysed that the policy-makers turn to the maps on the wall or to the geographical realities on the ground to discover the limitations imposed by geography on their choices. In other words, geography affects, and in certain cases even decides, the outcome of choices, but it does not *create* the choices. Thus, seen through Cold War lenses, the geographical properties of the Arctic acquired a specific meaning for the purposes of geostrategic deterrence.

In the Antarctic, as the next chapter will show, even though Cold War-related considerations were not entirely absent, it was still politically possible for the USA, the USSR and Norway to agree to disagree on the problematic question of who owns Antarctica and keep the region non-militarized while opening it to all for science. Among the geopolitical factors that made the superpowers cooperate in Antarctica, while taking threatening positions in the Arctic, was evidently the geographical fact of the location of the Antarctic *vis-à-vis* the two adversaries. Equally decisive for keeping Antarctica out of the Cold War contest was their desire to contain each other geopolitically rather than geostrategically; that, ironically, could be done geopolitically, and not by geostrategic deterrence. Antarctic geography, therefore, was perceived and represented differently from Arctic geography and subjected to a different kind of politicization.

Suggested reading

Archer, C. (ed.) 1988. *The Soviet Union and Northern Waters*. London: Routledge.

Archer, C. and D. Scrivener (eds) 1986. *Northern Waters: Security and Resource Issues*. London: Croom Helm.

Hogan, M.J. (ed.) 1992. *The End of the Cold War: Its Meaning and Implications*. Cambridge: Cambridge University Press.

Tamnes, R. 1991. *The United States and the Cold War in the High North*. Aldershot: Dartmouth.

Tunander, O. 1989. *Cold Water Politics: The Maritime Strategy and Geopolitics of the Northern Front*. London: Sage Publications.

5

The Antarctic Treaty System and multinational governance

The Antarctic, non-militarized, non-nuclear and subject to multinational governance for the last three decades and more, merits the serious consideration of those interested in the political geography of conflict and peace. The ATS, an interlinked network of substantive agreements, including the Antarctic Treaty of 1959, and that body of agreed recommendations, agreed measures and additional instruments which have been concluded pursuant to the Antarctic Treaty, is one of the few international arrangements of the present century that has succeeded. It has achieved its major political objectives; it has sustained a cooperative spirit on the continent; and it has brought together a very diverse group of states in a geopolitical framework in which they seem willing and able to cooperate. This is not to deny the legacy of the old geopolitics – the territorial claims in the Antarctic that continue to bedevil international relations in the region – but to submit that at least until now the new in geopolitics has had an upper hand over the old. And it is to be hoped that this ideal state of affairs will continue to sustain the spirit underlying the Preamble to the Antarctic Treaty of 1959: "It is in the interest of all mankind that Antarctica shall continue forever to be used exclusively for peaceful purposes and shall not become the scene or object of international discord" (*Handbook* 1990: xiv).

This chapter argues that little purpose is served by praising the ATS without (a) accounting for its success so far and (b) assessing its limitations. As pointed out by one of the most prolific British experts on this subject,

> In many respects, the ATS has proved to be a victim of its success. The establishment and preservation of a zone of peace has encouraged commentators to equate government policies of military and nuclear abstention with Antarctica's basic insignificance. It has proved easy to overlook the possible scenario if no

Treaty existed to keep the lid closed on tensions arising from security, sovereignty, resources and other issues. (Beck 1990c: 507)

It has proved equally easy to overlook the enormous geopolitical constraints within which the ATS has operated ever since its inception. The reference here is to the obvious conceptual inconsistency, in Article IV of the Antarctic Treaty, that on the one hand preserves the territorial claims and on the other denies and defers them. Ironically, it is this intentional ambiguity that has been instrumental in keeping the Antarctic experiment alive. An uncritical, even if positive, evaluation of the ATS can be deceptive, especially when it fails to stress adequately the pragmatic geopolitical reasoning behind its success.

At a time when the geopolitical isolation of the Antarctic is being increasingly eroded, not only because of an impressive expansion in the membership of the ATS in recent years (see Appendix) but also because of growing international interest in its ecology and resources, it is worth re-examining the following questions.

Is it due to physical isolation and relative "remoteness from the world's centres of population and of political, economic and military activity" that peace and cooperation have been maintained in the Antarctic? (Glassner 1993: 507). Or is it because, so far, the major export from the Antarctic has been science – unlike the Arctic, where it has been, still is, and is likely to remain resource exploitation – and it is relatively easier and painless to cooperate in the realm of science than in domains like mineral-resource development (Peterson 1988: 2), where the allocation of scarce rights could well be difficult? Or is it due to the persistent Pandora's box vision, shared by the claimant and non-claimant states alike, of what might happen if the ATS were to collapse or were seriously questioned? Or is it on account of the geopolitical consensus underlying the ATS, which in turn "rests on a fair degree of symmetry between the major constellations of power in the world" (Falk 1986: 283)? Or is it because of yet another common perception of the lack of an alternative, realistic or idealistic, system?

Indeed, is it because of a combination of most, or all, of the above-mentioned factors that the condition termed "stable peace" by Boulding (1979: 13) has so far been successfully maintained in the Antarctic? This is a condition in which war is unlikely not because of the threat of mutual annihilation ("unstable peace") – as was the case in the Arctic throughout the Cold War – but because of "mutual satisfaction with the prevailing situation". It is peace based on positive relationships rather than on threats and fears – even though the latter have not been entirely absent from Antarctic-related images, behaviour and interactions. Moreover, it is peace characterized by functional success in the domain of conflict management and conflict anticipation and not by the total absence of conflict.

The principal purpose of this chapter is to account for the "stable peace" in the Antarctic and for the political success of the ATS in maintaining it:

first, by highlighting the Cold War origins of the Antarctic Treaty and tracing the evolution of the ATS, focusing on its key geopolitical landmarks; secondly, by making a cut into the complexity of Antarctic geopolitics and examining the ways in which those active and/or interested in the Antarctic have so far perceived the power- and capability-generating aspects of its physical setting in general and dealt with the geopolitical problems of resource development *vis-à-vis* environmental conservation in particular. It is left to Chapter 8 to examine the management needs of increasingly diverse uses of the Antarctic environment and to undertake an environmental audit of the ATS.

The Cold War origins of the ATS

In order to appreciate the strength and limitations of the Antarctic Treaty, it is important to understand its origins in the Cold War (Mitchell 1984: 13; Beck 1986: 22; Parsons 1987: 4). In sharp contrast to the Arctic, in the Antarctic the Cold War led to politicization rather than militarization. By late 1947, Antarctic affairs assumed immense significance in the foreign-policy considerations of the USA and the "impetus for this shift in focus had more to do with the Soviet Union than with events on the ice" (Klotz 1990: 18). The US Department of State, in mid-February 1949, suggested that perhaps the best way of effectively dealing with the problem of conflicting claims – for the sake of being able to pursue science in the Antarctic – was by way of some form of internationalization and it approached the other interested governments, excluding the Soviet Union (Hayton 1960: 352). By late March, all the responses were in. Argentina categorically rejected the proposal on the grounds of her "incontestable sovereignty" over Antarctic territory; Chile, in putting forth her "Escudero Declaration", on similar grounds of national sovereignty, entered strong objections to any attempt at internationalization. The Chilean government favoured the "celebration of a *modus-vivendi* which would remove the danger of international disturbance or incidents, and which would not postpone the individual rights of the nations concerned" (De La Barra 1955: 59). France and Australia welcomed the US proposal for scientific cooperation but saw no need to include the question of sovereignty. New Zealand alone stated that it was not averse to the US plans, though Norway indicated that it was amenable to persuasion. In the circumstances, the USA concluded that no plan that talked about internationalization had any chance of acceptance.

The US proposal to internationalize Antarctica was probably also motivated by the broader goals of the containment strategy: keeping the Soviet Union out of Antarctica and its affairs. Antarctica, however, presented a special set of problems. Whereas in the Arctic the reasoning behind the policy of containment was primarily geostrategic, driven by the geopolitical vision of a threatening heartland, in Antarctica it was more geopolitical, even though military considerations were not entirely absent. American military planners were by and large of the view that the Antarctic had marginal strategic significance in peacetime (Klotz 1990: 21) – apart from its value as a training ground for cold-weather operations which for political reasons could not easily be conducted in the Arctic. However, if the strategic value of the region, especially of the Drake Passage, were to change dramatically, in the event of the Panama Canal becoming inaccessible due to conflict, the US Defence Department would find it imperative "that sovereignty or active participation in control of the Antarctic, under trusteeship arrangement or otherwise, should be denied to groups of nations which include our most probable enemies" (quoted in Ibid.: 21). The Department of State took the same position (Ibid.). It made little practical sense to argue for a permanent military presence in the Antarctic in view of the enormous costs involved. *Operation Highjump* in 1946–7 – with a dozen naval ships (including an aircraft carrier and a submarine) and 4700 personnel – would have been enough to change the minds of those who doubted the US capability of transporting military forces to the Antarctic.

The Soviet Union of course had no intention of being left out of Antarctic geopolitics, especially on account of an American-engineered solution to the claims dispute. While diplomatic dialectics, now well documented (see Hayton 1960; Triggs 1986; Peterson 1988: 36–41), would continue well into the spring and early summer of 1950, the USSR officially came on the scene (on 9 June 1950) with a memorandum simultaneously addressed to the governments of Argentina, Australia, France, Norway, New Zealand, the UK and the USA (but not Chile – the Soviet Union had no diplomatic relations with Chile at that time). The note was, apparently, the direct outcome of the widely publicized Leningrad discussions and resolutions (of 10 February 1949) of the Soviet All-Union Geographical Society, in which it was claimed that the Russian sailors Thaddeus von Bellingshausen and Mikhail Lazarev had in fact been the first to discover parts of the Antarctic continent during their voyage of 1819–21. Underlining the scientific and economic importance of the area, the memorandum documented Moscow's past insistence on international consultation, pronounced the "illegality of a separate solution" and asserted: "the Government of the U.S.S.R. cannot agree that such a question as the regime for the Antarctic should be decided without their participation" (Kulski 1951; Toma 1956; Hanessian 1960: 444). The United States' initiative was characterized as a "fig leaf to cover the American imperialists' design to seize the whole of the Antarctic" (quoted in Jessup and Taubenfeld 1959: 157).

The arrival of the Soviets on the Antarctic chessboard and the USA's perceived need to reach some kind of settlement about the claims dispute combined to put pressures on the US national security bureaucracy formally to assert an American territorial claim (Klotz 1990: 24–5). Some felt that such a move might also give the United States added influence in negotiating a new international regime for the region.

Despite the opinion in some quarters that US rights in the Antarctic Peninsula could be defended on solid legal grounds, the Central Intelligence Agency argued against a US claim to the Peninsula, anticipating that this would only antagonize American allies and further complicate what was already a messy dispute (Sahurie 1992: 36). The USA hesitated to stake a claim in Antarctica also because it felt that it had demonstrated interest in the continent as a whole, its activities having gone far beyond the unclaimed area of Marie Byrd Land. A claim to one particular part of the continent could be construed as recognition of the lawfulness of existing territorial claims to Antarctica. By such an action the USA could justifiably be excluded from the areas already claimed. There were still serious reservations about the possibility of establishing effective occupation and valid legal claims, coupled with the apprehension that a US claim could well prompt the Soviet Union to take the same path. It was finally concluded that American interests lay more in access to the whole continent than in exclusive control of a part of it.

The tensions between Britain and Argentina on the Antarctic Peninsula were highlighted by the Hope Bay incident of 1 February 1952, when Argentine soldiers fired shots over the heads of the British as they were landing to rebuild one of the stations that four years earlier had been destroyed by fire with the loss of two lives. Just a year later, British forces on Deception Island removed Argentine and Chilean huts that had been built only a few hundred yards away from the British stations. Subsequently, two Argentines were arrested and deported. In 1955 Britain applied unilaterally to The Hague for arbitration but in vain.

Towards the end of 1955, the question of international control of Antarctica was also raised in the British House of Commons. In February 1956, India proposed that the "question of Antarctica" be considered by the UN General Assembly, with the aim of realizing an international treaty according to which the resources of Antarctica might be developed for peaceful purposes and the area closed for testing nuclear weapons or for military activity (Chaturvedi 1986b: 4–8; 1990: 70–2). Several nations, including Sweden, showed interest, but the proposal was withdrawn, largely because of opposition from Chile and Argentina and lack of support from the USA and the UK (*International Conciliation* 1956: 35–43). By then, a number of nations were actively planning their scientific programmes for the biggest-ever international scientific venture, the International Geophysical Year (IGY, July 1957 to December 1958). There was more or less tacit agreement among the participating countries that the political problems of the Antarctic ought to be shelved for the duration of the IGY.

The IGY highlighted the value of Antarctica as a laboratory for fundamental science and gave the politicization of Antarctica a totally new, unprecedented direction. The political need to preserve Antarctica as such and in its pristine form now became apparent, urgent even, in the Cold War conditions pervading the world (Shapley 1985: 84–8). Efforts to launch a parallel joint effort in the Arctic, however, were unsuccessful. In the north polar region, as Sollie (1984: 29) points out, "national politics and strategic considerations were so strong that the essential standard of free access, joint planning, free exchange of personnel and close co-operation set for the Antarctic could not be accepted by all governments". The Soviet Union, which controlled nearly half the Arctic land and coast area, consistently opposed multilateral cooperation in the Arctic.

Against this background, in May 1958 the USA invited 11 other countries – this time including the USSR – to a conference on Antarctica. The invitation, perhaps deliberately, avoided suggesting a prominent position or role for the United Nations in the envisaged arrangement. Instead, the USA preferred an "agreement to disagree", that preserved the legal status quo in Antarctica, not only with regard to sovereignty claims but also with regard to the rights of other interested parties accruing from their stake and activities in the south polar region, including, of course, those of the USA.

Strictly from the viewpoint of US interests, this was the best possible option. The conclusion of a treaty would provide the USA with a feasible way of protecting its potential claims from relative deterioration, while providing sufficient time in which to gauge the situation as it developed and formulate an appropriate strategy for the unique, multifaceted Antarctic reality in which geography, science, law and politics were so inextricably intermeshed. Moreover, the treaty would help avoid further conflict between the Latin American claimants and Britain – all close allies of the USA at that time – and prevent a direct conflict with the Soviet Union.

In the prevailing Cold War context, the Soviet Union apparently found merit in taking the position it did in the matter. Like the United States it "sat on the fence" with regard to the issue of the claims, for the simple reason that it did not wish to – nor perhaps could it – stretch its military, technological, economic or political resources. It was content to obtain universal recognition of the Soviet stake and stance in the Antarctic (Boczek 1984: 839–40; Chaturvedi 1985a: 222–5).

Quite obviously the interests of the USA and the USSR converged. The full measure of the nature and potential of the area was unknown to both. In the midst of their large commitments in the rest of the world they could not find any strategic considerations that made it necessary to involve Antarctica in the Cold War. Both found the proposed treaty the best possible way of avoiding a confrontation, while at the same time guaranteeing and safeguarding their own strategic positions.

In the case of claimant states, what so obviously influenced their willingness to discuss a political arrangement for Antarctica was not just nagging uncertainty about the future of their claims in the event of a concerted occupation of the continent by the United States and the Soviet Union but also the utter impracticality of defending national interests in Antarctica by conventional military means. Both Argentina and Chile, probably others too, concluded on the basis of pragmatic geopolitical reasoning that their Antarctic claims would be advanced more effectively within rather than outside a treaty (Morris 1988: 358).

The Antarctic Treaty of 1959: focus on peace and science

The Antarctic Treaty, with a preamble and 14 articles, was signed on 1 December 1959 in Washington DC by the representatives of the 12 countries that had participated in the IGY. It took effect on 23 June 1961 (text in *Handbook* 1990: xiv–vi). The text of the Antarctic Treaty (cited hereafter as the Treaty) can also be found in some recent books (Quigg 1983; Parsons 1987; Chaturvedi 1990; Watts 1992) together with a discussion of its various legal and political aspects.

Article I of the Treaty declares that "Antarctica shall be used for peaceful purposes only". All activity of a military nature, such as the establishment of military bases and fortifications, the prosecution of military manoeuvres as well as the testing of any weapons, is strictly prohibited. This Article had the strong and vociferous support of the British, French and the Soviet delegations at the Treaty Conference, as well as those from the southern hemisphere. The superpowers were equally keen to keep the region out of the Cold War. The expression "peaceful purposes" thus seems to have been intentionally undefined and unelaborated. The signatories apparently intended that it should include all activities not clearly, visibly, identified as military.

Early agreement seemed to materialize also on the principle of non-militarization. This understandably pacified the Argentine and Chilean delegates. Strategic and security considerations had obviously compelled these two countries to press for the non-militarization of the region next door. The use of military personnel and equipment is, however, permitted (in recognition of the inhospitable environment of the region) as long as it supports scientific research or other peaceful purposes. Geographical compulsions have here obliged political actors to devise ways and means of cooperation.

Article I is complemented by Article V, which prohibits any nuclear explosion in Antarctica and the disposal there of radioactive waste material. The initiative for banning all kinds of nuclear explosions in the Antarctic came primarily from the nations of the southern hemisphere (*Conference on Antarctica*/COM.II/SR/2 (Final) 1 November 1959). So even though the nuclear powers of that time, all located far away from the

111

continent, were not enthusiastic about it, the provision was incorporated into the Treaty. Geography intervened once again.

Article VII provides for wide rights of inspection of all areas of Antarctica by the Antarctic Treaty Consultative Parties (ATCPs). The right of inspection was included primarily to monitor non-militarization and to generate and promote mutual trust, the very foundation of any cooperation. As the British representative at the opening plenary session of the Conference on Antarctica put it, "the principle of non-militarization is still so new in international practice and it would surely be wise to eliminate from the outset the possibility that the actions of one or other of the parties, including the United Kingdom, can give rise to doubt or suspicion, among other powers as to whether it is being observed" (*Conference on Antarctica Documents* 1959: Doc. 15: 3). The United States too, from the very beginning, insisted on incorporating an inspection clause in the Treaty (Bush 1982a: 70). It was made clear that without it there would be no Treaty. In any case, it was inconceivable that the Cold War attitudes in the rest of the world would not also surface in Antarctica, however unattractive or uninhabited it might be for the time being.

Under Article III, the contracting parties agree that, to the greatest extent feasible and practicable: (a) information about plans for scientific programmes in Antarctica shall be exchanged to permit maximum economy and efficiency of operations; (b) scientific personnel shall be exchanged in Antarctica between expedition and station; (c) scientific observations and results from Antarctica shall be exchanged and made freely available. The remaining articles concern the ways and means of making the system function in the desired manner.

The ATS as a system of governance

The Treaty accords its original signatories, the 12 countries that actively participated in the IGY, a special position in relation to the so-called "acceding" states. In contrast to the obligation of the latter to carry out "substantial scientific research activity" in Antarctica, understood to mean the establishment of scientific stations or the dispatch of scientific expeditions (Article IX), the original signatories are not obliged to do so. Whether the activities demonstrated by a country contending for "consultative status" in fact constitute "substantial scientific interest" or not is collectively decided by the consultative powers (Auburn 1979).

According to Article XIII, the Treaty is open for accession by any state which is a member of the United Nations, or by any other state which may be invited to accede "with the consent of all the Contracting Parties whose representatives are entitled to participate in the meetings provided for under Article IX".

The administrative arrangements provided for in Article IX of the Treaty lack formality in the sense that there are no established procedures nor indeed any specific agencies charged with the task of implementing them. There are to be periodic Antarctic Treaty Consultative Meetings (ATCMs) among the ATCPs to recommend measures in furtherance of the objectives of the Treaty. As pointed out by Watts (1992: 12), the hallmark of the ATS appears to be "institutional caution, coupled with institutional accretion". In order to become legally effective, each recommendation has to negotiate successfully the threat of "double veto": the recommendation must be approved first by the national representative at the Consultative Meeting and then by the respective legislatures on the domestic front.

The *ad hoc* decision-making mechanism for the ATS, it would seem, is more a technique of coordination than an institution of management endowed with independent authority. The system lacks the authoritative and effective institutionalization necessary for resolving conflicts. Typically, in systems of this type changes in an existing political arrangement flow from *ad hoc* bargaining rather than clear-cut legislative procedures. Such bargaining exercises do sometimes prove effective, but they seldom yield the unambiguous or trustworthy results that would accrue from proper legislative processes. In decentralized systems such as the ATS numerous unresolved conflicts are bound to emanate from competing claims or interpretations.

According to Article VI, the Treaty's provisions apply to the area south of 60°S latitude. At the same time, however, Article VI disavows any incursion upon the rights of the high seas as recognized by international law. The Treaty in no way attempts to define explicitly just which maritime areas of the Southern Ocean below 60°S latitude are, or should be, considered high seas. The primary reason for this ambiguity is that five of the seven countries which claim sovereignty over portions of the Antarctic continent demarcate their claims in such a manner as to include areas of the Southern Ocean (Joyner and Lipperman 1986: 13).

The most significant feature of the ATS, as a conflict-avoiding mechanism, is that it has been devised by shelving the complex and emotionally charged issue of Antarctic sovereignty. At the final meeting of the Plenary Committee, on 30 November 1959, the statements made by both claimants and non-claimants (see Bush 1982a: 38–9) left no doubt whatsoever that this unresolved – albeit now frozen and dormant – conflict was going to remain a major reality of Antarctic geopolitics. Article IV of the Treaty explicitly declares that "nothing contained in the present Treaty shall be interpreted as: a renunciation by any contracting party of previously asserted right or claims to territorial sovereignty".

The First ATCM at Canberra in 1961 augured a mechanism, a process, to assist the ATS in its unimpeded functioning, which has continued to produce a whole series of regulations covering various aspects of the Treaty.

The Antarctic Treaty – resources and conservation

The Treaty had wisely left the issue of resources alone and chosen to remain silent about it. Rushing what had not yet gone beyond speculation would certainly have exacerbated the suspicions and fears of the claimants and jeopardized management of the very issue that was to be diffused: conflicting positions on territorial sovereignty. The highest priority at the time was, naturally, the generally accepted need to establish a lasting political basis for international cooperation and to avoid excitement of conflict. The Treaty did not contain a statement of the objectives or principles of environmental protection. This is quite understandable given the Treaty's Cold War-related origins and concerns. Moreover, environmental concerns were not a salient component of the international agenda in the late 1950s.

Agreed Measures for the Conservation of Antarctic Fauna and Flora, 1964

The sovereignty issue surfaced soon after the Treaty came into force, albeit in a surreptitious way. The United Kingdom, it appears, was one claimant state that came to Canberra convinced that "the most explosive issue facing the Treaty, and the one with which it probably could not manage, was anything to do with minerals . . . the thing that was likely to tear the Antarctic Treaty apart" (Heap 1992: 37). Is this why the United Kingdom decided to raise the issue of the conservation of Antarctic wildlife at the very first ATCM? In a subtle but significant way, therefore, the problem of sovereignty was approached at the very outset, albeit apparently in a conservation context. The geopolitical reasoning behind the Agreed Measures for the Conservation of Antarctic Flora and Fauna 9 (cited hereafter as the Agreed Measures), subsequently concluded at the Third ATCM in Brussels in 1964 (text in *Handbook* 1990: 2402–6), is neatly summed up by John Heap (1992: 37), formerly the head of the Polar Regions Section of the UK Foreign and Commonwealth Office:

> There was no objective need to conserve Antarctic wildlife, no one was doing anything to Antarctic wildlife which required that we react by setting out to conserve it. It was almost something of a confidence trick because what we said was "we dare anyone to say that they are against the conservation of penguins" and we looked each one in the eye and no one dared. The Agreed Measures for the Conservation of Antarctic Flora and Fauna raised the issue of issuing permits. This was an issue which touched upon the sovereignty issue because we had to say who could issue these permits and we used the phrase "competent authority". To the Chileans the competent authority in the Chilean territory was the Chilean government, but the Chilean territory was partly British territory in the view of the British and partly Argentine territory in view of the Argentines. So the competent authority, in the areas of overlapping claims had to be Britain, Argentina and Chile – there was no getting away from that. That was a big step

to have taken, to get these three governments to agree that they would in effect, base their actual operations of these agreed measures on the basis of nationality rather than territory.

The Agreed Measures were the first relevant exercise of prescriptive power in respect of conservation within the purview of the ATS (Sahurie 1992: 522). The principle of conservation established in Article 6 prohibits "the killing, wounding, capturing, or molesting of any native mammals . . . except in accordance with a permit", which might be issued only for scientific purposes or to provide otherwise unobtainable food for parties operating within the Treaty area.

To protect the fauna and flora, the categories of Specially Protected Areas (SPAs) and Specially Protected Species (SPSs) were established. The former were designed to protect unique natural ecosystems. At the same time there was no way of enforcing the Agreed Measures in practice nor anything to ensure consistency of implementation by all the states party to the Treaty. There was no central authority for issuing permits and no way of monitoring cumulative impact. As Bush (1990: 126) points out, sensitivities about sovereignty and jurisdiction led to an "unwillingness . . . to have any but the most rudimentary institutional structure to oversee [their] implementation".

From a geopolitical angle it is the very first Article of the Agreed Measures that is of interest. Even though, under the Agreed Measures, the entire Treaty area is to be considered a "Special Conservation Area", the scope of their application was restricted to land and to ice shelves. Not only fish and whales in the entire Antarctic area but also mammals in the high seas were excluded. The reason for not covering the high seas was said to be the continuing resolve of the ATCPs not to "prejudice or in any way affect the rights, or the exercise of rights, of any State under international law with regard to the high seas within the Treaty Area, or to restrict the implementation of the provisions of the Antarctic Treaty with respect to inspection" (Article 1, *Handbook* 1990: 2403). The implementing legislation of some of the signatories to the Agreed Measures, however, is conspicuously lacking in uniformity. As Bush (1982a: 147) comments, whereas the implementing legislation of New Zealand, the UK and Belgium specifically excludes the high seas, the legislation of both Australia and the USA applies to the whole area south of 60°S, although "in neither case is it clear whether this extension of legislation to the high seas followed from an interpretation of the Agreed Measures or whether it was decided as a matter of policy that the regime should be so extended".

Nevertheless, when the ATCPs, including the so-called "ABC countries" with overlapping claims, had agreed to deal with the issue of conserving Antarctic wildlife on the basis of *nationality* rather than *territoriality*, the stage was set for further expansion of Antarctic Treaty jurisdiction into the high seas in future conventions.

The Convention for the Conservation of Antarctic Seals, 1972

The Scientific Committee on Antarctic Research (SCAR) had tabulated and arranged for the publication of statistics on seals and birds captured within the Treaty area during 1964–9, and reported in 1972 that at that time there was no "serious direct threat to Antarctic seals and birds and in particular no species was endangered, although the possibility of over-exploitation of some local populations of seals could not entirely be ruled out" (*Handbook* 1990: 2409). How did the 1972 London Convention on the Conservation of Seals come about?

Was it only because the fixed geographical scope of the Treaty, despite the initial stretching attempted under the Agreed Measures, had brought to light an important omission by which the seals on the Antarctic pack ice had been left unprotected? Since about 80% of the seals, including the particularly threatened Ross seal, live on pack ice there was an obvious need to expand the area of operation of the Antarctic Treaty, notwith-standing its Article VI, to include the seas south of 60°S. Or could it have been the possibility of renewed sealing in Antarctic waters? Although sealing was becoming much more politically unacceptable in the Arctic areas, Antarctic seal populations were now recovering from the reckless exploitation of the 19th and early 20th centuries, so there was indeed the possibility that commercial sealing might reappear. Moreover, outsiders could easily invoke the saving provision on the freedom of the high seas in Article VI of the Treaty, which certainly included freedom to hunt seals. Or could it have been due to the hidden, though not entirely selfish, motive of some of the Antarctic powers to achieve with a single stroke of diplo-matic genius an expansion in the geographical scope of the ATS while preparing the ground for dealing with the krill issue? Relatively speaking, the krill issue was much more compelling and contentious than the issue of protecting the seals. For the others in the ATS, there was simply no way of avoiding the problem, especially when the language of conservation was used to push through what was yet another attempt to stretch the Treaty further beyond its original jurisdiction.

Be that as it may, the Convention for the Conservation of Antarctic Seals (cited hereafter as the Seals Convention) was negotiated in London in 1972 (text in *Handbook* 1990: 4104–16). Its objectives from a conserva-tion point of view are the protection, scientific study and rational use of Antarctic seals, guided by the general principle that "this resource should not be depleted by over exploitation and that harvesting should therefore be regulated". It sets out rules on closed and open sealing seasons, sealing zones and reserves and provides an indicative list of other protection mea-sures which parties may adopt. Special permits allow seals to be taken for food, for scientific research or as specimens for museums, educational or cultural institutions. Catch levels are established for crabeater, leopard and

116

Weddell seals, whereas Ross seals, southern elephant seals and all fur seals are to be fully protected. Commercial sealing has not taken place in Antarctica in modern times.

The Seals Convention had made a significant contribution to the ATS, with its recognition of pre-emptive management. From the point of view of the ATCPs its significance also lay in the fact that the area of operation under the ATS, notwithstanding Article VI of the Treaty, had been further expanded to include the seas south of 60°S (Heap 1992: 37). But this time, instead of drafting another set of recommendations or agreed measures, the ATCPs decided to produce a convention outside the consultative process. This approach not only promised to avoid the legal and political problems posed by the geographical scope of the Treaty, it also opened the new sealing regime to non-Treaty states. Now that the substance of sovereignty, i.e. resources, had become the manifest focus of negotiations among the ATCPs, both claimants and non-claimants found it essential to affirm the provisions of Article IV of the Treaty for the purposes of the Seals Convention. As if Article 1 of the Convention was not sufficient, the representative of Chile made the following statement at the final session:

> The Delegation of Chile states that the reference to Article IV of the Antarctic Treaty contained in Article 1 of the present Convention signifies that nothing specified therein shall confirm, deny or impair the rights of the Contracting Parties *as regards their maritime jurisdictions and their declared juridical position on this matter*. (*Handbook* 1990: 4104) [emphasis supplied]

The Chileans, by mentioning maritime jurisdiction, had made a point with far-reaching geopolitical implications. Since the statement had apparently been made on behalf of all the ATCPs, including non-claimants, the American representative, in a statement soon afterwards, had no reason to contest or qualify the Chilean comment. He therefore confined his remarks to the regret felt by the United States about the lack of stronger provisions in the Convention for the observation of operations and enforcement of regulations which in his view had "chiefly arisen not from commercial but from juridical interests". He also made it clear that his delegation had decided to sign the Final Act "in order not to diminish the progress achieved by the Conference in international co-operation for effective conservation in the Antarctic" (Ibid.).

Growing focus on resources: CCAMLR

By the 1970s a rather impressive and definite outline of Antarctic resources had emerged as a result of extensive geological and biological research on and off the Antarctic continent. This was soon to be filled in by perceptions of the accelerating growth of the population in terms of consumption and the depletion of resources in the wake of the oil crisis. The ATCPs perforce saw the Antarctic in a new light and focused their attention on its resource aspects. Minerals are fixed and finite, in contrast to the resources of the Antarctic seas, which are renewable and in constant flux. There was therefore little hope for an agreement on Antarctic minerals if the Antarctic powers could not devise a regime for marine resources first. A marine regime thus acquired higher priority and did in effect overtake the minerals talks.

At a time when it had become quite common to maintain that the total world fish catch could easily be tripled by harvesting Antarctic krill, evidence that non-Treaty actors were taking an active interest in Antarctic resources was enough to galvanize the ATCPs into action. They saw the need to have a regulatory framework in place before the krill fishery, the dynamics of which were not fully understood, was actually overexploited (Hofman 1993: 534). Moreover, in the mid-1970s northern hemisphere countries such as the USSR, Poland and Japan – also South Korea and Taiwan – were excluded from their traditional fishing grounds after the proclamation of 200-mile fishing zones (Rowland 1988: 13). The United Nations Environment Programme (UNEP) and the Food and Agriculture Organization (FAO) also indicated research interests in the area.

Such a curious mix of political compulsions and ecological imperatives convinced the ATCPs early on that priority would have to be given to the protection of the ecosystem as a whole; and while the geographic boundaries of the Treaty were further stretched to coincide with the ecological boundaries, the special legal and political status, or rather the status quo, of Antarctica, under Article IV of the Treaty, would have to be preserved at all costs (IX-2, *Handbook* 1990: 4204).

In 1976, in accordance with Recommendation VIII-10, a SCAR initiative launched the BIOMASS programme, which conducted two experimental programmes on the Antarctic ecosystem. After two negotiating sessions in Canberra and Buenos Aires during 1978, and additional sessions at the Tenth ATCM in 1979, CCAMLR was formalized in Canberra in May 1980. After due ratification, it came into force in 1982 (text in Ibid.: 4209–17).

Although created at least in theory outside the ATS, in reality CCAMLR had to be organically linked to it. This geopolitical link has been forged at three major levels. First, the geopolitical consensus underlying Article IV of the Treaty was not only retained but explicitly reiterated, together with its concomitant ramifications for the freedom of the high seas. The jurisdiction of the ATS, which had steadily been creeping into the seas south of 60°S, was further extended to the Antarctic Convergence, this time with the aid of a sophisticated version of functional ambiguity. Secondly, the political pre-eminence of the ATCPs within the ATS was preserved. Finally, institutions set up under CCAMLR were meticulously tailored to take account of Antarctic-specific geopolitical realities rather than to forge linkages with other international agreements.

Given that the Southern Ocean ecosystem with which the ATCPs were now concerned goes well beyond the artificial boundary laid down under the Treaty, CCAMLR made good ecological sense in going as far as the Antarctic Convergence. To exclude the high seas from a conservation regime for the Southern Ocean would have been an obvious absurdity. The negotiations, however, proved far more difficult than had been anticipated.

France insisted that its islands of Kerguelen and Crozet, both lying well within CCAMLR's sphere of influence, be excluded from the Convention. As a consequence, CCAMLR had to be drafted so that while it made unambiguous exceptions for islands with undisputed sovereignty – such as Kerguelen and Crozet – the moratorium on claims south of 60°S was unaffected. A highly sophisticated and subtle formula of functional ambiguity was agreed upon for what has come to be known as the "bifocal approach to interpreting CCAMLR's jurisdictional purview" (Barnes 1982: 280–1; Bush 1982a: 406). Joyner (1992: 226–7), in his acclaimed study on Antarctica and the Law of the Sea, has succinctly summarized it as follows:

> In the view of states with territorial claims in Antarctica, Article IV, paragraph 2(b) in CCAMLR protects the rights both above and below 60° South. Conversely, non claimant states are able to contend that this provision pertains to claims south of 60° South latitude, which remain subject to Article VI of the Antarctic Treaty. Only claims north of 60° South therefore are valid and undisputed, where they remain unaffected by either agreement. The caveat here is waters adjacent to disputed claims may not necessarily be considered high seas. While Article VI in the Antarctic Treaty does preserve high seas freedoms below 60° South, it neither elaborates on the definition of high seas for the region, nor clarifies the legal implications of Antarctic claims there . . . This built-in ambiguity permits parties to CCAMLR to avoid a potentially contentious issue . . . The bifocal approach affirms the moratorium on claims – a key to ATS viability – for living resources, but leaves open the possibility that a state might forgo conservation should exploitation become commercially viable.

The United Kingdom, adopting the bifocal approach, would also claim that according to Article IV(2) of CCAMLR British territorial sovereignty over South Georgia and the South Sandwich Islands is unaffected.

CCAMLR leaves no doubt whatsoever that its architects had no intention of compromising their control over Antarctic decision-making. As Joyner (1992: 229) points out, "it reflects traditions and institutions established by the Antarctic Treaty". Yet there was no escaping questions such as: On what political or legal grounds could the ATCPs impose their terms on the non-member countries in respect of fishing in the high seas? How could these countries be compelled to abide by the rules unless they had a part in making them? On the other hand, how could the Treaty powers compromise their privileged position by admitting other nations on equal terms? Faced with such dilemmas, the ATCPs, in order to preclude the development of an alternative legal regime for Antarctica, decided to extend the opportunities for non-Treaty governments to contribute to the making of CCAMLR.

A special ATCM meeting was to be called to prepare a draft and to decide which other countries "actively engaged in research and exploitation of Antarctic Marine Living Resources" would receive an invitation to the decisive meeting at which the Convention would be negotiated. The same meeting would also determine which international organizations were entitled to attend "on an observer basis".

It has been pointed out that the so-called "two-stage process", ending with a "decisive" negotiating session, was largely a fiction. As had been intended from the beginning, the Convention was drafted entirely by the ATCPs. By the time of the final conference, ostensibly open to other nations fishing in the Southern Ocean, there was little left to negotiate and no substantive changes were tolerated (Quigg 1983: 189–90).

The requirements, of course, did not apply to the ATCPs, some of whom engage in neither research nor fishing in Antarctic waters. Signatories of the Treaty (the ordinary members, so to speak) were not guaranteed an invitation to the conference on any basis. The Netherlands, which acceded to the Treaty in 1970, and the Republic of Korea were refused observer status, as was the Antarctic Southern Ocean Coalition (ASOC), representing more than a hundred environmental organizations claiming a membership of more than two million.

The United States led a majority favouring the accreditation of all three, while the Soviet Union led the opposition. ASOC was not entirely excluded, since its executive head was a member of the US delegation. Organizations that were accredited as observers, in addition to the European Economic Community (EEC), were the FAO, the International Whaling Commission (IWC), SCAR, the Standing Committee on Ocean Research (SCOR) and the IUCN.

CCAMLR must surely be the first fishing convention in which the majority of drafters and charter members have no active interest in the fishing covered by the agreement. One might say that to involve countries like the USA, which had no financial stake in the fishing, should guarantee that the parties' foremost concern was conservation and the protection of the total ecosystem of the southern polar region.

Another major problem faced by the ATCPs involved the position of the then EEC in relation to the Convention. In the original 1978 draft, the EEC had been ignored on the grounds that British and French Antarctic territories are specifically excluded from the EEC. When the EEC insisted on participating, the Soviet Union took the position that it would include either the Community as a whole, or its individual members with interests in the Antarctic, but not both. The compromise finally worked out recognized that the EEC had mixed competence, i.e. while it has no uniform policy on scientific research and conducts no research in the southern seas, it does have a common policy on fishing. Thus the Community is allowed to participate in making decisions on some issues but not others. Article XII of the Convention gives no additional vote to the EEC. As a compromise, the European Economic Community, which was not an original signatory, became a participating member when the Convention came into force on 7 April 1982, after ratification by eight of the 15 signatories (Bush 1982a: 393–425).

CCAMLR aims at developing suitable mechanisms and measures for the conservation of Antarctic marine living resources. It adopts an innovative ecosystem approach rather than a single-species model, based on the principles that ecological relationships between harvested and dependent and related populations be maintained. Central is the idea that harvesting does not undermine stable recruitment levels, and any changes in the marine ecosystem which result from harvesting must be reversible. Although CCAMLR represents, without doubt, a significant advance in the protection of the living marine resources of the Antarctic, a number of questions (to which this study returns later) remain open and unanswered.

Behind the congealed appearance of the ATS in the 1960s – a placidity that is inevitable in legal formulations and definitions – one could detect a geopolitical reasoning directed at stretching the juridical scope of the Antarctic Treaty. If the creators of the ATS wished to create a legal framework within which a unique, challenging area could be explored, understood and, if possible, harnessed for human use, they were equally prepared to touch upon the soft underbelly of the Treaty, the inescapable reality of disputed ownership, via the resource issue. The negative implications of a mismatch between constantly evolving geopolitical realities and legal formulations for the functional viability and continuing success of the ATS were well appreciated by the ATCPs early on. The parameters of intended activity laid down in the Treaty were consequently modified with great caution and only after careful consideration. Political and all other ambitions and interests were balanced with the main objective of scientific cooperation for the understanding and use of Antarctica. It was natural that within the defined parameters of the Treaty the range and pace of activity was limited, slow and lacked the daring that later years would bring. This was to change qualitatively and fairly rapidly in the 1970s and 1980s, when increasing pressure on global resources focused international attention on the Antarctic (Wassermann 1978; Zumberge 1979).

The rise and decline of the minerals issue

When the initiatives for a minerals regime surfaced in the early 1970s, hardly anybody thought that commercial activity was likely or feasible. In the economic, technological and geopolitical climate of the time, mining the Antarctic was simply inconceivable. Why did the ATCPs not defer consideration till more adequate knowledge of the economic, technological and environmental aspects of mining the continent, and the means to pursue such activity, became available to them?

It was generally felt that once commercial curiosity was excited, interests awakened or mineral deposits on a commercial scale found, consensus would be the first casualty and thus more difficult to achieve; the question of territorial sovereignty would inevitably surface, jeopardizing the ATS. Under the circumstances, it was just as well that precise or full knowledge of the minerals map of the continent was not to hand. This geopolitical reasoning clearly illustrates that the reality with which the ATCPs were concerned, while negotiating the minerals issue, was not the reality as it *existed*, but a *future* reality which they wished to realize in the form of an agreement on the minerals issue. At the same time, they wished to prevent a *future* reality from happening: the breakdown of the ATS for the reasons mentioned above.

When the issue was first informally raised by the UK and New Zealand in 1970 at the Tokyo ATCM, it not surprisingly took the meeting virtually by storm. But scientific–technological and geopolitical developments in the world at large had been so rapid that even delegates who were negative in 1970 realized the urgency of the problems during the Seventh ATCM in Wellington in 1972 (Butler 1977: 46). By this time the Antarctic as a possible repository of vast resources had attracted enough anxious attention to demand, for the first time, that the subject "Antarctic Resources – Effects of Mineral Exploration" be carefully studied and included on the agenda of the Eighth Consultative Meeting (VII-6 1972; see Bush 1982a: 275–6).

The majority at that time favoured a moratorium on exploration in the Antarctic until the environmental, technological and political problems were sorted out. The Soviet Union expressed support ostensibly on the grounds of ecological–environmental considerations but probably because of its inferior technological capability *vis-à-vis* the USA, which handicapped it in benefiting adequately from the envisaged arrangement. Only the United States – technologically better equipped than the rest – opposed:

> There was a feeling [on the American side] at that time that a moratorium was not so much a delay to permit rational consideration as a decision not to examine the issue at all, at a time when perceptions of resource scarcity and hydrocarbon scarcity were dawning. (Quigg 1983: 194)

Nevertheless, the ATCPs decided upon voluntary restraint (VIII-14; see Bush 1982a: 328–9) until some basic ground rules could be agreed upon. On their recommendation, SCAR appointed a special committee to prepare for the consideration of the next (1977) ATCM in London a preliminary assessment of the environmental implications of mineral exploration and exploitation.

The special preparatory meeting in Paris in 1976 could not go beyond enunciating four guiding principles for the proposed minerals convention: (i) maintaining the Treaty in its entirety; (ii) retaining the pre-eminent role of the ATCPs; (iii) according top priority and special consideration to protecting Antarctic ecosystems; and (iv) accommodating the interests of all mankind.

In London, governments were asked to urge their nationals and other states to refrain from all exploration and exploitation of Antarctic mineral resources while progress was being made towards the timely adoption of an agreed regime for Antarctic mineral-resource activities (Bush 1982a: 343–5). In sharp contrast to the 1960s, the majority of the Treaty powers in the 1970s projected narrowly perceived and vociferously defended national interests in the matter of Antarctic resources. These changing attitudes caused considerable alarm and apprehension within the ATS. The majority (New Zealand, Japan, South Africa and Australia among them) were energy-dependent nations who probably perceived in the Antarctic the last hope of satiating their thirst for oil.

An Australian spokesman was quoted as saying: "The Treaty did not freeze territorial claims; it merely put them on the back burner to keep warm" (Quigg 1983: 196). Ambassador Keith Brennan of Australia too is on record as having argued that the claims issue was postponed only for those matters specified in the Treaty – and the Treaty did not say a word about Antarctic minerals. Hence, Australia felt that every drop of oil that may be found in her claimed territorial waters belongs to her, and thus the unilateral exploration and exploitation of resources by claimant states are entirely legal and legitimate, subject only to temporary and voluntary restraints. He also contended: "the validity of a claim does not depend on recognition . . . the existence of a claim is a reality. You cannot extinguish sovereignty by vote." Chile and Argentina were also adamant (Santa Cruz 1978: 451–61). The head of the Argentine delegation at the Washington Consultative Meeting (1979) distributed recent legislation entitled "Risk Contracts for Exploration and Exploitation of Hydrocarbons" and made it abundantly clear that his government considered the law applicable "in the sector of Antarctica over which it (had) reserved sovereign rights".

In contrast the United States supported the principle of "free non-discriminatory access". Antarctica should be left open to all, with the benefits going first to the nation(s) with the most advanced technology (Auburn 1977: 145–6). This was in line with the position the USA had adopted in the ongoing UNCLOS. The Soviet Union, on the other hand, conscious of its relatively disadvantageous position in offshore oil-drilling technology in the Antarctic, pleased the conservationists by advocating indefinite postponement of mineral exploitation and giving top priority to the fragile south polar environment, at least for the time being.

By the time of the serious discussions in Washington and Buenos Aires (December 1980–March 1981), however, almost all the extreme positions had mellowed considerably. The growing sense of urgency had induced the feeling that consensus and accommodation had to be achieved at all costs (see Wolfrum 1991: 11–15). If the ATCPs pulled in opposite directions and failed to make a joint stand before the Law of the Sea Convention concluded, all sorts of pressures would emanate from the Group of 77.

The division between claimant and non-claimant states that emerged at these discussions was even sharper than expected. The key question appeared to be whether the legal status quo under the Treaty could be reconciled with an equitable plan to develop mineral resources. And what about the interests of the developing countries, now that India, China and Brazil were part of the game? No wonder that the ATCPs felt obliged to reiterate in Wellington that any agreement that might be reached on a regime for mineral exploration and exploitation in Antarctica elaborated by the ATCPs should be acceptable and without prejudice to those states which had previously asserted rights of or claims to territorial sovereignty in Antarctica (XI-1; reprinted in Bush 1982a: 442).

Evolving consensus in this respect was indeed a formidable task (see Orrego Vicuña 1988: 356–61). The negotiators over the next six years or so (see Wolfrum 1991: 3–11) would first have to find a way of adjusting and reconciling the diverse views on the territorial status of Antarctica. The question of ownership of the subsoil is so directly connected with the concept of territorial sovereignty that a mere reiteration of Article IV of the Antarctic Treaty would not do. The claimant countries wanted a more specific manifestation of their position, but a direct reference to their claims might imply "recognition" of some sort of preferential position for them which the non-claimants would certainly interpret as prejudicial to their own.

The group of developing (Third World) countries did, however, acquire their own influence base during the negotiations. In 1982, when the talks about Antarctic minerals began, the only developing countries to have consultative status were the two claimants, Argentina and Chile. Their attitude and contribution to the talks were conditioned more by the fact of their being claimants than by any particular sentiment of fraternity with the developing countries. India, Brazil, China (see Keyuan 1993) and Uruguay, after admission as consultative members, formed a lobby of countries in their position that watched and promoted Third World interests in the minerals negotiations. Without doubt, a great deal of give and take was called for.

The imperative of devising effective means of protecting the Antarctic environment was universally and unanimously recognized. The challenge was to arrive at environmental provisions which would work in practice. In the absence of a total ban, provisions would be required to guarantee and ensure that no activity could be allowed to proceed which did not satisfy some fairly stringent conditions.

Agreement on the text for a new minerals regime came in June 1988, and in November 1988 the Convention on the Regulation of Antarctic Mineral Resource Activities (CRAMRA) was opened for signature in Wellington, New Zealand (text in *Handbook* 1990: 4311–34). CRAMRA closed the Antarctic to all exploitation or development activity unless there was consensus that such activity had satisfied the prescribed rules.

Provisions having direct or indirect bearing on the environmental (protection) aspect of potential minerals activity abound throughout CRAMRA. Some of these provisions could be characterized as purely environmental in nature, while others were general but certainly had implications for the environment. CRAMRA prescribed tough procedures to be followed before any patch of land or offshore area could be identified for exploration and development. The preamble to the Convention unequivocally states that protection of the environment has to be a "basic consideration" in decisions about mineral activity. There appears to be no suggestion whatsoever that the Convention aimed to promote minerals development or to open Antarctica for mineral-resource activities. Here too the special responsibility of the ATCPs to protect the environment and to "respect Antarctica's significance for, and influence on, the global environment" had clearly been recognized.

It is difficult to deny that the final text of CRAMRA had emerged from an elaborate process of balancing and accommodating divergent – often conflicting – positions and interests. The eventual solutions hammered out under CRAMRA were in many ways ingenious, for there was no attempt to give special status or consideration to anyone on mere legal grounds. Solutions were finally reached which could satisfy everyone: the distribution of authority among the institutions in CRAMRA was one such element; the decision-making process was another; the shape and the structure of its institutions yet another.

In January 1988, when CRAMRA seemed a virtual certainty, the dispatch of an expedition to service Greenpeace's World Park base at Cape Evans highlighted the persistent and well-articulated campaign of the Greenpeace movement, and many other national and international environmental groups, against the very idea of mining the Antarctic (see Greenpeace International 1985: 15–17, 26–7).

CRAMRA's prospects darkened, eventually to disappear, when in May 1989 the government of Australia announced that it would not sign since it now felt strongly committed to the view that no mining at all should take place in and around Antarctica. Australia would pursue instead urgent negotiations for a comprehensive environmental protection convention within the framework of the ATS; it would canvass international support for this position, which included the establishment of an "Antarctic Wilderness Park". French support for the Australian position promptly followed.

125

In order to enter into force, CRAMRA needed to be ratified by all the countries with territorial claims in Antarctica. Consensus within the ATS was obviously threatened. Absence of agreement on either CRAMRA or on an alternative regime to control minerals development in Antarctica would inevitably cause a geopolitical void in the Antarctic. Consequently, there would be nothing to prevent any nation from carrying out minerals development activity. Even a ban on such activity would not do, for it would be vulnerable to a possible change of heart or of government. Unregulated, or insufficiently regulated, activities might result, as would disputes or conflicts over rights to mineral resources. Under the circumstances, the ATCPs were left with two options: either restore the consensus, on the verge of collapse in the ATS, or face the consequences of the dismantling and eventual breakdown of the ATS.

Indeed CRAMRA could have made a significant contribution to the further evolution of the ATS and to its political viability. To the gradually, if unsteadily, evolving sovereignty–resources–conservation interface within the ATS, it would have brought stability by way of a negotiated, agreed-upon consensus approach for dealing with the regulation of an activity that impinges directly upon complex questions of national sovereignty and environmental protection in Antarctica.

It would have filled the gaps left by the earlier instruments in the expanding jurisdiction of the ATS. Its area of application would have brought within the juridical scope of the ATS, in addition to the continent itself, all the Antarctic islands and their associated ice shelves south of 60°S latitude, as well as the seabed and subsoil of the adjacent offshore areas (Article 5). Whereas CCAMLR extended as far as the Antarctic Convergence, CRAMRA would have extended to Antarctica's continental shelf.

Antarctica and its resources: common heritage? whose heritage? common to whom?

The discussion so far may give the impression that the Antarctic and its governance have throughout been the exclusive concern of those inside it. On the contrary, as noted earlier, "outsiders", such as India, took an interest in the icy continent as early as the mid-1950s. During the Antarctic Treaty Conference, it was the British delegation that raised the issue of "safeguarding the interests of countries other than those represented at the Conference":

> We are concerned that no misunderstanding should arise as to the motives of the Twelve Powers; we should not wish our deliberations to raise doubts in the minds of other nations, and particularly of those who, although hitherto not interested in the Antarctic, may question the right of any single group of countries even to give the appearance of legislation on a matter of worldwide concern.

... *The Treaty is, in fact, to be almost entirely a self-denying ordinance on the part of the signatories, who will derive from it virtually no privileges but only obligations. In order to ensure the smooth working of the practical arrangements which will give effect to the principles underlying the Treaty, it is desirable that arrangements should be in the hands of those Powers having experience of physical conditions of the Antarctic. The Twelve Powers participating in this Conference have that experience, and it is surely reasonable that they should be charged, initially, with the responsibilities which will devolve upon them as a consequence of this Treaty.* (*Conference on Antarctica Documents* 1959, Doc. 15: 4) [emphasis supplied]

It is unfortunate indeed that the world community is badly divided over the management of Antarctica, especially at a time when the importance of the south polar region to the overall health, even survival, of our planet has been increasingly established and universally acknowledged. Both the UN and the so-called "Third World" are divided over the "Question of Antarctica". It is no accident that the more developed among the developing countries – which include India, China and Brazil – are in the ATS. The majority of countries in the so-called "critical lobby" in the United Nations are among the least developed, who have recently become aware of both the multidimensional promise of the Antarctic and the serious limitations in respect of their economic–scientific–technological condition that prevent them benefiting from the Antarctic opportunity.

The conflict over acquiring meaningful physical as well as political access to Antarctica, and its present as well as potential resources, is not so much ideological as geopolitical. The reality is that the persisting divide in the international community is not due to "value conflict"; it is caused by the mismatch between, on the one hand, the growing interest of developing countries in the Antarctic and, on the other, the lack of opportunity to participate in the decision-making about the present and future of Antarctica.

Is the ATS "legitimate" or "illegitimate"? Does it or does it not represent the interests of mankind as a whole? How "effective" or "ineffective" is it as a caretaker of Antarctic science as well as the environment? And, most explosive of all, should the ATS continue to exist, or be replaced by some UN-based system of management for the Antarctic? Answers to these and similar questions, from both the critics and the supporters of the ATS, continue to highlight the persisting divide in perceptions as well as the prescriptions on these issues (see Chaturvedi 1986a; Hayashi 1986; Beck 1992, 1993; Sahurie 1992: 72–3). Here I attempt a brief geopolitical assessment of the UN debate on Antarctica.

The Malaysian Prime Minister, Dr Mahathir-bin-Mohammed, launched his offensive on the ATS just a few months before the Law of the Sea signing ceremony. In a speech to the UN General Assembly on 29 September 1982 he dismissed the Antarctic Treaty as an agreement between a select group of privileged nations which did not represent the true feelings of the members of the UN and expressed the desire for a new international agreement (UNGA 1982: 17–20). Ever since, Malaysia has been the most vociferous among the critics of the ATS. On the question of territorial claims in Antarctica, Malaysia took the position that if non-claimant ATCPs assert that the entire continent and its resources are open for their use, then "why should such assertion not be made applicable to the international community?" The validity of these claims is, according to Malaysia, suspect under international law: if such claims to sovereignty have not been recognized, then why should Antarctica not be a "common heritage" invested in the UN? Malaysia was also quick to urge that the scope of CCAMLR and its legal implications for the high seas be examined, the ongoing negotiations between the ATCPs for a minerals regime be reviewed and the whole question of international management, national exploitation and benefit-sharing carefully investigated.

The first resolution on this matter was adopted by the General Assembly on 30 November 1983, calling upon the Secretary-General to prepare a "comprehensive, factual and objective study on all aspects of Antarctica, taking into account the Antarctic Treaty System and other relevant factors" (UNGA 1983). That it was a negotiated resolution passed without vote reflected the feeling among ATCPs that the commitment of the Secretary-General would not imply any criticism of the Antarctic Treaty itself. Prepared under the direction of the UN Under-Secretary for Political and Security Affairs and completed in October 1985, the study did seem to acknowledge, though tacitly, the merits of the ATS (see UN Secretariat 1984).

The Malaysian position reflected, in part or in whole, that of most of the developing nations, including Antigua, Barbuda, Pakistan, Bangladesh, Cameroon, Cape Verde, Egypt, Ghana, Nigeria, the Philippines, Sri Lanka and Zambia, to name but a few. All were critical of the allegedly exclusive nature of the system, the membership of South Africa (no longer an issue in the UN debate) and the distribution of Antarctic resource benefits.

Of the 54 states that submitted replies to the Secretary-General, as many as 24 happened to be consultative as well as ordinary members of the ATS. All rejected as "misconceived" and "misrepresentative" the accusation that the ATS is anachronistic, discriminatory, harbours colonial territorial claims, is exclusive and thus should be replaced by the "common heritage of mankind" (CHM) principle. It was also pointed out that divergent positions within the ATS on Antarctic claims must be accepted as "a fact of life" by everyone (Woolcott 1984: 227). The growing membership of the ATS, including the accession to the Antarctic Treaty of India and China among others, was cited in rejection of the charge of exclusiveness (UNGA 1984: 87–8).

The following year, demanding a management system for the Antarctic that would be characterized by accountability, the involvement of developing countries and equity, the Malaysian spokesman presented the viewpoint of the critics:

> Why should the United Nations be excluded from involvement? . . . We wish to see that the system for management of that continent is one which would be accountable to international community, which would make it possible for the relevant international agencies to be more directly involved and which would ensure that the fruits of the exploitation of its resources could be more equitably shared as the common heritage of mankind. (UNGA 1985: 67–70)

The 1985 session marked the end of a dialogue that had begun in the UN during 1983–4 in the hope of creating better international understanding on the subject. Instead, a polarization of views on how to manage Antarctica emerged despite the agreed objectives of preserving it as a zone of peace, environmental protection and international scientific cooperation in "the best interests of all mankind". It was obvious that the ATCPs perceived no real role for the UN except as a forum for the international exchange of views or an occasional dialogue – strictly within the parameters of the ATS. From now on, they would choose merely to reiterate the virtues of the ATS and refuse to participate in votes taken on the item.

By 1986 a shift of attitudes within the critical lobby was distinctly discernible. For example, Antigua and Barbuda now seemed to be in favour of a "reformist" approach rather than the radical restructuring of the ATS, and not everyone seemed to be supporting the application of the CHM principle to the Antarctic. The ATCPs, emboldened by the accession of South Korea, North Korea and Greece to the Antarctic Treaty, seemed further united in their opposition to the moves to replace the ATS by some UN-based model of governance.

In 1987, a grey area could be seen emerging, despite the black-and-white impression given by the debate. This took the form of enhanced appreciation of the ATS in the realm of international cooperation and regional peace. Ghana, one of the most vociferous critics of the ATS, acknowledged that any attempt to bring Antarctica under UN purview should take into account the "legitimate rights" of the Antarctic Treaty parties, including their desire "not to overturn or do away with the Antarctic Treaty System" (UNGA 1987: 41, 46). This view was seconded by Sri Lanka, which suggested that the present Antarctic regime should be made more acceptable to the wider international community (Ibid.: 29–31).

At a time when the sterile debate in the UN seemed to be drifting and reacting to major geopolitical decisions within the ATS, being taken far away from New York, the most eventful of such decisions was the adoption of CRAMRA in June 1988. CRAMRA was bound to reactivate the otherwise receding attack on the alleged exclusivity of the ATS, now additionally sustained by the escalating pressures exerted by the Non-Governmental Organizations (NGOs) on the ATCPs, relating to the environmental protection of the Antarctic in general and the minerals regime in particular. CRAMRA was being perceived by many critics as a serious threat to the polar environment, in line with the NGOs' support for declaring Antarctica a "world park" with a total ban on mining. Antigua and Barbuda would not "accept the right of a small group of countries to arrogate to themselves the exploitation, and probably the devastation, of a continent" (UNGA 1988a: 11).

The defence of the ATCPs came as usual from the Australian delegate, although Michael Costello could hardly be expected to know that his country would soon contradict the position he was adopting with regard to CRAMRA: "the Antarctic Minerals Convention has been designed to protect the Antarctic environment to the maximum extent possible and to ensure that any minerals activity takes place . . . in a manner that does not cause conflict or discord" (UNGA 1988b: 32–4).

By the end of the 1980s it was becoming quite obvious that the demand for an alternative regime to the ATS, the possible framework for which was never even outlined, was as much a geopolitical move to acquire a share in decision-making for Antarctica and access to its resources as it was a strategy to deny those in the ATS the opportunity to take advantage of their privileged position in this respect. No wonder that, well up to the point when the greening of Antarctic geopolitics caused serious cracks within the ATS and eventually led to the abandonment of CRAMRA, the critics talked more about the minerals than about the environment, and the vocabulary of criticism was applied accordingly.

Owing to the much enhanced visibility of Antarctica in the global environmental context on the one hand, and the breakdown of consensus within the ATS over the adoption of CRAMRA on the other, the context for applying the CHM principle to Antarctica (advocated by the anti-ATS lobby in the UN), having been resource-driven for many years, is now clearly environment-oriented. For example, during the 1990 session, Antarctic science activities were being criticized on account of the rapid growth in the number of base stations, and the resulting overcrowding, notably on King George Island (UNGA 1990a: 3). Adverse environmental impacts arose, it was alleged, from waste disposal, constructional and other activities at base, oil spills from the ships (e.g. the *Bahía Paraíso* incident of 1989) and the alleged infringement of conservation measures (Ibid.: 4). The overcrowding of scientific stations was linked to the need to satisfy the "substantial research activity" required for ATCP status in Article IX(2) of the Treaty. ATCPs were also being blamed for unnecessarily duplicating research and logistic activities. Some critics maintained that a number of ATCPs were prospecting and exploring for minerals under the cover of scientific research (UNGA 1990b: 29).

Quite obviously, there has been a shift in the strategy of the critics, in that a point-by-point criticism of the "legitimacy" and "effectiveness" of the ATS is now to be cemented by the direct action in Antarctica itself of setting up a UN-sponsored station. From the point of view of the ATCPs an obvious geopolitical implication of having a UN-sponsored "international base" on Antarctica is that in a way it symbolizes the contention of the critics that the ATS is not "international" and that there is a dichotomy between the ATS and the international community at large. They therefore remain strongly opposed to the whole idea, pointing to the UN's scarce resources, the Antarctic research data already being made publicly available to the UN and the existing framework of cooperative relations with the UN specialized agencies (UNGA 1990c: 12).

A majority of the ATCPs have always perceived a threat to the legitimacy and functioning of the Treaty system from the CHM principle. Both the claimants and the non-claimants remain convinced that any attempt to bring the south polar region within the scope of the UNCLOS III would raise questions for which there are simply no answers. The claimants perceive in that principle an outright rejection of their claims, and not without reason.

The concept of the CHM as it was understood and applied in the context of the deep seabed, and its resource management by the proposed International Seabed Authority under the Convention, could not be applied to the Antarctic without radically restructuring, or replacing, the existing geopolitical arrangement for the region. The ATCPs did express their willingness to continue the dialogue about Antarctic matters so as to generate a better understanding of the Antarctic and its affairs in the international community, but on condition that the legitimacy and merits of the ATS should be neither questioned nor unduly criticized, as that was obviously becoming a routine feature of the UN debate on Antarctica.

The linkages as well as contradictions between economic growth and the imperatives of environmental conservation, sometimes so casually covered by the term "sustainable development", are also reflected in the UN debate on Antarctica. Should Antarctica be mined if the rapidly depleting marine and mineral resources elsewhere on the planet so demand, or should it be preserved as a natural-scientific laboratory? Those supporting CRAMRA interpreted it in such a way as to demonstrate that "sustainability" in the context of the resource development–environmental conservation interface was desirable as well as practical only by imposing CRAMRA. The majority outside the ATS did not agree because their perception was that sustainability, however defined, must be matched by considerations related to "equity". In other words, who decides who gets what, when, where and how from the various "exploitations" of Antarctica, especially the resource-related ones? Whereas the ATPs emphasize the need for expert handling of Antarctica and its affairs, and would insist that the ATS is open, fair and capable of providing both "sustainable" and "equitable" management for the Antarctic, critics in the UN – by and large the less developed among the developing countries, and those lagging behind economically as well as technologically – want a system of Antarctic governance that gives them a say in decision-making.

Considerations of *Realpolitik* nevertheless seem to dictate that whereas the UN would continue to be used as a platform for critics to express dissent and disagreement about various institutional and functional aspects of the ATS, the decisions that actually matter in the case of the Antarctic would continue to be taken in the ATCMs, and *not* in the UN. But then, how desirable or meaningful is this deadlock over an experiment, the joint management of a disputed sovereignty, that so far has insulated a huge continent from international discord and conflict? The ATS is far from perfect, and many of the views of the "critical lobby" are valid and even constructive. In demanding the replacement of the ATS, however, the critics must also carefully and realistically consider whether their proposed alternative will be at least as viable as, if not actually superior to, the ATS – one which would include, of course, a mechanism to provide for the "freezing" of claims and counterclaims of sovereignty over Antarctica as well as the "rights" asserted there.

In the opinion of this author there is great merit in the solution proposed by Østreng (1991a: 445–6) for bridging the widening gap between critics in the UN and the ATCPs. According to him, a beginning could be made by exploring ways and means of accommodating the reasonable concerns of all sides and by increasing further functional cooperation between the ATS and the UN in the form of information exchanges and cooperation on a technical level on matters of environmental, meteorological and other interest. This could be expanded if, for example, a Treaty Secretariat were set up, if the UN agencies devoted more funds to matters of Antarctic interest, and if international organizations became more involved in meetings held under the auspices of the ATS. Antarctic politics will doubtless become even more internationalized and that may add a new dimension to the long-standing disagreement between claimant and non-claimant states about the legality of sovereignty claims.

The U-turns in the ATS: crisis of consensus

The U-turns on CRAMRA by Australia and France called into question the collective understanding that the ATCPs abide by the norms of the system and seriously undermined the capability of the ATS to resolve intra-system conflicts. Australia asserted, quite simply, that even when undertaken under the stringent environmental regulations and controls embodied in CRAMRA, mining was environmentally unacceptable.

Apparently, in Australia, Antarctica was slowly but surely emerging as the touchstone for "green credentials" in Bob Hawke's government, especially in the wake of the Tasmanian state election results of 13 May

1989. As the five newly elected "green" members were crucial for the incoming minority Labour administration, the need for Hawke's government to foster the national perception that "the environment is Labour territory" became imperative. It became politically obligatory for the government to oppose those thinking of mining in the Antarctic. If the Australian rejection of CRAMRA was motivated by political and electoral considerations, it is equally obvious that the environment aspect too was a major, if not decisive, consideration (see Beck 1990b: 115).

It has also been suggested that the Australian shift was motivated by a selfish desire to protect Australia's own mining industry from being disadvantaged in the future as a result of subsidized activity in the Antarctic by non-Australian companies. The Australian delegation to the minerals negotiations argued, unsuccessfully, for an anti-subsidy clause. The Treasury in particular was unhappy about the absence of provisions in CRAMRA for specific royalty payments to claimant states. The Australian Mining Industry Council, on the other hand, while certainly preferring an anti-subsidy clause in the Convention, was particularly critical of the Australian government's position on CRAMRA (Dunn 1989).

France joined Australia in opposing CRAMRA, it is believed principally on environmental grounds, but the rise of pro-environmentalist political parties in the country and the concomitant desire not to relinquish its claim of sovereignty in the Antarctic were also instrumental.

One of the earliest reactions to the shift in the Australian position, and perhaps the strongest, came from Britain. During the second reading of the Antarctic Minerals Bill in the House of Commons (vol. 156, col. 218, 4 July 1989), the Under-Secretary of State for Foreign and Commonwealth Affairs stated:

> The Australian case rests on an unsubstantial assertion that Antarctic mineral activity is now suddenly environmentally unacceptable. The idea of maintaining the Antarctic as an unsullied frozen paradise free of environmentally damaging mining activities is attractive . . . .
>
> But . . . the purpose of the convention is precisely to avoid environmental damage from mining in Antarctica.
>
> Even if an outright ban on mineral activity could be negotiated – we do not believe that it could – it would be extremely unlikely to work. In a world of increasing population and increasing pressures on a finite resource base prospecting for minerals would continue. Instead of such prospecting being carried out openly within Antarctica and subject to proper control, as laid down in the convention, it would be done covertly under the guise of scientific research.

About the same time, the USA too came under pressure at home either to strengthen the environmental safeguards of the existing ATS or to negotiate a new comprehensive environmental convention. Such negotiations, it was urged, should form a major item in the agenda of the XVth ATCM; the President of the United States was asked not to submit the Convention to the Senate for ratification. Further delays to US ratification were caused by requests from the Council on Environmental Quality and the Environmental Protection Agency for a review of US Antarctic policy prior to submission of the Convention to the Senate. In addition, the State Department was asked to prepare a Legislative Environmental Impact Assessment as required by the National Environmental Policy Act (*Eco* 1989: 2).

On 28 September 1989 the Italian parliament unanimously forbade the government to sign or ratify CRAMRA and requested it instead to support and promote in international forums the proposal for the creation of a World Park in Antarctica (Ibid.: 1).

Against such a backdrop, the XVth ATCM in Paris (in October 1989), revealed both agreement and disagreement among the ATCPs over many substantive issues. Even though everyone seemed to accept in principle the need for comprehensive measures for the protection of the Antarctic environment and the dependent and associated ecosystems, sharp disagreement arose over the best ways to obtain them. France and Australia advocated the elaboration of an exhaustive convention; Chile pleaded for some kind of agreement similar to the Agreed Measures of 1964. Many contested the proposal for a new, single, comprehensive regime on the grounds that it would necessarily entail yet another time-consuming and arduous process of reconsidering carefully crafted compromises incorporated into existing agreements. Some, if not all, of the claimants feared that their position would be prejudiced by the form in which the environmental protection measures, proposed and contemplated, might eventually be cast.

No one, however, could afford to brush aside the fear that with the collapse of CRAMRA and the absence of a consensus on minerals development in Antarctica, the moratorium on minerals prospecting, exploration and development in the Final Act of the IVth Special ATCM would also cease to exist. Prospecting, at least in theory, could proceed subject only to controls, if any, enacted by national governments. Once there is a tangible manifestation of interest in the development of Antarctic minerals – perhaps consequent upon a galvanizing discovery – it would be extremely hard to negotiate under pressure a regime like CRAMRA, with the environmental safeguards CRAMRA contained. Will the ATS be capable of bearing the strain at that time? Perhaps not all the ATCPs were as anxious about such possibilities as those critical of the changed positions of Australia and France. Yet even others could not afford to ignore the implications of a breakdown of consensus within the ATS on such vital issues as environmental conservation *vis-à-vis* resource management in the Antarctic. The delegations left the French capital in a state of high anxiety. The polarization of views in the ATS clearly indicated that the problem defied simple or hasty solutions.

The ATCPs assembled in Viña del Mar, Chile, from 19 November to 6 December 1990 for the XIth Special ATCM. Delegations included the

26 ATCPs – Ecuador and the Netherlands were admitted to consultative status on 19 November at the same venue by the Xth Special ATCM, but the merging of the German Democratic Republic with the Federal Republic of Germany increased the total by only one – and the ten non-ATCPs (Switzerland having joined the Treaty on 15 November 1990). In addition, observers from CCAMLR, SCAR, the Commission of the European Community (CEC), the Inter-governmental Oceanographic Commission (IOC), IUCN and ASOC – a coalition of some 200 non-governmental environmental protection organizations, of which Greenpeace is the most prominent and best known – were also present at this ATCM. The invitation to ASOC was a recognition by the ATCPs of the arrival of a new actor on the Antarctic geopolitical scene. From now on the views and concerns of so-called "Green politics" will have to be accommodated by the ATS in all future decisions on Antarctica.

By the time this first special session devoted exclusively to the environment got down to business, the nature of alignments within the ATS over the question of CRAMRA and its future had changed considerably. In 1990 Italy and Belgium had joined Australia and France in proposing formally that a permanent ban on mineral-resource activities be incorporated into a comprehensive convention on environmental protection. The permanent ban was supported in addition by New Zealand and Sweden among the ATCPs, and by Denmark, Greece and the Democratic Republic of Korea among the non-ATCPs. The countries at the other end of the spectrum were the UK, the USA, Argentina, Norway and Uruguay. The rest were more or less of the view that the issue should be resolved before it damaged the viability and the achievements of the ATS.

Most participants in the meeting agreed that conservation and environmental protection measures under the Treaty have been developed haphazardly and in a rather *ad hoc* fashion. As a formal system for protecting the Antarctic environment these measures could be regarded as reasonably effective, but there was need of rationalization and consolidation. There were also gaps: for instance, there was no mention of compliance or liability, not even an explicit requirement of environmental inspection and no infrastructure that could make its operation more efficient. Yet, on the question of whether to mine Antarctica, under stringent regulations of course, or not mine at all, the ATCPs found themselves badly divided.

Among the proposals circulated at Viña del Mar (Bonner 1991: 12–17) was a "four-power" draft of a convention sponsored by Australia, France, Belgium and Italy which dealt with Antarctic mineral resources and called for a permanent ban on all activity with regard to these resources. Another draft proposal of exhaustive measures for environmental protection was submitted by the government of New Zealand. This also proposed a ban on mineral-resource activity as an alternative to CRAMRA.

There was also the "five-power" draft protocol, submitted jointly by the USA, Argentina, Norway, the UK and Uruguay, which contained institutional provisions and principles, and specified in appendices measures to deal with marine pollution, waste disposal, environmental impact-assessment procedures and the question of agreed measures for the conservation of flora and fauna.

The differences in the various texts were primarily two. First, the four-power "convention approach" called for the application of a set of decision-making procedures for all activity in Antarctica. This meant that scientific research activities there could be subjected to some form of collective decision-making. The five-power "protocol approach", on the other hand, implied that the decision-making competence of the parties would not extend to a requirement for prior permission or authorization for research activity, nor would the freedom of scientific research, guaranteed by the Treaty, be affected by new agreements. The second major difference between the convention approach and the protocol approach concerned institutions: what sort of new institutions will have to be evolved within the ATS to perfect its ability to deal with environmental protection in the Antarctic?

The outline proposal submitted by India deserves mention because it took the optimistic view that the differences among the various proposals could be reconciled "if the different views on substantive issues" were harmonized (XI ATSCM/7 26 November 1990: 1). As a possible way out of the impasse it suggested a legally binding moratorium on mining for a specific period, extension of which may be reviewed taking into account the factors prevailing at the time of review, including the availability of fail-safe technology. The idea of a prohibition or moratorium for a specific period was indeed a clever way out of the stalemate. This would enable both sides to circumvent a complete-loss-of-face situation and agree on a meeting point somewhere in the middle of the extremes of their positions.

As the discussion progressed at Viña del Mar, there was apparent convergence in a number of areas (see Interim Report, XI ATSCM/9 Rev. 1 5 December 1990: 1–6). In the first place, there appeared to be strong preference for a protocol, rather than a convention, as the most desirable form of agreement for protecting the Antarctic environment. The general view was that a protocol with annexes that could be updated from time to time as the need arose would be the most effective means of realizing environmental protection in Antarctica.

As for decision-making, the prevailing view appeared to be that the elaboration and effective implementation of the EIA procedures, and the commitment of all participants in this respect, could well become a basis for consensus in this problem area. It might make possible a compromise between those seeking additional control over environmentally sensitive, science-supported activities and those who feared that this would undermine the freedom of scientific research in the Antarctic.

In respect of institutions, one of the two broad problems again concerned decision-making. Differences arose on the demarcation of decision-making authority between the consultative mechanism of the ATS and its subsidiaries and the extent to which it could be vested in the advisory, the scientific and the political bodies.

Secondly, some of the Latin American countries particularly had reservations about establishing extensive and costly new machinery. All the claimant states were also worried about the implications of the authority of the new institutions *vis-à-vis* assertion of their respective sovereignty in the Antarctic. What eventually emerged, in outline, was the view that the ATS needed an environmental advisory body – not duplicating SCAR – to offer advice about implementing and assessing the effects of environmental regulation, and a secretariat that would provide the information and data-support functions necessary for an effective system of environmental protection (Scully 1991: 9).

Yet, the issue that was at the very heart of the whole debate – Antarctic mineral resources (still deep in the realm of the unknown and the unrealizable) – continued to generate high political temperatures among the Antarctic players. Those seeking an alternative to CRAMRA in terms of a permanent ban on mining insisted on an explicit declaration of this ban in the form of a written agreement. Those on the other side of the fence resisted. Unless this basic, first-order issue was first settled, the arguments about the terms of the proposed environmental regime could not make much sense at Viña del Mar.

Shortly before the meeting at Viña del Mar ended, Ambassador Rolf Trolle Andersen of Norway, one of the old Antarctic Treaty hands, produced an informal draft text of a protocol which later came to be known as the "Andersen Text". A clever, fair and balanced blending of the various proposals, it established a set of legally binding principles to the effect that the protection of the Antarctic environment with its dependent and associated ecosystems remains the fundamental consideration in planning and conducting all activity in Antarctica.

By the time ATCPs assembled in Madrid for the second session of the XIth Special ATCM (April 1991), the alignments within the ATS over the question of CRAMRA had once again undergone a change. The British government now announced its willingness to support a fixed-term moratorium – no period was specified – on condition that the moratorium would be kept under constant review and would be replaced by a minerals regime prior to its expiry. Curiously, Germany announced its support for a permanent ban in the week before the Madrid Meeting, which took the USA and the UK, the known stalwarts of CRAMRA, by surprise.

The Andersen draft, then, became the basis for further negotiations in Madrid, and by the time what is known as the "April Text" on the "Protocol to the Antarctic Treaty on Environmental Protection" was ready, one could broadly identify the areas where significant advances had been made since the Viña del Mar Meeting.

Significantly, Article 24 produced a carefully worded compromise package involving two stages: first, after 50 years, agreement of 51% of the ATCPs was required for the ban to be lifted; secondly, 75% of ATCPs, including all 26 states that were ATCPs at the time of the adoption of the Protocol, must ratify the amendment to allow it to enter into force. Any lifting of the prohibition must also include the negotiation of a legal regime on mining so as to avoid creating a vacuum. The package was designed to give something to both sides: those wanting a permanent ban, and those willing to accept only a moratorium on mining activities. Quite obviously CRAMRA was not in the picture any more: dead in letter, but not so much in spirit, as paragraph 4 of Article 24 insisted on there being a legal regime of a binding nature on mining before the prohibition could be lifted.

The ATCPs agreed to meet again in June to finalize the text of the new Environmental Protocol, thinking that it would be a good idea to sign the new agreement on 23 June 1991, the 30th anniversary of the Antarctic Treaty. Instead, what was in store for them was the announcement by the United States government, on the evening of 12 June, of its inability to accept the Articles in the Protocol relating to minerals prohibition. More specifically, serious reservations were being expressed about the "near-permanent ban" on mineral-resource activities as outlined in the April text. The USA decided to reserve its position on Article 6 (pertaining to the prohibition on mineral-resource activities) pending resolution of the Amendment provisions. It argued that these provisions made it virtually impossible to lift a ban as any of the 26 countries had the opportunity to block any proposed amendment. The USA government accepted the 50-year ban, but proposed an addition to these "Amendment or Modification" provisions (Article 26) to allow a nation to "walk away" from the ban provisions, if ratification of an amendment is held up for more than three years.

The changed US position fractured the carefully worked out and skilfully negotiated package of compromise among diverse positions, and effectively reduced the ban-lifting provision to only the 51% required to permit the lifting of the ban. As few countries would be prepared to allow unregulated mining activity to occur outside the Treaty, any country threatening to use the "walk away" clause would almost guarantee a smooth path to lifting the ban, assuming support from just 51% of the ATCPs.

At the Third Session of the XIth Special ATCM in Madrid (19–22 June 1991) the instant reaction of the ATCPs to the changed US position was that it had undermined the stability as well as viability of the ATS by attacking the principle of consensus that had sustained the entire edifice of cooperative arrangements for the Antarctic over more than three decades.

Moreover, a "walk away" clause relating to the minerals provision might also encourage other countries to "walk away" from other obligations. Italy argued that the US proposal was contrary to the Vienna Convention on the Law of Treaties because the USA wanted a country to be able to withdraw from some of its obligations under the Protocol while remaining a full and functioning member of the Protocol. Most delegations, however, believed that no agreement would be possible without accommodating the US concerns in some form.

It is reported that at the informal Heads of Delegation dinner, the French produced a compromise proposal that raised from 51% to 75% the number of parties required to adopt an amendment and called for the Review Conference to be reconvened if an amendment had not entered into force within three years. The Review Conference would then attempt to find new wording for the amendment and, if this was not possible, the entry-into-force provisions would be reduced to 75% of the ATCPs, without the requirement that all 26 existing ATCPs had to be party to that ratification. The objective of the French proposal appeared to be to make it difficult and time-consuming to lift the prohibition, without requiring a consensus to do so. It failed to elicit an enthusiastic response from any quarter. A major difficulty for many countries was what they perceived to be the weakening of the decision-making process in the absence of a reference to the negotiation of a legal mining regime in the event of the prohibition being lifted. This was particularly difficult for the claimant states, who required a veto over mining activities, at the very least if they occurred in their claimed territory.

Ambassador Andersen, assisted notably by New Zealand and the UK, then drafted an alternative proposal. This raised to 75% the figure required for the adoption of an amendment but called for the amendment lifting the prohibition to require "agreed means of safeguarding and applying the principles embodied in Article 4 of the Antarctic Treaty, including procedures by which decisions to be taken for determining whether, and, if so under what conditions, any fresh activities could be acceptable". This text, based on the wording of CRAMRA, was designed to be "constructively ambiguous", being interpreted as requiring a consensus to permit mining without actually stating as much.

On the evening of 19 June, the Plenary reportedly took up the Andersen compromise text for discussion. The reactions to it were marked by both annoyance and confusion: the first, because many nations felt that they were not being made a party to it; the confusion was caused by the ambiguity in the proposal. Both this compromise proposal and many others following it – including the one from Argentina which proposed to increase the requirements for adopting an amendment but at the same time reduced the ratification requirements – were dismissed by the majority present. The agreement finally reached was that the numbers needed to adopt an amendment would be 75%. It underlined the need to safeguard all interests in accordance with Article 4 of the Treaty in negotiating an amendment, retained the ratification quota of 75% of all ATCPs, including all 26 existing ATCPs, but allowed a nation to "walk away" from the provisions of the entire Protocol (not just Article 6 of the Protocol as desired by the United States) if ratification was not completed within five years; notification of intent to withdraw was to be given after three years.

The announcement, by President Bush on 4 July 1991, of the US decision to sign the Protocol on Environmental Protection to the Antarctic Treaty marked, in a way, the end of the most critical trial of the inner strength and viability of the ATS. This crisis of consensus over the minerals issue had been much more threatening than the campaigns of the critical lobby in the UN, for the obvious reason that, this time, the dispute was an internal one and not between the ATS and those opposed to it.

The Protocol on Environmental Protection to the Antarctic Treaty (hereafter cited as the Protocol) was concluded by consensus on 4 October 1991 in Madrid. It was opened for signature in Madrid on that date and, thereafter, in Washington until 3 October 1992. Twenty-three of the ATCPs, including the United States, signed on 4 October, together with eight of the non-ATCPs. The Protocol will come into force after ratification, acceptance, approval or accession by all the current ATCPs. This may take some considerable time, on account of the ratification procedures followed by the legislatures of the individual state parties.

In the final analysis, the reasons for adopting a protocol, rather than an independent instrument, can be stated as the formal reaffirmation of the dominant role of the ATCPs in the matter of Antarctic governance. The decision-making process for protecting the Antarctic remains firmly in the hands of the ATCPs; the ATCMs are to continue as the exclusive forum for deliberation about both the creation of new norms and the inspection and supervision that ensure compliance with the Protocol. The only exceptions to the perceived requirement of continuity and supervision – by now a tradition within the ATS – are the projected establishment of a Secretariat and the decision to convene ATCMs annually instead of biennially. There are no reasons to believe that the Secretariat will have any more than a general competence in matters concerning the Protocol.

Another noteworthy aspect of the Protocol is that its membership is open only to sovereign states. The exclusion of international organizations, especially the ones with undisputed environmental credentials, is rather hard to understand from an ecological point of view. This also affects the European Union which, especially after the Single European Act of 1986, has autonomous competence in environmental matters and has already adhered to CCAMLR. How long the EU can be kept out of mainstream Antarctic geopolitics, law and diplomacy as a political actor in its own right remains to be seen.

Summary and Conclusions

"So far, so good" for this early experiment in the new geopolitics. The international system has always been described by both Doctrinal Realists and the old geopolitics, in its condition of "anarchy", as one in which the threat and use of force is inevitable. The state system is believed to be intrinsically a "war system". The Antarctic experiment in the joint governance of disputed territory supports the reality that "even though the contemporary world remains a long way from having a 'peace system', even if there is a long way to go, before such oases of stable peace [the Antarctic being one] spread to create a wider peacefulness, it is still too soon to declare that the state system is immutably a war system" (Booth 1991: 337).

What also emerges from this chapter is that the passage to peace and cooperation in the Antarctic has been neither straightforward nor problem-free. It is equally obvious that more than one factor has contributed to the political success of the ATS. Even though geography continues to pose enormous challenges in such a harsh environment, the advances of science and communications have opened up Antarctica today so that it can no longer be regarded as separate from the rest of the world. Although the ATCPs have coped with the enormous pressures that the erosion of geopolitical isolation has brought in its wake, especially on the floor of the UN, they have barely survived the crisis of consensus within the ATS on the minerals issue. The strain imposed by the efforts to achieve "internal accommodation" among the ATCPs indicates that it is relatively easier to cooperate in the realm of science. At the same time, the manner in which CRAMRA was negotiated, difficult accommodations arrived at and consensus lost and restored shows that if political will and political commitment are present it is well within the realm of possibility to negotiate and conclude an agreement on the issue of Antarctic mineral-resource development. Whether such an agreement will actually be possible further down the road is difficult to say.

What appears to have brought the ATS back on the rails, after consensus was lost over CRAMRA, is not merely the Pandora's box vision shared by all the ATCPs but also the continuing consensus among the ATCPs that there are no viable alternatives to this system of functional cooperation, now far removed from the initial Cold War context and considerations of the Treaty. The external relations of the ATS with at least a segment of the UN therefore continue to be based on *confrontation*. Everyone seems to agree nevertheless that the benefits of maintaining the ATS far outweigh the costs of agreeing to disagree on who owns the Antarctic and its resources, even if it means injecting a few more intentional ambiguities into the system.

With the aid of the ATS as a conflict-avoiding mechanism, the ATCPs have over the years successfully negotiated and adopted *by consensus* a variety of international instruments to regulate activity in the Antarctic. These instruments have been developed by a strategy of addressing matters before they turned into problems which might threaten the prospect of consensus. To stay ahead of possible conflicts thus seems to have become a guiding principle for the ATCPs in tackling new issues and problem areas.

It has been observed that "regimes institutionalize and constrain international behaviour; they therefore direct behaviour away from the narrow self-interest of 'state of nature' into paths of order and ultimately community" (Ibid.: 346). Where does the ATS stand today in this respect? Whereas some people might still question the state and status of the ATCPs as a community within the ATS, the success of the latter in directing the behaviour of its participating members away from Cold War geopolitics towards peaceful productive geopolitics is hard to dismiss. The cooperation so far realized within the ATS has gone far beyond cooperation arising solely out of self-interest. This is not to deny the continuing resilience of the problem of territorial claims, and the role played by the aggressive South American variety of geopolitics until recently in this context, but to highlight the compromise that seems to be possible between this kind of behaviour and the principles and norms of the ATS.

Suggested reading

Beck, P.J. 1986. *International Politics of Antarctica*. London: Croom Helm.

Herr, R.A. and B.W. Davis (eds) 1994. *Asia in Antarctica*. Centre for Resource and Environmental Studies, The Australian National University with Antarctic Co-operative Research Centre.

Jørgensen-Dahl, A. and W. Østreng (eds) 1991. *The Antarctic Treaty System in World Politics*. London: Macmillan.

Joyner, C. 1992. *Antarctica and the Law of the Sea*. Dordrecht: Martinus Nijhoff Publishers.

Peterson, M.J. 1988. *Managing the Frozen South: The Creation and Evolution of the Antarctic Treaty System*. Berkeley: University of California Press.

Sahurie, E.J. 1992. *The International Law of Antarctica*. Dordrecht: Martinus Nijhoff Publishers; New Haven: New Haven Press.

Watts, A. 1992. *International Law and the Antarctic Treaty System*. Cambridge: Grotius Publications Limited.

6

Indigenous peoples: consciousness, assertion of identity and geopolitical ferment

Arctic indigenous peoples, with a long history of colonization, economic and political marginalization and deprivation of legitimate rights to their lands and resources, are now demanding effective participation in the sustainable development of their homelands and in the making of decisions that affect their political rights as citizens and their status as human beings with a distinct cultural identity.

Without going into the problem of how to define the term *indigenous* (see Burger 1987: 6–11; Morse 1989: 1–12; Glassner 1993: 194), indigenous peoples are defined in this study as those who: continue to adopt and adapt to processes which sustain rather than limit development; observe and situate those processes within an ecological system for which they serve as stewards; originate and implement management strategies based on spiritual rather than material economics; recognize equity of opportunity for all elements and contributors to this economics; and encode this generally in a socio-cultural form rather than a power-political one. As Lynge (1985: 22) puts it, "they are distinct peoples on distinct land with distinct traditions – but never recognized as such". However, it is important to bear in mind that substantial differences exist among the Arctic indigenous communities in socio-cultural, economic, demographic and geopolitical terms (see Dahl 1992; 1993). Contrary to what is too often expected, they do not speak with a single voice, have the same objectives or have one vision of the future (Morse 1989: 12).

This chapter surveys recent indigenous movements across the Circumpolar North, paying particular attention to the facets that are both spatial and political, such as: (i) the relationship of the indigenous peoples with their land and physical environment; (ii) indigenous demands for control over land, water and other resources; and (iii) the political movement towards self-determination and self-government.

Land and physical environment: subsistence, territoriality and self-determination

The United Nations Meeting of Experts on Self-Government for Indigenous Peoples, held in September 1991 in Nuuk, Greenland, recognized that indigenous peoples are historically self-governing, with their own languages, cultures, laws and traditions (UN 1991: E/CN.4/1992/42). The meeting emphasized that the right of indigenous peoples to traditional lands, resources and economies is integral to the very idea of self-determination and stressed that the autonomy and self-government of indigenous peoples are beneficial to the protection of the natural environment and the maintenance of an ecological balance, thereby helping to ensure sustainable development.

To all indigenous peoples land is much more than a commodity, a provider of material things. It is their spiritual sustenance, the very heart and soul of their culture, their history and their very existence as distinctive peoples (Spencer 1978: 9–16; Dahl 1989; Gray, 1991: 8). Although it is a fact that most indigenous people in the Circumpolar North today live in large modernized communities firmly situated within the contemporary cash economy, "subsistence" remains a distinctive and vital part of their culture. Whaling, sealing, land-game hunting, fur trapping, fishing and family reindeer herding are an important component of cultural continuity and ethnic identity as well as their customary diet.

Subsistence has never been a steady state. What we see today is a "mixed subsistence–market economy" (Krupnik 1993: 263–4), an adaptation brought about by contact with other cultures, technological development, changing ecological conditions and population growth. Subsistence activities alone can no longer sustain a rapidly growing population in northern villages, nor can they provide indigenous people with an exclusive choice for the future. Only with control over non-renewable resources, particularly minerals and hydrocarbons, will they be in a position to determine the proper balance between subsistence activities and resource development (Osherenko and Young 1989: 97).

Consequently, while the question of maintaining meaningful access to grazing lands for reindeer, salmon-spawning streams, caribou calving grounds and ice-covered waters with seals and walrus continues to be of immense significance for the circumpolar indigenous peoples, ensuring effective control over non-renewable resources has become equally important in an age of industrialization and "modernization". Clearly, this would imply acquisition of territoriality, "the attempt by an individual or group to affect, influence or control people, phenomena, and relationships, by delimiting and asserting control over a geographic area" (Sack 1986). According to this definition, territoriality is a primary geographical expression of social power, the means by which space and society are interrelated.

Indigenous peoples were in continuous occupancy and full usage of their lands long before the assertion of European sovereignty (Elliott 1989: 48; Usher *et al.* 1992: 113). With the decline of nomadic societies and the rise of the Westphalian sovereign territorial state system, the relationship of humans to land also underwent a fundamental change, resulting in the assertion of control of land by individuals as private property at one level, and the control of land by the state at a higher level (Goertz and Diehl 1992: 1). However, what lies at the core of the modern assertion of "aboriginal title" is a very different notion of territoriality. It is the territoriality of hunters, gatherers and trappers which, having survived for millennia, is now increasingly subsumed under the territoriality of the modern nation-state. But not without resistance and conflict. What lies behind the mobilization of various indigenous groups along the lines of ethnicity is an expression of "unresolved territoriality", ethnic identity being a precondition for political identity and political claims (Dahl 1988: 315). Territoriality in this context is much more than the geographical expression of social power and control; it acquires cultural connotations as well (Nuttall 1992: 57–8).

Making ethnic and/or cultural identity a precondition for political identity, as well as a prerequisite for geopolitical give and take (giving up aboriginal land titles in exchange for undisputed land ownership and financial compensations), proves that modern nation-states continue to employ the strategy of political reductionism against their indigenous minorities. Manipulated in this way, indigenous groups continue to mobilize their own political forces around the principle of ethnicity on the premise that as long as the territorial question remains unsolved, the question of ethnicity will remain alive. This is often at the cost of division and fragmentation among indigenous groups, creating minorities within minorities. It also gives rise to a geopolitical discourse that rationalizes and justifies claims to separateness, exclusivity and difference, as a matter of both cultural difference and self-expression.

Indigenous peoples are today confined to merely a fraction of the land they originally occupied and used. Indeed, most environmental problems in the Arctic today, such as the destruction of forests and tundra, the reckless exploitation of resources, the testing of nuclear weapons and disposal of hazardous waste, occur on the land of indigenous peoples or on land from which they have been evicted in the past. Accordingly, territorial questions assume unprecedented significance on the indigenous agenda of self-government and self-determination (Rosing 1985: 309).

Since not all Arctic land is equally desirable from the point of view of settlement and development and since resources are not evenly distributed, who gets what, when and how from such a landscape becomes vitally important. The struggle that begins with the demand for a fair land-claims settlement is by no means over with the formal agreements. The issues of environmental protection, indigenous rights, cultural preservation, language retention and health, which all Arctic peoples currently face, continue to pose new challenges, demanding the translation of battles won on paper in the courtrooms or at the bargaining tables into concrete actions and effective implementations. When indigenous peoples talk about self-government, they talk in terms of "restoration and management of the land base", and according to "their ideas of indigenous political autonomy" (Simon and Stephens 1993: 1).

There are considerable variations not only in the way in which the question of ethnicity has been related to that of territoriality across the Circumpolar North but also in the present geopolitical state and legal status of indigenous peoples' lands and resources.

American Alaska: settled claims, new realities

During and after World War II Alaska experienced a construction boom, and as a result of in-migration its population almost doubled. Although they constituted 45% of the territory's population in 1940, indigenous people were reduced to as little as 26% a decade later (Korsmo 1994: 90). Even though demographic shifts continued to make increasingly high demands on land and resources, aboriginal land rights were not addressed in the new constitution when Alaska became a state in 1959.

It was only in 1971 that the Alaskan Native Claims Settlement Act (ANCSA) was passed, prompted by the discovery in the late 1960s of massive oil deposits in Prudhoe Bay and the proposed construction of the Trans-Alaskan Pipeline. ANCSA assigned title to about 40 million acres of native lands (about 11% of Alaska) to profit-making regional and village corporations with indigenous shareholders and provided $962.5 million in compensation for renouncing the remaining native claims to land as well as hunting and fishing rights in Alaska (Burch 1979: 7–30; Burger 1987: 182). After 20 years, shares in the corporations which own the retained lands could be sold to non-natives, and the lands could be taxed.

Land-claims settlement in Alaska demonstrates that focusing merely on the amount of land and resources to which indigenous people hold title is inadequate for measuring the extent to which that land is protected (see McNabb 1992). The corporations that were assigned title to the land through ANCSA were generally undercapitalized, short of trained and educated people, located long distances from markets and dependent on naturally occurring resources for access to markets, poorly developed in terms of infrastructures and lacking in political influence. In addition, the corporations' pursuit of economic profit meant they were at odds with villagers who were chiefly concerned with subsistence activities. Eventually the corporations foundered, which led to widespread concern among Alaska natives that the future might see the demise of those communities as independent entities enjoying unencumbered use of traditional hunting and fishing territories (Young 1992: 52–3; Korsmo 1994: 95). According to Osherenko and Young (1989: 100–1), "the greatest threat to Native land in Alaska is not large-scale resource development but loss of land owned by Native corporations through sale, foreclosure, or bankruptcy". Today's adults may choose to sell off the whole patrimony of an indigenous village or nation, once held for the common good (Sambo 1989: 191–2, 197).

ANCSA doubtless represents a policy of assimilation. It does not recognize special rights. Congress viewed special rights as being inegalitarian and, moreover, special rights and racially defined institutions were regarded as tending to isolate the native peoples from the mainstream of society; this was thought to be counterproductive. The *Realpolitik* behind the ANCSA was probably that assimilation into industrial society would eventually tear apart the traditional native social fabric. Once sucked into the wage economy, indigenous people would be transformed into well-to-do Alaskans, shareholders and businessmen, and enter the national commercial and corporate mainstream of the United States.

In 1983, on the initiative of the Inuit Circumpolar Conference (ICC), the Alaska Native Review Commission (ANRC) was established in order to conduct a comprehensive review of ANCSA. With Thomas R. Berger as Commissioner, it held a series of hearings culminating in the report *Village Journey*, concluding that Alaska's native nations must assume title to their corporately owned lands as soon as possible in order to retain their land base and preserve land-rooted native culture or face imminent threat from non-renewable resource development (Berger 1985a: 186; 1985b; 1985c: 4).

Today, no public issue divides Alaskans more deeply than that of prioritizing subsistence hunting and fishing for Alaska's rural residents (Caulfield 1992: 23; Nakazawa *et al.* 1992: 117–22), given the predominance of a geopolitical vision demanding equal and unrestricted access to land and resources in the name of individualism and equality. After extensive lobbying of both the state and federal governments by indigenous groups, Alaska adopted a subsistence law in 1978 which gives priority to subsistence use in rural areas. The federal government followed two years later with its own subsistence law. Title VIII of the 1980 Alaskan National Interest Lands Conservation Act (ANILCA), which set aside public lands in Alaska for national parks, forests and wilderness preservation, recognized the priority of rural residents, both native and non-native, who depend on local resources, over sport and commercial uses.

Disagreements about the definition of rural areas and the subsistence criterion have given rise to a legal shambles – while the federal government uses the rural criterion for subsistence hunting and fishing on federal lands, the State of Alaska recognizes all Alaskan residents as potential subsistence users. The State of Alaska is being lobbied to amend the constitution to permit subsistence preference, and the Alaska Federation of Natives and Alaska Inter-Tribal Council are demanding that the federal government assume control of fishing regulation on major rivers in the state so that the subsistence rights promised in Title VIII of ANILCA are guaranteed.

In April 1994, a federal district court judge ruled that the priority given to subsistence fishing by federal law applies to all navigable waters in Alaska (*Tundra Times*, 6 April 1994: 1, 16). According to this judgement, which has far-reaching implications for Alaska native subsistence users, all navigable waters are "public lands" as defined by ANILCA. The court accordingly ordered the government to take over management of subsistence fishing in navigable waters. In a related ruling, the court also rejected the State of Alaska's claim that the state, not the federal government, is entitled to manage subsistence hunting and fishing on public lands in Alaska. It held that since the state could not implement a priority for rural residents in Alaska, as mandated by ANILCA, the federal government was entitled to take over management of subsistence hunting and fishing so that it could establish that priority. The government of the State of Alaska has decided to file an appeal against the judgement.

Advocates of native rights maintain that the best way out of this political–legal impasse would be to have local control of resources. For the majority of Alaskan natives, the most desirable form of self-government would probably be native boroughs. The North Slope Borough has been one of the strongest and most effective native local governments in Alaska. These forms of regional government are, however, vulnerable to demographic uncertainties (Korsmo 1994: 100). Native dominance depends entirely on maintaining a majority population in the region. An alternative is tribal governments, with participation limited to native people. Villages with recognized tribal governments would then levy taxes, operate their own schools, administer their own legal codes and regulate hunting and fishing.

In October 1993, the federal government confirmed tribal status for Alaskan native villages through the publication of a list of federally recognized tribes. Around 250 Alaska native villages were listed as recognized and eligible for funding and services from the Bureau of Indian Affairs. The historic significance of this event is obvious: the State of Alaska, since its inception in 1959, had not recognized the tribal authority of rural villages governed by a tribal government. Despite the massive ambiguity surrounding the current debate on native rights in Alaska, many villages are now becoming self-reliant and seem determined to establish or strengthen their own institutions such as courts, councils and schools. Two different forms of government coexist in these villages, with the municipal government in a majority of cases assuming the responsibilities of the tribal government (Kasayulie 1992: 44).

The Canadian North: a new partnership

The Canadian North, comprising about 40% of the land area of Canada, if only about a third of 1% of its population, is complex in both demographic and cultural terms. The Yukon, the western regions of the Northwest Territories and the Nunavut region of the eastern Northwest Territories are very different social, economic and political environments. Though sparsely populated, the region's complex population is composed of Indians, Inuit, Métis and non-natives, scattered in communities ranging from isolated native villages, built around harvesting natural resources, to ultra-modern transportable mining camps, staffed by people flown in on rotation.

The nature of the relations between aboriginal peoples and public government in northern Canada differs significantly from that which has emerged in other regions of the country. Parliament retains jurisdiction over all aspects of governance, and territorial government budgets are massively dependent on financial transfers from the federal treasury. Unlike the situation in the southern provinces, control of natural resources as well as the control of the Crown's interest in unpatented lands is in federal hands. The reinforcement of public government in the North through territorial government is currently a high priority of the federal government, which regards it as a "democratic institutional framework for the social and economic development of Aboriginal peoples residing in Canada's northern regions" (Canadian Government 1993d: ii).

Despite a history of denial, abrogation, encroachment and indifference, aboriginal tenure and management systems survive, albeit in modified and sometimes covert fashion (Usher et al. 1992: 122).

The current status of aboriginal land rights in Canada reflects the complexity of the northern region, very different scenarios being contemplated by the various aboriginal communities. Over the last two decades or so, political demands have been skilfully represented by aboriginal leaders, making full use of opportunities opened up by land-claims negotiations and by the strong presence of aboriginal representatives in territorial legislative assemblies and other regionally and locally elected bodies.

In retrospect, the 1950s and 1960s were landmark decades in cultural and political revival, administrative recognition, legal enforceability and the practical value of aboriginal rights and title. The dominant vision in Canada at that time was that economic growth represented progress and that the North was a hinterland for the support of the southern urban metropolis. In the 1960s, exploration permits for northern Canada were made available on easier terms than anywhere else in the world, without any prior land-use planning or environmental regulation (Cumming 1989: 697).

In the 1950s, the Canadian government embarked on an ambitious experimental programme of resettling Inuit in unoccupied regions of the

Arctic, often far from their original homelands. Relocation affected the entire Inuit population of Canada. It was an infringement of civil rights, causing anguish, deprivation and often sickness or death. The Canadian government justified the relocations as a means to encourage Inuit living in "overpopulated" areas whose natural resources had been overharvested to "migrate" to areas which were rich in resources, and thereby "improve their living conditions". Other motives were economic-policy incentives, moral convictions and sovereignty concerns (see Marcus 1992: 77).

Those who escaped relocation were evacuated from their homelands, clustered in settlements and expected to begin a new life. To enter the modern age, they were encouraged to abandon the traditional native subsistence economy, based on hunting, fishing and trapping, which had sustained them for centuries. Economic opportunities were limited, however, by factors such as the climate, the enormous distances and the sparse population. In the villages there were few jobs, and most went to white people. The net result for indigenous people was dependence and powerlessness (Berger 1988: 4).

In opposition to new, large-scale plans for resource development the indigenous peoples of the Canadian North mobilized themselves under the leadership of a cadre of young, politically aware, "educated and often angry native activists" (Coates and Powell 1989: 100–1). This fast-accelerating activity with respect to indigenous land rights received a further impetus in 1969, when the "white paper" on Indian policy proposed terminating aboriginal rights and treaties and launching a programme of assimilation and incorporation. Throughout Canada, it met with stiff resistance from indigenous groups, who finally succeeded in reversing the government's initiative. Eventually, and for the first time, "existing aboriginal rights" were recognized in the 1982 Constitution Act. Thereafter, in the evolution of institutions and patterns of government in the Canadian North, it was not possible to brush aside indigenous aspirations and needs.

Through comprehensive claims settlements, the federal government seems set to resolve the legal ambiguities associated with the common-law concept of aboriginal rights and to reach an agreement on special rights for aboriginal peoples with respect to land and resources (Canadian Government 1993b: i, 5). However, the federal government emphasizes that "uncertainty with respect to the legal status of lands and resources, which has been created by a lack of political agreement with Aboriginal groups, is a barrier to economic development for all Canadians and has hindered the full participation of Aboriginal peoples in land and resource management" (Ibid.). For aboriginal leaders, on the other hand, claim settlements involve more than real-estate transactions or compensations extinguishing title. They view them as historic opportunities to secure their future as a people.

The James Bay and Northern Quebec Agreement (1974)

The catalytic event leading to negotiations and eventually to this first so-called comprehensive claims settlement was the James Bay Hydroelectric Project, which the Quebec government began to set up in 1971 in an area not yet ceded, and still used by indigenous people engaged in a traditional hunting economy. This project involved the damming and diversion of several major rivers flowing into James Bay and the flooding of several thousand acres of land. In the process the livelihood of the indigenous people affected would be destroyed (Moss 1989: 685).

The James Bay and Northern Quebec Agreement was a once-for-all deal that exchanged aboriginal rights for a package of benefits, thus freeing the land for development (Berger 1988: 219). The benefits included ownership of 8737 sq km by 15 Inuit community corporations with a population of approximately 5000 and exclusive hunting and fishing rights over some 98 398 sq km. Mineral rights remained with the Quebec government but could only be exploited with the consent of the Inuit community corporation and upon payment of compensation. Total compensation paid was well over C$225 million.

Like ANCSA, the objective of the James Bay Agreement was to facilitate resource development on the terms and conditions laid down by the Province of Quebec. While the Agreement has contributed to an increase in the services provided to the residents of Inuit Quebec, it has also intensified the region's fiscal dependence on the provincial government (Duhaime 1993: 22–5). Furthermore, it has not generated increased political responsibility to the region nor any increase of local power in collective decision-making. Both Cree and Inuit feel that they have had a raw deal (Diamond 1991). The Agreement is vague in many respects and thus vulnerable to different interpretations and has led to bureaucratic wranglings between the federal and Quebec governments over responsibility for some of its provisions (Moss 1989: 688–9; Purich 1992: 124; Creery 1994: 117). Meanwhile, as the Quebec government develops plans to proceed with the James Bay II (Great Whale) project, the eventual success of the Agreement will depend on who wins the battles over implementation – which are likely to continue for some time.

The Yukon

The key catalyst for the assertion of aboriginal rights during the 1970s in the Yukon was the dramatic rise in the production of oil and gas from deposits in the northern part of the region. Significant transfers of land and resources to territorial control were causing tensions between the territorial government and the Council for Yukon Indians (CYI). An agreement-in-principle on land claims was reached in 1984 and approved by both the federal and

Yukon cabinets. However, the package was rejected because the Yukon Indians felt that it was tantamount to surrender of their aboriginal rights and also that their divergent interests could not be effectively addressed in that fashion. Significantly, Yukon Indians have shown no strong inclination to regional or community government, preferring instead to focus on individual First Nation self-government agreements.

Talks were resumed in the spring of 1985, focusing on agreements specific to each First Nation, to be negotiated under a broad umbrella agreement. In December 1991, an Umbrella Final Agreement (UFA) was ratified by the CYI. It entitled them to 41 440 sq km of land, C$248 million in financial compensation, a share of Yukon government resource revenues if and when these are transferred to the Yukon and guaranteed participation in land and resource management (Canadian Government 1993e).

The emphasis at present is on hammering out 14 First Nation Self-government Agreements, four of which have been concluded so far, with the Champagne-Aishihik, Nacho Nyak Dun (Mayo), Teslin and Vuntut Gwich'in (Old Crow) First Nations (see Smyth 1993). These will give a considerable range of powers to the respective First Nation governments in areas such as community development and social programmes, communications, culture and aboriginal languages, economic development and relations with Canada, the Yukon and other local governments. The complexity of the Yukon situation is likely to increase when the First Nations act to exercise the self-government provisions in respect of their individual land claims.

The Northwest Territories

Indigenous communities in the Northwest Territories (NWT) have shown a preference for a consensus style of government rather than for party politics, and the political culture is far more closely associated with aboriginal aspirations (Dacks 1990: 109). Striking variations are to be found among the Inuit, Inuvialuit, Dene and Métis within the NWT.

In June 1984, the federal government signed the Inuvialuit Final Agreement, with the Committee for Original Peoples' Entitlement (COPE) representing the Inuvialuit of the Western Arctic. The Inuvialuit relinquished their claim to lands in the Western Arctic in exchange for legal title to 91 000 sq km of land, mineral rights in one-seventh of that area, and C$152 million in compensation for other land. They also received C$10 million for economic-development initiatives, C$7.5 million for various social programmes, such as housing and health, and guaranteed harvesting rights and decision-making participation in wildlife management and environmental conservation (Dickerson 1992: 103; Purich 1992: 122–3).

One of the practical consequences of the Final Agreement is that the oil and gas industry now has to deal with a new private land-holder, the

Inuvialuit, and has to abide by environmental screening and consensus-based decisions about some of the issues related to land use (Keeping 1989: 156–7). There is, however, no provision for local government under the Agreement, and the Inuvialuit Regional Corporation has been demanding more direct public government, in the form of a regional government structure with substantive powers of a territorial nature to address the special interests of the Inuvialuit and other residents of the region.

In the wake of the discovery of oil and gas in Alaska, Canadian Arctic Gas announced in March 1974 that a pipeline stretching 2600 miles from Prudhoe Bay, Alaska, across northern Yukon, then south from the Mackenzie River Delta to the mid-continent would be built at an estimated cost of C$10 billion.

Having gone through the socio-cultural dislocations caused by the influx of a large number of outsiders since the time of the Yukon gold rush, the Dene of the Mackenzie Valley protested and formed their own political organization, the Indian Brotherhood, to fight for their cause. It pressed for a quick settlement of land claims, lobbying the federal government forcefully to ensure that the views of the Dene and Métis were recorded and taken into account.

In March 1974, Justice Thomas Berger of the Supreme Court of British Columbia was appointed by the government to conduct an inquiry into the proposed Mackenzie Valley pipeline. His 1977 report, *Northern Frontier, Northern Homeland*, concluded unequivocally that the pipeline should be delayed for 10 years to allow the natives to settle land claims and to prepare for the project. He stressed that native people do not want a settlement that will extinguish their rights to the land but rather one that will reinforce their rights to the land and lay the foundations of native self-determination under the Constitution of Canada. He also emphasized the need to establish institutions that can act as pillars for self-determination.

While the recommendations of the Berger Commission were accepted by the federal government, the Dene/Métis decided to negotiate separately with the federal government throughout most of the 1970s, differences having developed over the construction of the pipeline. The Dene political leadership became much more radical and vocal. It changed the name of their organization from the Indian Brotherhood to the Dene Nation, withdrew an earlier land-claims proposal, declared unwillingness to give up aboriginal rights in exchange for land and sounded a strong note of dissent in the Dene Declaration of 1975: insisting on the right to self-determination as a distinct people, it demanded recognition of the Dene Nation (Creery 1994: 120). It has been said that the Dene problem has probably been to "locate sufficient power with themselves while dominating an entire territory in which they were outnumbered by whites" (Jull 1991: 48). The Dene later moderated their stance considerably and established a single claims secretariat with the Métis Association of the NWT in 1983, in the hope of negotiating collectively with the government. However, such negotiations have not been successful (Devine 1992). The Gwich'in (Delta Dene) were the first to withdraw support for a joint negotiation and to conclude an agreement with the federal government and the government of NWT in April 1992, setting the stage for the settlement of other regional claims (Canadian Government 1993d: 28).

The Nunavut

A fundamental reordering of the political map to accommodate the distinctive aspirations of an aboriginal minority became a reality with the passage of the Nunavut Land Claims Agreement Act in July 1993, after the signing in May that year of a historic agreement between the Prime Minister of Canada and other federal government representatives, ministers of the government of the NWT and elected leaders of organizations representing the Inuit of Nunavut (Canadian Government 1993c). The Act will come into force in two stages: initially through the establishment of a special commission to organize the new Nunavut government, then through a formal change in the political map of Canada and the assumption of legal responsibilities by the new government on or before 1 April 1999.

The significance of this breakthrough for the Inuit of Nunavut goes far beyond the borders of Canada, providing practical inspiration for other indigenous peoples (Merritt 1993b: 2–3). The very scale of the Agreement is remarkable. It covers the ownership and management of lands and waters in an area of roughly 1 500 000 square miles, all that portion of the existing Northwest Territories north and east of the tree line, divided almost equally between onshore and offshore components, with an onshore area constituting about 20% of the landmass of Canada and comparable in size to Western Europe, inhabited by only 22 000 people. In addition, the creation of the Nunavut territory and government will give a single aboriginal people political control over government machinery exercising substantial jurisdiction and will endow them with commensurate financial and bureaucratic resources in a large part of a modern industrialized state.

The Inuit of the Eastern Arctic had long argued that there was a natural division in the NWT along the tree line which ran from the Mackenzie Delta diagonally to the NWT–Manitoba border, separating the tundra, land of the Inuit, from the forests, home of the Dene. They argued that the people of the two regions had different histories, cultures and languages and would always be different. The capital of the NWT, Yellowknife, lay south of the tree line and was run by non-indigenous civil servants with no understanding of the Inuit and their land. The Inuit saw land-claims negotiation with the federal government as an opportunity to push for more representative government closer to home and accordingly proposed a division along the tree line, with a new government in the eastern territory, which would be called Nunavut – "our land".

The national Inuit organization, Inuit Tapirisat of Canada, adopted a very pragmatic geopolitical approach to the options for Nunavut. Home rule as achieved by neighbouring Greenland would require the creation of a political entity with powers extending considerably beyond those enjoyed by any Canadian provincial government and would require Nunavut to deal with the federal government outside the context of Canadian federalism. Such an approach would undoubtedly be construed by a majority of people in Canada as a threat to the geopolitical integrity of the nation and hence be unacceptable (Inuit Tapirisat of Canada 1979: 14).

The Nunavut Land Claims Agreement and the accompanying legislation establishing the Nunavut territory and government hold the promise of a new political and jurisdictional order in the Canadian Arctic. Some key features of the Agreement are: the vesting of title to 136 000 square miles of land in Inuit organizations; title to the mineral estate of more than 14 000 square miles of land to Inuit organizations; a 5% Inuit share in resource revenues obtained by the Crown from development of resources on Crown lands; guaranteed Inuit hunting, fishing and trapping rights throughout Nunavut, with an Inuit monopoly on trapping, absolute priority of use of wildlife for local consumption and first priority in all commercial ventures involving wildlife; provision for compensation to Inuit hunters, trappers and fishers in the event of loss due to industrial development (Canadian Government 1993c).

In exchange for the rights and benefits provided under the Agreement, Inuit (under a provision entitled "certainty" in Article 2) agree to live by the terms of the Agreement and to "cede, release and surrender to Her Majesty the Queen in Right of Canada all their aboriginal claims, rights, title and interests, if any, in and to lands and waters anywhere within Canada and adjacent offshore areas within the sovereignty or jurisdiction of Canada" (Ibid.).

From a geopolitical point of view, it is not only the impressive package of rights for the Inuit in respect of ownership and use of northern lands, waters, wildlife and other resources that is noteworthy in the Agreement but also its emphasis on wildlife management and conservation. The wildlife sections took many years to negotiate, as Inuit negotiators had to overcome strong resistance from the federal departments of Fisheries and Oceans and the Environment, whose officials did not want Inuit to have decision-making power (*Nunatsiaq News*, 28 January 1994). The right of each Inuk to harvest all species of wildlife to the full extent of his or her "economic, social and cultural needs", throughout all undeveloped lands in the Nunavut Settlement Area (including parks and conservation areas), is acknowledged and protected. Even where conservation measures require limitations to be imposed on the harvesting of a particular species of wildlife, Inuit are given an absolute priority to all wildlife needed to sustain their families and communities.

Given the severity of its climate, the harshness of its physical environment and the dispersal of its residents throughout more than two dozen communities in three time zones, between which communication is exclusively by air and, seasonally, boat and snowmobile, the depth and diversity of the Nunavut economy is seriously constrained by the high costs involved in the circulation of goods, ideas and people. The non-renewable economic sector of Nunavut none the less features several operating lead, zinc and gold mines, and there are significant proven reserves of hydrocarbons and hard minerals awaiting extensive exploration which may one day prove an important addition to the Nunavut economy.

Nunavut provides practical inspiration for other indigenous peoples at least as a precedent (Jull 1993: 15). According to a Russian scholar (Cherkasov 1993: 69): "This cautious step by the Canadian government, shifting the emphasis from the 'national/ethnic' to the 'territorial' aspects of autonomy, deserves our attention in examining analogous problems of regional government in the Russian North."

Demographics is on the side of the Inuit in Nunavut, and should remain so well into the indefinite future, helping them maintain control over the legislative and executive institutions of the new government. With implementation of Nunavut on the way, one major challenge is to prepare a skilled indigenous workforce to make good use of the opportunities that the creation of a new government will eventually bring. One of the reasons the Inuit of Nunavut have asked that the territorial government be set up in 1999 is because they hope to have their own workforce in place by then. To breathe life into the Agreement will require continued clarity of vision and plain hard work from Inuit politicians and dedicated staff (Fenge 1992: 137; Merritt 1993a: 12–14). The Agreement provides many tools that can be used to chart a better future in the Arctic. It now remains for Inuit to use these tools to their best advantage.

Labrador

Reluctance on the part of the Newfoundland government to consider the question of aboriginal rights, even after their formal recognition by the federal government in 1973, led to the formation of the Labrador Inuit Association, representing approximately 3800 Inuit (Haysom 1992: 181). This was followed in 1978 by the submission of a proposal to the federal government for the settlement of claims, demanding rights to land, compensation, the right to manage resources and regional government. In 1990, the Newfoundland and federal governments finally hammered out an agreement on how to handle the claim. Negotiations are now on the agenda but proceeding slowly.

While land claims continue to generate controversy throughout the Canadian North, divisions among the indigenous peoples themselves, opposition from many non-indigenous individuals and groups and the lack of resolution of outstanding claims bode ill for amicable settlements. It is also uncertain just how much, if any, benefit will accrue to the underdeveloped communities as a result of current and future settlements or how payments received in the settlements will affect local and regional economies (Hamley 1993: 277).

Greenland: going beyond Home Rule?

In 1979, Greenlandic Inuit, outnumbering Danes by around 45 000 to 10 000, became the first Inuit population to achieve Home Rule. Ever since, Greenland has been universally praised for having set an exemplary precedent for aboriginal self-determination and self-government. Greenlanders are determined to play an effective and meaningful role in shaping their future and have embarked on a firm course of nation-building. Because of the extensive system of self-government that has developed under Home Rule, Greenland Inuit today have more constitutionally protected rights than any other indigenous people, and it is in fact no longer justifiable to view them as an oppressed minority in relation to a dominant nation-state (Nuttall 1994: 1).

During World War II, with Denmark under Nazi occupation, Greenland had its first, albeit short-lived, taste of independence from the Danish kingdom. Having survived the complete breakdown of communications with Denmark during the war, Greenlanders were quick to realize that the historical dependence on Denmark might not be the only option for the future (Dunbar 1950: 133).

In the 1950s, there was a wave of change in Greenland in almost all walks of life (Sugden 1982: 263–4). Housing, health conditions and education were dramatically improved, life expectancy rose and administration was improved. However, these improvements meant that Inuit had to put up with an invasion of Danish skilled workers, schoolteachers, doctors and administrators which posed a dilemma for them. Inuit craved more self-determination and autonomy, for which they required better education and therefore mastery of Danish, since the Greenlandic Inuit language was unsuited to handling modern subjects like medicine or engineering, but they ran the risk of becoming increasingly alienated from Inuit culture. By the late 1960s and early 1970s, however,

> . . . Greenlandic society had been overwhelmingly transformed from one based on small-scale subsistence hunting and fishing to a modern, export-oriented economy. The majority of the population was now living in the fast-growing west coast towns and this demographic transition brought its own problems. Life in the settlements had been characterized by, and organized around, kinship and other networks of close social association. But movements to the towns led to the fragmentation of kin-based groups and individuals now experienced alienation, social and economic marginality and discrimination, accentuated by ethnic divisions between Inuit and Danes. (Nuttall 1994: 8)

157

Towards the end of the 1960s, a new political phenomenon surfaced to shape and change the course of Greenland's future, namely a growing political awareness among bilingual Greenlandic students in Denmark (Taagholt 1980: 295). They were the first to protest against the official Danish integration policy and to defend the role of their native language in a modernization process that was fast transforming their society. Increasing assertiveness on the question of self-government manifested itself in many ways. The 1971 elections to both the provincial council and parliament saw the new generation of protesters capturing seats, and in Denmark the new social-democratic government appointed a native Greenlander as Minister for Greenlandic Affairs.

The 1970s witnessed enhanced political activity in Greenland. While Denmark was engaged in a political debate about its accession to the EEC, Greenlanders showed their reluctance to join through a negative vote of 70.3% in the 1972 referendum on the issue. However, since a majority in Denmark had voted in favour, Greenland also had to join. In 1974 concessions were granted to multinational oil companies to explore for oil in the fishing grounds off the west coast of Greenland – another factor contributing to dissatisfaction with the Danish administration of Greenland (Nuttall 1994: 8). Eventually, the Minister for Greenlandic Affairs was asked by the provincial council to examine the prospects for home rule in Greenland which he did by creating, in 1973, a special Greenlandic committee to look into the matter. A Home Rule Commission was set up by the Danish government in 1975, and the Home Rule Act was passed three years later. In January 1979, the Act was submitted to a referendum in Greenland. With 70% of the votes in favour, Home Rule was introduced on 1 May 1979.

From a geopolitical point of view, it is important to note that the rights and powers of the Home Rule agreement were granted to Greenlanders not as a people or ethnic group but as inhabitants of a discrete landmass. Greenlandic Inuit are very fortunate in that they have always been in a clear majority within a well-defined geographical area, an island, and have thus never had to deal with the problems of fuzzy demarcations (Johansen 1992: 33–4). This has been of the utmost importance to their recognition as an indigenous people. The Home Rule Act does not refer to the collective rights of the Inuit population. Instead, it is a law for everyone living permanently within the geographical entity of 840 000 square miles known as Greenland, including the Danish minority of 20%. Danes living in Greenland have voting rights and are eligible for the Greenland Assembly (*Landsting*) according to the same rules as the rest of the population.

The issue of natural resources and the assertion of newly acquired national identity and autonomy led in January 1982 to a referendum to determine Greenland's continued membership of the EEC. The Home Rule authorities felt that Greenland's fish resources, particularly cod, redfish and shrimp, were being abused by the EEC, threatening the sustainability of the stocks. The fact that Greenlanders were not in political control of a resource which was the basis of the country's only industry was perceived as a serious problem. Moreover, there was a contradiction in an integration policy vis-à-vis Brussels and a devolution policy vis-à-vis Copenhagen. Greenland was not attracted to the prospect of being governed from the continent by former colonial powers (Lynge 1993: 29–30). The referendum resulted in Greenland's withdrawal from the EEC. Since then, Greenland's relationship with the EEC has been regulated by a special protocol and by an agreement and protocol concerning fisheries for a 10-year period from 1985, by which Greenland took over responsibility for fisheries management in Greenlandic waters, obtained almost free access to the EEC market and continues to receive financial compensation worth around DKR 270 million per annum for access to limited quotas in Greenlandic waters (Johansen 1992: 33–7; Martens 1992: 200).

Greenland celebrated its first National Day and flew its own flag for the first time in the summer of 1985. The same year, Greenland joined the Nordic Council and was granted two seats in the Nordic Parliamentary Assembly. In 1988, the Landsting instituted a committee for security policy and foreign affairs, although the Home Rule Act of 1978 clearly defined these as matters for the Danish government. The Danish government, however, accepted the arrangement on condition that the committee would have a consultative role only. In 1989, Greenland and Canada concluded an agreement on the scientific monitoring of the stocks of beluga and narwhal shared by the two countries in the Davis Strait and Melville Bay.

In addition to nation-building, Greenlanders are struggling to match the high cost of modern living in the Arctic with the present income from the country's potentially enormous resources. Foremost is the issue of critical economic dependence on two key factors: a block grant from Denmark and the income from shrimp fisheries (Greenland Home Rule Authority 1992: 18–19). An increasing proportion of the Danish government contribution is paid by way of a block grant which the Home Rule Authority is practically free to use as it wishes. Of the total government expenditure of DKR 2.9 billion in 1990, the contribution from block grants was to the tune of DKR 1.5 billion, accounting for about 27% of total public expenditure. Shrimp exports are the other major source of income. Of total exports worth DKR 2178 million in 1991 (which was 22% lower than in 1990 due to the closure of zinc and lead mines at Marmorilik and a drop in the export of fish products), shrimps alone brought in DKR 1.7 billion. However, there are indications that the contribution of the shrimp fisheries is set to decrease to somewhere between 50% and 80% of the present contribution (Martens 1992: 194). If this happens, in addition to the closure of the zinc and lead mines at Marmorilik and the near-disappearance of cod from Greenlandic waters,

159

the question is whether the loss to the Greenlandic economy will be met by Denmark through an increase in the block grant.

So far, the Danish government and parliament and public opinion support continued transfers to Greenland. However, a standing dispute between the Greenland Home Rule government and the Danish political authorities about the rights to mineral resources in Greenland makes the answer to the above question uncertain (Jull 1979: 6–7). At its 1991 spring session, the *Landsting* unanimously agreed that the time is now ripe for Greenland to take over the administration and ownership of mineral resources, a bid which the Danish government strongly resists. The potential exploitation of mineral resources and hydrocarbons is the key not only to future relations between the kingdom of Denmark and Home Rule in Greenland but also to independence for the Greenlandic economy. According to Gunnar Martens (1992: 202), a senior civil servant in the Prime Minister's office in Denmark,

> . . . the removal of the only potential Greenlandic contribution to the solidarity of the Realm – the mineral resources – and undue discrimination of Danes living in Greenland, may weaken Danish solidarity with Greenland . . . In this context it should not be forgotten that the reason why Denmark entered into the experiment of trying to make Greenland an industrialized society was the expectation that over a span of years the Greenlandic economy would be self-supporting – at least to a wide extent. This utopia today seems far away, unless important mineral, gas or oil deposits are discovered.

Quite obviously, Danish expectations of a surplus-generating Greenlandic economy have not so far been met. As the last remaining mining activity in Greenland, at Marmorilik, ended in 1990, and the development of tourism is unlikely to have any major impact at least for a number of years, the extent of this dependence has increased and is unlikely to diminish in the immediate future (Poole 1994: 22). At the same time, the shrimp fishing and processing industry is still facing some very serious problems, having reached a point of crisis by the end of the 1980s. Greenland faces deep recession. It will also probably have to bear with its dependence on expertise from abroad at least until far beyond the year 2000, although from the point of view of the Inuit of Greenland, "real" Home Rule will obtain only when Greenland reaches an educational level equivalent to that of the Western world, and dependence upon foreign expertise is minimal. It can reasonably be argued that all these factors limit the political independence of Greenland and undermine the content of Home Rule. What are the scenarios for the future?

During the February 1991 session of the Nordic Council, the Danish Prime Minister stated that Greenland is free to leave the realm if it so desires. A federation between Iceland, Greenland and the Faeroes or an Arctic state consisting of Greenland, Nunavut and the Inuit part of Alaska are possibilities that have been suggested (Martens 1992: 199). However, any such venture is unrealistic at present, considering the web of dependencies in which Greenland finds itself entangled. What is essential now is pragmatism. The Greenland Home Rule Authority has emphasized the need for new forms of economic activity, laying particular stress on the development of mining and tourism. This poses a serious dilemma: how best can the Home Rule Authority reconcile the interests of the Inuit population with the need for increased revenue from resource development and the further social, economic and ecological change this will entail?

In Greenland immediate threats to Inuit cultural survival emanate not from land grab by outsiders but from an animal-rights campaign that at present shows no sign of abating, and there are genuine fears that it will continue to undermine the subsistence economy (see Wenzel 1991; Lynge 1992). Given its exceptional significance, it will be necessary to return to this issue later in the study.

The Sami homelands: dividing boundaries, unifying issues

The Sami live in an area spanning Finland, Norway, Sweden and the Russian Kola Peninsula but have been a minority there since the "civilization" of the Scandinavian north in the 14th century (Johansson and Myrlund 1992: 212). Democratically elected representative Sami institutions have today been established in the Fennoscandian countries, and significant steps are being taken to harmonize Sami policies within the Nordic framework. However, closer inspection reveals that they have not only been denied rights to land ownership but are also being subjected to powerful policies of assimilation and integration (Cramer 1988; 1993). For the Sami of the Kola Peninsula, the collapse of the Soviet Union has brought problems as well as new opportunities. What Sami appear to have in common is continuing uncertainty about their territorial rights and the resulting threat to their cultural survival.

The policy of the Fennoscandian nation-states has been to confer resource rights exclusively upon reindeer-herding Sami and to regard these as privileges which can be revoked through simple policy adjustment, without due process of law or just compensation. While it is true that reindeer herding is what keeps Sami identity alive (Beach 1994: 152), the reality today is that only a small minority of Sami are directly involved in this activity. To confuse the matter further, there is continuing disagreement in these countries about the definition of the Sami as a population. It is significant that all Sami associations have been established as a result of political mobilization among the Sami themselves against government authorities that either were largely insensitive to Sami interests or tried to suppress them (Brantenberg 1991: 76–7).

A Sami movement claiming special indigenous rights for the Sami people, including territorial rights, was organized in Norway during the 1950s as a reaction to a liberal government committed to large-scale integration of the northern regions and their population into the national welfare state. Sami organizations from Norway, Sweden and Finland met in Norway in 1953 to address issues of common concern. This led to creation of the Nordic Sami Council (*Nordiska Samerådet*) in 1956: delegates from the three countries meet every three years and an executive council promotes the organization's objectives. In 1976, the Nordic Sami Council joined the World Council of Indigenous Peoples. Today, Sami maintain close contacts with the United Nations Working Group for Indigenous Populations in Geneva as well as other international bodies, and they also took part in the United Nations Conference on Environment and Development in 1992. The Sami Council has NGO status within the United Nations, and quite often Sami representatives send their national delegations to the United Nations as experts. Sami have therefore gained considerable experience of lobbying for indigenous peoples in general, and the Sami Council has been advising the national development agencies and foreign ministries of the Fennoscandian countries about the application of funds dedicated to the promotion of indigenous causes.

The 1980s witnessed a landmark event in the evolution of Sami political consciousness, in the form of a major conflict over the damming of the Norwegian Kautokeino–Alta waterway (Paine 1989: 190–235). Running from the interior plains to the coast, this riverway had provided sustenance for Sami hunters, gatherers and herders for thousands of years. There was serious concern among Sami about the consequences this project would have for their culture (Paine 1982). They joined with environmentalists and fishing organizations in non-violent protests and placed two new and troubling questions on the Norwegian political agenda: Who are the Sami? What are Sami rights? Although they lost the legal battle over the construction of the dam, their cultural pride and political awareness received a tremendous boost (Osherenko and Young 1989: 90).

Soon afterwards, the Norwegian Sami Rights Committee (1980–1) was appointed to look into the questions of Sami rights to natural resources and to recommend appropriate legislation (Brantenberg 1993: 27–8). The Committee ushered in a new era in Norway's Sami policy. Its recommendations became the basis of the new Sami Act in 1987 and for a constitutional amendment (110a) which recognizes two different ethnic groups in Norway: Sami and Norwegians. A principal conclusion of the Committee was that the Norwegian state is responsible for protecting Sami culture and that the Sami should be provided with the means to safeguard their natural resources and enhance their own culture. As a result, the Sami Parliament was created in 1989. However, it failed to meet Sami expectations in that it could not veto land encroachments injurious to Sami land usage. Sami did not qualify as a "people" under the terms of the 1966 United Nations International Covenant on Economic, Social and Cultural Rights and were therefore not considered by the Committee to possess the right of self-determination.

Sami land claims in Norway are still a matter of uncertainty. Recently, the Sami Rights Committee's subcommittee on property rights concluded that the state has property rights to Crown land in Norway, thereby endorsing the status quo. In the county of Finnmark, where the majority of Sami live, Crown land constitutes approximately 97% of all land – as well as substantial areas of land in other northern counties like Troms and Nordland. The fact that Sami interests in land and water are still disputed may not only damage Norway's reputation as a champion of indigenous peoples elsewhere but may also provide an excuse for other nation-states to continue to neglect and abuse their own indigenous minorities (Ibid.: 40).

In Finland, the question of the cultural and economic survival of the Sami minority became an issue in the 1940s and led to the establishment of a State Committee on Sami Affairs (1949–51). A second committee (1971–3) managed to persuade the Finnish government to set up a Sami Parliament and to define the "Sami Homeland" (Müller-Wille 1979: 66). The growing political stature of the Sami in the international arena also contributed to these developments. The Sami Committee concluded that the Sami are the original owners and users of the Sami Homeland. However, the state has not established what rights this would secure for the Sami (Beach 1994: 194). It is important to note that in Finland there are no general laws governing Sami rights. Instead, they are regulated by a variety of specific laws such as those pertaining to water, timber and fishing. Reindeer herding is not an occupation reserved for the Sami.

In 1989 Kaisa Korpijaakko wrote a pioneering doctoral dissertation on the legal rights of the Sami in Finland during the period of Swedish rule. Her extensive research into the taxation records of that period reveals that Swedish/Finnish governments did recognize that Sami people owned their lands. They were not considered landless nomads at that time; their land titles were incorporated into the state's land-tenure system.

Finland's Advisory Board on Sami Affairs decided in 1978 to examine the question of rights to natural resources administered by the state that could be transferred to the Sami. In 1990, it proposed that a Sami Act be enacted to restore collective Sami ownership of the lands formerly owned by the Sami which now constitute state forests. The Board also proposed that the Act confirm the rights of Sami to herd reindeer, hunt and fish. The property rights of the non-Sami local population and their rights to fish, hunt and move freely would be safeguarded. The question of Sami land rights has been referred to the Sami Parliament for further study, and the organizational and administrative issues are presently under investigation by the Finnish Ministry of Justice.

In Sweden, the negative effect of extractive industries on Sami grazing lands and the environment, which had alarmed politically aroused reindeer herders for several years, was finally recognized in 1983 as an issue worthy of inclusion on the national political agenda. That same year, the Sami Rights Committee was appointed by the government to consider the possibilities of strengthening the legal position of Sami with regard to: reindeer herding; whether a democratically elected Sami organization should be established; and measures for preserving and developing the Sami language. At a later stage, the mandate of the Committee was extended to consideration of the state and status of the Sami as an indigenous people. However, like its Norwegian counterpart, the Committee limited itself to studying the status of Sami in the light of the minimal requirements of international conventions on human rights, ignoring the legal issues of land ownership and resource rights (Ljungkvist 1988: 247; Beach 1994: 189).

In August 1993, the Swedish Sami Parliament was opened by King Carl XVI Gustaf, who described the event as "a watershed in our common history". The publicity generated by the occasion was exploited by Sami activists, who protested about the deterioration of Sami hunting rights by way of hunger strikes and by pitching their tents outside the parliament building. Hunting in the mountain regions had previously been permitted only to members of Sami communities. A recent move to open up hunting of small game to anyone purchasing a licence was perceived as a potential threat to reindeer herding. The issue is essentially a question of land rights. While the Swedish government claims to have the right to permit hunting on state-owned land, Sami dispute state ownership of Sami land. The newly elected Sami Parliament was quick to pass a resolution which expressed suspicion of the government's handling of Sami hunting and fishing rights and also of the government's action in indigenous questions, both nationally and internationally.

Although the Sami parliaments in Finland, Norway and Sweden are still far from being vehicles for meaningful and proactive change, the very existence of such democratically elected bodies does open up challenging avenues for indigenous participation in the political process. The prospective establishment of a Nordic Sami Assembly, comprising representatives from all three parliaments, also presents interesting opportunities. The Sami parliaments have the possibility of creating hitherto non-existent channels of political communication between the Sami and the state on the one hand and between various factions among the Sami themselves on the other. The path is not without hurdles, however. Political apathy on the part of the Sami could lead to a situation whereby their parliaments, handicapped by limited powers and advisory roles, may fall short of representing the entire spectrum of Sami interests.

In the wake of glasnost and perestroika, the Sami of the Kola Peninsula have established their own ethnically defined political organization, the Kola Sami Association, based in Murmansk. In theory, with the dissolution of all reindeer-herding collective farms, where workers owned the means of production collectively, worked collectively and shared their production, the herders might now claim the right to own an unlimited number of reindeer. In practice, they cannot afford to buy the animals. There are also several unresolved questions such as who controls grazing rights and to whom their meat produce can be sold now. Bleak employment prospects, combined with the extremely low price of reindeer meat in Russia today, means that the future of the Kola Peninsula Sami is very precarious.

The only silver lining in the dark cloud seems to be that the cultural and political interaction between the Sami of Russia and those of the Fenno-scandian countries has increased. Having joined the Sami Council, the Russian Sami will probably not be long in establishing a Sami Parliament and cooperating with the other Sami parliaments in a pan-Sami Parliament. An important question for the Russian Sami will be how to balance the priorities of protecting native culture and the transition to a market economy.

The "small peoples" of the Russian North: from collectivization to privatization

No indigenous group in the Arctic is so precariously placed today as are the Small Peoples of the Russian North. Outnumbered by an overwhelming preponderance of incomers, they are presently facing a crisis of identity. The indigenous population of Siberia was a mere 5% of the total population towards the end of the 1980s (Forsyth 1992: 405), and the linguistic base of all the indigenous communities, with the exception of the Nganasans, Nentsy, Khants, Dolgans, Chukchi and Koryaks, is shrinking so rapidly that extinction of their native tongues seems imminent (see Golovko 1993; Pentikäinen 1993: 23). Most ill-placed are those too small in numbers to be granted any form of national autonomy. Ironically, the source of their misery today is what could have been the source of their prosperity, namely Siberia's fabulous natural resources. Having paid in cash as well as kind the penalty of being resource-rich, and having been treated by their Russian masters as an internal colony ever since the beginning of the century, these numerically small, economically marginalized and culturally threatened communities are now struggling to survive economic and political chaos in Russia (Shnirelman 1994).

After the October Revolution, the indigenous peoples of Siberia and the Soviet Far East were cast in the role of colonial natives whose interests were subordinated to those of the Soviet State. State-run industries encroached on their remaining land base and ousted indigenous people all over the North. State farms with imported labour recklessly exploited the natural resources which formed the basis of the traditional native economies. State deer-breeding farms arbitrarily used any pastures they wished, and fishing farms blocked the rivers with fishing nets, openly flouting all the rules and violating the seasonal fishing periods, thereby depriving indigenous people of their traditional food.

The key objective of the Russian Communist Party's social policies in the 1930s was collectivization. Land, animals and buildings were all seized from their owners and "collectivized" in the sense that they became the property of the state (Forsyth 1992: 290–320; Schindler 1992: 56–7). The fact that reindeer herders and hunters were also subjected to this radical "social engineering" indicates that collectivization had very little to do with agriculture as an economic activity of the local community, since almost none of the Siberian natives cultivated crops, and even those who reared cattle, such as the Yakuts and Buryat Mongols, were basically nomadic with little or no interest in farming. Whatever the justifications offered by the Communist Party for its policies, the collectivization of the hunting, fishing and herding activities of the indigenous peoples in the Russian North was intended to discipline them, deprive them of leadership and reduce them to the level of serfs handing over their produce, especially furs, to the Soviet Russian State (Forsyth 1992: 291). At the beginning of 1934 about 12% of deer herds were in collective ownership, by 1936 about 50%, and by 1943 as many as 89.2% (Vakhtin 1994: 50). To protest was very dangerous, and those who dared were ruthlessly suppressed and severely punished.

From the mid-1950s, the region was subjected to industrial assault on an unprecedented scale, with serious ecological consequences. It was discovered to be extremely rich in timber, gold, coal, ore, oil, gas and other natural resources. However, laws were flouted. A new mine or a new timber-cutting site could be started at any time, in any place, on the decision of the Moscow administration. Any parcel of land could be alienated from the native people by a stroke of the pen, justified by the extraordinary state importance of the task. The fragile ecological systems and the small ethnic groups of the North were severely affected by this industrial pressure and ecological aggression (Ibid.). The rights and needs of the indigenous people were simply ignored as their lands and their culture were mercilessly destroyed before their own eyes.

The most graphic example is that of the Khants, whose land has the largest oil deposits, and who have never received any compensation for the oil extracted from their land, which itself was destroyed. Similarly, when large oil and gas deposits were found on the Yamal Peninsula, and a technical plan was drawn up, including a south–north railway which cut off the summer deer pastures from the winter ones, no attention was paid to the rights and needs of the indigenous peoples concerned.

Between 1950 and the mid-1980s, Soviet influence on the indigenous peoples of Siberia and the Far East was institutionalized and inescapable. Traditional livelihoods came under threat. The socio-economic restructuring that followed involved the amalgamation and even total destruction of many small villages and settlements, which were viewed as having little chance of becoming "worthwhile" communities, and the relocation of their inhabitants to larger, more "suitable" settlements. Nomadic people were forced to settle, with disastrous consequences for their traditional vocations and subsistence economies. At the same time, state and collective farms were closed in the villages, leading to massive unemployment, alcoholism and other related problems.

Then came *perestroika* and *glasnost*. Restructuring and openness were, however, no more than the inevitable result of dry Siberian oil wells and exhausted gas deposits and coal fields (Fotinov 1991: 10). By the mid-1980s, it was revealed that gigantic projects in Siberia and the Far East had been undertaken without any concern for either the environment or the indigenous peoples whose livelihood was imperilled by them. Some of the worst industrial damage to nature and the native economy occurred in the tundra, where large areas of reindeer pastures have been turned into wastelands. The number of reindeer was less than at any other time in the 20th century. Not only had the Khants and Nentsy of Western Siberia, for example, been ousted from their devastated homeland; they had received no compensation from the oil and gas industry for this "development".

On Sakhalin Island today, more than half of the spawning grounds for salmon have become too toxic or choked with plant life for the salmon to return; the timber lumber industry practises no form of reforestation, which has led to widespread desertification in the northern territories of a once exceptionally beautiful island; and antediluvian pulp and paper plants continue to release catastrophic levels of dioxin into the island's largest fresh-water rivers (Grant 1992: 73).

In 1988, two Russian scholars from the Institute for Social and Economic Problems of the Russian Academy of Sciences in Moscow asked: "How are the interests of the people of the North being looked after in our country?" and provided the answer themselves:

> . . . deplorably. They were ignored when nuclear testing was conducted in the Arctic in the fifties, and they are being ignored now in the search for economic minerals in the taiga and tundra, in the production of oil and gas, and in the construction of giant pipelines across pastures and hunting grounds.
>
> The situation in the Khanti-Mansi National District is highly typical of the North as a whole. The Khants and Mansi now live in 72 settlements. Many of these are to this day without electricity, and people use kerosene and oil lamps as in the old days . . . There are also some communities that are considered officially to be "dead", non-existent, but which continue to be populated. These communities have no facilities whatsoever, and the inhabitants are forced to rely on their resources or the help of their neighbours. (Pika and Prokhorov 1989: 137)

In the late 1980s, indigenous movements began to emerge in many parts of the Russian North, led by native writers taking advantage of a more liberal official press. Their concern soon went beyond cultural matters to the question of native rights, particularly with reference to territory. In 1989 they protested about the ecological destruction of the Yamal Peninsula. In Kolpashevo, a village in Tomsk Oblast', a constituent assembly of 87 delegates established the Society of Tomsk Sel'kups, demanding restoration of ethnic Sel'kup village soviets in areas of high-density Sel'kup population. In 1990, a constituent assembly of the Regional Society of the Eskimos in Provideniya, Chukotka, demanded native priority to land usage, the imposition of tax on all external organizations using the land and freedom to pursue traditional industries. In the emerging movement for greater regional autonomy and the assertion of identity, the Republic of Yakutia emphasized its autonomy by adopting the new name of Sakha in 1990. Declarations of autonomous status by the Yamal–Nenets Republic, the Chukchi Republic and the Koryak Republic on the Kamchatka Peninsula, and the declaration of national sovereignty by the Buryat Autonomous Republic, followed and are suggestive of renewed national and regional self-awareness (Wood 1993/94: 73–80).

The spectre of some kind of real political separation of Siberia from Moscow has already made its appearance (Ibid.: 80–5). The radical Far Eastern Republic Freedom Party envisages total denationalization in a future independent republic, together with the priority of individual rights over those of society and freedom of enterprise and initiative. Although the Siberian intelligentsia is becoming increasingly vocal about Siberia's rich resources and their use for the benefit of Siberia itself, and about foreign banks and businesses trading directly with their Siberian partners, bypassing Moscow altogether, the prospects of absolute political separation from Russia are highly speculative.

> . . . Siberia, including the Far East, is really too huge and too heterogeneous a territory to unite or co-ordinate its political, economic and national interests in any coherent way . . . There are too many inter-regional, inter-ethnic and inter-sectoral conflicts of interest for any kind of coherent programme for total regional independence to work successfully in the immediate future. (There is, too, the danger that in an independent Siberia the old colonialism of Moscow could be replaced by a new economic imperialism, as the country's resources fall prey to international and multi-national business interests which, in the rush to exploit the emerging market, may be no more solicitous of Siberia's interest than they have shown themselves to be elsewhere in the developing world where fat profits are made at the expense of the natural environment and indigenous population). (Wood 1993/94: 83–4)

What are the alternatives for the Small Peoples of Siberia and the Far East? The first major non-governmental attempt to address the problems of the indigenous peoples was made in March 1990, when the first Congress of Small Peoples of the North was held in Moscow. At this congress, the

Association of Small Peoples of the North was created as an organization uniting the Small Peoples of the North so that they can take an active part in the development of the economy, improve their social and cultural living standards and defend their rights (IWGIA 1990: 47). One major demand concerned ownership of land. Similar questions dominated the 1989 meeting in Tyumen' of 35 scholar experts on Northern minorities. At both meetings, there was general agreement that what is needed first and foremost is a profound legislative change, giving effective autonomy to the areas populated by indigenous peoples. These areas should also be decentralized to the extent possible in the form of indigenous villages, agreements should be underpinned by legal guarantees to land, and budgetary allocations made directly to the indigenous minorities.

Summary and conclusions

Indigenous peoples the world over are under acute pressure today. Governments by and large seem bent upon integrating and assimilating them, and entrepreneurs, transnational corporations, development agencies and other economic forces are too eager to exploit the mineral and other resources located in their habitats. It is no surprise, therefore, that indigenous peoples everywhere – the Arctic being no exception – consider the geopolitical imperative of having an effective say in the development and management of their lands, waters and other resources as integral to any meaningful democratization that promises to go beyond the establishment of new institutions or simply the replacement of old ones. The emerging strength of the indigenous perspectives, evidenced by the growing acceptance of the validity of indigenous people's interpretation of events that heretofore had been in the exclusive (interpretive) domain of non-indigenous elites, does suggest, however, that the marginal site occupied by the indigenous experience and knowledge is becoming less marginal in the dominant, state-centric geopolitical discourse. In the case of Antarctica one can exclude the human–cultural parameter while talking about either environmental security or stable peace or sustainable development, but that is not possible in the Arctic.

This survey of indigenous movements in the circumpolar world, from North America to the Russian North, demonstrates that stable peace and comprehensive security for the Arctic can only result when people reach out to cooperate with one another across political divides, provided that the domestic political system is capable of sustaining a civil society in which economic and cultural security go hand in hand with civil and political liberties. In contrast to the conventional geopolitics of state power and its Cold War variety, new thinking in geopolitics, as emphasized in Chapter 1, must therefore go both below and beyond the state level. It should examine the proposed alternatives to an excessively state-centred geopolitics. Indigenous discourses on nature, land use, economic regulation and management offer alternatives to Western theories of development and propose new perspectives on the issue of sustainable development that can no longer be disregarded. As Wilmer (1993: 36–7) puts it: "Indigenous peoples' demand for inclusion in global civic discourse not only challenges the status quo but it is in some ways an exercise in the deconstruction of meaning attached to international values such as modernization and development." We will return to this theme in Chapter 9.

In view of the intimate relationship between the natural environment and the cultural, social, economic and physical well-being of indigenous peoples, it is imperative that national and international efforts to implement environmentally sound and sustainable development recognize, promote and strengthen the role of indigenous peoples and communities. This chapter reveals the fundamental importance of settling the territorial question as a prerequisite for any effective participation of indigenous peoples in the sustainable management of their natural resources. It also emphasizes that the settlement of aboriginal land claims is not a mere transaction. Intrinsic to settlement is the establishment of new institutions that can form the basis of native self-determination.

The indigenous movements of recent years not only constitute a radical critique of the history and society of the Arctic-rim states; they also propose some radical alternatives, opposing many fundamental features of modern, Western life (Jull 1985: 11). They demonstrate clearly that ethnic identity and ethnic relations are not easily divorced from the question of land rights. Most important of all, despite significant variations in terms of their scope, objectives and strategies, they all appear to emphasize the point that without a distinct territorial base, no meaningful political autonomy is possible for the indigenous peoples of the Arctic. And without political autonomy, they will at best be either passive objects or mute spectators of the development process, and not active participants as they would like to be. Whatever the final outcome, these struggles for grassroots democracy and "self-government" in the Arctic and elsewhere will remain worthy of comment and study by political geographers far into the future.

Suggested reading

Berger, T. 1988. *Northern Frontier, Northern Homeland. The Report of the Mackenzie Valley Pipeline Inquiry.* Vancouver/Toronto: Douglas & McIntyre.

Lynge, F. 1992. *Arctic Wars, Animal Rights, Endangered Peoples.* Hanover and London: University Press of New England.

Minority Rights Group (ed.) 1994. *Polar Peoples: Self-determination and Development.* London: Minority Rights Publications.

Nuttall, M. 1992. *Arctic Homeland: Kinship, Community and Development in Northwest Greenland*. London: Belhaven Press.

Smith, D. 1993. *The Seventh Fire: The Struggle for Aboriginal Government*. Toronto: Key Porter Books.

Wilmer, F. 1993. *The Indigenous Voice in World Politics*. Newbury Park: Sage Publications.

7

The post-Cold War Arctic: international cooperation and dispute management

A dynamic conception of geopolitics recognizes that throughout modern history there have been distinctive geopolitical orders, characterized by specific patterns of geopolitical rivalries between world powers, and punctuated by transitional periods of geopolitical disorder (see Agnew and Corbridge 1989, 1995). Associated with each geopolitical order is a dominant discourse about the spatial division of the world and its geographical orientation and a set of geopolitical practices to maintain the viability of that discourse. Whereas the old geopolitical order created and sustained by the Cold War – characterized by a "stability that was based on very strict ideological adherence to an antagonistic alliance system" (Taylor 1993b: 38) – is on the decline, the new one is yet to emerge in concrete terms. The Circumpolar North too is affected in numerous ways by the geopolitical transition, defined by Taylor (1993a: 330) as "the short period of rapid change between one geopolitical world-order and the next". During periods of transition, it is quite unclear what new geopolitical order will emerge, hence the dominant discourse of the previous geopolitical order tends to persist (see Taylor 1990).

However, the key difference between then and now is that there are no enemies to confront across the artificial "East–West divide" in the Arctic, which again was largely a creation – and now a legacy – of the Cold War. The old threat perceptions having become more or less redundant, the dividing line between military security and civil security is much less blurred now than it could ever be during the Cold War.

Thus, in today's Arctic a variety of bold initiatives promises to usher in a new era of bilateral as well as multilateral cooperation. If sincerely implemented, and taken to their logical conclusions by those concerned, these initiatives hold the additional promise of creating an amicable political–

diplomatic environment for the peaceful resolution of some of the long-standing Arctic disputes, frozen earlier in the Cold War psychosis. The new geopolitics and policy-makers are now face to face in the Arctic.

Nevertheless, despite quite obvious perceptual and behavioural indicators of change in the post-Cold War Arctic, are past structures, attitudes and patterns of behaviour, especially since World War II, still embedded, and is there still opposition from both "East" and "West" to meaningful change in the Arctic? Does the Cold War discourse persist? Change is apparent, but will uncertainty be the major characteristic of the geopolitical as well as the geostrategic environment of the Arctic for some years to come? In what ways is this period of geopolitical transition, particularly in the former Soviet Union, going to affect the new opportunities emerging for international cooperation in non-military realms and for seeking solutions to long-standing disputes?

This chapter has two parts. In part one, a brief overview of cooperative efforts currently under way in a relatively less problematic area like science is followed by an analysis of the key political initiatives for building Arctic regimes for international cooperation in the light of the questions above. Part two provides an overview of some of the maritime boundary disputes pending in the Arctic and explores the possible relevance of Antarctic Treaty-type solutions to their resolution.

Scientific cooperation

The establishment of the International Arctic Science Committee (IASC) in 1991 should certainly help build bridges between the scientific communities throughout the Circumpolar North, especially across the "East–West divide" (Roots 1992; Young 1992: 186; Franckx 1993: 257–61). The importance of international cooperation and coordination of scientific research in the Arctic can hardly be exaggerated. During the Cold War, chiefly organized under the auspices of national regimes – where, more often than not, hegemonic military interests called the tune in the allocation of both projects and funds – it was seldom binational and even more rarely multinational (Østreng 1992a: 32). Comparisons between Arctic and Antarctic science, in terms of motivations and the practice of polar research (Bohlin 1988; Elzinga and Bohlin 1993), also reveal that the value of Arctic scientific research to the funding authorities has primarily been tied to commercial, military and social interests and thus has been concerned mainly with the practical application of new knowledge.

During the SCAR meeting in San Diego in 1986, an informal assembly to consider the question of cooperation in Arctic science was chaired by Dr J.H. Zumberge, then chairman simultaneously of SCAR and the United States Arctic Research Commission. The prevailing international political situation in the Circumpolar North seemed favourable for exploring the possibility of institutional cooperation in Arctic science. A series of meetings followed (Franckx 1993: 258–9).

In November 1987, a detailed report, "International Communication and Coordination in Arctic Science" (prepared at the request of an informal consultative meeting held in February 1987 by a working group of three experts from Canada, Norway and Denmark), outlined the prevailing situation and the needs of Arctic science, and made a strong case for the creation of the IASC (Roots *et al.* 1987).

Undoubtedly, Gorbachev's historic Murmansk speech, in which he also proposed to host a conference of Arctic countries on the coordination of Arctic scientific research, provided an important impetus to the planning of the IASC (Issraelian 1992). However, as one of the members of the working group mentioned above reflected later, the key challenge was (and probably still is) "to search for an international mechanism that would not displace or discredit the various bilateral and specialized arrangements for Arctic co-operation that exist, that would truly represent varied national and international interests and could be supportive of national policies, and that would still meet the need for effective co-ordination of important science and keep it at arm's length from political interference" (Roots 1992: 148).

Once the Soviet side could overcome its initial reluctance to make future membership of the proposed scientific body available to non-Arctic countries engaged in significant Arctic research, the door was open for the formal creation of the IASC, eventually established at Resolute Bay (Canada) on 28 August 1991.

In a bipolar study of this nature it is tempting to ask whether the SCAR model was of any inspirational or practical value in the creation of the IASC. As Young and Cherkasov (1992: 17–18) have shown, initially there were two distinct and competing visions of the proposed committee. According to one it was to be a non-governmental organization that concentrated on identifying and refining research opportunities and was open to all parties engaging in Arctic research. In some ways this committee would resemble SCAR and might in due course merge with the latter as a constituent element of the International Council of Scientific Unions (ICSU). The other view envisaged the IASC as an intergovernmental organization that would focus on the management and logistic support of Arctic research and would restrict membership to the eight countries on the Arctic rim. The tension between the two was finally resolved through a "complex hybrid" which dealt with managerial issues as well as the design of scientific research.

The geopolitical, national-policy and research-support situation in the Arctic is quite different from that in the Antarctic. An international committee modelled directly on SCAR thus does not seem feasible for the

Arctic, unless of course there is to be an intergovernmental political instrument equivalent to the Antarctic Treaty to provide some sort of policy umbrella.

This raises some pertinent questions for science in general and for polar science in particular. In the first place there is the complex issue of the desirability and practicality of divorcing general science from its broader political and policy setting. A complete "depoliticization" of science, if feasible at all, would perhaps create apathy among the politicians and policy-makers; it would also add to their ignorance of what science has to offer in solving local and transborder ecological problems. At the same time, using science simply as a tool for obtaining short-term political gains, or perceiving science through the narrow prism of national interests, could demoralize scientists and seriously affect their professional competence, their capability to contribute to scientific knowledge. A balance ought to be achieved between enlightened national interest and the imperative of promoting science in the best interests of humanity within innovative national, regional and global frameworks. Given that such an ideal is difficult to realize, it is not surprising that the process of establishing the IASC was marked by a number of problems, such as the choice of actors to participate in that initiative (as noted above in the case of the Soviet Union), and "division between Canadians who hoped to promote their nation's political agenda regarding Arctic sovereignty and those who wanted to separate scientific goals from the rest of the agenda" (Young 1992: 188–9). The Soviets wanted the IASC to be inaugurated on their territory, where it would advance their zone-of-peace initiative, but the United States objected, and eventually the Committee was actually founded in Canada. Apparently, geopolitical thinking in some of the Arctic states has so far failed to recognize that it does not matter who takes the initiative as long as it promotes mutual benefit.

The IASC currently comprises a council, a regional board and working groups as the main working organs, together with the so-called Arctic Science Conference and a Secretariat. On membership a compromise was reached that the founding articles would be signed only by the national scientific organizations of the eight Arctic countries involved, and from the first meeting of the IASC the agreement would be open for other interested parties to join. As expected, at the very first meeting of the IASC, held in Oslo in January 1991, national scientific organizations from France, Germany, Japan, the Netherlands, Poland and the United Kingdom successfully applied for membership of the council. However, only the national organizations of the eight Arctic countries can appoint representatives to the regional board, which works on consensus. The board has the right to make recommendations which the council will take into account if the proposed programmes or projects are likely to affect the economic, social, environmental and other major interests of the Arctic countries.

The following programmes are currently (IASC 1994) being regarded by the IASC as *Science Priority Initiatives*: (i) Global Change Research in the Arctic; (ii) Effects of Increased UV-radiation in the Arctic; and (iii) the International Science Initiative in the Russian Arctic (ISIRA). The ISIRA is meant to ensure that the achievements of Russian scientists and institutions – currently facing enormous economic hardship due to political reorganization in Russia – and their contributions to solving some of the vast environmental and other problems in the Russian Arctic are brought to the attention of Western scientists. There is also felt to be "a special need in some sciences to make Russian Arctic data available to the international science community" (Ibid.: 3). How is this going to be realized in practice? Will the old power structures in Russia, such as military establishments, offer any significant opposition to the sharing of data? Will Russian scientists and their financially starved organizations feel able to cooperate with their Western counterparts without fear of unexpected political reversals within Russia? Questions such as these, although hard to answer at this stage, remain none the less.

The long-term strategy of the IASC includes the provision of a mechanism for planning and promoting international circumpolar research by establishing working groups, providing access to all areas and sharing technologies, logistics and other resources.

Northern Forum: promoting a northern dialogue

Established in November 1991 to identify areas of transregional, pan-Arctic interest for future cooperation, the Northern Forum has been described by its founders as "an international organization of leaders from northern and arctic regions of the world" (*Northern Forum* 1994: 2). What distinguishes this initiative from those discussed so far is that its membership is drawn not only from the Arctic-rim states but also from the northern parts of Japan, China, Mongolia and South Korea. Currently it has 19 members, including: Alaska (USA); Lapland (Finland); Hokkaido (Japan); S. Trøndelag and the Northern Counties Association of Northern Norway; Dornod (Mongolia); Heilongjiang (People's Republic of China); the Republic of South Korea; and regions within Russia, including the Chukotka Autonomous Okrug, Kamchatka Oblast', the Sakha Republic, Sakhalin Oblast', the Komi Republic, St Petersburg Oblast', the Khantiy–Mansiysk Autonomous Okrug and the Jewish Autonomous Region. The General Assembly, the supreme administrative body, which meets biennially, represents all full members. The Forum also has a corporate secretariat in Alaska and a board of directors, comprising governors and top-ranking political officials, who represent northern regions. Associate membership is available to businesses, universities and special-interest groups.

The wide spectrum of Northern Forum membership makes good geopolitical sense and gives an Asia–Pacific dimension to circumpolar co-operation. Once we place the Northern Forum and its various international priority projects (see Ibid.: 4) in the wider context of the emerging regional dynamics of the global geopolitical economy, and of the ecological implications, the need to extend the scope of international Arctic cooperation by involving non-Arctic actors becomes more obvious. Another notable aspect of the Forum is its emphasis on providing a cooperative framework for the business, scientific and environmental communities to interact with one another. The Forum has also set up a branch secretariat in Yakutsk, the capital of Sakha, whose economy is already fully integrated in the global economy.

The Forum has also decided to support the initiative by the Sakha Republic to establish the Arctic Bank for Reconstruction and Development. According to the President of the Republic of Sakha, Mikhail Nikolayev (1993: 1), "As Yakutia and the other arctic and northern regions are coming into the world economic foreground, they need a basis for the implementation of their ideas and projects approved in the Arctic Basin. All interested parties shall voluntarily pool their finances for this purpose . . . for an International Bank for Arctic Reconstruction and Development, to be patterned after its functioning European counterpart."

Towards an Arctic treaty? The case for an Arctic Region Council

The need for, and the rationale behind, an Arctic treaty has been succinctly summed up by Professor Donat Pharand (1992: 168–9), a Canadian expert on international law and one of the enthusiastic advocates of the idea:

> The adoption and signing of Declarations, strategies and Action plans have real merits and are evidence of serious intentions, but there is a need for an Arctic Treaty which would give legally binding effect to the political will of Arctic States. A treaty system has worked well for the Antarctic and is being proposed by the European Parliament to replace the Ministerial Conference system for the protection of the North Sea which has been in place since 1984. Such a treaty, establishing a Council with its own structure and implementation mechanisms, would permit a much needed co-operative and holistic approach for the fulfilment of the various purposes of the Council . . . .

Professor Maxwell Cohen (1970–1: 74–5) of Canada was the first to propose, in 1971, institutionalization of cooperation in the Arctic Basin, in the form of a treaty – 10 years after the Antarctic Treaty came into effect. Although Cohen's vision was geographically restricted to the Arctic Basin, it failed to find support among the Cold War-obsessed policy-makers of the Arctic-rim states throughout the 1970s. Incidentally, at that time as many as four of the Arctic-rim states (the United States, the Soviet Union and

Norway as original signatories to the Antarctic Treaty, and Denmark, which joined later, in 1965, as an ordinary member) were actively contributing to the evolution of a multinational system of governance in the southern polar region. But in the case of the Arctic, the idea of non-military cooperation at the height of the Cold War clashed head-on with the conception of the Arctic Ocean as a frontal strategic zone during armed conflict. It was in the second half of the 1980s (by then two more Arctic-rim states, Sweden and Finland, had acceded to the Antarctic Treaty) that the idea was revived in academic circles.

In 1987, a working group of the National Capitalist Branch of the Canadian Institute of International Affairs, of which Cohen was a member, discussed further the concept of an Arctic System or Council and made specific suggestions to the government of Canada. The Canadian Prime Minister, during his visit to Russia in November 1989, raised the question of a "council of Arctic Countries coming into existence to co-ordinate and promote co-operation among them" and an independent panel, co-chaired by Professor Franklyn Griffiths, a Canadian expert on Arctic matters, and Ms Rosemary Kuptana, President of the Inuit Tapirisat of Canada, was established soon afterwards (Pharand 1992: 166). Following the recommendations of a preliminary report prepared by the panel, the government of Canada announced on 28 November 1990 that it would seek the creation of an Arctic Council for circumpolar cooperation. The official Canadian view of the Arctic Council is that its agenda should be flexible, allowing for growth with success, as confidence grows. In addition, the Council should allow Northern peoples to contribute to decisions affecting their lives and interests. Finally, the Council should be designed to permit appropriate input from non-member countries outside the region which have interests in the Arctic and whose activities could affect the region "for better or worse" (Griffiths 1992a: 283).

Indeed, a strong case for an Arctic Region Council has been presented, with renewed emphasis on unifying circumpolar, rather than divisive north–south and/or east–west, geopolitical reasoning (Griffiths 1992a; Pharand 1992). It will be useful to consider some of this positive thinking, the driving intellectual force behind the initiative: first and foremost the attempt to reformulate the notion of security in general and security for the Circumpolar North in particular. To quote Griffiths (1992a: 300):

> . . . it is *we* who are the prime danger to ourselves where overpopulation, unsustainable development, global warming, ozone depletion, and many other nontraditional threats to "security" are concerned. A concept that alerts us essentially to danger emanating from elsewhere is no longer appropriate to the needs of humankind. Nor is an understanding that biases action towards resistance rather than accommodation.

In a word, Griffiths asks for *civility* (Ibid.: 307), which requires southern majorities and the governments that speak on their behalf to give progressively greater respect and attention to one another, the circumpolar environment, Arctic populations and above all to the aboriginal peoples.

The establishment of an Arctic Region Council, it is strongly felt, will be a significant step in the direction of achieving that civility simultaneously with equitable and ecologically sustainable development and management of the Circumpolar North (Pharand 1992: 177–81).

According to the blueprint for the Arctic Region Council, in the form of a Draft Arctic Treaty (see *Northern Perspectives* 1991: 20–3; Pharand 1992), the Arctic Region will comprise the area north of 60°N latitude (including Labrador and the region in northern Quebec known as "Nunavik"). It will include all the areas covered by tundra or continuous permafrost, except for parts of northern Quebec and of Labrador. By contrast, it is pointed out, a limit of the Arctic Circle would exclude significant bodies of water and large areas of the tundra and of sea ice. In geopolitical terms, the Canadian model of the "Arctic Region" would include the Yukon, NWT (including Nunavut), all of Greenland, all of Finland, all of Iceland, all of Svalbard and most of mainland Norway (north of Oslo), most Swedish territory north of Stockholm, virtually all of Alaska, and roughly the northern half (counting the archipelagos) of Russian territory, including the numerous rivers emptying into the Arctic Ocean.

With reference to the structure of the Arctic Council, the Arctic Council Panel (see *Northern Perspectives* 1991: 10–12) has indicated a preference for a model that goes beyond the conventional state-centred processes and apparatus of decision-making, one that would yield to innovative forms of collective action adapted to the special circumstances of the Circumpolar North. According to such a "compact structure", the Arctic Council would consist of 10 delegations, acting on the basis of consensus. The Arctic states would account for eight, the ninth would represent the indigenous peoples, and the 10th delegation, nominated by the Northern Forum, would speak on behalf of the circumpolar territorial governments. Non-Arctic states (for example, Germany, Japan, Poland and the United Kingdom) "could also be invited individually to attend as observers with the right to speak in Council as they do in the Rovaniemi process" (Ibid.: 11). The non-Arctic states and non-state actors could also be invited to participate in the work of Arctic Council Working Groups as appropriate. Thus, in the opinion of the Panel: "The option of a compact Arctic Council offers an efficient means of ensuring that the northern voice is heard while at the same time keeping the human resources, interaction, and financial costs of participation to a minimum" (Ibid.).

Additionally, the Arctic Region Council will promote the use of the region for peaceful purposes. This immediately raises the difficult question of interpretation. Will "peaceful uses" imply comprehensive *demilitarization* of the area in the sense in which it has been understood and practised in the Antarctic? The terms "non-militarization" and "non-nuclearization" are not appropriate in the case of the Arctic, since (unlike the Antarctic) it is already militarized and nuclearized. Not surprisingly, the expression "peaceful purposes" is deliberately vague in the draft treaty (Pharand 1991: 21).

Complete demilitarization of the Arctic or, for that matter, a complete ban on nuclear weapons north of 60° would require, *inter alia*, a political agreement among all the Arctic states, backed up by legal force, and a system of verification and control. Such a radical departure from the past also makes imperative the release of political will and attitudes from Cold War psychosis – in itself quite a revolutionary change in the notion of national security (see Boulding 1991: 150, 152).

Total or partial demilitarization of the Arctic has been suggested by a number of scholars and organizations over the years: most noteworthy is the idea of establishing a Central Arctic Demilitarized Zone beyond the 200-nautical mile EEZ of Arctic Basin states, covering the seabed and subsoil, the water column and the air space, with a verification system for both the surface and subsurface waters and the air space (see Purver 1988). This idea is in need of further serious consideration by all the Arctic states as the first step towards confidence-building measures in the Arctic.

Some observers might even argue that in order to realize cooperation in non-military matters, it would be prudent to exclude military matters from the mandate of the proposed Arctic Region Council. The Arctic Council Panel strongly disagrees on the grounds that this would not only imply acquiescence in discriminatory and prejudicial military use of the Arctic but also underwrite the continued marginalization of the region and compromise the inherent interrelatedness of circumpolar issues (*Northern Perspectives* 1991: 15).

> Is not the removal of toxic materials from military sites around the region an environmental and also a human rights issue? Does not the same apply to low-level flight training, and to the testing of nuclear weapons? Should we be prevented from considering the use of a small number of decommissioned U.S. and Soviet nuclear-powered attack submarines as platforms to monitor critical arctic processes of global warming and the oceanic transport of pollutants? (Ibid.)

As the proposal stands, the Arctic Region Council could in principle be open to the discussion of any topic, including security and sovereignty issues, although negotiations on collective undertakings would be by consensus. Perhaps this is why the idea of the Arctic Council has so far received a cool response from most of the Arctic-rim states. The USA has argued that given the existence of the Arctic Environmental Protection Strategy (AEPS) (see Chapter 9) and the IASC, there is no need for an Arctic Council. It has also resisted in the past strong indigenous participation in the Council (Ibid.). The US Navy in particular is said to have serious reservations in this respect. Obviously, a transnational institution with such a comprehensive mandate would pose a direct challenge to those who are still captives of the old paradigm of national security, clinging to the conventional notion of state sovereignty.

Despite the virtually flawless eco-geopolitical reasoning on which the concept of an Arctic Region Council rests, serious differences continue to be expressed about the need for this body, what should be included in its discussions and who should be represented on its proposed organs. Most problematic of all appears to be the question of its mandate, despite the qualifier that "the Acts of the Arctic Council will be taken by a procedure that includes consensus among the eight arctic states once all members have made their views known" (*Northern Perspectives* 1991: 15). Given the conflict between the strong feeling on the part of the indigenous peoples as well as territorial governments that no major issue or problem should be excluded from the scope of an Arctic treaty and the reluctance on the part of the hegemonic interests within the Arctic states to be bound by such dictates, the Panel may have felt compelled to adopt a conciliatory tone, that "the mandate of an Arctic Council be an open one that allows for growth in the Council's agenda with the growth of consensus" (Ibid.: 14). Apparently this too has failed to generate so far the necessary political will on the part of most Arctic-rim states to negotiate an Arctic treaty.

The second Framework Report of the Arctic Council Panel, published in May 1991, noted, on the question of the mandate of the Council: "currently, the Arctic States are unanimous in tacit opposition to negotiations among Arctic States on confidence-building and arms control measures affecting the region, and would see such issues treated in non-arctic negotiation forums only" (Ibid.: 13).

A series of recent developments, however, has brightened the prospects of the Arctic Council. Foremost is the announcement, on 29 September 1994, of a new US policy, outlined in a Fact Sheet issued by the Department of State (US Department of State 1994), declaring that the United States has six principal objectives in the Arctic region: (i) protecting the environment and conserving its biological resources; (ii) assuring that natural-resource development is environmentally sustainable; (iii) strengthening institutions for cooperation among the eight Arctic nations; (iv) involving indigenous peoples in decisions that affect them; (v) ongoing scientific monitoring and research into regional and global issues; and (iv) meeting post-Cold War national security and defence needs.

In February 1994 the Clinton administration had circulated a Presidential Decision Directive (PDD) on US policy for the Arctic and Antarctic regions which reflected current thinking in Washington (US Government 1994). Not made public, the PDD recognized the need for "international co-operation in both regions and the role for U.S. leadership in these co-operative international efforts", and underlined the "important differences between the two regions: the Arctic is an inhabited area in which environmentally sustainable development must occur; the Antarctic is to be maintained as a relatively pristine reserve principally devoted to scientific research" (Ibid.: 1). It points out that the United States "must maintain the ability to protect against attack across the region, to move ships and aircraft freely under Law of the Sea principles, to control our borders and areas under our jurisdiction, and to carry out military operations in the region". At the same time, there is an acknowledgement that "the end of the Cold War, however, allows a significant shift of emphasis in US Arctic policy".

While the US government is willing to work towards a legally binding agreement among the Arctic states as explicitly mentioned in the PDD, the policy that has been made public (a shortened version of the PDD) only says that "the United States will seek to create a more formal policy forum through which Arctic nations can oversee implementation of Arctic strategy" (US Department of State 1994: 2). The Arctic Council is not specifically mentioned and probably what the policy-makers in Washington have in mind is the AEPS. Be that as it may, it is worth noting that the US government is prepared to go beyond pledges and declarations in Arctic matters. No less encouraging is the evidence that the distinction between civil and military security, which had virtually evaporated during the Cold War, is now visible again. It is precisely here that a window of opportunity has opened up. At the same time, one might question the need to "maintain the ability to protect against attack" in the region. Geostrategic thinking is obviously still alive in certain corridors in Washington.

Yet another important development is the creation by Canada (thereby joining the Nordic countries) of a special ambassadorial position for circumpolar issues. The appointment to this post of Mary Simon, whose dedication to the advancement of Inuit rights is widely acknowledged and highly regarded, is significant for more than one reason. The "number one task" that has been assigned to her by the present government in Ottawa is the establishment of an Arctic Council. Furthermore, there are encouraging signs that the idea of an Arctic Council has finally received a favourable response from the United States. Whether the US support is unconditional remains to be seen; it may be linked to the issue of the Beaufort Sea dispute with Canada. The competing views on this long-standing jurisdictional question are well documented (see Rothwell 1988). Canada maintains that the international boundary, on both land and sea, was established along the 141st meridian by the Treaty of 1825 between Great Britain and Russia by which both Canada and the USA are bound. The USA holds that the boundary line should be drawn perpendicular to the coastline at the point where the boundary meets the sea. Both states have offered gas and oil rights in the overlap area between the two claims, but no drilling has yet been authorized.

It is unlikely that Canada will agree to a trade-off of US support for the Arctic Council in return for recognition of its position on the Beaufort issue; otherwise the Arctic Council would become politically suspect at the very outset. If unconditional and unequivocal US support for the Arctic Council is forthcoming, the other Arctic-rim states are likely to join. Whether the Arctic Council will eventually be able to negotiate a legally binding treaty remains to be seen. The idea, nevertheless, is worth exploring further and we will return to it towards the end of the study.

Cooperation in the Barents Euro-Arctic Region: problems and prospects

The new geopolitical thinking in the post-Cold war Arctic has also gone *beyond* the nation-state level, towards regionalism and regionalization (Chapter 1). Most noteworthy is the Norwegian initiative for realizing transborder cooperation through the creation of a Barents Euro-Arctic Region (Stoltenberg 1992). The Barents Sea is becoming a unifying element instead of a dividing one (Tunander 1994: 40). Formally established at a meeting of Ministers of Foreign Affairs from the Nordic countries and Russia, held in Kirkenes in January 1993, this innovative and brave effort addresses the following areas: environment, economic cooperation, science and technology, regional infrastructure, indigenous peoples, cultural relations and tourism. The Kirkenes Declaration was signed by all the participating countries and the European Commission. These are all members of the Barents Euro-Arctic Council, which may convene at Foreign-Minister level or other relevant ministerial level, with a rotating chairmanship among the four core countries: Norway, Finland, Sweden and Russia. Currently, the United Kingdom, France, Germany, the Netherlands, Poland, the USA, Canada and Japan participate as observers.

Duality is said to be "the key element of the Barents concept" and the "interplay and tension between regional and central governments interested in cooperation in the region" (see Holst 1994: 11) is said to have given rise to an organizational structure with two pillars: an international government-level pillar (the Barents Council and, for instance, the Norwegian/Russian Mixed Commission) and a transregional municipal pillar (the Regional Council and bodies covering individual issue areas). The key actors are the nation-states, the eight administrative regions directly involved: the counties of Nordland, Troms and Finnmark in Norway, Norbotten in Sweden, Lappland in Finland, the Russian districts of Murmansk, and Arkhangel'sk and the Republic of Karelia (Map G) and the European Union (EU). The indigenous peoples too will have one representative on the Regional Council. It has been described (in terms of its key features and objectives) by its architects (Jervell 1994: 6, 11) as *a mixture of vision* and *realpolitik.* The vision was of peace-promoting, confidence-building cooperation in the north, to be achieved by linking the northern parts of the Nordic area with northwestern Russia. The realpolitik (meaning a policy aiming at pursuing national interests and firmly anchored in political realities) from a Norwegian perspective consisted of making this a multilateral cooperation forum involving other Nordic and European countries.

The establishment of the Barents cooperation provides a basis for north European dimension to the common foreign and security policy that Nordic countries will encounter as members of the EU. The Barents cooperation could become a northern extension of a Moscow–Brussels dialogue, and could also make a specific contribution to future cooperation based on a partnership agreement between the EU and Russia.

The quotation raises a series of questions: what constitutes a political region? What is the essence of regionality in the context of Barents cooperation? What are the major driving forces behind emerging regionalism in the Barents area? What is going to be the geopolitical configuration of the Barents Region in terms of the polarization of the actors, divisions between the core and the periphery, power stratification, the integration between the actors and levels of development? What is the current extent of cohesion (in other words, the degree of homogeneity and similarity) among the actors in the region? What promise does this initiative hold for the indigenous Sami peoples as well as for the socially equitable and ecologically sustainable development and management of their homelands?

There is an excellent discussion of the concept of a "political region" in Thompson (1973). Restricting the term to a cluster of at least two actors, he focuses on three properties: (i) geographical proximity; (ii) significant interactions in one or more spheres, either conflictual or cooperative; and (iii) recognition of the area in question by the regional actors themselves, and by outsiders, as standing out from its surroundings: the discursive aspect of regionality (Castberg *et al.* 1994: 71–2). The core of regionality therefore seems to lie in both "the interactive and discursive distinctiveness of a more or less clearly defined geographic area" (Ibid.).

What might add yet another interesting geopolitical dimension to the concept and practice of regionality is that in some cases a "political region" may not be a reality as it actually *exists* but a *future reality* which certain political entrepreneurs, policy-makers and others wish to realize. This is precisely what makes region-building, under the circumstances, some kind of a *project*, which, once established and accepted in its discursive sense by all concerned, will promote, or alternatively impede, certain outcomes. As Tunander (1994: 36–9) points out, mobilization for region-building may also rely upon evoking historical myths to generate certain symbolic unifying elements and perspectives. In the case of the Barents Region, the use of historical analogies by Norwegian Foreign Ministers to revive memories of the Pomor or coastal trade (*pomor'e* is "coastal area" in Russian) in the 18th and 19th centuries – when the Russian merchants along the White

185

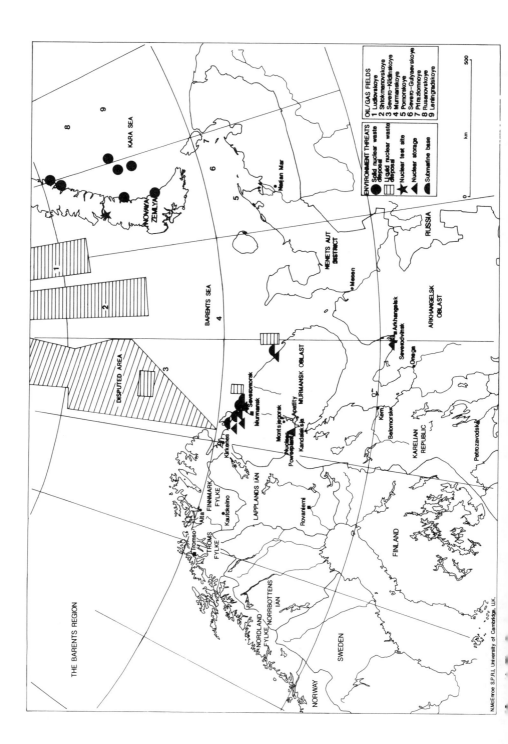

THE BARENTS REGION

ENVIRONMENT THREATS
Solid nuclear waste disposal
Liquid nuclear waste disposal
Nuclear test site
Nuclear storage
Submarine base

OIL/GAS FIELDS
1 Ludlovskoye
2 Shtokmanovskoye
3 Severo-Kildinskoye
4 Murmanskoye
5 Pomorskoye
6 Severo-Gulyaevskoye
7 Prirazlomnoye
8 Rusanovskoye
9 Leningradskoye

KARA SEA
NOVAYA ZEMLYA
BARENTS SEA
DISPUTED AREA
NENETS AUT DISTRICT
Mezen Mar
Mezen
RUSSIA
ARKHANGELSK OBLAST
Arkhangelsk
Severodvinsk
Onega
MURMANSK OBLAST
Severomorsk
Murmansk
Montajegorsk
Apatity
Nuclear Poertresse
Kandalaksja
Kem
Belomorsk
KARELIAN REPUBLIC
Petrozavodsk
Kirkenes
Alta
Tromso
FINNMARK FYLKE
TROMS FYLKE
Kautokeino
LAPPLANDS IÄN
Rovaniemi
FINLAND
NORDLAND FYLKE
NORRBOTTENS IÄN
SWEDEN
NORWAY

0   km   500

N.McEnroe S.P.R.I. University of Cambridge, U.K.

186

Sea, together with the Norwegian fishing communities and Finnish and Sami settlements in the North, formed a trade area far away from capitals and state authority – is not purely accidental.

Regionality can be identified at several levels. At an international level, a region can be any particular territory delimited on account of various ordered and intensified interactions among at least two international political cal actors in geographical proximity. As the level, quantity and frequency of these interactions intensify, so does the level of regional cohesion (Naveh 1994). The key example here, and so far an obvious success story, is the Western European region, emerging out of integration processes in the EU involving abolition of a multiplicity of barriers between national states. As a result, many border regions which have had peripheral positions for geopolitical reasons in the past are steadily acquiring "important bridging roles in new transnational macroregional formations characterized by multifold interaction and co-operation" (Wiberg 1994: 1).

The "hybrid" nature of the Barents Region project, in relation to the levels of regionality described above, is reflected in its institutional structure. Whereas the transnational dimension is projected in the Regional Council, composed of representatives of province authorities and indigenous peoples, the international or inter-state dimension is reflected in the ministerial-level Barents Council, which also includes a representative of the European Commission.

Both the spatial scope and the functional mandate of the Barents Region are worth noting. As observed above, the mandate of the Barents Council is strictly confined to civilian matters, in sharp contrast to the all-encompassing mandate of the proposed Arctic Region Council. This may to some extent explain why the proposed Arctic treaty is still awaiting political consensus among the Arctic-rim states, while the Barents Region initiative is already functional. The Norwegian government has also emphasized that collaboration in the Barents Region should mainly be restricted to land-based activities so as to avoid the disputed maritime boundary line between Norway and Russia in the Barents Sea and the controversial legal status of the zone around Svalbard. This would seem to exclude cooperation in the fisheries and the offshore petroleum sectors – which is precisely where the Barents Region is particularly well endowed in terms of natural resources and cooperation would appear to be "natural". According to expert opinion on this subject (Castberg et al. 1994: 73), however, this restriction should not be viewed as a blanket one, for: (i) environmental concerns have already been exempted from it, and (ii) for more than a decade, it has been Norwegian policy to encourage cooperation with its large eastern neighbour as long as this does not touch on the unsettled sovereignty issues. Finally, as long as the Barents Region remains little more than an arena where parties can come together to identify projects of joint interest, it is doubtful if activities within it can compromise the legal claims to sovereignty of any participant.

This leads naturally to a discussion of the major driving forces behind Barents Region cooperation, because it is the interplay among these forces that is likely to decide whether the issue of sovereignty can be kept at bay, and for how long, or whether it will have to be confronted and tackled in one way or another. What does stand out in this context is the resource dimension, the abundance and significance of which was noted in Chapter 2. At the same time it could be argued that no other place in the Arctic poses as formidable a challenge as the Barents area does for realizing the ecologically sustainable development and management of the environment and its resources. In addition to being rich in resources, it is the most heavily militarized as well as polluted part of the Circumpolar North.

The Russians have stressed that the Barents cooperation will not only give the central authorities in Moscow a chance to support the development of various subregions, it will also contribute to: (i) economic and social stability; (ii) a stronger regional perception among people in the North; (iii) demilitarization of industries and people's attitudes of mind in the North; and (iv) the process of solving environmental problems in the area. In the Russian part of the region, large-scale efforts are necessary to deal with environmental damage, calling for efficient production methods and the upgrading of the existing infrastructure. The industrial sector must transform its role from raw-material supplier into producer of diverse manufactured products. Needless to say, most (if not all) of these cases require substantial financial resources. Investment, skill and technology from the Western countries can play an important role in supporting the collapsing economies of the Russian North and transforming the political economy of the region as a whole. For Russia "cooperation in trade and economy is the matter of highest priority" (Kozyrev 1994: 27). Nordic enterprises are showing interest in cooperating with Russian enterprises in the exploitation of various raw materials, but there is also interest in selling consumer goods and know-how. Where Nordic enterprises can be very effective and competitive is in the implementation of environment-friendly technologies.

At the same time, there is a risk of conflicts of interest in the Barents Region in the case of shared raw-material resources. One obvious example is the fish-processing industry. Modernization of this industry on the Russian side is likely to be perceived as a threat to the fish-processing industry on the Norwegian side. Similar problems exist in the case of the forestry resources in the southern part of the region. Informed anticipation of conflicts of interest and rivalries, and collaboration and joint ventures in the region have been suggested as possible solutions, together with training entrepreneurs and managers in the skills of operating in the different social, political and economic environments (Wiberg 1994: 10–11). Given the enormous cultural differences and other incompatibilities between Russia and its Nordic partners (see Bathhurst 1994), it has rightly been stressed that the success of the Barents cooperation will depend as much upon cultivating cross-cultural understanding and education as "upon moving quickly to create, strengthen, and defend new institutions which can operate within the complex, political cultures" (Ibid.: 55). The experience of the Nordic attempts to integrate the Barents or the North Calotte in a functional sense so far indicate that there are numerous difficulties in the way of proceeding from vision to reality. These include: (i) the small and dispersed populations in the Nordic part which form a weak base for mutual trade and other types of interaction; (ii) strong national north–south orientations of dependencies, transport infrastructure and physical flows; (iii) a rather chaotic economic, ecological and political situation in Russia that calls for strategies to cope with the great uncertainties and lack of general institutional arrangements; and (iv) few higher-education and research institutions, of limited scope, within a region comprising the peripheral parts of all the national states involved (Ibid.: 12–13).

Nevertheless, the process of Europeanization has undoubtedly reached Northern Europe. The Barents Region Project is based upon a reasonable premise that in a Europe of regions, on certain issues the Barents Region is likely to find better allies in other European regions and in the European Commission than in its own capitals. One could even argue that in the event of full integration of the Nordic countries into the EU, although Norway recently voted not to join, there will be a very important role for the countries of the Barents Region as direct links between the EU and Russia, since they may also benefit from long-term subsidies from EU Structural Funds.

The very first question, then, is whether the Barents Region cooperation will/can be in a position to realize the critical shift from domination to non-domination as the governing principle within it. The question acquires additional significance because this cooperation is a top-down political project, even though it has a footing on the regional and local levels. From this flow other questions relating to the present and future prospects for ecologically sustainable and equitable development and management of the Barents Region.

Will the Barents Region eventually evolve into a political unit of an entirely different order, with its own spatial structures and, as a consequence, acquire a different range of possibilities for developing lasting transborder cooperation? It is difficult to say at this stage. It is, however, quite certain that the answer will depend on the effectiveness of regionalism as a component part of any new order in the Euro-Arctic. Sceptics may ask whether it will represent something radically "new" in terms of the transformation of the geopolitical surface of the Arctic or whether it will just be the old order transferred to a new regional and international dimension. Much of what comes out of this project is no doubt going to depend on the centres of power located to the south: would they be willing to compromise their sovereignty as understood and practised in the traditional sense? Will it be able to usher in a new era for the Sami peoples by ensuring their full and effective participation in the making and implementation of its policies? At present there is just one representative of the indigenous peoples on the Barents Regional Council. Is this enough? Will it allow grassroots-based regionalization to gather its own momentum, even if it means a head-on collision with many facets of the state-centred political order?

According to a noted Sami scholar, so far there is not much enthusiasm among Sami politicians for the Barents cooperation (Helander 1994), although its general objectives – environmental security, regional stability, a regional network and the possibilities for active participation by the indigenous peoples – are viewed positively. One reason could be that, in comparison with the Sami of Norway and Russia, there is little awareness of the Barents cooperation among the Sami in Sweden and Finland (Ibid.), which may be due to relatively less media coverage in these countries. Political opinion too is divided about how the Sami will benefit. Whereas some people feel that the cooperation will indirectly lead to the identification of the Sami region, and will generate beneficial law-making as well as some profit from resource exploitation, others seem to fear that expectations should be limited to some political influence or some sort of educational and cultural exchange. Many Sami politicians argue that there should be greater indigenous representation on the various bodies and at all levels within the Barents system. According to one viewpoint, the Sami peoples are already marginalized within their respective national states and will continue to remain a minority even within a regional cooperative framework, so the Sami population may not improve its position radically (Käkönen 1994: 13).

Jyrki Käkönen (1994) has some interesting new ideas on the subject of regionalism and regionalization. He insists upon drawing a clear distinction between civil-society-based "regionalization from below" and "state centred regionalism". In the latter, states remain the major actors, they cooperate with one another in a certain region, or encourage (even push) their internal regions to cooperate with neighbouring regions. Regionalization from below, with its emphasis on changing the "essence of politics" and "creating new forums for politics" (Ibid.: 4), has altogether different connotations, since it brings new actors into the international forum and challenges the traditionally dominant and dominating role of the states. Ideally speaking, therefore, it should change the role of the former peripheries of the "unified" states, giving them more power and autonomy as the role of the states themselves declines due to this shift of power. According to Käkönen (Ibid.: 12–13), this alternative reflects the principle of subsidiarity which is adapted by the EC and also "strengthens the development of common economy in the Calotte area, i.e. economy for the region itself instead of being a periphery in four different national economies".

Accordingly, Käkönen finds the idea of Calotte cooperation much more promising than the idea of the Barents Region, which he feels is a model based on state-centred regionalism intended to extend and promote national interests (Ibid.: 9–10). The North Calotte is a political term, first launched by the Nordic Council in 1957. It includes the northern counties of Norway (Finnmark, Troms and Nordland), Sweden (Norbotten) and Finland (Lappland) and, for the last few years, the Murmansk district. There is an official body, called the North Calotte Committee, under the Ministerial Council of the Nordic Countries.

Käkönen fears that, in the Barents cooperation, states are going to control the utilization of resources by dictating the conditions for their exploitation and controlling the development of the infrastructure, including harbours and airports. In the long run, then, the Calotte or Barents area will "remain as a gateway which means that the goods will flow via the Calotte region but very little will remain in the region" (Ibid.). The idea of regionalization from below, currently being expressed through Calotte cooperation, points in a direction worthy of serious consideration by the Barents Region initiative.

Dispute management in the Arctic: relevance of the Antarctic experience?

In both polar regions sovereignty continues to be an issue. The prospects for international cooperation and the ecologically sustainable development and management of resources in both regions are seriously constrained by disputes about who owns what and where. Whereas in the Antarctic sovereignty concerns have been predominantly territorial – though maritime dimensions are becoming increasingly important – in the Arctic the maritime issues are the source of greater conflict and invariably tangled with geostrategic, "security" considerations. In contrast to the Antarctic, sovereignty over land areas is reasonably well established in the Arctic, with the exception of Svalbard. Some of these disputes are indeed difficult to solve to the complete satisfaction of all parties, especially when natural resources are an issue as well as military security. This has led to a stimulating debate about whether a frozen sovereignty approach, like that in the Antarctic, could also be appropriate in the Arctic (Stokke 1991; Rothwell 1993, 1994). While the question is worth exploring from a geopolitical perspective, it is important to bear in mind the diverse contexts and characteristics of the two polar regions.

Exhaustive treatment of each one of the maritime disputes in the Arctic is far beyond the scope of this chapter. The account below is therefore limited to a brief overview and analysis of three outstanding unresolved disputes in the Arctic. It also discusses whether the dispute-management strategies of the ATS could be of some relevance, particularly in the Barents Sea, where an agreement between nations to cooperate in mutually beneficial activities is held up by the disagreement.

Boundary delimitation in the Barents Sea

Norway and the USSR, later Russia, have been negotiating a maritime boundary in the Barents Sea for over 20 years. While Norway holds that the boundary should be drawn in accordance with the median-line principle under international law, the other side has maintained that owing to "special circumstances" (i.e. the form and length of the Barents coastline, ice conditions, the greater population of the Kola Peninsula as compared with northern Norway, shipping and fishing interests in the area, the vulnerability of marine ecosystems, the geostrategic importance of the waters to Russia and the sector decree of 1926), the boundary line should follow the sector line (Scrivener 1992; Moe 1994: 133). It should be remembered that, in order not to compromise its legal position as well as its political interests *vis-à-vis* Russia in the Arctic, Norway had deliberately avoided asserting a sector-shaped claim in Antarctica and left both its northern and southern terminus undefined.

While there is no justification whatsoever in international law for the sector line being the boundary (Churchill and Ulfstein 1992: 89), the median-line principle, as defined by the 1958 Convention on the Continental Shelf, has passed into customary law under Article 76 of the UNCLOS III but with important modifications (Glassner 1990: 25). The continental shelf is now defined as the seabed out to 200 miles or the edge of the continental margin, whichever is further. Not only have the 200-m isobath and the exploitability clause been dropped, the geological definition has also been ignored. Given that the Barents Sea is comparatively shallow – only about half of its expanse (about 1 405 000 sq km) is deeper than 200 m, and the average depth is 229 m – from a geological as well as from a legal point of view, the whole of its bed is continental shelf.

In short, given the vagueness and generality of the rules relating to maritime-boundary delimitation, international law is not of much help in deciding where the boundary should lie in the Barents Sea. By implication, the states concerned, in this case Norway and Russia, must make a genuine effort to negotiate and reach an agreement, which is most likely to be influenced by the prevailing geopolitical and economic circumstances and the related perceptions. The problem is much less of *what* the law is than of *how* it should be interpreted and applied in the Barents case. Accordingly, the bone of contention is whether or not there are "special circumstances" in the Barents Sea that validate departure from the median-line principle.

The disagreement has resulted in a sizeable disputed area of about 155 000 sq km, causing tensions between the two countries from time to time (Traavik and Østreng 1977: 343–4). However, with the exception of the *Valentin Shashin* incident in 1983, when a Finnish-built Soviet drilling ship strayed about 2 km over the median line, since the early 1980s both countries have refrained from conducting seismic surveys in the disputed area.

The establishment of the Barents Region, and the generally conducive political climate at present, has at least transformed the delimitation issue "from an over-arching problem in Norwegian-Soviet/Russian relations to a more limited, area-specific problem" (Moe 1994: 134). The exclusion of the offshore sector from the area of Barents cooperation, it is hoped, might offer an incentive to the Russians to reach an agreement. The key question, however, is whether in the Russian perception the changes brought about by the end of the Cold War are compelling enough to allow a change in its earlier policy or not. In any case, it will be far more difficult for Russia to argue that her geostrategic stakes in the Barents Sea continue to provide justification for the "special circumstances" argument and, therefore, the sector principle.

The Grey Zone Agreement

The legal–geopolitical complexity of the Barents Sea is further enhanced by creeping coastal-state jurisdiction, with implications for marine-resource management. After the introduction of a 200-nautical mile EEZ by the two riparian states, the area which remained international waters shrank drastically to about 64 000 sq km. Since most of the former international waters now come under the jurisdiction of Norway and Russia, the unsettled maritime boundary has also caused problems for the regulation of third-country fishing. In 1977, a "Grey Zone" agreement was concluded, enabling Norway and Russia to regulate and control their own fishermen, as well as third-country fishermen licensed by each of them (Hoel 1994: 116). Under the agreement, while the joint Fisheries Commission would decide total allowable catches and quotas for fishing, each of the two states would separately inspect its own vessels and those of the third parties. Despite the absence of a maritime boundary, the need for joint management of the fisheries in the area was thereby met. It is worth noting, however, that the accord, strikingly similar to the CCAMLR arrangements for the Southern Ocean, specifically avoided the joint enforcement of regulations which coordinated inspections would have involved, and opted instead for a management regime of separate jurisdiction. Thus the Grey Zone accord could not prejudice in any way either party's stance on the location of the maritime boundary in the Barents Sea. Renewed annually since its inception, the accord seems to have fulfilled its geopolitical and ecological functions reasonably well as far as the southern part of the Barents Sea is concerned.

The "Special Zone" proposal

In January 1988, Soviet Premier Ryzhkov proposed, as an interim solution to the Barents boundary dispute, the establishment of a "Special Zone" of economic cooperation and confidence-building that would include the disputed shelf area. In this zone the two sides would jointly conduct oil and gas activity on an equal basis, without prejudice to either side's position on where the boundary should be drawn. Accordingly, both sides would agree to disagree on the sovereignty question while proceeding with resource development in the area.

A Special Zone might have provided Norway with greater opportunities to ensure that Soviet offshore practices in the Barents and Kara Seas were ecologically safe, as well as to secure investment opportunities for its oil companies (Scrivener 1992). Yet the proposal, broadly based on the Antarctic Treaty solution, was promptly and firmly turned down by Oslo. Norway insisted, and continues to insist, on a clear, treaty-based boundary. This might possibly include a "utilization clause", i.e. where petroleum fields straddle the agreed maritime boundary, exploitation would take place on a joint basis. Why did Norway turn down the freeze solution in the case of the Barents Sea petroleum area while agreeing to it decades previously in respect of its Antarctic territorial claim?

Plausible explanations may be provided by both geohistorical and geopolitical factors. It is worth recalling that territorial claims in the Antarctic, including that of Norway, were not only legally dubious and politically suspect at the time of their assertion; they were not worth a conflict in the Cold War environment. In other words, the benefits of freezing the territorial claims were perceived by all the parties as far greater than the costs. Although the geopolitical interests involved were quite complex, no natural resources were at stake. Equally conspicuous by their absence were geostrategic concerns. In the case of the Barents Sea dispute, however, the interests involved are clear cut, with oil resources at stake. For Norway, as Stokke (1991: 360) has argued, "the cost of pursuing a policy of wait and see is lower, because of low oil prices, no offshore oil hits in Norway's part of the Barents Sea so far, and huge areas that are yet to be explored in undisputed waters".

In 1993 the foreign ministers of Russia and Norway declared that "a solution of the delimitation issue would further the development of cooperation in several areas, especially the Barents Region" (Moe 1994: 133). Apparently, the confidence-building measures taken as part of the Barents cooperation and the transformed post-Cold War geopolitical realities have created an environment that is far more conducive to solving the delimitation issue. Significant advances have been reported, but consensus has yet to be achieved on the delimitation of the part of the shelf lying nearest the mainland (Hanevold 1994: 230). Is a solution finally in sight?

It is fairly clear that both Norway and Russia would prefer to resolve the dispute through bilateral negotiations, rather than going for third-party settlement. However, the pace and tone of further negotiations, as well as the likelihood of their successful conclusion, will depend to a large extent on how strongly the two parties perceive the need to explore the new sites for seabed hydrocarbons. Equally important, if not more so, will be the extent to which Russia maintains a distinction between economic interests (oil, gas and fish) and military-security-related interests in the Barents Sea. This will depend on how notions about the "security" of the country have changed in terms of: (i) Russian threat perceptions, (ii) the national interest, and (iii) the means of guaranteeing national security. While the Barents is not mentioned specifically in the "new" Russian military doctrine, military-threat perceptions are still important even if they are no longer solely associated with the West (see Mironov 1994). Some experts within Russian military circles even maintain the possibility of long-term rivalry with the United States, thus indicating that the Russian Barents region, together with the area of operation of the Northern Fleet, will continue to have military-strategic significance (Jonson 1994: 175). This is not to deny the existence of a broader view of the question of national security in today's Russia but to suggest that traditional notions of security continue to impose serious constraints on cooperation and conflict resolution. The long passage to international cooperation in the Euro-Arctic region has just begun.

Dispute over the Svalbard shelf

The key question here is whether the provisions of the Svalbard Treaty of 1920 extend to Svalbard's EEZ and continental shelf or whether some other arrangements are needed to establish resource jurisdiction beyond the territorial sea (Glassner 1990: 97). In other words, can the Treaty be used as a basis for claiming a 200-mile EEZ around Svalbard and its resources? If so, by whom? Will all the signatories to the Treaty have equal rights to these resources? The Norwegian position is that Svalbard does not have its own continental shelf – it rests on a shelf stretching northwards from mainland Norway, and the natural resources outside the 4-mile territorial waters of Svalbard therefore belong to Norway (Østreng 1982b: 80–1). According to Norway, the restrictions on sovereignty imposed by the Svalbard Treaty apply only to the areas explicitly mentioned in the Treaty and cannot be extended.

The Soviet Union/Russia has strongly disagreed, asserting the existence of a Svalbard shelf of unspecified size and arguing that the "equal access" provisions of the Svalbard Treaty and the Mining Code for Svalbard are equally applicable in this area. While Norway continues to maintain that the Treaty's provisions for a non-discriminatory resources regime referred only to the islands and territorial waters of the archipelago (Traavik and Østreng 1977: 362), Moscow has rejected this interpretation of the geographical coverage of the Treaty. Most major Western powers reserve their final judgement and their rights under the Svalbard Treaty.

The uncertain legal situation in the Barents Sea will become even more tangled if the Norwegian government decides at some stage to establish an EEZ around Svalbard. So far this has not happened, perhaps because, despite some oil prospecting on Svalbard itself, no significant oil exploration has occurred offshore, and the presence of extensive energy resources has yet to be established. At the same time, the dispute has prevented the commencement of oil drilling on Svalbard's continental shelf, to the benefit of the local ecology. It would certainly be to the advantage of Norway to seek a diplomatic solution whereby its sovereignty over the EEZ and the continental shelf is acknowledged unconditionally. This would allow Norway greater access to the resources of the area, apart from making it easier for Norway to prescribe and enforce regulations.

At the same time, "there are potentially some fairly strong economic reasons for the other parties to the treaty could be expected to dispute the Norwegian view" (Ibid.: 364). If major reserves of oil, for example, are found around Svalbard, and if the shelf happens to be within the Svalbard Treaty area, countries like Germany, France, Italy, the United Kingdom and the United States, among others, will have secured participation in the exploration and exploitation of the resources. The idea of securing access to Svalbard oil under the non-discriminatory, indeed extremely favourable, conditions of the Treaty and the Svalbard Mining Code must have become more appealing to the oil-starved industrialized countries of the West after the Gulf crisis. Consequently, it is very likely that most Western governments will continue to "reserve" their views on the Norwegian position, which is probably an indication that they would much rather wait and see. Moscow, however, has explicitly rejected the Norwegian claim. Why should the Soviet Union, later Russia, give such high priority to the resource potential of Svalbard when it has abundant oil and gas reserves in other parts of the Arctic? Would it not make better sense for Moscow to support the Norwegian position and thereby deny the Western oil companies access to an area that continues to be militarily important? Or could it be that Russia, like the Soviet Union, is using the Svalbard issue to make its position on the delimitation dispute more acceptable to Norway?

Supposing the Norwegian position on Svalbard is accepted by Russia in exchange for recognizing a dividing line in the Barents Sea "closely approximate to the sector line", how much does it gain or lose? The difficulty for Norway is that recognition of the dividing line would compromise its long-standing position on the delimitation issue, and Russian support on its own does not guarantee that other signatories to the Svalbard Treaty will also support the Norwegian stand. Probably this explains to some extent why Norway has traditionally favoured treating the various disputes in the North as separate issues.

It could be, and has been, argued that there are good reasons for other states to support the Norwegian position that "the treaty does not apply" and thereby prevent rivalry over the Svalbard shelf (Churchill and Ulfstein 1992: 151). In this case none of the parties, including Russia, would have any legal basis for claiming a presence on the shelf. Russia's fear may well be that whereas the Western oil companies, or rather their Norwegian subsidiaries, will probably be licensed by Norway to operate on the Svalbard shelf, the same opportunity may be denied to Russian companies. Russia may also be concerned, as the Soviet Union was, to keep Western oil-rig density low in an important transit area for her nuclear submarines.

On the other hand, it could be argued equally forcefully that if the Treaty does apply, it does not follow that the outcome would inevitably be discord. It should be possible to establish a moratorium until a more orderly system of exploitation has been developed. This could be done by revising the Mining Code or by negotiating a new arrangement broadly along the lines of CRAMRA, with stringent environmental provisions on the one hand and acknowledging Norway's special status on the other. The latter would probably be the only, even if not the ideal, option if there is a sudden eruption of serious international interest in Svalbard on account of a major oil discovery, and Norwegian efforts to win the others over to its side fail. Some scholars (Ibid.: 153) do not recommend such an alternative, fearing that "the outcome of such a conference would, however, be unpredictable and it would probably be more likely to produce uncertainty than an improved Treaty". The CCAMLR experience so far has also shown how difficult it is to implement conservation measures in situations of disputed sovereignty. Agreement and consensus is a far better option, if it can be realized, than agreeing to disagree.

It is worth bearing in mind, however, that (whatever may happen in the future) the Svalbard Treaty as it stands will not be enough to deal with large-scale mining activities. It is here that the key feature of the ATS as a dispute manager, often overlooked while exploring its relevance for the Arctic, stands out: conflict anticipation or pre-emptive strategy (Stokke 1991: 362). At the same time, "if no viable resources exist in this area, the problem of jurisdiction need not arise and a preemptive strategy may even be counterproductive in triggering an unnecessary conflict" (Ibid.: 363). It is to be hoped that before the Svalbard issue becomes too complex and induces conflict, solutions will be in place. From Norway's point of view, the time is right to try to settle the Svalbard issue now.

At issue in Svalbard is not just the Norwegian position, or the reservations expressed by the other parties but also the conservation demands of the fisheries and the integrity of local ecosystems. While there does not appear to be an immediate crisis over fisheries management in the 200-mile zone around Svalbard, the situation is far from satisfactory (Ibid.). Accordingly it has been suggested that for this particular reason "Norway should accept the application of the Svalbard Treaty and commence full enforcement of its regulations, including the arrest of fishing vessels which violate regulations in the zone" (Ibid.: 151).

In more than one way the Svalbard issue resembles the Antarctic situation. Does the legal freezing of the territorial dispute on Antarctica under Article V of the Antarctic Treaty apply to the maritime areas? In other words, can the claimant states, including of course Norway, argue – as Norway has done in the case of Svalbard – that the mandate of the Antarctic Treaty is limited only to the areas mentioned in its provisions?

The Canadian–US Northwest Passage dispute

The origins of the dispute between two friendly neighbours over the Northwest Passage lie in a curious mix of geohistorical, geopolitical and legal factors (Larsen 1989: 177–84; Franckx 1993: 75–107; Rothwell 1993). As a shipping route, the Northwest Passage is a series of connected straits, but not all of them are navigable, due to heavy ice conditions and shallow draught. This handful of viable combinations of straits and channels allows shipping to pass from the North Atlantic Ocean up the Davis Strait between Canada and Greenland, through the Arctic Archipelago to the Beaufort Sea, and then to the Chukchi Sea and the Bering Strait into the North Pacific.

In Canada's view the waters of the Northwest Passage are its internal "historic waters", especially since the declaration of baselines around the edges of the Canadian Arctic Archipelago in 1986. Accordingly, the passage does not qualify as an international strait for the purposes of navigation or otherwise. Since coastal states have complete sovereignty over their internal waters, Canada is said to be fully justified in regulating or prohibiting the passage of international vessels in the Northwest Passage for safety or environmental reasons.

As noted in Chapter 3, the first positive evidence of a Canadian claim to the islands of the so-called "Arctic Archipelago" and the waters which lie immediately north of continental Canada came in 1909 with the assertion of the sector principle by Senator Poirier. Ever since, Canada has sought to assert its claim in various ways, the most recent geopolitical–legal expression of which has been the Nunavut Land Claims Agreement.

The United States has consistently challenged the Canadian claims and the related legal–political assertions *not* by staking a rival claim to the Arctic Archipelago but by claiming that the waters of the Northwest Passage are part of an "international strait" through which there is freedom of navigation. As a maritime power, it has been the policy of the United States to maintain that international straits (some of which are perceived to be critical "choke-points") must remain open for maritime commerce and naval use. In the case of the Northwest Passage, US concern has been further enhanced by technological advances over the past three decades that have substantially improved the prospects of using the Passage as a commercial shipping route from Alaska to the east coast of the United States.

The first major events to trigger strong Canadian reaction were the voyages of the American tanker *Manhattan* in 1967 and 1970. Franckx (1993: 76) points out: "If the challenges to the Canadian sovereignty over the Arctic had until then mainly been territorial in nature, the voyage of the Manhattan had definitively relocated the crux of the problem to the maritime aspects of the matter." According to Rothwell (1993), despite Canada's best efforts throughout the 1970s and 1980s to assert more actively sovereignty and jurisdiction over the waters of the Archipelago and surrounding islands, the legal validity of these claims remains uncertain in many ways. On the other hand, persistent rejection by the United States of absolute Canadian sovereignty over the Northwest Passage has made this dispute "one of the most significant bilateral legal issues in the Canadian–United States relationship" (Ibid.: 332).

What, then, are the prospects for resolving this dispute? Rothwell has cogently argued (Ibid.: 368) that the dispute "appears to be ready-made for the application of an Article IV Antarctic Treaty-type solution". A "Northwest Passage Treaty" might allow the sovereignty issue to be "resolved" in favour of the existing sovereign, Canada, while permitting international navigation in the Passage that does not affect the status of that sovereign. The treaty would: (i) allow Canada's pre-existing sovereignty claim over the waters of the Passage to remain intact; (ii) disallow any activities of the United States or its nationals, taking place for the duration of the Treaty, to affect the status of Canada's pre-existing, present or future sovereignty over the Passage; (iii) allow both the parties to maintain previously held views on the validity of each other's differing claims; and (iv) allow the United States and its flagged vessels to "use the waters of the Northwest Passage without permission from Canada, thereby overcoming any impression that the United States acknowledges the Canadian claim" (Ibid.: 369). The only limitation on United States vessels, under the proposed treaty, would be an obligation to respect Canadian laws and regulations dealing with transit passage as recognized by the UNCLOS.

The proposed solution has substantial merit, but a number of issues require further consideration. To state the most obvious first, Article IV of the Antarctic Treaty has at best "shelved", not "resolved", the first-order problem of territorial sovereignty in Antarctica. The calculated ambiguity of this "solution" has also revealed its inherent negative side-effects over the past three decades. Although the apparently robust principle of "agreeing to disagree" has so far been instrumental in maintaining the geopolitical equilibrium established by the ATS, in reality it has proved to be extremely fragile and vulnerable to diverse interpretations, as demonstrated by the events leading to the rise and fall of the minerals convention (see Chapter 5).

In the case of the Northwest Passage, both the parties first have to be convinced that the cost of maintaining the status quo, in both the short and the long term, is going to be far less than the current impasse created by the dispute. From Canada's point of view, this may not necessarily be so. An Article IV type of solution would not resolve the dispute in Canada's favour. On the contrary, Canada might feel that it was the United States that was going to benefit far more by way of shelving the dispute on the one hand and obtaining access to the Northwest Passage on the other. The success of an Article IV type of solution depends to a large extent on the perception, common to all the parties to the dispute, that the cost–benefit ratio is more or less equally shared. Once they recognize that for Canada the Arctic Archipelago and the fabled Northwest Passage are "also a significant part of the Canadian national psyche" (Ibid.: 331), it is arguable whether the proposed solution would receive the necessary official and public support.

It might well be that Canada would respond more favourably to a solution that recognizes its sovereignty but subject to certain conditions. That is to say, the Svalbard type of solution might be more acceptable to Canada. One of the major conditions of Canadian sovereignty would be more or less the same as stated under (iv) above. Either way, the solutions proposed by Rothwell and this author can only be "types", for the simple reason that the issues at stake, as perceived by the parties to the dispute(s), vary considerably from case to case. Both authors, however, emphasize the need for innovative and unconventional approaches to the solution of pending boundary disputes in the Arctic which will depend for their success on the political will of both the United States and Canada.

Summary and conclusions

In the post-Cold War Arctic there are obvious indicators of change in favour of the themes and thrust of new thinking (Chapter 1), both *below* and *beyond* the nation-state level. Nevertheless, it is probably true that old habits and attitudes die hard. Given the resilience of the nation-state system, it is quite likely that whereas state-centred geopolitics in practice will continue to respond reactively to various demands arising from environmental change and the increasingly felt need for comprehensive security, traditional methods and tactics will be employed in pursuit of so-called "national interests" as far as possible. The transition from the old geopolitics to the new geopolitics in the Arctic may not be as smooth as one would wish.

Most of the initiatives discussed in this chapter have yet to go beyond declarations and pledges, giving some cause for scepticism on account of the continuing reluctance of the Arctic-rim states to accept conditions on their sovereignty and opposition from what Stokke (1992: 10) calls "the ideological hegemony of economic and security concerns" in the Arctic. Scepticism, however, ought to be tempered with the realization that the Cold War had not even ended a decade ago, and it is perhaps unrealistic to expect instant replacement of "confrontation with co-operation and dialogue, enemy images with partner images, the arms race with arms control and disarmament, divided security with shared security" (Østreng 1992b: 13).

As O'Tuathail and Agnew (1992: 190–204) point out: "The Cold War as a discourse may have lost its credibility and meaning as a consequence of the events of 1989 but it is clear from the Gulf crisis that intellectuals of statecraft in the West at least, and the military-industrial complex behind them, will try to create a new set of enemies."

While policy-makers in the Circumpolar North will have to put up, for the time being, with the nagging uncertainty of geopolitical transition in and around the Arctic, especially in Russia, they cannot afford to miss the opportunities now at hand for bilateral as well as multilateral cooperation. They should also bear in mind that civil society in Russia is facing a traumatic transition and is in need of understanding and support. The mass media too have a significant role to play in the creation and projection of images of peace and friendship. Such positive images are among the most effective tools in the hands of a civil society struggling to overcome undesirable elements in its past and to lay the foundations of comprehensive security for its present and future generations. The Arctic can ill afford to be subjected to yet another geopolitical discourse of domination, fragmentation and militarization.

Suggested reading

Griffiths, F. (ed.) 1992. *Arctic Alternatives: Civility or Militarism in the Circumpolar North*. Toronto: Science for Peace/Samuel Stevens.

Osherenko, G. and O.R. Young 1989. *The Age of the Arctic: Hot Conflicts and Cold Realities*. Cambridge: Cambridge University Press.

Stokke, O.S. and O. Tunander, (eds) 1994. *The Barents Region: Cooperation in Arctic Europe*. London: Sage Publications.

8

Conservation and management of the environment in the Antarctic

As Antarctic activities multiply, their ecologically sustainable development and management require a more advanced, comprehensive and forward-looking perspective. Political success in *governance*, although a vital pre-requisite, does not necessarily guarantee that the ATS is going to be equally successful in *managing* increasingly diverse, in some cases even conflicting, uses of Antarctica. For the first time, the provisions of the Protocol on Environmental Protection are *mandatory* rather than *hortatory*, regulating the impact of tourist and scientific activities on the environment. Enforcement, however, is to be in the hands of the national governments of the countries from which these human activities originate. Can the Protocol cover all activities adequately? What new issues and problems are likely to arise in future decades such that a new Convention or the equivalent should be considered now? Is tourism such an issue? What about other components of the ATS, i.e. the Agreed Measures, CCAMLR and the Seals Convention? How efficiently and effectively have they performed?

In the light of the Protocol and the prohibition it has imposed on all mineral activities for at least 55 years, attention is now sharply focused on the *here* and *now* in matters Antarctic. Does the Treaty need a Secretariat, if only to handle the flow of information between member states and the planning and recording of ATCMs? For scientific activities the SCAR Secretariat performs the appropriate role, but the activities of the ATS go way beyond collaborative research. Where should it be situated? What more is needed?

The major objective of this chapter is fourfold. First, to assess in some detail the strengths as well as limitations of the Protocol; secondly, to point out the changing nature and directions of Antarctic science; thirdly, to discuss the management needs of the fast-growing tourist industry in the

Antarctic from the angle of ecotourism; finally, to take note of progress made so far towards establishing a permanent Antarctic Secretariat and to undertake a brief "environmental audit" of the Agreed Measures, CCAMLR and the Seals Convention, all of which fall outside the scope of the Protocol.

The Protocol on Environmental Protection: breaking new ground

The Protocol designates Antarctica as a "natural reserve devoted to peace and science" (Article 1) and commits its present and future signatories to total protection of the Antarctic environment – its intrinsic and extrinsic worth, including its wilderness, its aesthetic value and its value as an area for scientific research, especially research essential to understanding the global environment (text in *Handbook* 1994; Bush 1992: 1–77). The text of the Protocol can also be found in some recent books (Verhoeven *et al.* 1992; Watts 1992; Elliott 1994), together with a discussion of its various legal and political aspects.

The Protocol sets out some basic environmental principles by which to regulate all human activity in Antarctica. It supplements the Antarctic Treaty, does not derogate rights and obligations enjoined by other instruments in force in the ATS and calls upon its Parties to consult and co-operate with the contracting Parties to other international instruments in force within the ATS and their respective institutions (Article 5).

Article 6 calls upon the ATCPs (i) to promote cooperative programmes of scientific, technical and educational value; (ii) to provide appropriate assistance to other parties in the preparation of EIAs and information relevant to any potential environmental risk; (iii) to provide help for mitigating the effects of accidents which may damage the Antarctic environment; (iv) to consult other parties in choosing sites for prospective stations and other facilities so as to avoid the cumulative impact of their excessive concentration in any single location; and (v) wherever possible to undertake joint expeditions and share the use of stations and other facilities.

The Protocol categorically prohibits any activity relating to mineral resources, "other than scientific research" (Article 7), but its full implications become clear only when read in conjunction with the provisions dealing with modification or amendment (Article 25). According to the latter, if, after the expiry of 50 years from the date of entry into force of the Protocol, any of the ATCPs so requests, a conference shall be held to review the operation of this Protocol. If a modification or amendment is proposed, it can only be adopted by a majority comprising 75% of the states that were ATCPs at the time of the adoption of the Protocol. Furthermore, modification or amendment shall enter into force only upon ratification by 75% of the ATCPs, including the ratification of all the 26 states that were ATCPs at the time of the adoption of the Protocol.

All this is well in the future, but the present position with regard to the unequivocal, unambiguous Article 7 of the Protocol emphasizes the consensus among the ATCPs that the prohibition on Antarctic mineral-resource activities contained therein shall continue unless there is in force a binding legal regime on Antarctic mineral-resource activities. Such a regime would also include an agreed means for determining the conditions under which mineral activities will be acceptable and shall fully safeguard the interests of all states referred to in Article IV of the Antarctic Treaty. If a modification or amendment to Article 7 of the Protocol is proposed at a Review Conference, it shall include such a binding legal regime. If, however, any such modification or amendment has not entered into force within three years of the date of its communication to all Parties, any Party may at any time thereafter give notice to the Depositary of its withdrawal from this Protocol, and such withdrawal shall take effect two years after receipt of the notice by the Depositary.

Article 8 of the Protocol, headed "Environmental Impact Assessment", deals with what is perhaps one of the most crucial, complex and challenging areas: prior assessment of the likely impact of any activity in the entire Antarctic Treaty area which may be adjudged to have: (a) less than a minor or transitory impact, (b) a minor or transitory impact, or (c) more than a minor or transitory impact (Francioni 1993: 62–5). This Article, however, needs to be considered in conjunction with the provisions of Annex I, integral to the Protocol, in order to understand the full extent of the Article's scope and spirit.

Annex I divides EIA procedures into three categories: (1) a Preliminary Stage, at which the environmental impact of a proposed activity can be considered at national level according to established procedures before commencement of that activity. If it is determined as having less than a minor or transitory impact, it may take place, subject to monitoring and verification; (2) Initial Environmental Evaluation, which will assess in sufficient detail whether the proposed activity is likely to have more than a minor or transitory impact – there will, accordingly, be a full description, including its purpose, location, duration and intensity, together with a consideration of alternatives to the proposed activity; and (3) Comprehensive Environmental Evaluation, which will come into operation if an initial environmental evaluation shows, or if it is otherwise determined, that a proposed activity is likely to have more than a minor or transitory impact. The proposed activity will not proceed unless a draft Comprehensive Environmental Evaluation has been considered and approved by the ATCM on the advice of the Committee for Environmental Protection (CEP).

The CEP, comprising all signatories to the Protocol, is a new institution of immense value and considerable competence established by the Protocol, *vide* Article 11. The functions of the Committee (Article 12) include offering advice to the ATCPs on the effectiveness of measures taken pursuant to the Protocol, the application and implementation of EIA procedures to mitigate the environmental impact of approved or proposed activities, the operation and further elaboration of the Antarctic Protected Area System and the state of the Antarctic environment, etc. The ATCMs, drawing upon the best scientific and technical advice available, will define, in accordance with the provisions of this Protocol, the general policy for the comprehensive protection of the Antarctic environment and adopt measures under Article IX of the Antarctic Treaty for the implementation of this Protocol.

The Protocol establishes binding and compulsory dispute-settlement procedures with respect to the prohibition on mineral activity, environmental impact assessment, emergency response action, the Annexes (unless they provide otherwise) and compliance with those particular provisions. Any Party, including a non-ATCP, can raise the issue of a violation of the Protocol under these procedures.

The Protocol is incomplete without its five Annexes (text in Bush 1992: 83–128; *Handbook* 1994: 2018–261), which improve upon existing measures for environmental protection. The first, on "Environmental Impact Assessment", has already been noted. The second, on "Conservation of Antarctic Fauna and Flora", updates the Agreed Measures, although the provisions on SPAs have been removed from the latter and incorporated into an Annex (later adopted at the XVIth ATCM in Bonn in October 1991; Ibid.: 2045–59) on "Area Protection and Management". However, permits for taking native fauna and flora are still to be issued by national authorities, but on stringent conditions and on quite a limited scale. The third, on "Waste Disposal and Waste Management" (which is also to apply to non-governmental activities), strengthens existing management provisions and adds to the list of materials which must be removed from the Antarctic. The fourth, on "Prevention of Marine Pollution", sets out much more specific details than the recommendations adopted to this effect at the Ninth ATCM and includes details of prohibited practices. Some of its provisions have been inspired by – if not actually derived from – the international Convention for the Prevention of Pollution from Ships, 1973, as amended by the Protocol of 1978, and called MARPOL 73/78.

An assessment of the Protocol

Organically linked to the Antarctic Treaty and other components of the ATS, the Protocol in no way alters the "special legal and political status of Antarctica". Still, it does break new ground. An immediate question that springs to mind is whether the present ATS has the capacity to monitor key environmental parameters and ecosystem components in order to be able to detect and issue early warning of any unauthorized adverse activity. At the same time, are effective, environmentally safe and technologically foolproof procedures available to tackle the tasks? Or must the method of trial and error be the only tool at our disposal? In that event, can the risk be taken and by whom? In addition, there are questions arising from the goals set by the Protocol, particularly about the objective of realizing environmental principles through EIAs (see Lyons 1993). Article 3(2) of the Protocol states that:

> activities in the Antarctic Treaty area shall be planned and conducted on the basis of information sufficient to allow prior assessments of, and informed judgements about, their possible impacts on the Antarctic environment and dependent and associated ecosystems and on the value of Antarctica for the conduct of scientific research . . .

How much is sufficient information and who can provide it? (Ibid.: 116–17). What are the key environmental parameters, and how are they to be defined? Or, for that matter, how are the adverse effects of a particular activity defined, detected and identified according to the blanket categories of "minor or transitory impact" or "less or more than a transitory impact"? How does one ensure that "appropriate national procedures", in accordance with which the different stages in the EIA are to be carried out, are otherwise appropriate as well? This is further complicated by the fact, as Lyons (Ibid.: 117) puts it, that "the preparation and circulation of an Environmental impact assessment is partly a public relations exercise, that is, to reduce political risk rather than to reduce environmental risk". Given the complexity, in places even ambiguity, in such crucial areas, how does one mitigate conflict potential among the ATCPs in this context? One can foresee, of course, the desirability of a more active role for organizations like SCAR in reconciling differences caused by diverse perceptions of, for instance, what constitutes a significant impact on the Antarctic environment.

One obvious flaw, certainly in comparison with the decision-making process in CRAMRA, is that the activity can be continued while the Comprehensive Environmental Evaluation procedure is still incomplete. Therefore, "the first thing that should be added to the Protocol is a provision that the start of the activity has to be postponed until a decision about a CEE is taken" (Bennekom 1992: 46).

The Protocol embraces some of the features of CRAMRA and applies them to all human activities in the Treaty area "which take place on the continent of Antarctica and all Antarctic islands, including all ice shelves, south of 60° south latitude and in the seabed and subsoil of adjacent offshore areas up to the deep seabed", as was the case under CRAMRA. As noted earlier, the waiver of the prohibition on mineral-resource activities in Antarctica has been made dependent upon the fact that a binding legal regime on Antarctic mineral-resource activities be in force, including an agreed means for determining whether (and if so, under what conditions) any such activity is acceptable. CRAMRA may be dead as a document, but it is alive in spirit. Hence, each ATCP with this status when the

Protocol is signed has in effect a double veto with which to block any mineral-resource activity even beyond the 50-year period, by failing to ratify the instrument on the regulation of mineral-resource activities (Wolfrum 1991: 88–9, 93).

The Protocol does not clearly say who is actually responsible for planning human activity in Antarctica. It relies upon its state parties to address questions of monitoring and compliance; they must take "appropriate measures within [their] competence" to ensure compliance with the provisions of the Protocol. Each Party is obliged to ensure that the prescribed EIA procedures are employed when planning scientific research and other government operations, tourism, the associated logistic support, etc., in the Treaty area. The actual wording of the relevant provisions seems to suggest that scientific research is a governmental operation that excludes private research activity, but all research projects may not qualify as "governmental" under the national laws of some Contracting Parties.

Each Party must take measures to ensure compliance with the Protocol and the principles governing it. Like CCAMLR and CRAMRA, the formulation of the provision here adopts a bifocal approach. The key question is whether the Party's competence to ensure compliance with the Protocol is to arise from – or be judged in terms of – its recognized or claimed territorial jurisdiction or from both. The Protocol does not rely upon the exclusive mechanisms of a sponsoring state. As a result, both forms of jurisdiction may be invoked in the matter of conducting activities in the Treaty area, but the power to control activity in Antarctica will rest with the state as it is recognized internationally. Apparently even the Protocol has not been able to escape the shadow of the unresolved question of jurisdiction.

This lacuna quite clearly has considerable potential for causing conflict. In contrast to CCAMLR, or even CRAMRA, which covered specified activity, the Protocol covers *all* human activities. Moreover, in another deviation, the system of a sponsoring state, which was identified as the state primarily responsible for activity in the Treaty area, has been abandoned. The resulting disputes can now only be resolved by consultations among the ATCPs themselves, or by a mutually agreed formal means of settling disputes, since these are not covered by the mandatory dispute-settlement procedures in Article 19 of the Protocol. The jurisdiction in the case of marine pollution, on the other hand, is clearly defined: responsibility for lapses or violations falls upon the flag state or the port state.

The system of inspection laid down in the Protocol also leaves much to be desired. Inspections are to be conducted under the terms of the Antarctic Treaty, on an individual and collective basis. Generally following the CRAMRA approach, Article 14 of the Protocol sets up a two-tier system of inspection. Observers may be nominated either by the ATCPs – as under Article VII of the Antarctic Treaty – or by the ATCMs. The procedure in the latter case still needs to be worked out. As a result, at present only the inspection procedures of the Treaty's Article VII, following the rule of consensus in nominating observers, are applicable.

The Protocol lacks details in respect of responsibility and liability too; these, ultimately, are the two means to enforce whatever rules there are for the protection of the Antarctic environment (Francioni 1993: 71). Article 16 in the Protocol contains much that needs to be elaborated. During the Venice ATCM, a Group of Experts was created, under the chairmanship of Germany, to work out the details of the proposed liability Annex. The task of elaborating a "satisfying" liability regulation was then assigned to Professor Rüdiger Wolfrum, Director of the Max Planck Institute for Comparative Public Law and International Law in Heidelberg. The deliberations (see ATCM 1994b: 1–6; ATCM 1995b) so far have revealed the complex nature of the liability question, especially in respect of the following: (1) Which damages are to be covered by the future liability regime? (2) Is it appropriate to provide uniform liability regimes for different activities or should each activity be dealt with separately? (3) How is the notion of "damage", as used in Article 16 of the Protocol, to be defined? (4) What is the appropriate standard of liability? Do different activities or different damages require different standards? (5) What are the appropriate means of calculating the amount of compensation, given that the major objective of the liability regime is to strengthen the protection of the Antarctic environment? (6) Who is the proper plaintiff in the case of damage to the Antarctic environment, and who will pay compensation after the reimbursement of restoration costs? (7) Who is the appropriate debtor in the case of the environmental damage? (8) What are the appropriate institutions to decide upon claims for compensation?

Most problematic, however, appears to be the notion of damage (see ATCM 1995b: 3–4). The majority of ATPs appear to be of the view that minor or transitory impacts on the Antarctic environment, whether assessed or accepted, should not be regarded as damage. As Wolfrum (1991: 12) himself admits, "the question of damage cannot be properly dealt with without relevant advice from scientists having a profound knowledge of the parameters of the Antarctic environments".

Assuming that scientific advice on the Antarctic environment becomes available somehow, together with consensus on damage, liability and the relevance of state liability in this whole system, the difficult issue of compensation remains. How do we calculate compensation? Who is to undertake the removal action or the restoration, if any? And, most complex of all, how do we define irreparable damage? Most ATCPs seem to be in favour of calculating compensation in accordance with the costs of removal. However, damage may be irreparable for physical reasons, for technical reasons and perhaps even for economic reasons. There is no precedent in international law to guide the ATPs on this subject.

All attempts to create an institution with effective law-making or enforcement powers under the Protocol seem to have been thwarted by the claimant states perceiving a threat to their declared sovereignty in Antarctica. As a result, the CEP has been assigned certain advisory functions *vis-à-vis* the ATCMs – the latter retaining final responsibility and powers in respect of the environmental protection of the Antarctic.

The geographical–jurisdictional boundaries of the Protocol are similar to those of the Antarctic Treaty, i.e. south of 60°S latitude, short of the Antarctic Convergence, that happens to be the northern limit of CCAMLR and forms part of the Antarctic marine ecosystem. Given the objectives of the Protocol and the fact that the problems of marine pollution are as serious, if not more serious, than the pollution caused by human activity on the continent, and are likely to increase with growing commercial fishing, it is difficult to see the reason for not extending the jurisdiction of the Protocol to the Antarctic Convergence.

Thus the Protocol, in spite of its substantial promise, remains inadequate and incomplete in many ways. It also suffers from a host of handicaps and hazards caused by the sovereignty-related realities of the ATS. At the same time, the value conflict – to borrow the terminology coined by Willy Østreng – between the demand for a permanent, total ban on mining the Antarctic and the support for a minerals regime with stringent environmental safeguards – is *shelved*, not *resolved*, by the Protocol. This reality, further complicated by the complexity of some of the provisions of the Protocol, is likely to become the soft underbelly of the ATS in years to come. Nevertheless, there is little doubt that the Protocol has introduced a new environmental ethic into both science and politics in the Antarctic. As Elliott (1992: 287) puts it, in a recent study on this subject: "Political interests still dominate (although the initial defection showed that the collective political values could be questioned), but the acceptance of an overarching instrument, imposing 'top-down' principles and rules, signals that environmental interests are no longer subordinate."

Undoubtedly, the Protocol constitutes the most important normative and institutional innovation in the history of the ATS. Yet fear has been expressed that this "innovation may become a victim of its own success", for at least two reasons (Francioni 1993: 72). First, a moratorium on mining could paradoxically exercise a negative influence on the scale and intensity of scientific commitment because of the diminished incentive to invest in a normative framework that no longer allows the prospect of future remuneration in terms of mineral resources. After all, it was no coincidence that there was a quite dramatic increase in Antarctic programmes during the 1980s, the decade dominated by the minerals issue. Secondly, the transformed post-Cold War geopolitical realities which accompanied the collapse of the Soviet empire renewed world-wide emphasis on domestic economic reform under the pressure of an emerging global market economy, and the regional and global alignments at political and economic levels may push the Antarctic further down on the priority list of most countries if the continent "loses its stature as an arena for the geopolitical rivalries of the major powers" (Ibid.: 72).

The "Green" critique of the Protocol

At the Bonn ATCM, ASOC submitted its critique of the Protocol (ATCM 1991b). The document praised the Protocol as "a giant step toward a comprehensive approach to environmental protection in Antarctica" but regretted at the same time that the environmental principles it established had been "watered down due to undefined terms and weak language" like "limit", "significant adverse effect", "detrimental changes", "substantial risk", etc. The most objectionable clause in the Protocol, according to ASOC, is the one that allows a Party to withdraw from the Protocol if a modification or amendment has not entered into force within three years of its adoption. Should a Party opt to withdraw, it will no longer be bound by the environmental rules of the Protocol, including those that prohibit mining in the Antarctic. ASOC has also demanded that "the deep seabed, as defined in the 1982 UN Law of the Sea Convention, should be specifically included within the terms of the mining ban" (ATCM 1995c: 3), and the domestic legislation should not limit the minerals ban to any particular period of time (Ibid.).

At the Bonn meeting, ASOC circulated another document, entitled "Initial Environmental Evaluation", about the removal of its World Park Base at Cape Evans, Ross Island (ATCM 1991c: 1–3). It outlined the objectives of the Greenpeace Antarctic Expedition Programme as follows (Ibid.): (i) draw the attention of the public, media and Antarctic decision-makers to present and future threats to Antarctic wildlife and wilderness, including possible commercial minerals activities in the Antarctic (in the light of the new Protocol, in the long term), overfishing, non-compliance with environmental regulations and other environmentally detrimental human activities; (ii) promote the "World Park" option for Antarctica; (iii) investigate, monitor and document disturbance of the Antarctic environment by human activities and establish scientific data on environmental impacts; and (iv) monitor compliance with existing environmental regulations at scientific bases in the area south of the Antarctic Convergence.

The objectives of the Greenpeace Antarctic Expedition Programme, for which no time limit is suggested, underline Greenpeace's resolve not only to sustain but, in fact, to increase its inspection activities in order to monitor the implementation of the Environmental Protocol and CCAMLR.

It is obvious (see ATCM 1994a: 216–17; ATCM 1995c) that hopes expressed in some quarters that the successful conclusion of the Protocol would placate the fears of the environmentalists, and reduce the aggressiveness of their campaigns, are likely to be belied. This raises the possibility of dispute over the inspection provisions set up under the Protocol and the "monitoring" carried out by Greenpeace "watchdogs". How are the ATCPs going to respond? What will be the impact of the presence and activities of these NGOs on the viability of the ATS?

In the context of interaction between states and NGOs in the Antarctic, it is useful to bear in mind that for many years after the Antarctic Treaty came into force in 1961, SCAR, despite the quasi-governmental aspects of its membership, was not only the sole NGO of significance, it served as a central organ of the ATS, capable of mobilizing considerable resources to achieve cooperative scientific objectives. In recent years, however, against the backdrop of the Antarctic resource diplomacy of the 1970s, many more NGOs have become active in the Antarctic arena (see Kimball 1988a). Most notable are IUCN and ASOC, followed by Greenpeace, Friends of the Earth, the World Wildlife Fund (WWF) and a few other environmentally oriented groups.

Nation-states continue to be *the* guardians of the ATS (Herr and Davis 1992: 15). Even though the exercise of territorial sovereignty has been quite problematic for the nation-states in Antarctica, the experience of Antarctic NGOs so far has shown how thoroughly the sovereignty discourse has governed the behaviour of the ATPs. The "freezing" of sovereignty in Antarctica under Article IV of the Treaty might have been expected to offer fertile ground for experimentation with non-state instruments such as NGOs. In reality this has not happened. For example, whereas ASOC has been accorded observer status in the ATS, probably in the hope that the presence of this "umbrella organization" might contribute positively to the image of the ATS as an open and adaptable system, Greenpeace, a constituent member of ASOC, has been excluded. Perhaps the active assertion by Greenpeace of its ethos as a direct-action NGO in the Antarctic, especially at a time when the ATCPs were negotiating a minerals regime, and later its alliance with the "critical lobby" in the UN, made its acceptance as a "legitimate player" in the ATS a difficult prospect.

The supremacy and resilience of the state actors within the ATS is thus hard to ignore. At the same time, political pressures exerted in recent years on the member governments, individually and collectively, to acknowledge and cooperate with a range of NGOs is beginning to produce results. The success of the NGOs in opposing CRAMRA, and in forcing some of the ATPs to reverse their position on this issue, has contributed significantly towards making the ATS more tolerant of the presence of the NGOs on the Antarctic geopolitical scene. However, the cooption of some of the NGOs could be made possible only by changing the core values of the Antarctic Treaty itself and by introducing a new environmental ethic into Antarctic geopolitics. Whether these changes would eventually lead to more dramatic institutional change in the ATS, so that some of the NGOs would be granted consultative status, is difficult to predict. What does appear certain is that Antarctic geopolitics can no longer be as state-centric as it has been in the past.

Management of Antarctic science: changing nature, priorities and directions

Antarctic science is profoundly affected by the changing geopolitical setting of the Antarctic, which itself has been transformed by the ongoing debate – both within and outside the ATS – about resource exploitation *vis-à-vis* environmental conservation, and the emergence of new actors on the Antarctic scene, including the environmentalist interest groups and tourism-related organizations. The collapse of the Soviet Union too has deeply affected the scale and intensity of Antarctic science.

Science in general has never been apolitical, and the same can be said of Antarctic science. This is not to suggest that science done in the Antarctic has not been motivated by human curiosity or what may be called the basic research considerations. The contributions of the Antarctic science community to enriching human knowledge of the inhospitable south polar region are universally acknowledged and praised. Yet it is difficult to overlook the fact that Antarctic science has often been driven by non-scientific factors, perceptions and motivations. Consequently, the basic research motives have occasionally been tempered by commercial, political and (latterly) environmental motives – so-called "external factors". To illustrate this point, we may first briefly recapitulate the various stages in the development of Antarctic science since the early period of political tensions that threatened to turn the continent of Antarctica into an arena for Cold War machinations.

The IGY (1957–8), and the drawing up of the Antarctic Treaty soon afterwards, undoubtedly instrumental in the reduction of tension, also augured a new period of relative stability with a strong focus on science. The Antarctic Treaty made the performance of "substantial scientific interest" a mandatory qualification for acquiring fully-fledged membership of the ATS. Science therefore acquired a symbolic value as political capital, a passport for entry to the ATS, as it remained without too many external pressures of a direct kind during the sedate 1960s.

If the 1970s were the decade of the "Club of Rome Report", with its alarming and pessimistic forecast of fast-depleting global resources, and the "oil crisis" that sent energy prices rocketing, the late 1980s and the early 1990s belonged to the concerns expressed in the "Brundtland Report", and "Green developments". Both were to have great influence on the nature, priorities and management of Antarctic science. When the

213

world at large seemed to be more concerned with the realities of and the speculations about resource depletion, geophysical and geological research was being generally promoted on the science agenda of many a state active in the Antarctic. The same was the case with the biological sciences, which were required to respond to the needs of states fishing in the southern seas. In today's world of instant communications and high-tech-based mass media, the geopolitical fall-out from the circulation of the "actualities" or "myths" of Antarctica as a reservoir of fabulous resources was considerable for both Antarctic science and politics.

The ATCPs were quick to negotiate and conclude resource-management treaties during the 1980s. Much more dramatic and influential were the "Green developments" in the Antarctic from the mid-1980s onwards that led to CRAMRA being set aside and the void filled by the Madrid Protocol. Some of the issues, concerns and challenges that this new development has thrown open for the Antarctic science community have already been touched upon in Chapter 2. Let us now turn to some of the most likely future challenges for Antarctic science.

According to the former Director of the British Antarctic Survey, David Drewry (1993: 39), "many new avenues for productive, innovative, frontier research will open up in Antarctic science from the persistent harnessing and adaptation of technology" such as: satellite remote sensing, automation (for example, autonomous submersibles and remote unmanned observatories), the miniaturization of electronic and mechanical systems and devices, increased supercomputing power and modelling tools. In his view, today's fashionable topics (such as global warming, ozone reduction and bio-diversity) will eventually fade from the scientific agenda after they have been translated into political action, accompanied by a range of monitoring and other routine technical and scientific activities. Their place may well be taken by the study of the coupling between presently diverse whole-earth systems. Furthermore (Ibid.: 39–40),

> . . . such research may become focused increasingly upon the provision of new food resources to meet the demands of world population in exponential growth. The Antarctic region will not remain untouched by such circumstances and indeed may be central to many . . . *In the first few decades of the twenty-first century I predict that there will be considerable harvesting activity in the Southern Ocean, which will require, if it is to have any chance of being sustainable, a massive extension of current ecological research, as well as firm regulatory mechanisms developed through the Commission for the Conservation of Antarctic Marine Living Resources (CCAMLR).* [emphasis supplied]

As Antarctic science steadily becomes more interdisciplinary, highly sophisticated and global in scope, unfamiliar intricacies, unwelcome tensions and difficulties in its management are likely to surface. Conducting sophisticated high-tech science today is a costly affair; its results are long term and its productivity characterized by low visibility. Only a very select class of countries can afford to indulge in it, especially when for obvious reasons budgetary allocations for Antarctic research have been further reduced. Not only aircraft and shipping, which traditionally have consumed a disproportionately high percentage of Antarctic science programme funds, but also the application of state-of-the-art satellite and computer technologies are likely to add to the cost of Antarctic infrastructure, equipment and logistics. The impact of these rising costs is multiple.

Multinational projects are likely to be affected as shrinking budgets will compel states to reserve for their own nationals the slots available. Yet conversely it might also happen that some countries will be obliged to operate their facilities at less than full capacity, opening new opportunities for participation by foreign nationals. The third adverse impact of the rising cost of Antarctic science – and it is already showing – will be on the states trying to establish their credentials and qualifications for consultative status in the ATS. The quality of both science and environment are bound to suffer as the new aspirants inevitably tend to focus more on the easily accessible coastal regions of Antarctica for setting up scientific stations. This has already led to a concentration of such stations in choice areas, which in turn diminishes scientific returns, duplicates scientific research and has adverse environmental effects arising from their cumulative impact. The situation has little prospect of being corrected or reversed unless certain immediate steps are taken both at the individual governmental level and by the ATS.

This has also led some to argue that the criterion of acquiring consultative status in the ATS needs to be reviewed (Pannatier 1994). The interpretation of "substantial scientific research activity" needs to be re-examined and imaginatively reformulated, taking into account new directions in Antarctic science that would enable a country to undertake substantial research activity, or substantially add to Antarctic scientific knowledge, through satellite programmes or ship-based activities or multinational collaborative projects, without the need to set up a base in Antarctica. Since science has ceased to be the only reason for states to express or demonstrate interest in the Antarctic – commercial fishing in Antarctic waters is already under way and the onset of tourism has been practically simultaneous – the ATCPs will have to consider, sooner rather than later, whether the science-based criterion can remain the only legitimate criterion for sharing in Antarctic decision-making.

The much-needed shift from exclusive state-centred Antarctic science to more open and flexible multinational scientific cooperation also requires the development of effective channels of communication, and much more systematic and effective exchange of information than has been the case so far, both in respect of Antarctic scientific activities in general and in relation to identifying opportunities for coordination and collaboration among various national scientific programmes and between these programmes and the relevant international organizations (Kimball 1990: 3).

The tenor of scientific collaboration in the Antarctic is likely to be set by those nations which possess major logistics capabilities (Drewry 1992, 1993). The high cost of logistics and station facilities puts them increasingly out of reach of most countries today. Increasing interest in the Antarctic may not quite match the ability of states to operate there. If countries guided by political rather than scientific objectives employ inadequate, inefficient logistics, or lack sufficient experience and capability to carry out a science programme in Antarctica, science will automatically become increasingly politicized, thereby enhancing the political role of Antarctic logistics and the political significance of coordinating logistics. It is against this background that we need to look at a new actor on the Antarctic science scene: the Council of Managers of National Antarctic Programmes (COMNAP).

Federated to SCAR and said to incorporate the functions of the former SCAR Working Group on Logistics, COMNAP addresses itself to issues related to resource allocation and sharing costs and practical "know-how" among countries. Its principal task is the support of science, which it achieves through regular exchange of information on operational matters, seeking solutions to common operational problems, reviewing major logistic requirements for international scientific programmes and by supplying coordinated responses to questions and requests for advice from various sources by creating the necessary subgroups (ATCM 1991d: 245). The close working relationship of SCAR, COMNAP and the ATS will no doubt be of considerable value to the viability of the ATS and central to the realization of the principles and objectives of the Antarctic Treaty.

The pre-eminence of science in the Antarctic, and SCAR's contribution to it over 30 years, was spelt out at the Bonn ATCM. In his opening address, the then SCAR President R.M. Laws stressed the role of SCAR in the ATS in providing advice on the development of the Agreed Measures for the Conservation of Antarctic Fauna and Flora (1964), in concluding the Convention for the Conservation of Antarctic Seals (1972) and in its responses to requests for advice on the possible range of the environmental impact of mineral exploration and exploitation in reports published in 1979 and 1985 (Ibid.: 230–1; Bush 1994a: 26–7). He regretted, however, that:

> . . . SCAR is now very much concerned at the diminution of its role in relation to the ATS and the effect this may have on freedom of scientific investigation and co-operation. Excessive regulation or direction could lead to unproductive use of scientific capacity and funds. It is ironic that, just when the value of Antarctic research to understanding global problems has begun to be recognised, the environmental impact of scientific activities in the Antarctic has begun to be questioned . . .

> Among SCAR's concerns are: its inadequate funding, which may limit the advice it can give in future; duplication of scientific effort in management; possible diversion of funds from primary science to monitoring; the influence of environ-

mental pressure groups; misconceptions about the nature of Earth science re-search in the Antarctic. (Ibid.)

SCAR was not prepared to accept that "there is a significant widespread environmental impact problem" in the Antarctic but instead would rather claim that a minute fraction of the Antarctic environment is affected by human activities originating in the region, and that the more serious impacts on the Antarctic originated in the wider world (Bush 1994a: 36).

Whereas governmental support of SCAR's activities still leaves much to be desired (ATCM 1994a: 128), there seems to have been some positive change in the relationship between SCAR and ASOC since the Bonn Meeting. For example, in Kyoto (Ibid.: 215) ASOC declared its support for Antarctic science and complimented SCAR's crucial scientific work in coordinating global-change research through its Group of Specialists on the subject. It is to be expected that cooperation between SCAR and environmental organizations will grow in a spirit of mutual understanding and accommodation.

Whereas science and science-related activities continue, by and large, to be the *raison d'être* for the ATS, the nature, context and focus of Antarctic science is changing fast. Even though science-oriented activities continue to be mandatory for acquiring and maintaining political influence within the ATS, the commercial attractions of the southern seas and the more recent lure of profits from tourism are additional reasons for national involvement(s) in the Antarctic. It is to the latter that I turn first.

Regulating "ecotourism" in the Antarctic: problems and prospects

Tourism in the Antarctic and Subantarctic contexts has been defined as "all existing human activities other than those directly involved in scientific research, and the normal bases" (Hall 1992: 4). Ecologically sustainable tourism, it is hoped, can be instrumental in conserving the "productive basis of the physical environment by preserving the integrity of the biota and ecological processes, maintaining diversity, and producing tourism commodities without degrading other values" (Hall and Wouters 1994: 369). In the long run it might even "save" Antarctica from commercial exploitation by generating among the tourists strong political commitment to conservation policies (Smith 1994).

Managing tourism in extremely scenic but ecologically sensitive Antarctica has emerged in recent years as one of the key questions facing the ATS: a "front-burner issue" (Beck 1994: 375). The increasing number of tourists visiting specific – or select, more accessible and (logistically) safe – areas on the continent or its surrounding islands has led to serious concern about the likely environmental, legal and geopolitical implications. The numbers have increased sixfold between 1981 and 1993 (8460 tourists in 1992–3) and are expected to grow in the future (Naveen 1991; Enzenbacher 1992: 17; 1993; Kiernan 1993: 7). The number of tourists who have visited the Antarctic now exceeds 52 000; 50 710 seaborne tourists comprise more than 96% of that total (ATCM 1994c).

The changing face of Antarctic tourism, with new operators entering the market, "often with little or no experience of the area" (Ibid.), raises a number of pertinent questions: What makes Antarctic tourism distinctive or different from tourism elsewhere in the world? What is its role within the ATS? What kind of challenges does it pose to the ATPs and the tour operators? With what measure of success has the ATS responded to these challenges so far? What more is needed?

What makes Antarctic tourism different from tourism in other parts of the globe is the peculiar geographical and legal–geopolitical setting of the region. Despite revolutionary improvements in technology and logistics in recent years, it is the physical geography of the area that dictates the *when* and *where* of Antarctic tourism. As a result, tourists tend to visit the most accessible parts of the Antarctic (such as the Antarctic Peninsula and the Subantarctic or peri-Antarctic islands, particularly South Georgia, Macquarie Island, the South Shetland Islands and the New Zealand Subantarctic islands) and coincide – even clash – with the most productive period for scientific research, the Antarctic summer.

Seaborne tourism dominates (Enzenbacher 1992: 180), is considered the more "appropriate" form of tourism (Bauer 1994), happens to be the fastest-growing element of the Antarctic economy (White 1994), generates both real and potential ecological concerns (Enzenbacher 1994; Splettstoesser and Folks 1994) and raises the most complex politico-legal issues (Beck 1994) in comparison to other forms of human activity in the Antarctic.

The arrival of commercial tourism on the Antarctic scene dates back to 1966 (Reich 1980; Hart 1988; Headland 1994: 270–5); before then virtually all expeditions to the Antarctic were organized by governments or had some measure of governmental backing (*Handbook* 1994: 2287). In subsequent years commercial tourism increased, using ships and aircraft.

The earliest tourist flight was in 1956 when a Douglas DC-6B of LAN Chile flew over the South Shetland Islands and Trinity Peninsula carrying 66 passengers. Qantas (using Boeing 747 aircraft) and Air New Zealand (using a Douglas DC-10) began overflights in 1977 and by February 1980 had made a total of 44 excursions, using wide-bodied jet aircraft (Swithinbank 1993: 103). The tragic air crash on Mount Erebus, in 1979, highlighted the inadequacy of planning, traffic control and rescue services in the harsh Antarctic environment. Since 1984, the only reported overflights have been rare passenger-carrying excursions, by Boeing 737 aircraft of the Chilean airline LADECO. The future of airborne tourism in the Antarctic will perhaps depend largely on the development of additional airfields. However, the last few years have also witnessed an increase in adventure tourism, using aircraft to penetrate deep within the continent, and even offering the possibility of visits to the South Pole itself.

It is important to bear in mind the difference between commercial tourism and non-governmental activities. The former is mostly recreational and adventurous; what chiefly distinguishes it from the latter is that it is "heavily dependent on sponsorship or other private contributions in cash and kind" (*Handbook* 1994: 2287).

The present characterization of Antarctic tourism as a "problem area" by the ATPs relates also to the complex question of who should be identified as the recipient state of this human activity. As Vidas (1992: 8) points out: "Therefore, nothing but a notion of a *recipient base* is applicable in Antarctica."

The jurisdictional and liability-related uncertainties of Antarctic tourism are further complicated when third parties are involved (Boczek 1988: 466; Beck 1994: 382). The dilemma that the ATPs continue to face in terms of all third-party activities in the Antarctic – but more so in the case of tourism, due to its multinational character – is that it is generally accepted in international law that no treaty creates obligations for any third party without its consent (Watts 1992: 294–8). If that is so, what kind of "appropriate efforts" should the ATPs be making, under Article X of the Antarctic Treaty, to ensure that tour companies and/or tourists do not engage in "any activity contrary to the principles or purposes of the Antarctic Treaty"? Even though tourism-related activities in the Antarctic are being accepted by the ATPs as a peaceful use of the Antarctic, many potential problems remain:

> . . . future problems can be anticipated because of the multinational character of tour groups, the predominance of seaborne tourism, the registration of tour ships in non-ATP states like Liberia, and doubts about their ability and will to enforce requisite safety and conservation standards. One possible legal nightmare might result from an accident in, for example, an area claimed by both Argentina and the United Kingdom involving a Liberian registered vessel, with an Italian captain, a Filipino crew, and a multinational tour group organized by a US travel agent jointly with other agents in Australia, Britain, Japan, and the United Kingdom. There would seem no easy answer. (Beck 1994: 382)

Tourism was not discussed when the Antarctic Treaty was negotiated in 1959. It was simply a non-issue then. Although the existing recommendations date back to the 1960s and 1970s (see *Handbook* 1994: 2287–9; Beck 1994: 378), they lack "conceptual rigor" (Boczek 1988: 465) and by and large appear "too vague to be enforceable" (Auburn 1982: 280). The hectic pace of the 1970s and 1980s, dictated first by the question of marine resources and then dominated by mineral resources (Chapter 5), led to no more than an acknowledgement by the ATCPs of the "rapid increase in tourism and other non-governmental activities in Antarctica" (ATCM 1987: 120; *Handbook* 1994: 2296–7), and a general appeal for responsible and organized tourism. At the same time, perhaps, the ATPs found the existing framework satisfactory and hoped that tour operators and non-governmental activities would be self-sufficient, adequately insured and well equipped.

Regulation of Antarctic tourism has apparently never been approached systematically by the ATCPs (Boczek 1988: 465; Wace 1990; Beck 1994: 379). Enzenbacher (1992: 22) too has pointed out that to date no comprehensive tourist impact assessment has been undertaken in Antarctica. Antarctic policy-makers and tour operators are in fact "regulating" a commercial industry whose effects are not yet fully understood. Vidas (1992: 15) says that "the trend is usually in the opposite direction", meaning that environmental impact assessments are undertaken by and large after the damage has been done. Effective management of Antarctic tourism requires adequate information from all concerned, be they government agencies or commercial tour operators.

After the crisis of consensus over the minerals issue had been successfully resolved, the ATCPs started paying serious attention to the issue of growing tourism in the Antarctic. At the XVIth ATCM in Bonn in 1991, flooded with numerous working and information papers on the subject, the Chairman acknowledged: "There are still some sensitive and tricky problems like . . . how to tackle tourism in Antarctica." Indeed, serious differences about tourism and non-governmental activities in the Antarctic Treaty area soon surfaced among the ATPs. Whereas the working papers of France, Chile and Italy proposed an Annex on Tourism to the Protocol, many saw no need for a separate Annex, on the ground that the Protocol refers to all human activities, thus including tourism. NGOs have also opposed a separate annex, fearing that this could give ATCPs an effective veto over any NGO activity in the Antarctic (Elliott 1994: 202). SCAR's position is that provisions of the Protocol should apply equally to governmental and non-governmental activities, including tourism (Bush 1994a: 44–5).

Even though the Bonn Meeting could not reach consensus over the need for a separate annex on tourism integral to the Protocol, there was a shared concern to regulate this new problem area within the framework of the ATS. The following issues came up for immediate consideration: supervision of tourists on the continent, registration and licensing of shipping, provision of air-navigation arrangements and emergency and rescue services, the need to educate those involved in all aspects of tourism, the creation of specific tourist sites so as to avoid interference with the sites of scientific research and the need to integrate both existing and new recommendations in a single code.

It was revealed in a document submitted by the United Kingdom at the Bonn Meeting (ATCM 1991e: 29) that in "an unprecedented move, tour operators who, for many years, have operated environmentally sound expeditions to Antarctica, have founded the International Association of Antarctica Tour Operators (IAATO)''. And the guidelines endorsed by IAATO urged that its members should also "know and understand the relevant provisions of the Protocol on Environmental Protection to the Antarctic Treaty and Annexes, and shall wherever practicable fully comply with those provisions, whether or not their own country has issued legislation to require compliance, and ensure that all staff and clients are properly briefed on those provisions that might affect them''.

An Informal Meeting on Tourism was held in Venice, on 9–10 November 1992, with the intention of hammering out a consensus policy on tourism (Vidas 1992; *Handbook* 1994: 2300). Instead, a sharp polarization emerged between two groups of ATCPs: the "Group of Five" (Chile, France, Germany, Italy and Spain) and the United States and New Zealand. Whereas the former sought to deal with tourism within the framework of the Protocol through an additional Annex, the latter, believing that tourist activities were already adequately regulated, saw the problem as essentially one of implementation.

The UK emphasized that any judgement about the adequacy of the existing framework, as embodied in recommendations, should be made only after assessment of: (1) the nature and scale of the potential problems and impacts of tourism and non-governmental activities; and (2) the adequacy of existing provisions. In response to the French proposal, the United Kingdom's argument was that since the ATS already had one document, the Protocol, it was neither necessary nor desirable to talk about a specific policy for Antarctic tourism. Instead all efforts should be directed towards giving the Protocol legally binding force as well as implementing and enforcing it. Australia too saw little need for a new legal instrument dealing specifically with tourism but emphasized the need to develop a clear guiding statement applicable to all tour organizers. In short, no consensus emerged.

The XVIIth ATCM in Venice achieved little more than enabling participants to reiterate their respective positions. The key positions remained unchanged, while the polarization between them was reinforced. The outcome of the XVIIth ATCM with regard to Antarctic tourism was rather poor (Vidas 1992: 29–32; Bush 1994b: 30–1).

At the XVIIIth ATCM held in Kyoto, 11–22 April 1994 (ATCM 1994a: 14), the only general agreement was that "the objective at this Meeting was not to create new rules and regulations but to provide guidance to those visiting Antarctica and those organizing and conducting tourism and non-governmental activities there" (Ibid.: 14). Accordingly, Recommendation XVIII-1 elaborates the obligations of organizers and operators (Ibid.: 41) as follows: (1) to provide prior notification of, and reports on, activities to the competent authorities of the appropriate Party or Parties; (2) to conduct environmental impact assessment of planned activities; (3) to ensure effective response to environmental emergencies, especially with regard to marine pollution; (4) to respect scientific research and the Antarctic environment, including restrictions regarding protected areas, and the protection of flora and fauna; and (5) to prevent the disposal and discharge of prohibited waste. At Seoul it was stressed that "the effective management and monitoring of tourism and non-governmental activities in Antarctica can only be achieved by the collation and analysis of systematically collected data" (see ATCM 1995d: 1; also ATCM 1995a).

In the prevailing circumstances it is clear that regulation of Antarctic tourism will continue to take place at: (1) the ATS level, (2) the governmental level and (3) the tourism industry level. All three have their own contributions to make in realizing the objectives of ecotourism.

Whereas guidelines accepted voluntarily by the tourist operators, as well as by their clients, should be encouraged by the ATCPs – also because there are no centralized enforcement mechanisms within the ATS – much more needs to be done to regulate their environmental impact and avoid the political–legal complications arising from the increasing number of tourists bound for the Antarctic. It would also be useful for the Antarctic policy-makers to note the location of various tour operators, as the latter are likely to lobby their respective governments for various concessions and thereby contribute to the decision-making processes of the ATS. For the ATS as a whole, the challenge will be to balance tourism-related interests with the interests of scientists and environmentalists, which can sometimes be different.

In recent years, the IUCN has adopted a most thoughtful approach to the proactive management of Antarctic tourism. Its report on Antarctic conservation (1991: 70) recommended that controls should be augmented by:

(1) instituting a comprehensive review of procedures;
(2) promoting interaction between those involved, with the aim of developing tour management guidelines;
(3) proactive planning and selection of tourist destinations, followed by careful monitoring of subsequent impacts; and
(4) controlling the choices of tourist destinations.

The most timely research project to monitor and assess the effects of tourist activity in Antarctica is currently based at the Scott Polar Research Institute, Cambridge (England). Entitled *Project Antarctic Conservation*, and independently funded, it aims to discover: (1) how parties of tourists are managed afloat and ashore; (2) the impacts they have on plant and animal communities and other facets of the environment; (3) the impact of tourists on all recorded landing sites; (4) effective ways of controlling tourism within the means, and consistent with the objectives, of the Protocol; and (5) the management procedures that are most likely to be effective in minimizing undesirable impacts by tourists on the environment (Stonehouse 1992: 216–18). The results of this project will help to define the impacts generated by large-scale commercial tourism in Antarctica.

Antarctic secretariat in search of a location

Of late there has been widespread support among the ATCPs for the establishment of a small, modern, cost-effective Secretariat, responsible to and under the authority of the ATCMs, to facilitate the operation of the ATCM mechanism in view of expanding agenda of the ATS and the CEP. However, there are differences on a number of substantive issues. Those in favour of the Secretariat have agreed that costs should be kept to a minimum. Some of the ATPs have favoured a weighted division of costs, while others have argued for an equal division. There are those who argue that all or part of the costs of holding ATCMs should be included. More complex differences emerge on the question of the location of the proposed Secretariat. Argentina has long been insistent on Buenos Aires, in sharp contrast to the demand by Peru (for example) that it must not be located in the "claimant states".

At the Bonn Meeting, however, some delegations were of the view that this question could remain open for the time being, while others held that no aspect should be isolated. There appeared to be no consensus on the immediate establishment of a Secretariat; some delegations maintained that the study and consideration of this subject had not proceeded to the point where a concrete decision could be taken. Instead, these delegations emphasized the preservation of the present working structure, which includes a network of direct diplomatic contacts that precede, and determine the contents of, formal decisions. Some even supported, in principle, the creation of an administrative support unit to assist the Environmental Committee.

Consensus on the issue continued to evade the ATPs at Kyoto. Most noteworthy in this context, however, was the withdrawal by the United States of its offer to provide the site for the Secretariat and offering instead "support for its location in Buenos Aires" (ATCM 1994a: 101). The American announcement, especially the second part of it, must have taken the majority of the ATPs, in particular the United Kingdom, by surprise. The United Kingdom's policy has been that the Antarctic Secretariat must not be located in any of the claimant states. Whereas Argentina expressed its "satisfaction and gratitude" for the almost "unanimous support the offer of Buenos Aires as headquarters for the Secretariat has received", only the delegations of Peru, Spain and Greece explicitly mentioned their support for the Argentine bid (ATCM 1994a: 89, 96, 108).

No decision on the site of the Secretariat could thus be reached in either Venice or Kyoto. However, there seems to be general agreement in favour of locating the Secretariat in the South American subcontinent or in the southern hemisphere. According to a working paper on the organizational aspects of the proposed Secretariat, submitted by Italy in Kyoto (ATCM 1994d: 1–6), while there is considerable agreement among the ATPs with regard to the functions of the secretariat, the staff complement and method of financing, several questions remain open with regard to the legal status. These relate essentially to: (1) the nature of the instrument by which privileges and immunities should be granted, (2) the scope of such immunities, (3) whether they should be enjoyed only in the territory of the host state or in the territory of all ATCPs or ATPs and (4) the way in which pertinent regulation could be uniformly implemented in the domestic law of state Parties (also see ATCM 1995e).

The Agreed Measures and the Protected Area System: a reassessment

Chapter 6 has already noted the geopolitical context in which the ATPs negotiated the first environmental protection agreement in 1964, in the form of Agreed Measures for the Conservation of Antarctic Fauna and Flora. The Agreed Measures designated the Antarctic Treaty area a Special Conservation Area – although the concept was never defined – and introduced a system of protected areas with scientific and environmental objectives. The first of such mechanisms, which provided only for the protection of flora and fauna, was termed "Specially Protected Areas" under Article VIII of the Measures.

Conflicts of interest soon arose between environmental protection and protection for scientific purposes within the ambit of SPAs. It was decided, therefore, to establish SSSIs as a separate protection mechanism for some scientific activities of particular interest (Orrego Vicuña 1992: 10). The SSSIs were to be protected from harmful interference and were to be subject to periodic revision so as to avoid curtailing the freedom of scientific research provided for under the Antarctic Treaty (listed in *Handbook* 1994: 2083–4). Another noteworthy development at this level has been the creation of Marine Sites of Special Scientific Interest (Ibid.: 2098–9).

During the XVth ATCM in Paris (October 1989) it was decided to designate other areas for protection. Since neither the Agreed Measures nor the Recommendations adopted by the ATCPs had provided a "specified mechanism for identifying and protecting areas of outstanding geological, glaciological, geomorphological, aesthetic, scenic, or wilderness value" (ATCM 1989 [Rec. XV-10]: 82; *Handbook* 1994: 2108–9), the concept of Specially Reserved Areas (SRAs) was introduced. There was no mechanism for the protection of areas in the vicinity of scientific stations – where, it was felt, the combined and cumulative effect of human activity could result in mutual interference or in harmful impacts on the environment – so the concept of Multiple Use Planning Areas (MUPAs) was brought into being. Recommendation XV-11 (ATCM 1989: 84–6; *Handbook* 1994: 2109–12) underlines that each MUPA shall be designated pursuant to a management plan developed through consultations, as appropriate, among interested Parties and approved by the ATCPs.

It is important to bear in mind that the issue of protected areas was taken up by the Paris ATCM in the context of a broader debate about environmental protection in the 1980s. The provisions of the Agreed Measures had come under increasing scrutiny from non-governmental organizations as well as from environmental management experts (Elliott 1992: 119).

A review of the Protected Areas was thus undertaken at the XVIth ATCM. It was also felt that the existence of many types of legislation had caused considerable confusion about the regulations relating to protected areas. The United Kingdom, with the full support of the United States, emphasized that the "system should be concise, unambiguous and in conformity with the existing Annexes to the Protocol" (*Handbook* 1994: 2119). Finally, two main types of area were introduced by way of Annex V to the Protocol (Ibid.: 2125–9): ASPAs and ASMAs. According to Article 3 of the Annex (Ibid.: 2125), "any area, including any marine area, may be designated as an Antarctic Specially Protected Area to promote outstanding environmental, scientific, historic, aesthetic or wilderness value, any combination of those values, or ongoing or planned scientific research". The SPAs and SSSIs designated by past ATCMs were now designated ASPAs and were to be renamed and renumbered accordingly. Entry into an ASPA shall be prohibited except in accordance with a permit. On the other hand, under Article 4 of the Annex (Ibid.: 2126), any area, including any marine area, where activities are being conducted or may in future be conducted, may be designated an ASMA "to assist in the planning and co-ordination of activities, avoid possible conflicts, improve cooperation between Parties or minimize environmental impacts". ASMAs may also include areas where activities pose risks of mutual interference or cumulative environmental impact, and sites or monuments of recognized historical value. Entry into ASMAs will not require a permit.

It is worth mentioning that in accordance with the Convention on Seals, special areas have been established for sealing which are subject to periodic seasonal closure, as well as Seal Reserves, where hunting is forbidden because they are reproduction and breeding areas or sites where long-term scientific research is being carried out (Orrego Vicuña 1992: 11; *Handbook* 1994: 2261). CCAMLR too provides for the closure of excessively exploited fishing areas. Of late, ASOC members have been working on the idea of creating a whale sanctuary in the Southern Ocean. According to ASOC (ATCM 1994a: 216), "recent reports of under reporting of past commercial whale catches highlight the need for a cessation of commercial whaling and the imposition of a sanctuary in the Southern Ocean. Creation of the sanctuary would also greatly assist in achieving the objectives of the Protocol and CCAMLR."

The environmental protection system described above has been criticized on the grounds that it lacks both comprehensiveness and precise elaboration of environmental criteria, since most measures have arisen from isolated concerns expressed by the ATCPs, "which in turn influenced an erratic application and evolution" (Orrego Vicuña 1992: 11). Whereas from the legal point of view the measures in question lack force or are too general (Ibid.), from a geopolitical standpoint it has been stressed that "this exercise should not result in denial of access to any country" (Sreenivasan 1994: 77).

CCAMLR and the Seals Convention: science, politics and conservation

We have already observed (in Chapter 5) that CCAMLR (with its 21 participating members) is one of the four conventions regulating conservation and resource management in the Antarctic which has distinctive politico–geographic characteristics. It applies to all marine resources inside an area that is approximately delineated by the mean position of the South Polar Front, and as such its northern boundary differs from that of other conventions (60°S). The principal institutions of CCAMLR are the Commission as the policy-making and regulatory body and the Scientific Committee as an advisory body and a forum for consultation and cooperation concerning the collection, study and exchange of information.

As outlined by IUCN (1991: 59), CCAMLR's main provision is that harvesting of any population should be on the basis of sustainability in the long term. It has rightly been emphasized that large-scale exploitation, in some cases overexploitation, of most of the fish stocks in the Southern Ocean precedes CCAMLR (Kock 1994: 3). The Convention, therefore, cannot be blamed for what happened before it came into force in 1982. Soon afterwards, two urgent priorities for the Scientific Committee and the Commission were to assess the state of Antarctic fish stocks and attempt their recovery through conservation measures. However, efforts in the direction of applying more rigorous conservation measures were thwarted by one or more of the fishing nations for the sake of short-term economic gain. Some fishing countries even refused to adopt conservation measures on the pretext that scientific advice, on which those measures were largely based, could not be regarded as reliable since it was based on inadequate information. Strangely enough, this information was to be provided only by the fishing countries themselves. Since conservation measures required agreement among all the members, and agreement was mostly lacking, CCAMLR was unable to realize its objectives throughout the 1980s.

The decision-making system in the Commission, as set up under CCAMLR, has therefore been criticized as a serious flaw in the regime designed to conserve living resources. It has a majority-based system of voting; substantive decisions must be made by consensus; the question of whether a matter is one of substance shall itself be treated as a substantive matter, a rule analogous to the "double veto" formula in the Security Council (Auburn 1982: 245). Non-substantive decisions are taken by a simple majority of the members present and voting. The consensus decision rule carries the risk that the interests of the majority can be blocked by a single participant. However, it could be argued that no decision-making procedure can, of itself, force a state to accept a conservation measure that it deems to be contrary to its vital interests (Orrego Vicuña 1991).

In view of the urgent need to acquire more data about the Antarctic marine ecosystem, the Scientific Committee would be expected to play a key role in implementing and maintaining the conservation system. However, its functions fail to include conducting scientific research and are limited to data collection and analysis, providing scientific advice and developing standards for conservation measures. Moreover, its decision-making structure is not clear and is probably based on consensus. It has no sound financial and logistic basis, and the participation of scientists from other organizations, such as the FAO and various non-government organizations, is not guaranteed. Finally, it is altogether possible that recommendations or advice from the Scientific Committee might be ignored by the Commission. The Convention's mechanism for dealing with compliance and enforcement is, to say the least, rather weak and decentralized. At the same time it is difficult to assess to what extent the Scientific Committee has influenced the behaviour of the fishing nations.

The key issue in any resource-management system, however, is the enforcement of conservation measures. Article IX of the Convention (*Handbook* 1994: 181–2) lays down that measures, once agreed by members, and to which no objection is received within 90 days, become binding on all members after 180 days. It is worth noting that, like other Antarctic Treaty provisions, the Convention is not enforceable, even on members, and relies on voluntary compliance. Hence CCAMLR suffers from a tremendous disadvantage in respect of the enforcement of its conservation measures.

Despite the obligation imposed by Articles IX and XXIV of the Convention, no system of inspection was in place before 1989/90. In total, 20 inspections of fishing vessels have been carried out since then by inspectors working under the System (ATCM 1994a: 118). On-board inspection visits normally last a few hours. Inspectors are appointed by national authorities and not by the Commission, which inhibits truly independent monitoring. Constrained further by the remoteness of fishing grounds in the Southern Ocean, inspections involve enormous logistic costs. Unless it is backed by strong national interests, as in the case of the Kerguelen fishing zone, effective implementation of the inspection system under CCAMLR is un-likely to be possible. In several cases, however, non-compliance with the conservation system has been reported and legal action taken against the alleged offenders by the governments of the flag state of the vessels. At the same time a large proportion of the violations with respect to fishing and incidental mortality was not brought to the notice of CCAMLR at all in the 1980s (Kock 1994: 14).

Whereas it is quite reasonable to hope that inspections as a compliance mechanism will prove to be adequate for ensuring compliance with en-vironmental rules, or for pointing out violations, the results so far have been rather disappointing. Maybe, as Kimball (1988b: 18) observes, "par-ties to the treaty have traditionally been reluctant to 'rock the boat' by asking too many questions about each others' activities in Antarctica".

A report on the functioning of CCAMLR was submitted to the Bonn Meeting (ATCM 1991a: 210–15). In view of the fact that fishing is concen-trated in a few relatively small areas (although the current level of catch is quite small when compared with the most conservative estimates of the global sustainable yield of krill which themselves vary greatly), concern was expressed about its impact on krill predators which forage within these areas. It was pointed out that, given the current knowledge of krill biology and ecology and thus the ability to estimate its abundance and distribution, it is not possible now nor likely to be possible in the near future to provide more precise estimates of the sustainable yield (Ibid.: 211).

Consequently, at the 1990 meeting of CCAMLR it was proposed that precautionary measures should be adopted for krill fishery until such time as more precise information is available. Such measures then would serve as a safeguard against a sudden increase in the level of catch, which may be detrimental to krill predators and would allow the krill fishery to develop in a controlled manner. However, contrary to the advice of the Commission, the krill-fishing members were arguing that current scientific evidence does not support the imposition of regulatory measures, and since it was not their intention to increase their fishing effort or their catches dramatically in the near future, there was no need to regulate krill harvesting. The disagreement continues.

With regard to fin fish, the CCAMLR observer was to point out that current harvesting of fin fish in the Convention area is now focused on three species (mackerel icefish, Patagonian toothfish and the lantern fish) and is confined to the South Atlantic and around Iles Kerguelen in the Southern Indian Ocean. Whereas fishing for icefish and toothfish is regu-lated by the Commission through the establishment of total allowable catches and prohibited areas, no regulations have been made as yet for lantern fish. At the same time, scientific survey results have provided little or no evidence of the recovery of populations of fish species that the Commission has sought to protect through regulation. This may be due to the accidental taking of young fish in krill trawls, and therefore the Commission has agreed that it might be necessary to close the krill nursery areas to harvesting for certain periods in the future. Whether the krill-fishing members would adhere to the advice of the Commission in this respect remains to be seen.

The Antarctic Seals Convention

The review of the operation of the Convention for the Conservation of Antarctic Seals came at the Bonn Meeting by way of a report submitted by the United Kingdom, the depository government for the Convention (ATCM 1991f: 1–3; Bush 1994a: 24–5). It was also reflected in the report of the meeting of the SCAR Group of Specialists on Seals (held in São Paulo, Brazil, from 16 to 18 July 1990), presented at the ATCM by SCAR as one of its information papers. Whereas the United Kingdom claimed that there has been no commercial sealing in Antarctica since the Convention was adopted in 1972, the SCAR Group expressed its concern about the recent decline in the stock of southern elephant seals in the Indian Ocean sector of the Southern Ocean. It said that while the causes of the decline in numbers of the elephant seals are not understood, past or present commercial fisheries and/or climatic changes could have caused perturbations of food supply which have contributed to it.

Accordingly, there is an urgent need to assess the current status of southern elephant seals and to collect additional information which will help to identify factors causing the decline. The SCAR report revealed further that a review of the returns of Antarctic seal takes indicates that some countries are submitting inadequate, incomplete or late returns. This is contrary to requirements under the Agreed Measures for the Conservation of Antarctic Fauna and Flora and the Convention for the Conservation of Antarctic Seals.

Summary and conclusions

The Protocol has introduced a new environmental ethic into all aspects of Antarctic reality, including its geography and geopolitics. In sharp contrast to the heady resource diplomacy of the 1970s and 1980s, that at one stage brought the ATS to the brink of collapse following a crisis of consensus, the 1990s appear to be characterized by the growing ascendance of environmental values over resource-driven geopolitical visions. This is not to suggest that the fundamental tension between commercial–exploitative values and conservation–ecological values has been fully resolved, nor to conclude that there is no conflict potential in the diverse uses of the Antarctic, but to stress that the terms of debate within the ATS appear to have been transformed dramatically over the past few years. As a result, all components of the ATS have come under some kind of environmental audit both by the ATPs themselves and by the NGOs. This has revealed, from the viewpoint of conservation, a number of shortcomings, not only in the Protocol itself but also in other components of the ATS; these will have to be corrected in the future.

The Protocol provides a fairly balanced, even though in some respects incomplete, framework for conserving the Antarctic environment and there is much in it that is new as well as promising, but it is not – and need not be – the last word on the subject, especially in respect of the management of tourism. Translation of the principles and purposes of the Protocol into efficient and effective management practices will largely depend on the political will of participant countries. The ATPs will not only have to ensure speedy implementation of legislation on their respective domestic fronts, they will have to ensure meaningful participation of both public and non-governmental organizations in the protection and management of the Antarctic. The task of managing increasingly diverse uses of the Antarctic in an ecologically sustainable manner is far beyond the individual capacity of the ATPs. The increase in tourism in the Antarctic has also underlined the need for cooperation not only among the state Parties but also between them and the tourist industry.

This chapter has revealed that the ATS in general is at a critical juncture: if it is characterized on the one hand by consensus among all its members in respect of preserving and strengthening this unique experiment in international cooperation, it is at the same time marred by disagreements about what the most urgent or immediate priorities on its agenda are and the appropriate ways of meeting those priorities. It is becoming increasingly obvious that the next 30 years are going to be more challenging than the past 30 have been.

Suggested reading

Eliott, L.M. 1994. *International Environmental Politics: Protecting the Antarctic.* London: Macmillan; New York: St Martin's Press.

Hall, C.M. and M.E. Johnston (eds) 1995. *Polar Tourism: Tourism in the Arctic and Antarctic Regions.* Chichester: John Wiley & Sons.

Harris, C.M. and B. Stonehouse (eds) 1991. *Antarctica and Global Climate Change.* London: Belhaven Press.

Verhoeven, J., P. Sands and M. Bruce (eds) 1992. *The Antarctic Environment and International Law.* London/Dordrecht/Boston: Graham & Trotman.

9

Sustainable development in the Arctic: options and obstacles

As an approach for "reconciling" economic development and environmental conservation goals, the concept of sustainable development has figured in a number of post-Cold War initiatives taken by the Arctic states, in the new US Arctic policy (Johnson 1994: 6) and in the emerging comprehensive native-claims settlements in Canada. Sustainable development has even been said to offer "an important integrating theme for a northern foreign policy" for the Arctic states (Doering 1994: 79). Yet, despite the increasing popularity of the phrase and its wholesale adoption by the Earth Summit in 1992 (see Johnson 1993), there is no consensus among scholars, let alone policy-makers, about the definition of the expression in the national or regional context (Bartelmus 1994: 69–78; Norgaard 1994: 17–20). In some cases, sustainable development has increasingly been "co-opted to mean sustaining conventional development rather than developing economic practices that are environmentally sustainable" (Käkönen 1993a: 23). Consequently, the term may lose all its force, also in the Arctic. There is an essential relationship between conservation and development, and unless development projects judiciously apply conservation principles, they will not be sustainable and Arctic ecosystems and resources may continue to be severely damaged (Arikaynen 1991; Roginko 1992; Brinken and Pyzhin 1993; Hoel 1993; Luzin 1993).

The major purpose of this chapter is to elaborate and examine the options for community-based sustainable development in the circumpolar Arctic. The main premise of this focus is that strategies of sustainability have to be based upon realities specific to the region in question – indeed, within the region one might encounter significant variations – emphasizing local control, local actions and local solutions (Pretes and Robinson 1989). This does not imply that all the issues related to sustainable development are exclusively local in nature and scope or that they can be tackled on that level alone. Even though more macro-level activities (national, regional, global) remain important, both as causes of and solutions to "unsustainability", without local-level participation no sustainable development is possible. At the same time, "an unfolding of the concept into practical guidelines calls for much more concrete conceptual considerations as well as functional framework" (Rasmussen 1994: 25).

The chapter has three parts. Part one identifies some of the preconditions for realizing community-based development and examines their prospects in the Arctic. Part two moves to the national and regional levels and offers an assessment of the more recent initiatives taken by the Arctic states under the Arctic Environmental Protection Strategy (AEPS). Part three emphasizes the need to treat sustainability as an operational, measurable concept and discusses various sectoral plans and national/regional initiatives in the Arctic for achieving sustainable development and management in specific policy and economic sectors – e.g. renewable resources, habitat conservation, tourism and transportation. The chapter concludes by making the case for a legally binding Arctic Treaty on Sustainable Development, leaving the concluding chapter of the study to comment on its prospects.

"Sustainability" in the Arctic: from the ideals to realities

What are we going to develop and/or sustain in the Arctic and how? Since sustainability cannot be defined without addressing the question of values (Käkönen 1994: 19), whose values should matter? Do we apply the values of the developed southern metropolis or those of the northern communities? According to diverse notions of sustainability (themselves influenced by the basic questions of sustainability of what, for whom, where and when), there are a number of answers with obvious geopolitical implications. Given that different groups tend to establish and "re-establish" power relations through their control of resources, and that local demands are often linked to wider social resistance, it is equally vital to explore whether the local communities are able to carry their alternative vision of sustainability into the organs of the state itself. If not, what is needed to "empower" those communities?

According to a recent study on the subject (Käkönen 1994), if growth-oriented modernization, state sovereignty, centralized systems, state-centred democracy and the exploitation of nature remain the driving forces behind the *old* paradigm of development thought, then under the *new* paradigm the key parameters of sustainability ought to be adaptability, civil society, decentralized systems, local democracy and new definitions of the human–environment relationship. Sustainable development demands, first and foremost, a cultural revolution, i.e. fundamental changes in thought and behaviour, "allowing humanity to create social and natural preconditions for an existence that respects and adapts to the natural environment" (Griffiths and Young 1989: 1). Where does the Arctic stand in terms of such a paradigm shift?

Ecological economics, community-based development and the dilemma of peripheries in the Arctic

While finite nature is increasingly exposed to many alarming trends that threaten the future viability of human life and civilization, the financial world is largely blind to natural limits and is concerned only with favourable long-term trends and gains. Neither economics nor ecology can provide an answer to the persistent human dilemma about sustainability. While conventional economics is unmindful of nature and its role as the foundation of all economic activity, conventional ecology appears to be equally ignorant of the special needs and potential of people, especially the indigenous communities. What is needed, therefore, is a new discipline of ecological economics that recognizes that the human economic system is embedded in the earth's natural ecosystem. Without this awareness, a sustainable economy, whereby human society attains a balanced relationship with the earth's ecosystems without compromising basic human needs and cultural diversity, may not be possible.

Most interactions between human activities and the natural environment are best observed, measured and managed at the grassroots level *in situ*, i.e. by those directly affected. This applies particularly to Arctic communities and calls for an alternative to state-centred, highly centralized and bureaucratized approaches to growth-centred development. One critical distinction between growth-centred and community-based development is that "the former routinely subordinates the needs of people to those of the production system while the latter seeks consistently to subordinate the needs of the production system to those of people" (Korten 1984: 300; Korten and Carner 1984: 201). Advocates of community-based development share the view that "smaller-scale, decentralized development aimed at the maximization of self-sufficiency is more supportive of human survival needs than are the dependency-producing dynamics of centralized economic consolidation" (Lockhart 1987: 393).

Broadly speaking, therefore, the objectives of community-based development in the Arctic are: (i) to operate within the limits of the biosphere and local ecosystems; (ii) to address basic local needs, strengthen shared commitments to the common well-being and encourage local initiative and self-reliance; (iii) benefit indigenous and other northern peoples and improve their quality of life consistent with obligations to future generations; and (iv) to encourage the use of local technologies and indigenous knowledge for promoting culturally appropriate development.

The United Nations Conference on Environment and Development has also emphasized the need to recognize and strengthen the role of indigenous peoples and their communities the world over in realizing sustainable development (see Johnson 1993: 415–18). Chapter 26 of Agenda 21 calls upon both the governments and the intergovernmental organizations to strive for the following objectives: (a) establishment of a process to empower people and their communities through measures that include: (i) adopting appropriate policies and legal instruments at the national level, (ii) protecting their lands, resources and environment from environmentally unsound practices, (iii) recognizing their traditional dependence on renewable resources and ecosystems, including sustainable harvesting, (iv) strengthening national dispute-resolution arrangements in relation to settlement of land and resource-management concerns, (v) supporting alternative environmentally sound means of production to improve quality of life and ensure effective participation in sustainable development; (b) establishing arrangements to strengthen the active participation of indigenous people and their communities in the national formulation of policies, laws and programmes related to resource management; and (c) involving those communities at the national and local levels in resource-management and conservation strategies.

The above principles and objectives have a special attraction for the communities living in peripheral regions such as the Circumpolar North. Moreover, recent years have witnessed the processes of devolution, land claims and self-government in many parts of the Arctic, inducing among the indigenous communities a desire for self-sufficiency (see Chapter 6). Although the northerners have not rejected outright the benefits of industrial development, they have shown greater determination to maintain and strengthen the indigenous social and economic systems, which are closely tied to the rhythm and productivity of nature. The need for sustaining northern economies is taking precedence over the glittering promise of megaprojects, with "empowerment", "involvement" and "participation" enabling local communities to achieve sustainable development as they perceive it.

So far, most Arctic development has run contrary to these principles, and the "tendency seems to be to follow the international market economy trend and to subordinate sustainable development to the market economy" (Lyck 1994: 20). It has indeed largely taken the form of megaprojects and large-scale industries, mostly concerned with energy and mineral-resource extraction – activities that, by and large, are capital-intensive, unsustainable and have adverse environmental impact (see Agranat 1991; Luzin 1993; Fenge 1993–4, 1994).

Throughout the Circumpolar North, small communities have suffered because "the Arctic is peripheral to metropolitan political, financial and manufacturing centres, and serves as a resource-producing hinterland of metropolitan regions" (Pretes 1993: 94). Since most capital is externally based, any proceeds from the extraction of raw materials, i.e. potential revenues or rents, are likely to leave the Arctic, finding their way to the south. Moreover, public- and private-sector investments in the Arctic have, for the most part, "not been oriented towards adapting southern production technologies for northern use, or establishing the infrastructure required to support economic diversification" (Stagg 1991: 20).

A stable and diversified secondary industry base has been difficult to achieve because of remoteness from markets, high operating costs and lack of adequate funding. Many northern communities have been forced to rely heavily on the extraction of non-renewable resources for their income and subjected to the cyclical vagaries of boom and bust at the expense of traditional land-based economies. With this kind of development have come "economic dependency, social disintegration and political paralysis" (Lockhart 1987: 398).

It has been proposed (Pretes and Robinson 1989) that "permanent trust funds" (a kind of investment and development fund) could be one way of contributing to sustainable development by: (i) transforming non-renewable resources into renewable financial resources, (ii) decentralizing the economy, (iii) transforming mineral and petroleum resources into investment and business development. Both Alaska and Alberta have acquired substantial revenues and thereby reduced their dependence on the central government. So long as no environmental trade-offs are involved in the pursuit of such funds and they are made available to communities, the idea appears to be worthy of consideration elsewhere in the Arctic. An additional merit of this approach is that the funds could be used to help indigenous entrepreneurs diversify local economies, thereby enhancing the social and cultural security of their communities.

Isolated community life is a major feature of northern existence, a feature reinforced by the infrastructural limits placed on transportation by geography and climate. Below-zero temperatures – in some places for 240 to 300 days a year – and long winter nights affect labour activities and modes of recreation. The extreme vulnerability of Arctic ecosystems to anthropogenic activities also has implications (see Chapter 2). In permafrost, for example, the erosion of soil and vegetation by transport and mechanical pollution causes lasting geomorphological, hydrological, geochemical, geocryological and biological changes (Arikaynen 1991: 18). Another Arctic-specific feature is the cohabitation of two radically different population groups, migrants and natives. Conflict often arises between the two cultural and economic modes, "demanding sound and wise policies for recruiting the labour force for the Arctic regions" (Ibid.). The indigenous people, particularly those who are mainly dependent on renewable resources, require a form of socio-economic development and education that takes into account their mode of life, traditions and needs.

At the same time, it is not possible to treat the Circumpolar North as one economy (Lyck 1990a: 311). The most characteristic economies in the Arctic are: (i) old, traditional economies developed from a barter economy, based on subsistence practices; (ii) public economies, based on transfers of capital from the metropolises located to the south; and (iii) private economies, principally based on large-scale production in the utilization of land resources. While such diversity rules out generalizations, it is hard to deny that so far economic strategies designed in the industrialized south have brought at best mixed results to the hinterland regions, undermining sustainability in every sense of the term.

For those advocating a return to traditional subsistence practices, in the hope of creating or re-creating self-sufficient hunter–gatherer systems in the Arctic, there is no escape from the reality that, by and large, the traditional economy today is integrated and dependent on the economy of the centres. Employment mobility is generally not an option in the Arctic because it disrupts family networks and the fabric of small communities. It is renewable resources that have to be given priority if northern communities are to ensure a viable future for themselves. However, while most of the means for pursuing traditional economic activities have to be imported, the products too are sold to the markets of the south:

> North Atlantic fish production is a good case to illustrate the integration of the local or even regional economy into the world market. For the Faroe Islands, Iceland, and Greenland fish products account for between 70 to 90 per cent of export earnings. Traditionally, the fish has been sold to European markets. Today these markets are also filled with fish products from various less developed countries. Prices go down, fishermen have to catch and sell more in order to maintain their incomes and the final result is over exploitation of the North Atlantic fish stock. (Käkönen 1994: 25)

Most Arctic communities – by and large linked to the advanced industrial societies to the south by modern telecommunication and transport systems – continue to experience the revolution of rising expectations. The so-called "new technologies", in combination with permanent settlements and a cash economy, have made even the subsistence economy capital-intensive throughout much of the Arctic. The labour force in many Arctic communities is also likely to grow dramatically by the end of the century, with fewer opportunities to pursue traditional subsistence activities. Consequently, for the vast majority of the young labour force "the only alternative to welfare and, therefore, a life of dependence on transfer payments from the southern metropolis will be migration out of the Arctic or greater integration into southern systems in the interests of expanding the cash sector of the economies of Arctic communities" (Griffiths and Young 1989: 14).

Are the Arctic communities capable of influencing the behaviour of the advanced industrial centres to the south (Griffiths and Young 1989;

Käkönen 1994)? Overcoming entrenched dependencies, minimizing the extent to which they are integrated into the economic and political systems of the principal Arctic states, and acquiring the freedom to design future options for self-management require political autonomy and an effective say in political decision-making. With some exceptions, indigenous peoples continue to struggle for the recognition of their rights to land as a precondition of any meaningful economic and cultural development (see Chapter 6). The authority to make decisions about the exploitation of Arctic resources still lies, in considerable measure, with those who may not be well informed about the social and economic conditions prevailing in the region or with those who have little incentive to show particular concern for the desires and needs of the Arctic communities.

Should these realities then lead us to conclude that the future of this 1% of the earth's population, living in eight different countries, is inevitably gloomy? While it is not realistic to expect that the Arctic communities will be able to go their own way, severing ties with the industrialized centres of power to the south, few would dispute the need for drawing on the substantial assets of the Arctic. What are those assets? What are the threats to those assets? Where do they come from and what can be done to counter those threats? While seeking answers to such questions it is vital to bear in mind the symbiotic link between the cultural and biological diversity of the Arctic and consequently the overlap that exists in terms of both the problems and the solutions.

The cultural diversity, indigenous knowledge and wisdom

The ability of mankind to adapt to changing environmental circumstances depends largely on protecting not just the biological diversity of our habitat but also its cultural diversity. Unfortunately, in "many instances the preservation and development of a traditional knowledge 'corpus' is still regarded as retrograde, an activity beyond the legitimate purview of modern science" (Fraser 1994: 122). In fact, sustaining and utilizing this knowledge ought to be the starting-point of what some would call "knowledge-based sustainable development" (House 1993). The question remains: "how can we best protect and capitalize on the natural environment [and our knowledge of it] so as to achieve sustainable development, that is economic development that at best enhances and is at worst neutral *vis-à-vis* the integrity of the natural environment" (Ibid.)?

From an indigenous perspective, as Keith (1994: 3) puts it, "traditional ecological knowledge" is a way of knowing and thinking about ecosystems. Despite the onslaught of industrialization and modernization, traditional knowledge systems and cultures still survive in many parts of the Arctic. We are particularly talking of settlements (often with populations of less than a thousand) and their environs, where "ways of life based on renewable resources and traditional cultures are most strongly reproduced and sustained" (Griffiths and Young 1989: 17). For example, nearly 42% of just over 50 000 people of the Northwest Territories of Canada live in settlements of under 600 people. These communities are composed of both natives and non-natives, who visualize their future and that of their children as intimately bound to the future of the North. Needless to say, protection of their cultural assets requires the protection of the communities themselves as well as the subsistence practices that remain at the core of their cultural identity.

Noteworthy in this context are the preliminary findings of the study of Traditional Ecological Knowledge (TEK) undertaken by the Canadian Arctic Resource Committee around Hudson and James Bays. The traditional-knowledge input from more than 20 communities there has revealed that a third population of beluga whales resides year-round in southern Hudson Bay and James Bay, whereas scientific evidence had indicated that there are only two populations and that they migrate out of the Bays only in winter. The findings of the Inuit hunters further reveal that the populations of beluga whales may not in fact be declining; they may only be seeking sanctuaries in new areas away from noise and disturbance. If confirmed, these findings might prompt modifications in the current regulatory and management policies for the beluga whales. The study has, therefore, already demonstrated the usefulness of traditional knowledge in the "co-management" of renewable resources, and there are encouraging signs that traditional knowledge is at last gaining a measure of respect and recognition as a legitimate complementary mainstream science (see Sallenave 1994).

The major threats to human–cultural assets can be grouped into two main categories. First, abrupt environmental and economic assaults can sever the umbilical cord of indigenous cultural identity and subsistence practices, causing the erosion and eventual loss of indigenous knowledge. Secondly, the penetration by market forces and consumer culture into these communities might add to the social pathologies (high rates of suicide, alcoholism, etc.) generally associated with the collective as well as individual dilemma of a community caught between the mutual contradictions of a traditional subsistence culture and the modern consumer culture (see Wilmer 1993: 6–14).

Among the major threats of the first kind, the growth in recent years of international anti-harvest groups, particularly the anti-fur movement in Western Europe and North America, is most notable. These campaigns continue to undermine the symbiotic relationship of the indigenous peoples with their land and resources. For the indigenous peoples, the trapping of fur-bearing animals is a way of life defined as aboriginal and is related to the harvesting of renewable resources (Lynge 1992).

Indigenous strategies to counter the campaigns of anti-harvest groups include: (i) ongoing collaboration among indigenous peoples to formulate and implement a common strategy; (ii) securing national and international support for the protection of indigenous subsistence rights; (iii) increasing public understanding of subsistence practices and their profound socio-economic and cultural significance for indigenous communities; (iv) securing expanded markets for products of indigenous harvesting; and (v) ensuring that Arctic and other state governments play an active supportive role (see Tauli-Corpuz 1993). The establishment of income-security programmes has also been suggested (Griffiths and Young 1989: 20), to provide support for the communities affected by the anti-harvesting campaign.

Abrupt socio-economic and cultural dislocation of northern communities, with concomitant adverse ecological impacts, can also be caused by megaprojects exploiting Arctic hydrocarbons and other non-renewable resources. There are no simple countermeasures to buffer the small Arctic communities against the overwhelming impact of these projects. It is precisely here that some of the major battles of "sustainability" are going to be waged in the years to come. The following select examples should suffice to illustrate the challenge that awaits the Arctic communities.

According to some scholars, after a decade of inactivity due to sagging demand, low prices, popular objections to northern pipeline construction and nationalist pressures against exporting energy to the United States, it appears that Canadian Arctic gas production – and the construction of pipelines to reach lucrative southern markets – is now imminent. If this is the case, what was once an ecological nightmare might soon become a reality. The voices that were heard during the days of the Berger inquiry in the 1970s are not heard any more. The Inuvialuit, originally the group most opposed to pipeline construction during the Berger inquiry, now support the Mackenzie Valley gas development. They do so because their land-claims settlement has provided them with some control over the pace and direction of development. On the other hand, the Dene and Métis are still awaiting the final agreement and do not want the gas development to proceed, but once their claims have been resolved, they will also probably prefer to support the project. Growing unemployment and poverty are forcing both groups to accept large-scale gas development in the expectation of providing their communities with long-term socio-economic security, although they hope that representation on the Environmental Impact Board will allow them to control the decisions that are likely to affect the natural environment and subsistence-related activities.

What about those parts of the Arctic where indigenous land rights are not recognized – for example, the Sami homelands? The biggest environmental threats have come from the radioactive fall-out from Chernobyl, which heavily contaminated reindeer pastures, and from acid rain, especially from Russia's Kola Peninsula. Now, however, diamonds have been found in the so-called "Baltic Shield" across Arctic and Subarctic Europe, raising the possibility of a Klondike-style rush to exploit huge mineral deposits, probably one of world's largest (*The Times* (London), 9 September 1994), and the Sami have been caught totally unawares. It has been reported that both the Norwegian and the Finnish governments have already given permission for prospecting (Pearce 1994: 59). This could mean an ecological catastrophe for reindeer herds that are already short of pastures. Mining will take over a lot of land, and pollution could threaten the Tana River, one of the world's richest salmon rivers. While there is said to be widespread opposition to mining among the local Sami Councils, the Norwegian government has so far refused to hold direct talks with the Sami Parliament or other representatives (Ibid.).

Similar ecological concerns have been raised about the cumulative effects of diamond mining in the Lac de Gras area near Yellowknife, in the Northwest Territories. Pending the verdict of a federal Environmental Impact Assessment Review Panel, the mining companies (BHP Minerals Canada Ltd, a unit of Broken Hill Proprietary (BHP) Co. of Australia, and its partner, Dia Met Minerals of Kelowna, BC), could be ready to begin production as early as 1997 (Hummel 1994: 13). Some of the most immediate concerns focus on the need for: (i) clear plans backed up by the necessary political will to complete a network of protected areas, particularly in the regions that are most likely to be affected by the mining; (ii) research on the regional grizzly bear population, and caribou herds, especially the Bathurst herd whose calving grounds and winter range encompass the Slave geological province; (iii) a policy on what impacts could be permitted on wildlife-sensitive parts of the tundra landscape; (iv) policies on access by winter roads versus permanent roads, on hydro development to service the very high energy demands of diamond mining and on kimberlite-tailing disposal; (v) assessment of the socio-economic benefits to northerners, coupled with efforts to train the local workforce for the employment opportunities (Ibid.). Imperatives of sustainable development demand that similar concerns should be met in Norway and Finland as well.

In northeastern Alaska, efforts to open up the Arctic National Wildlife Refuge to oil and gas exploration pose a threat to the Porcupine caribou herd, on which the people of the northern Yukon and the Mackenzie Delta depend. The US Department of the Interior is proposing to open up the last 10% of the Alaska coastal plain to development, despite the potential adverse effects not only on caribou but on the birds, the bears and the muskoxen which use the area. Opposing the development plans is one of the top priority items on the political agenda of the communities of the Vuntut Gwich'in of the Old Crow region in the northern Yukon.

To encounter the potential threats to small and predominantly native communities of the Arctic from megaprojects, there must be mandatory environmental and social-impact procedures which precede development activities. Such assessments must be made early enough in the planning process to be able to influence decisions and help formulate alternative approaches. Even after a specific project has been approved, evaluation and monitoring should continue. The Antarctic experience has shown that the implementation of EIAs can be seriously hampered by ambiguity about what constitutes a "minor" or "major" impact. Given the complex nature and range of actors and interests involved, obtaining consensus in this respect could be far more problematic in the Arctic. Therefore, impact-assessment procedures should be standardized across the region through the exchange of scientific knowledge, experience and techniques. At the same time, there must be active and effective involvement of Arctic communities in the EIAs on a regular and mandatory basis. At present, "most environmental assessments and most monitoring systems for northern development projects neither involve aboriginal communities significantly nor include northern aboriginal peoples' vast knowledge of the natural environment. As a result, most EIAs are ineffective" (Sallenave 1994: 16).

The discussion so far has shown that the common dilemma of the indigenous communities is how to sustain a way of life which is economically more progressive in the Arctic-specific context but politically and internationally less accepted. Yet it is *they* who in both the short and the long term must identify the problems for themselves, together with appropriate solutions. The community of about 500 Inuit of Clyde River, on Baffin Island in the Eastern Arctic, has successfully developed and implemented a conservation plan to protect the endangered bowhead whale and its critical habitat in the Isabella Bay (Igalirtuuq) area, in cooperation with the World Wildlife Fund, Canada. The community has not only sponsored the plan but has also identified how it wants to be involved in its implementation. The plan covers not only issues related to the survival of the bowhead but also the possibility of economic benefits through carefully developed and monitored tourism – an approach worthy of emulation by the others in the North.

Ecological assets, biological diversity and renewable resources

While it is true that vast tracts of the Arctic habitat remain more or less pristine, in many parts the damage is extensive and in some cases already irreversible. It is worth bearing in mind the distinction between (i) Arctic-specific threats and (ii) the threats that originate outside the Arctic but imperil the Arctic habitat and its biological–cultural diversity. We begin by citing a few examples in the first category.

In the Russian Arctic, oil and gas extraction over the last two decades has destroyed an estimated six million hectares of reindeer pasture in the Yamal–Nenets region alone. The gigantic oil fields in Western Siberia were developed without any EIAs. As a result, many valuable species of fish and fur have completely disappeared, and dozens of small rivers are polluted. In Chukotka the mining industry has destroyed the tundra cover of the land, and the rivers are without plankton, thus endangering salmon and other valuable fish. Destruction of tundra has not merely caused a decline in the number of fur-bearing animals, it has also seriously affected the health of the indigenous people, because greens and plant roots are widely used in traditional medicine. In the Murmansk region, industrial mining sites like Nikel' and Monchegorsk occupy vast areas of completely destroyed vegetation and soil. In Monchegorsk an area of nearly 300 sq km is just an ecological desert. Emissions of sulphur from the Kola Peninsula alone are twice as large as those in the whole of Finland. The so-called "industrial desert" in this region, which contains no living plants, covers an area of about 100 000 hectares. The area where sulphur deposits are estimated to be 1–2g/sq m annually is about 5 million hectares, approximately half the size of Finnish Samiland; the trees lack foliage and there have been drastic changes in the composition of lichen and mosses. It is feared that even if all industrial activity in this area were to cease immediately, the sulphur content of the soil would make cultivation impossible for another 100 years (Ibid.: 140). Unless the speed at which the boreal forest line is receding to the south is curbed, the Peninsula might turn into a rocky tundra within a few decades (Roginko 1992: 147). The Noril'sk area is in a similar state of devastation.

The most recent environmental disaster in the Russian Arctic is the leaking oil in the northwest Russian province of Komi. While estimates of the amount vary from 14 000 tonnes to 65 000 tonnes (about twice the volume in the *Exxon Valdez* disaster), it has been officially acknowledged that the leak has been a long-standing problem, which has increased substantially since February 1994 (Keller 1994b: 12). Given that the pipeline, patched at least 27 times, has been leaking periodically since 1988, the amount of oil involved in the current spill is only a fraction of what has leaked into the tundra and its rivers over the years (see Sagers 1994). When the oil company, Komineft, tried to contain the spill by constructing a dam, it probably did not anticipate that the dam would burst after heavy rains; it did, the resulting flood carrying oil into two tributaries of the Pechora – the Usa and the Kolva Rivers. As a result, the entire Pechora River basin – one of the most important salmon rivers in Europe, supporting the livelihood of local indigenous peoples, particularly the Nentsy who live downstream of the river – is under threat. The long-term implications of the spill for the Russian oil companies are obvious, as it "highlights a number of continuing weaknesses and problems that threaten the overall well-being of the sector" (Ibid.: 101). Growing concerns about Russia's rickety pipeline network might force the Russian government into accepting a larger role for Western companies, both in terms of oil development and the transportation system. The operators of Russia's crude-oil pipeline system fear that the major beneficiary will be a consortium of Western companies (led by Texaco, Exxon and Norsk Hydro) that hopes to construct its own oil-export terminal on the Barents Sea.

While it is in the Russian North that the most dramatic evidence of environmental devastation is found, destruction of the Arctic habitat is not confined to that area. In Alaska, massive oil development at Prudhoe Bay has destroyed thousands of acres of wildlife habitat and left hundreds of open pits containing millions of gallons of oil-industry waste (Chance and Andreeva 1993: 2). The James Bay hydroelectric power complex in northern Quebec has already inundated thousands of square kilometres of wildlife habitat; black spruce forests, which take over 100 years to grow, are being clear-cut at the rate of 600 sq km per year – the equivalent of one Cree family hunting ground (Diamond 1991: 93). According to the World Wide Fund for Nature, if wilderness areas are defined as "areas 5 km or greater from any road or major development" (which does not exclude houses or grazed areas), over the past decade alone the Norwegian wilderness has been reduced by approximately 5000 sq km (*WWF Arctic Bulletin* 1994a: 12). The prospects for the remaining wilderness in the Norwegian north do not appear to be very promising given the fact that nearly 10 sq km of such wilderness habitat is disappearing every week (Ibid.).

Wide-ranging Arctic-specific measures have been suggested to counter the threats outlined above. Griffiths and Young (1989: 6–11) emphasize the need: (i) to standardize Arctic environmental data in order to be able to develop a composite picture of the state of the Arctic environment; (ii) to establish uniform environmental standards specifying permissible limits with regard to the use of natural resources and environmental services; (iii) to develop common environmental assessment procedures; (iv) to introduce joint monitoring arrangements to verify compliance on the part of those engaged in industrial activities in the Arctic; (v) to form unofficial teams of environmental experts to ensure politically detached assessments of environmental protection measures and complaints about their violation; (vi) to establish an Arctic sustainable-development bank with the primary objective of offering investment capital to those interested in providing alternatives to alliances with powerful multinational corporations; and (vii) to introduce a system of SPAs to identify and protect areas of exceptional ecological importance.

Whereas most of the measures suggested above demand an important and active role for the Arctic indigenous communities at both the planning and the implementation stages, substantial economic investment as well as political effort are called for at national and regional levels. It is only recently that the Arctic states have responded politically to the need to address the common environmental issues on a regional basis. It is to this development that we turn next, bearing in mind the following questions: What is the nature and scope of this initiative? What are the major objectives of the initiative and where and how do they fit into the broader context of sustainable development?

Arctic Environmental Protection Strategy: going beyond the pledges?

On the initiative of Finland, the first ministerial meeting on the Arctic environment, involving all eight circumpolar countries, was held in June 1991 in Rovaniemi. Thus began the so-called "Rovaniemi Process", promising a new environmental ethic as well as functionally effective institutions for the Circumpolar North through a Ministerial Declaration on the Arctic Environment and an Arctic Environmental Protection Strategy (AEPS). The latter's objectives are: (i) to protect the Arctic ecosystem, including humans; (ii) to provide for the protection, enhancement and restoration of environmental quality and the sustainable utilization of natural resources, including their use by local populations and indigenous peoples in the Arctic; (iii) to recognize and, to the extent possible, seek to accommodate the traditional and cultural needs, values and practices of the indigenous peoples, as determined by themselves, related to the protection of the Arctic environment; (iv) to review regularly the state of the Arctic environment; and (v) to identify, reduce and, as a final goal, eliminate pollution.

It was also agreed to implement the Arctic Monitoring and Assessment Programme (AMAP), initiated in Rovaniemi in 1989 to monitor the levels and assess the effects of anthropogenic pollutants on all components of the Arctic environment. A task force was also set up (AMAP 1993: 3–5). The other working groups subsequently set up to implement the AEPS are: Protection of the Marine Environment, led by Norway; Emergency Prevention, Preparedness and Response, led by Sweden; and Conservation of Arctic Flora and Fauna (CAFF), to be led by the Arctic countries consecutively.

The objectives and principles outlined in the AEPS, together with the declarations and pledges made both at the first and the second ministerial conferences (the Nuuk Declaration 1993), establish that the policy-makers are aware that "the Arctic environment consists of ecosystems with unique features and resources which are especially slow to recover from the impact of human activities, and as such, require special protective measures" (Ibid.: 3). Much-needed sensitivity acknowledges the fact that "the indigenous peoples who have been permanent residents of the Arctic for millennia, are at risk from environmental degradation" and that "in order to achieve sustainable development, environmental protection shall constitute an integral part of the development process and cannot be considered in isolation from it" (Ibid.). Resources are being sought to enable full participation by each country in the programme activities so that "management, planning and development activities shall provide for the conservation, sustainable use and protection of Arctic flora and fauna for the benefit and enjoyment of present and future generations, including local populations and indigenous peoples" (Ibid.).

It is worth pointing out that in Rovaniemi, in September 1991, it was first decided to consider an Arctic sustainable-development strategy. However, it soon became obvious that some states preferred the term "environmental protection" to "sustainable development" as the key guiding principle for the proposed course of action (Griffiths and Young 1989: 17–18). Could this disagreement be due to a divergence of perception in terms of "comprehensiveness and readiness to address problems in their industrial origins *versus* functional selectivity and an inclination to deal with consequences rather more than the character of industrial activity" (Ibid.)?

Since 1991, when the AEPS was agreed, considerable progress has been made towards realizing ecological security for the Arctic as a whole (Prokosch 1994b: 4–5). It is hoped that this pan-Arctic cooperation will result in concrete action being taken by several governmental working groups, of which AMAP is reported to have achieved the most so far. At the same time, and despite the fact that at this level few non-environmental interests are affected, all attempts to introduce some kind of *regulative* elements into the Rovaniemi Process have failed. The lack of legal obligation under the AEPS, in sharp contrast to the obligations created by the Madrid Protocol in the case of the Antarctic, casts serious doubt on its implementation and enforcement. As Stokke (1992: 226) points out:

> One reason is the element of asymmetry present in this issue, in that various Arctic States will be affected differently by increased institutionalization. Generally, the Arctic rim States stress the difference between Antarctic and Arctic politics, especially the status of the sovereignty claims, and less explicitly, the strategic significance of the Arctic.

While there appears to be little disagreement among the Arctic states, at least in principle, that ecological problems require transnational strategies with sufficient regulative competence, differences persist over how best to realize the objective of ecological security for the Arctic without duplication of effort, excessive bureaucratization and the common political problems associated with the combination of asymmetry and competition.

The Rovaniemi Process is no doubt a concrete and relevant step in the direction of realizing environmental protection for the Arctic. However, given the linkages between economic development and conservation practices, and the need for proactive (rather than reactive) management of increasingly diverse exploitation of the Arctic natural environment, a far more comprehensive and legally binding regime is required. Arctic-specific realities require such a regime to be based on the principles of sustainable development outlined above. Treating the symptoms of unsustainability only, while the fundamental causes remain more or less untouched, may not lead the Arctic countries far enough on the road to sustainable development. Even the former require far more specific commitments of both a political and a financial nature from the Arctic states than has been the case so far.

While it remains to be seen whether the Arctic states will eventually take the Rovaniemi Process to its logical conclusion by creating a comprehensive circumpolar environmental protection regime for the Arctic, they have adopted a number of international instruments or entered into bilateral and multilateral agreements, protocols and conventions which have relevance for the Arctic. It is timely to look briefly at some of them.

Protected areas

Some progress has been made in respect of protected areas. Given the organic unity of the land and sea components of the Arctic ecosystems, the need to provide for the natural functioning of ecosystems is now widely recognized (see Arikaynen 1991). Certain areas of the Arctic have been declared protected areas (designated as national parks or reserves) as a consequence of either individual state legislation or international conventions (see CAFF-Report 1994: 53–8; Rothwell 1994). Approximately 14% of the terrestrial Arctic area is protected in some form, which is roughly equivalent to 5.5 million hectares (Prokosch 1994b: 4). These can range from very large national parks, such as the Greenland National Park, which is approximately 70 million hectares in extent, to small bird sanctuaries on Svalbard.

A group of American environmental organizations has proposed recently the establishment of several transnational protected areas in the Arctic (*WWF Arctic Bulletin* 1994b: 16). Among the terrestrial areas proposed are the large-scale Caribou Commons Biocultural Reserve, comprising the adjoining Arctic National Wildlife Refuge (US), Ivvavik and Vuntut National Parks (Canada) and the vital Porcupine caribou calving grounds. The group has also proposed an International Marine Biocultural Reserve (the "Arctic Ring of Life"), encompassing the dynamic and productive region shoreward of the permanent icecap, i.e. the zone of leads and polynyas parallel to the coastline of the Arctic Ocean. The proposal has extraordinary ecological merit because of the critical importance of this multipurpose habitat for birds and marine mammals and as a hunting ground for indigenous peoples. It also underlines the vulnerability of the "Arctic Ring of Life" to large-scale oil and gas development, mining, nuclear-powered transport and nuclear waste disposal.

From the perspective of the new geopolitics, however, the Beringia Conservation Program launched in 1989 by the National Audubon Society, an

American environmental organization, is the most challenging initiative. The principal objective of the programme "is to cooperate with Russian and Native partners to conserve a shared natural and cultural heritage in Beringia, that vast expanse of land and sea in Northwest Alaska and Eastern Siberia that constituted a land bridge between Asia and North America during the Ice Age" (Cline 1992: 71). Three key proposals under the programme are: (i) the Beringian Heritage International Park, (ii) the Bering Land Bridge World Heritage Site and (iii) the Beringia International Marine Biosphere Reserve. The presidents of both the USA and Russia have agreed to establish the international park as a formal recognition of the shared natural and cultural heritage of the Beringia region. The second proposal actually stems from the 1988 annual meeting of the IUCN which had passed a resolution urging both the USA and the USSR to designate the Barents Strait region as a World Heritage Site, in view of its significance as a global treasure trove of answers to questions about world palaeoecology, anthropology, archaeology and history. The objectives of the Beringia International Marine Biosphere Reserve have been described as follows: (i) according greater international recognition to the importance of the Bering Strait as an international crossroads for people and wildlife; (ii) officially recognizing the historic relationship between the wildlife and people of Northwest Alaska and the Russian Far East and their continued reliance on subsistence; (iii) encouraging greater international cooperation between the USA and Russia in the protection of a shared natural and cultural heritage in Beringia; and (iv) identifying opportunities for sustainable development for the indigenous communities as perceived by themselves (Ibid.: 71–2).

Despite the unmistakable ecological value as well as geopolitical significance of the above-mentioned proposals in weakening the Cold War mentality on both sides of the Bering Strait, the biosphere reservation idea has so far failed to generate support in Alaska (Ibid.). While some indigenous communities fear that a biosphere reserve might somehow undermine subsistence activities, mining interests anticipate that the reserve would interfere with oil development and mining. Doubts have also been expressed about the capability of the proposed reserve to deal effectively with the mounting threats of overfishing, air and water pollution and radioactive wastes.

The nature, scope and impact of human activities is far more diverse in the Arctic than in the Antarctic. In the case of the latter a balance is to be maintained primarily between environmental protection *per se* and protecting the natural environment for its scientific value, as opposed to "nonscientific" human activities, i.e. tourism. The range of interests to be reconciled in the Arctic is much wider: those of the mining industries, the environmental organizations, the ministries of the environment, the tourists and tour operators, and above all the indigenous people. To obtain consensus in the Arctic will thus be far more difficult.

The idea of an Arctic Protected Areas Network has been supported by the majority of indigenous people in the Arctic, provided the importance of these areas to their survival in terms of land, biological resources, hunting and fishing grounds and reindeer pastures is taken into account. It is felt that such networks can play a pivotal role in environmental management by safeguarding indigenous harvesting areas as well as the habitats that support them.

The management prospects of the protected areas appear to vary across the Circumpolar North. As of January 1994, the total area of all types of Arctic reserve (strict nature reserves, national nature parks, nature monuments, special-purpose reserves and nature–ethnic parks) was about 19.7 million hectares, comprising about 10.2% of the Russian Arctic (Volkov and Korte 1994: 299). However, prevailing economic and political uncertainty in Russia continues to cause "confusion about legislation, management, and authority in relation to the nature reserves" (Ibid.). Other problems include: (i) the remote location of the Arctic reserves and the difficulty and expense involved in linking them to the rest of the country; (ii) lack of detailed scientific information and the problem of gaining access to the relevant data in "relatively inaccessible archives"; and (iii) the problem of regulating tourism in nature reserves without undermining its income-generating potential. In the case of nature–ethnic parks, which aim to protect nature and the traditional use of resources by indigenous people, there are still no general rules for their management. Conflict has also arisen about the use of natural resources by, on the one hand, indigenous people and, on the other, local Russian people, who may have different rights. While much remains to be done by the Russian authorities themselves in managing protected areas in the Russian Arctic, the need for international financial and technical assistance is perhaps too obvious to be emphasized.

Despite the fact that marine and coastal waters are by far the most biologically productive of the Arctic ecosystems, they have received the least permanent protection. According to the WWF (Prokosch 1994b), the development of a much-needed comprehensive plan for protected areas in the Arctic must incorporate both marine and terrestrial environments, comprising at least 50% of the total Arctic. In addition to working out common conservation objectives within a common frame of reference, the plan should include: (i) mapping of marine ecosystems; (ii) establishing scientific and traditional knowledge criteria for the selection of protected areas; (iii) evaluating the comparative advantages of the various protected-area strategies adopted and implemented by different countries; (iv) establishing a target for a percentage of areas to be protected on a repre-sentative basis; and (v) considering various aspects of the said plan within the context of wider management strategies. Obviously, success on the ground will depend to a large extent on the political and financial commit-ment of the Arctic countries.

A proposal for establishing a Barents Sea International Park has also been put forward by the WWF and some other NGOs (*WWF Arctic Bulletin* 1994b: 17). The intention is that the park, which would extend from the summer limits of Arctic pack ice in the north to the winter pack-ice limits in the south (including the islands of Svalbard, Bear Island, Franz Joseph Land, part of Novaya Zemlya and the marine areas surrounding them), should include both marine and terrestrial ecosystems, since they are mutually interdependent. Whereas the idea appears to have gained some support within both Norway and Russia, the Norwegian government's response to the proposal so far is said to be both slow and cautious (Ibid.). Given that Svalbard falls within the scope of the Barents Sea Park, Norwegian hesitation is perhaps understandable. Norway is also concerned that the natural reserves on Svalbard "will necessarily entail restriction on the usage of possible natural resources in the protected areas; these are the resources in which the parties to the Svalbard Treaty could have a legitimate interest" (Hanevold 1994: 229).

Conservation and wildlife management

According to the 1992 Convention on Biological Diversity, which entered into force in late 1993, the state Parties are obliged to ensure conservation of "biological diversity, the sustainable use of its components and the fair and equitable sharing of the benefits arising out of the utilisation of genetic resources". The Convention, ratified by Canada, Denmark, Norway and Sweden, and quite similar to CCAMLR, is based on an ecosystem approach and therefore is of exceptional significance for the Arctic. Other conventions with global application, and relevant to the protection of Arctic wildlife, are the Convention on International Trade in Endangered Species of Wild Fauna and Flora (1973) and the Convention on the Conservation of Migratory Species of Wild Animals (1979). While the former has been ratified by all the Arctic states except Iceland, the latter has been ratified by only Denmark (excepting Greenland), Finland, Norway and Sweden. Specific management regimes for caribou, fur seals, polar bears and whales are already functional in the Arctic.

Caribou

Large caribou herds extend from Alaska across into northern Quebec. To ensure the sustainability of the herds, while allowing a subsistence take by the indigenous people, a number of management schemes have been implemented. In July 1987 Canada and the USA signed an Agreement on the Conservation of the Porcupine Caribou Herd, aimed at conserving the herds through bilateral cooperation and coordination, while also ensuring opportunities for customary and traditional uses of the herd by communities in Alaska, the Yukon and the Northwest Territories. The agreement, negotiated over a period of 10 years, with the strong involvement of local-user groups, represents only a formal commitment to co-operate between the two parties rather than a resource-management agreement. It fails both in providing specific habitat-protection measures or a clear procedure for determining or distributing an allowable harvest to users on either side of the international boundary and in establishing an authority with the capacity to make independent binding decisions on the allocation of the harvest (Bankes 1991: 20–1).

Fur seals

One of the earliest examples of multilateral cooperation to protect the Arctic environment is the 1911 Convention for the Preservation and Protection of Fur Seals, signed by Great Britain (for Canada), Japan, Russia and the United States. Seeking to prohibit pelagic sealing in the waters of the Pacific Ocean north of 30°N, including the Bering, Kamchatka, Okhotsk and Japan Seas, this was one of the first attempts to prohibit resource exploitation in areas beyond national jurisdiction, where the resources were traditionally regarded as *res communis*. After a short break during World War II, a new treaty, based on the same principles, was concluded by the same parties in 1957. The agreement finally lapsed in 1984, when the USA refused to approve a new four-year extension. This has led some scholars to conclude that instead of increasing international cooperation on this matter, "countries are sliding back from international to national regulation of fur sealing in the North Pacific" (Franckx 1992: 114).

Polar bears

The 1973 Agreement on the Conservation of Polar Bears is the first and only circumpolar, legally binding conservation agreement in the Arctic (see chapter 4). There appears to be near-agreement among the experts that the species – numbering between 25 000 and 40 000 – is at present increasingly vulnerable (Prokosch 1994a: 13). The IUCN Polar Bears Specialist Group indicated at its meeting in January 1994 that some of the polar bear subpopulation in Canada is already overexploited (Ibid.), and quota and reporting systems are still undeveloped. Although polar bear hunting in Russia is prohibited, conservation measures there are reported to be under increasing pressure due to illegal shooting by poachers, the pollution of Arctic waters by chlorine organic compounds, other pesticides and heavy metals, an increase in drilling activities and the extraction of hydrocarbons and oil products (Uspensky 1994: 14). Consistent political and financial commitment will be required from the Arctic states to ensure that the conservation and management of polar bears is not threatened.

Whales

The 1946 International Convention for the Regulation of Whaling and its management by the IWC have obvious relevance to the Arctic because of the large number of whales in Arctic waters, the commercial significance of whaling for Iceland and Norway and the economic–cultural importance of whales to indigenous people. As a result of the moratorium imposed by the IWC during the last decade, serious tensions have surfaced between whaling and non-whaling parties to the Convention. While Iceland has withdrawn from the IWC, Norway is thinking of resuming commercial whaling in the Arctic. Recently a North Atlantic Marine Mammal Commission (NAMCO) has been created, of which Iceland, Norway and the Home Governments of the Faeroes and Greenland are members. Regional in scope, the NAMCO admits only parties interested in resource management and is concerned with the conservation and management of seals and small cetaceans. NAMCO has yet to undertake regulating activities in Arctic waters.

Sustainable development and tourism in the Arctic

Over the past two decades or so a combination of factors – including the establishment of national parks, much-enhanced accessibility, increased visibility via all forms of the media, heightened awareness of indigenous issues and a dramatic increase in international interest in tourism in "wilderness" areas – has resulted in a rapid increase in the number of tourists bound for the Arctic (see Johnston 1995). Although numbers are still low compared to those experienced in other tourist destinations – with the exception of the Antarctic – the ecological as well as social impact of tourism is increasing. The problem is that of maintaining the economic benefits while minimizing or preventing adverse impacts on the natural and social environments.

In the context of sustainable development, one could argue that tourism should be "developed and maintained in an area (community environment) in such a manner and at such a scale that it remains viable over an indefinite period and does not degrade or alter the environment (human and physical) in which it exists to such a degree that it prohibits the successful development and wellbeing of other activities and processes" (Butler 1992). It is important to bear in mind the distinction between tourism that helps sustain the grassroots economies and benefits local communities, and tourism national governments see as contributing to the gross national product (GNP), hence far more desirable. Moreover, the principles of ecotourism, outlined in Chapter 8, should be integrated into the local-development programmes, in harmony with the principles of community-based sustainable development in the Arctic.

The steady growth of the tourist industry in both the polar regions has invited mixed reactions from the observer and the analyst. According to some the Arctic is in "danger" and "the tourist industry in general, and more frequently under the guise of ecotourism, is exerting more and more pressure on extremely fragile and irreplaceable ecosystems" (Colin 1992). For example, tourism is now the second largest source of income in the NWT, generating C$54 million in 1990, equal to 2.7% of the GNP, and an additional C$23 million in taxes. The tourism industry employs around 2500 people, approximately one-third of the workforce in the NWT (Butler 1992). More than 250 000 tourists visit Alaska every year, and the number might reach 500 000 by the year 2000.

The economic attraction of tourism for the Arctic economies, struggling against massive fiscal dependence on the outside and seriously constrained by limited prospects for diversification, is quite understandable. In 1992, the Greenland Home Rule Government established "Greenland Tourism", a firm wholly owned by the government, with the aim of attracting more tourists to Greenland. It is estimated that by 2005 the number of tourists visiting Greenland (currently between 5000 to 6000 a year) might reach an annual volume of 35 000. Although the boost to the overall GNP would be welcome, how much the communities outside the main population centres would benefit remains to be seen. From the point of view of the smaller communities, the hiking and trekking package tours in their areas would be a far more attractive proposition than other forms of high-profile tourism.

Each country, region and locality will need to adapt and define ecotourism in the light of their own circumstances. Nevertheless, there is a need for a set of common policy guidelines. The question or issue of prime concern in the Arctic (as in the Antarctic) is not whether or not there should be tourism in the high latitudes, but how it should be regulated. As Butler (1991) demonstrates, while some of the regulatory problems of Arctic tourism emanate from the policy-makers' ignorance of the scale, nature and power of tourism as a dynamic industry, and lack of appreciation that tourism can and does have impacts on the environment that may not be easily reversible, some problems are due to lack of agreement about the levels of development, control and direction of tourism. While local control of tourism, or at least substantial local involvement in decision-making about tourism, is extremely important, that alone may not be enough to ensure that tourism development will be appropriate. Moreover, it would be naive to assume unanimity in local attitudes to tourism; some local residents may desire extensive tourism development, while others may wish for little or none.

A number of very useful recommendations for managing tourism in the context of sustainable development have been made by Colin (1992). They include: (i) integrating tourism into traditional land-use planning; (ii) designing ecotourism programmes in such a way that they benefit the local people, thereby also helping to preserve natural areas and wildlife;

(iii) careful planning with local communities to ensure that tourist activities do not interfere with subsistence activities; (iv) providing better training for guides, tour operators, travel agents and members of host communities; and (v) establishing centres of information, data and studies on ecotourism, with the appropriate contracts. However, much more is required in order to achieve accountability and adequate planning, management and control of Arctic tourism. Although there are governments in the Arctic, unlike the Antarctic, it is the active involvement of the tour operators and local communities that holds the key to better prospects for ecotourism in the Circumpolar North. One would expect the tour operators in the Arctic, many with bipolar experience, to participate actively in the formulation and implementation of guidelines for the conduct of the tourism industries and the tourists (see Blangy and Wood 1992). This can be achieved by setting up an International Association for Arctic Tour Operators.

Development and management of circumpolar transportation/ communications networks

One of the legacies from the past is that communication and transportation networks in the Arctic are mainly intranational and flow in a north–south direction (see Kazantseva and Westin 1994). Barriers of a natural geographic, structural, administrative and cultural nature further perpetuate the role of the Circumpolar North as a mere supplier of natural resources and inhibit interaction among the northern communities at all levels. In order to travel to Anchorage or Fairbanks in Alaska from the neighbouring Whitehorse in Yukon, for example, one has to fly via Seattle. The same pattern can be observed in the Nordic countries and in Russia. Northern Norway is linked with Oslo, northern Sweden with Stockholm and northern Finland with Helsinki. The flow of air traffic in Russia also reveals that the Murmansk region is similarly linked with St Petersburg, and Arkhangel'sk with Moscow. The road networks fall into more or less the same national patterns and remain largely oriented towards the commercial requirements of the industrialized southern metropolis. Transformation of the Arctic into a truly circumpolar geopolitical region will demand not just investment in the transportation sector but also meticulously planned and judiciously implemented EIAs. A well-developed communications infrastructure will also be vitally important, especially for the Russian North (Putilov 1994).

The Northern Sea Route

As a result of the hegemonic conflict, the use of the Northern Sea Route (NSR) for international trade and commerce during the Cold War was strictly forbidden. However, in the radically transformed context of the post-Cold War era and the changing world economy (see Knox and Agnew 1994: 135–7) a very different picture emerges. One of the most far-reaching developments of the 21st century would be the NSR's availability to international shipping. There are obvious economic advantages for Russia, the other states on the Arctic rim and for "outsiders" in making this "shortcut" between the Pacific and the Atlantic a reality (see Østreng 1991b, 1994). The opening of the NSR would be the most obvious manifestation of the linking of the Russian maritime Arctic to the global economy, acting as a "catalyst for change in the Arctic and sub-Arctic regions of the globe" (Brigham 1993: 167). From the Russian point of view, the prime motivation is to link the "Northern Russian Zone" to Europe and the Far East and thereby contribute to the economic restructuring of the country (see Granberg 1993).

Historically, the NSR, which serves several large harbours and numerous smaller ones at the estuaries of the great rivers of Siberia, has been providing transit passage for Russia/the Soviet Union, while stimulating the expansion of regional commerce and industry. Now that the majority of the sea ports in the European part of the former Soviet Union belong to Lithuania, Latvia and Estonia, the importance to Russia of alternative Arctic harbour facilities, particularly in the context of the NSR, is that much greater. The significance of the route is further augmented by its potential for generating revenue for the cash-starved Russian economy through international commercialization. According to Brigham (1993: 168), the NSR can be used in three distinct ways: (i) to establish flows of materials, goods and services between European ports and Western Siberian cities such as Igarka and Noril'sk by linking maritime activities in the Barents and Kara Seas and on the Ob' and Yenisey Rivers; (ii) as a maritime economic link between the Far East and Pacific-rim countries and Russia's Far Northeast (in other words, to link natural-resource development on the Lena River, Laptev Sea and East Siberian Sea to Alaska, Korea, Japan, China and other Pacific countries); and (iii) ultimately as an international waterway for year-round transits by foreign and Russian ships between European and Russian ports and destinations throughout the Pacific Ocean.

However, there are problems too. Whereas shipping companies would like to ensure that reduced distances are also translated into reduced transit times, to ensure low costs on a year-round basis – which may well become possible, in the not too remote future, by a curious combination of much-improved icebreaking technology and less Arctic ice due to climate change and ice melting – improvements are also required in ice-warning and ice-surveillance capacity, as well as in the administrative and organizational efficiency of the Russian State. Assuming that the technology is available, or soon will be, using the NSR is still going to be very expensive.

Other limiting factors include: erratic deliveries from other regions to the NSR due to the dismantling of the state supply system, and the extremely difficult situation of industrial enterprises, the icebreaker fleet and the ports, due to price liberalization and inflation (Granberg 1993: 982). The present as well as future prospects of the NSR will depend to a large extent, therefore, on the scale of international investment and industrial activities in the Arctic and Subarctic regions as well as on the development of transit shipment. Lurking in the background, with its potential nuisance value, will of course be the persisting differences between the USA and Russia over the legal status of the passage (see Timtchenko 1994).

Yet another factor to be taken into account is the way in which the transformed position of the Kola Peninsula – from a geostrategic point of view perhaps far more important to Russia than it was to the Soviet Union – is going to affect the development and operation of the NSR. Will there be opposition from military interests to its internationalization? It is rather unrealistic to assume that there will be none (see Dawisha and Parrott 1994: 233–45). However, as long as Moscow continues to recognize the distinction between military and non-military uses of the NSR, and is prepared to stress economic interests rather than the importance of the NSR in strategic games, international cooperation should be forthcoming. The cooperation of the Navy and the Frontier Guard will of course be central to the whole enterprise in the context of monitoring and control of national ocean space. Equally crucial will be the success in realizing the rather complex and difficult process of converting military–industrial facilities, personnel and technologies for the production of civilian products and services to support the commercial use of the NSR.

From the standpoint of sustainable development, however, the two most vital considerations are the impacts of the project on (a) the Arctic environment (Hansson 1993a) and (b) the indigenous peoples of the region. The most immediate environmental consequences will probably flow from increased shipping activity and the potential for accidents associated with it. The incidence of sea ice and shallow waters, the limited possibilities for efficient prevention and clean-up operations and the inadequate maintenance of the ships (more than 50% of which are over 20 years old) must also be borne in mind, despite the universally acclaimed experience of Russian crews in large-scale operations in such harsh and remote conditions (Hansson 1993b: 12).

As forcefully argued by Osherenko (1993), "those planning for expanded use of the NSR have not yet addressed the environmental and social impacts of increased and internationalized use" (Ibid.: 116). According to her, the NSR can be expected to alter life in the small communities as they are drawn to the ports along the route. While the non-indigenous populations of the region involved are far more numerous than the indigenous population, the dependence of the latter on natural resources makes

255

them major actors as well as a key focus of social and ecological impact assessments. For example, as many as 10 indigenous groups live in the coastal areas from Norway to the Chukchi Sea alone (see Ibid.: 121–3). Since these and many other indigenous groups across the region show remarkable variation in terms of settlement patterns, nomadic practices and the relationship of clans and individual families to the settlements and communities, there is a need for both detailed and geographically wide-ranging baseline studies. To sum up: "If the proponents of the NSR take their commitment to sustainable development seriously, if they heed the international agreements signed by the eight Arctic states, and if they hope to steer a smooth course through the politically turbulent waters of devolution of power and authority from the central government to local and regional authorities and indigenous peoples . . . they will have charted a safer and more successful course" (Ibid.: 128–9).

The polar route: towards an "Arctic Mediterranean" community?

The physical logic of the northern-hemisphere air setting, the steady leaps of aeronautical science and technology, the end of the Cold War and the growing prospects of large-scale exploitation of mineral resources in the Arctic have combined to revive the idea of an "Arctic Mediterranean" as the focus of a future intercontinental civil aviation community. In the words of Henrikson (1992), who has followed the origins and evolution of this idea for nearly two decades, the question is whether this notion "could or should be developed in the technologically advanced and politically improved situation of the present". If so, "what should be the regulatory character, if any, of a civil-aviation order or 'regime' in the northern skies" (Ibid.: 108)?

As and when the vision of an "Arctic train of ships driving straight through the north polar ice, year round" from the Barents Sea to the Bering Strait is realized, the political geography of many parts of the Arctic will also change from the point of view of aviation. For example, the island of Svalbard, by virtue of its intermediate location, will become an important base for ice-reconnaissance aircraft and helicopters. Aviation and shipping in the Arctic will become increasingly associated. However, the ultimate driving force behind and the justification for a circumpolar aviation regime is likely to be the known riches of the region, especially the hydrocarbons. Where rail or road communications are not feasible, and where water links are seasonal, air transport will hold the key to the opening up of the gas and oil sector (Armstrong *et al.* 1978: 64–5). Moreover, the need for aviation services in the High North is likely to increase in the future due to the growth of tourism – likely to be the largest industry in the North by the end of the century. It is significant that, as a result of an increase in the number of overseas visitors to the Yukon by 152% since

1987, air travel has increased by 45% and is likely to grow further (Yukon Government 1995: 25). The requirements of the indigenous and other inhabitants, who at present are forced to go all the way down "south" in order to cover relatively short circumpolar distances, will also play an important role. As this classic pattern of centre–periphery spatial domination is increasingly challenged by the northern communities, and free-trade zones are established with neighbours, intra-Arctic hops will receive a further boost.

The question then becomes: should Arctic civil aviation be formally regulated? There is currently no specific regime for transarctic flying, despite the fact that the end of the Cold War has opened up new possibilities. Most notable is the Open Skies Treaty, signed in March 1992 in Helsinki, providing for general-purpose mutual observation, increasing transparency and enhancing confidence. As more great-circle routes are being contemplated (with transpolar flights into China, perhaps extending to Southeast Asia and India), it seems certain that "the web-like designs of both intra-Arctic and supra-Arctic air traffic are rather likely to thicken and to overlap in the future" and also that "the sheer complexity of these expanding aviation connecting routes, together with the social and natural side-effects of the growing system, suggest need for a cooperative supervision if not actual management of it" (Henrikson 1992: 129). The sustainable development and management of Arctic aviation will have to take into account the fact that air rules in the high latitudes are made not so much by "sovereign consent" as by natural laws and that there are important environmental concerns as well. Seasonal adjustments to routes, or even total avoidance, might be necessary in order to ensure that wildlife is not disrupted. Needless to say, the EIAs required to meet such concerns would also benefit from effective input from local communities.

Summary and conclusions

The northern circumpolar regions of the global economy present to the advocates of community-based sustainable development both unique options and unique obstacles. This chapter has shown that, among alternative models of development, the community-based, citizen-driven approach has the greatest potential for realizing fundamental changes in the socio-economic, ecological and cultural survival strategies for the circumpolar Arctic. It has emphasized localized, participatory economic planning as the most effective alternative to the insecurity, dependency and vulnerability typically inflicted by large-scale, remote, socially detached and politically non-accountable economic development. This in turn requires us to arrest, if not reverse, the dominant growth-oriented trends within the Arctic states on the one hand and to arm the local communities with genuine political autonomy and the financial and technical competence to re-establish their control over resources on the other.

While the creativity, innovative capability and traditional knowledge of indigenous people have a vital role, renewable resources should be given a central place if northerners are to ensure a viable future for themselves and for future generations. Strategies will have to be judiciously planned and implemented to ensure that the extraction of non-renewable resources is balanced against the impacts of such exploitation on the tenuous renewable-resource chain, without compromising the North's own future needs for such irreplaceable resources. It is crucial to ensure that if "indigenous people are not to be suppressed by the indiscriminate application of sustainable development, the concept must be given a dynamic dimension including the possibility for changes of traditional production as accepted in other industries" (Lyck 1990b: 7).

What emerges equally obviously from the chapter is that throughout the Circumpolar North the struggle between community-based economies and megaproject development is likely to intensify in the years to come. Prospects for sustainable development, therefore, will also depend upon the political will, efforts and intervention of the Arctic states themselves. Despite many innovative and promising initiatives in recent years with regard to environmental protection, the Arctic states so far have failed to negotiate a legally binding circumpolar arrangement which will take into account the multidimensional facets of sustainable development. The need for such a binding commitment is far more pressing in the context of the inadequacies of the prevailing bilateral and multilateral arrangements in terms of both their narrow scope and their ineffective implementations.

Suggested reading

Greiffenberg, T. (ed.) 1994. *Sustainability in the Arctic*. Proceedings from Nordic Arctic Research Forum Symposium 1993. Aalborg: Aalborg University Press.

Käkönen, J. (ed.) 1993. *Politics and Sustainable Growth in the Arctic*. Aldershot: Dartmouth.

The Commission on Global Governance 1995. *Our Global Neighbourhood*. The Report of the Commission on Global Governance. Oxford: Oxford University Press.

Simonsen, H. (ed.) 1993. *Proceedings from the Northern Sea Route Expert Meeting, 13–14 October 1992, Tromsø, Norway*. Lysaker: Fridtjof Nansen Institute.

10

Conclusions: the way forward

Politics, and political processes, rarely come to a natural end; they are essentially an ongoing activity. Vigorous or sedentary, politics is present whenever and wherever humans are organizing themselves and the space around them for the satisfaction of their wants – spiritual or material. The unceasing continuum between geography and politics does not permit "final", conclusive statements. The intention here is therefore not so much to "conclude" as (a) to summarize briefly the findings of the study in respect of the issues raised in the first chapter, (b) to assess continuity as well as change in the polar regions and (c) to comment on the prospects of the new geopolitics in the Arctic and Antarctic in the 1990s and beyond.

The polar regions: then and now

Chapter 1 has argued that the essence of a new geopolitics lies in the acknowledgement of both a new politics and a new geography. The study of politics is not only about power politics but also about the restraint of power, the use of power to achieve a vision of collective good and social justice and the channelling of power through decision-making institutions where values determine output. Similarly, geography is not just concerned with the disposition of states in relation to the layout of the continents and oceans, determining the strategic options of particular states, but also with human–environment relations at local, regional and global levels. The success of a new geopolitics on the ground thus depends largely on the ability and willingness of politics to transcend narrow state-centred, power-political concerns and to address the issues that concern humanity as a whole. Environmentally sustainable and socially equitable development and management were singled out as two of the major concerns of the new geopolitics in the polar regions, in contrast to the obsession of the old with territorial aggrandizement and domination.

The complexity of the natural environment in the Arctic and Antarctic was explored in Chapter 2, with reference to ecology, resource endowment and subjective human factors. Both polar regions were shown to be exceptionally important, highly vulnerable but inadequately understood *ecological regions* of our planet that have been profoundly affected by the sovereignty discourse, the geography of imperialism and the geopolitics of state power (Chapter 3).

After World War II the two polar regions were taken in opposite directions by the then major powers. The Cold War transformed Arctic circumpolar political geography into a militarized geography, disallowed international cooperation among the Arctic states in the civil domain and extensively damaged the ecology and resource base of the indigenous homelands (Chapter 4). In the Antarctic, though Cold War-related considerations were never absent, there were few compelling reasons for either the claimant or the non-claimant states, including the two superpowers, to drag the area into Cold War politicking. While the Arctic was extensively militarized, the major powers of the day found it convenient to keep the Antarctic non-militarized, non-nuclear, peaceful and open to science.

Antarctic geopolitics: continuity, change and challenge

What was initially, at the height of the Cold War, conceived and formalized in the 14 articles of the Antarctic Treaty, has over the years evolved and expanded far beyond those tentative, elementary objectives of gaining scientific access to the Antarctic. The ATS now encompasses and addresses a variety of issues on which the Treaty was either silent or ambiguous (Chapter 5). It has established itself as a pioneering experiment. The principles according to which the system has evolved are indeed unique: meaningful accommodation, together with the exceptional dispute-management strategy of *circumvention*, which consists of proceeding in the areas of agreement and possible cooperation while setting aside the contentious issues – in this case, the sovereignty dispute in Antarctica.

Maintaining peace and cooperation in the Antarctic has, however, not been an easy task for the ATPs. Whereas the harsh environment and relative isolation continue to impose serious limitations on what humans can achieve in the Antarctic, rapid advances in transport and communications technology have "opened up" Antarctica today as never before. Although the ATCPs have been able to present a common front against the mounting pressures caused by the erosion of geopolitical isolation, especially on the floor of the UN, they have barely survived the crisis of consensus on the issue of mineral-resource development.

The most significant element of continuity in Antarctic geopolitics relates to the array of territorial claims on the continent which, despite Article IV of the Antarctic Treaty, seems to have acquired new dimensions of complexity and contestation. The claimant states have not refrained from asserting sovereign rights over their claimed territories, be it by way of issuing postage stamps, increased activity by national scientific expeditions, increasing their Antarctic budgets or the application of domestic or territorial laws to the claimed sector. The unresolved and obviously intractable sovereignty dispute continues to impinge upon the evolution of the ATS. It is not without reason that, in all the instruments negotiated and concluded by the ATCPs thus far, "the special legal and political status of Antarctica" is invariably highlighted as a reminder to those within or outside the ATS that every development pursuant to the Treaty must avoid prejudicing the position of claimants or non-claimants in Antarctica.

What has made Antarctica and the ATS so special is neither the reality of the dispute about ownership nor the cooperation among the diverse states but the unique combination of the two. It is the fact that the two realities have been made to coexist, and have been subordinated to the pursuit of commonly "agreed" objectives, that has made the ATS a unique experiment in international relations and diplomacy. It is the philosophy of agreeing to disagree and yet not letting that disagreement get in the way of cooperation that makes the ATS worthy of consideration in very many parts of the world, including the Arctic.

Within this context, the perceptions of Antarctica in individual southern-cone countries are strongly conditioned by their respective geographical locations and overall geopolitical visions and are frequently different from those held by not only more distant nations but also other southern-hemisphere countries (for example, Australia). The return of democratic forms of government in Argentina and Chile, however, offers grounds for optimism and suggests that the evolving geopolitics of South American Antarctica will be cooperative and constructive in nature. Whatever the outcome, it is clear that an appreciation of the manner in which South American geopolitical thinking influences attitudes to Antarctica will continue to be an invaluable guide to the understanding of both perceptions and realities for the quadrant located between the Greenwich and 90°W meridians.

At the time of writing the final section of this book, the ATPs seem to be quite anxious that Pakistan – which sent a scientific expedition to Antarctica in 1991, and has set up a base there – has not, so far, disclosed its intentions *vis-à-vis* the ATS even though it has joined SCAR as an associate member (Rabbani 1994). The reasons for such anxiety become obvious when it is recalled that Pakistan aligned itself with the "critical lobby" in the UN. Will Pakistan join the ATS? Or will it choose to continue to challenge the ATS, at the same time maintaining its scientific presence in

Antarctica? Does this indicate that Pakistan wishes to demonstrate its commitment to the scientific value of Antarctica by showing interest in SCAR membership but to convey its political opposition to the ATS by deciding against adhering to the Antarctic Treaty? Or does Pakistan believe that it will improve its chance of joining the Treaty as a Consultative Member by causing the ATCPs to wonder about the geopolitical implications of a Pakistani presence on the continent but absence from the ATS? Since the Madrid Protocol, most of the reasons for the attack on the ATS in the UN have either ceased to exist or are questionable; it remains probable that Pakistan will join the ATS.

The concluding of the Protocol issue itself has blunted much of the attack on the ATS in the UN. Even its worst critics now seem to agree that over the years the ATS has served a useful purpose in securing peace, stability, scientific cooperation and environmental protection in Antarctica. No viable alternatives to the ATS have presented themselves, for fairly obvious reasons. In this ATS-versus-UN management controversy it must be asked whether the UN as structured at present (it is currently undergoing a "restructuring" process) is actually capable of better performance than the group of "professionals"/"experts" in the ATS. Not much in the UN record inspires particular confidence in that organization's ability to handle an entity and area like the Antarctic. That said, efforts to bridge the gap between the ATS and the critics in the UN should continue.

As the ATS moves into its fourth decade, some of its major challenges appear to be related to non-governmental activities in Antarctica, i.e. those of the environmental pressure groups and the tour operators. The overall impact of these new actors is likely to become much greater. The need of the hour is to transform these "challenges" into proactive cooperative partnerships. Antarctic geopolitics can no longer be a monopoly of nation-states, and the geopolitical isolation of the Antarctic is now a thing of the past.

For the ATPs, the 1990s are going to be a time for both reflection and action. Although no formal request has been made by any one of the ATCPs to convene, under Article IX of the Antarctic Treaty, a conference for review of the Treaty, one seems already to have started in an informal manner. The Bonn ATCM witnessed a healthy and timely action on the part of the ATPs. What appears to be under review is not just the Treaty but the ATS as a whole. A number of items on the agenda of the Bonn and Kyoto ATCMs clearly hinted at such thinking, which has obviously been prompted by the Protocol and the debate that preceded it. For example, the operation of the ATS has come under discussion with special reference to its organizational aspects, the public availability of documents, the examination of recommendations and the exchange of information, and of course the implementation of the Madrid Protocol. With the steady growth of Antarctic tourism, the ATPs will have to pay far more serious and systematic attention to its regulation than has been the case so far.

The viability of the ATS, in the context of the overall prospects for Antarctica and the ATS, will therefore continue to depend critically on its ability to respond to the new problem areas well before they develop into crises – assisted by imaginative and innovative dispute-management strategies and backed up by the necessary political will and commitment to continue to build further on the gains, to avoid conflict deriving from increasingly diverse uses of Antarctica and to demonstrate to the rest of the world that Antarctica shall always be used for peaceful purposes and in the best interests of humankind.

Arctic geopolitics: continuity, change and challenge

Whereas the tradition of a new geopolitics is well established in the Antarctic, the post-Cold War Arctic is in the midst of profound changes both below and beyond the nation-state level. These developments promise to usher in a new era of truly circumpolar cooperation, provided all the Arctic states have the political will to demonstrate their commitment to ecologically sustainable and equitable development of the Circumpolar North.

Over the past few decades the demands of the indigenous peoples for self-government and political autonomy have gained greater momentum and strength, providing new perspectives on security, sovereignty and development in the Arctic (Chapter 6). However, the pace and prospects of the indigenous movements are rather uneven and much needs to be done, especially in terms of capacity-building. The future is full of challenges for the indigenous communities, their leaders and organizations. In the 1990s and beyond, indigenous issues will continue to dominate the agenda of the new geopolitics in the Arctic as new alignments are sought and partnerships formed across national borders to fight entrenched dependencies and counter the forces unleashed by industrialization and modernization. The future of the so-called "small peoples" of the Russian Arctic, in comparison with that of other indigenous groups in the Arctic, however, appears to be rather bleak as Russia fumbles its way to a market economy and haphazardly "opens up" to multinational corporations and Western consumer culture.

Chapter 7 explored the nature and extent of change in the post-Cold War Arctic and found that despite the obvious, encouraging indications of change, the transition from the old to the new geopolitics might not be as short and smooth as one would expect. However, initiatives like the IASC, AEPS, the Barents Region, the Northern Forum and the Arctic Council, among others, indicate that politics in the Arctic has started responding in a big way to the new "circumpolar" realities. This positive change, however, is being undermined by certain continuities from the past: the continuing militarization of the Arctic, especially the Kola Peninsula; the persistence of the Cold War discourse among the old power structures, with its dividing "East–West" logic; the reluctance of the Arctic-rim states to accept any limitations on their sovereignty, which is also reflected in their failure to resolve long-standing disputes; and, last but not least, the uncertainty created by political and economic instability in Russia. It is probably unrealistic to expect far-reaching changes in the Arctic to occur overnight. In the foreseeable future, then, the "old" and the "new" might have to coexist, rather awkwardly, in the Arctic. Nevertheless, there is mounting evidence of the recognition, since the end of the Cold War, of a distinction between military and civil security in the Arctic: both state and non-state actors in the Arctic seem to be willing to act while the window of opportunity is wide open.

The long-standing image and reality of the Circumpolar North as a supplier of natural resources is currently being reinforced by the so-called "regionalization and globalization of the market economy", as exemplified by the Barents Region and the Northern Sea Route projects. The question is not whether economic development is going to take place in the Arctic (it most certainly will, especially in the Russian North) but at what further cost, by whom and for whom. In other words, will it be ecologically sustainable and socially equitable development for the benefit of northerners, especially the indigenous communities, or will it simply repeat the well-known history of boom and bust, leaving behind damaged ecosystems, increasingly dependent "empty" economies and shattered kinship?

Chapter 9 has shown that there are no simple answers to the contradictions arising from the desire for economic growth and the imperatives of environmental conservation – often casually compressed in the term "sustainable development". Nor is there a model that could be applied to the Arctic as a whole. Yet alternatives to the dominant paradigm of growth-oriented economic development in the Arctic must be found. Community-based sustainable development can alone provide meaningful solutions to the problem of political marginalization and the massive economic dependence of the northern communities on the southern, industrialized centres – which has been the norm rather than an exception in the Arctic. Despite the numerous obstacles, policies for sustainable development will have to be planned and implemented at local, national and regional levels. Although illuminating in some respects, the Antarctic experience in the area of environmental conservation and management is of limited value in the Arctic, because the latter is already integrated into the regional and global economy. Moreover, in the Arctic not only environmental impacts but also the socio-cultural impacts must be taken into account.

Despite the commitment expressed in various policy pronouncements, the Arctic states are inadequately placed at present, both in terms of policies and institutions, to tackle the multiple challenge of sustainable development. The AEPS has its merits, but the lack of legal obligations raises concerns about its implementation and enforcement. There is thus an urgent need for a legally binding circumpolar arrangement, at least as binding as the ATS, to address the environmental issues within – rather than outside – the context of sustainable development.

The prospects of a treaty that would translate the emerging realization of the circumpolar Arctic as a distinctive ecological region into enlightened policies and concrete actions for its sustainable and equitable development appear at present to be mixed. The necessary political will among all the Arctic states to be legally bound by such a treaty is still absent. Things might change, however, now that the US government is prepared to support an Arctic Council. To begin with, the Arctic Council is likely to be a flexible forum capable of evolving to reflect changing requirements, to advance common objectives in the Arctic region. As mutual confidence and trust grow among the participating actors, and perceptions of the common circumpolar stakes are translated into policy recommendations – which might not happen in the immediate future – the necessary political will to be bound legally might then manifest itself in concrete terms. Once the political will is there, the cooperation of existing initiatives and institutions will be necessary to avoid duplication of effort.

As progress is made in the direction of an Arctic treaty for sustainable development, it is to be hoped that many aspects of the ATS – its underlying political philosophy, its experience so far in conflict anticipation and management – and the Madrid Protocol will be helpful to the policy-makers in the Arctic. It is neither desirable nor feasible to export the ATS model to the Arctic. The two polar regions have quite diverse geopolitical contexts which will become increasingly diverse as the Arctic economy is further integrated into the global economy. Yet this study has shown that they are not "poles apart" either.

Both are integral parts of the global ecosystem and continue to reflect and respond to the larger political issues and economic trends in the global system. Both demonstrate that the conventional state-centric understanding of power, security and sovereignty is no longer adequate in a world where we humans, in our reckless pursuit of economic growth, make the earth yield more for wasteful consumption and diminish its ability to sustain life of all kinds, including ourselves. Evidence from both the polar regions leads us to conclude that a reconceptualization of sovereignty is necessary, timely and possible. Both illustrate that, despite the reluctance of the nation-state to accept limitations on its sovereignty, its failure to make adaptive responses to environmental issues will result in further delegation of tasks and resources to international and supranational forums and agencies. Finally, both the Arctic and Antarctic effectively demonstrate – together as well as in their own distinctive ways – that geopolitical processes are not merely power games between states and that the key to the survival and welfare of global civil society lies in the ecologically sustainable and socially equitable development and management of our common habitat.

11

Appendix: Antarctic Treaty and Scientific Committee on Antarctic Research

The Treaty, made on 1 December 1959, came into force on 23 June 1961. SCAR, formed on 3 February 1958, is part of the International Council of Scientific Unions.

Adherents and Members (in alphabetical order with *Y-M-D* dates):

	Antarctic Treaty		*SCAR*	
			Full	*Associate*
ARGENTINA	1961-06-23		1958-02- 3	
AUSTRALIA	1961-06-23		1958-02- 3	
Austria	1987-08-25			
BELGIUM	1960-07-26		1958-02- 3	
Brazil	1975-05-16	(1983-09-12)	1984-10- 1	
Bulgaria	1978-09-11			
Canada	1988-05- 4			
CHILE	1961-06-23		1958-02- 3	
China, Peoples' Republic	1983-06- 8	(1985-10- 7)	1986-06-23	
Colombia	1989-01-31			1990-07-23
Cuba	1984-08-16			
Czech Republic[4]	1962-06-14			
Denmark	1965-05-20			
Ecuador	1987-09-15	(1990-11-19)	1992-06-15	(1988-09-12)
Estonia			1992-06-15	
Finland	1984-05-15	(1989-10- 9)	1990-07-23	(1988-07- 1)
FRANCE	1960-09-16		1958-03- 3	
Germany BRD[1]	1979-02- 5	(1981-03- 3)	1978-05-22	
DDR[1]	1974-11-19	(1987-10- 5)	1981-09- 9	
Greece	1987-01- 8			
Guatemala	1991-07-31			
Hungary	1984-01-27			
India	1983-08-19	(1983-09-12)	1984-10- 1	

(*continued over*)

	Antarctic Treaty		SCAR	
			Full	Associate
Italy	1981-03-18	(1987-10- 5)	1988-09-12	(1987-05-19)
JAPAN	1960-08- 4		1958-02- 3	
Korea (Pyongyang)	1987-01-21			
Korea (Seoul)	1986-11-28	(1989-10- 9)	1990-07-23	(1987-12- 8)
Netherlands	1967-03-30	(1990-11-19)	1990-07-23	(1987-05-20)
NEW ZEALAND	1960-11- 1		1958-02- 3	
NORWAY	1960-08-24		1958-02- 3	
Pakistan				1992-06-15
Papua New Guinea[2]	1981-03-16			
Peru	1981-04-10	(1989-10- 9)		1987-04-14
Poland	1961-06- 8	(1977-07-29)	1978-05-22	
Romania	1971-09-15			
RUSSIA[3]	1960-11- 2		1958-02- 3	
Slovak Republic[4]	1962-06-14			
SOUTH AFRICA	1960-06-21		1958-02- 3	
Spain	1982-03-31	(1988-09-21)	1990-07-23	(1987-01-15)
Sweden	1984-04-24	(1988-09-21)	1988-09-12	(1987-03-24)
Switzerland	1990-11-15			1987-06-16
UNITED KINGDOM	1960-05-31		1958-02- 3	
UNITED STATES OF AMERICA	1960-08-18		1958-02- 3	
Ukraine	1992-10-28			
Uruguay	1980-01-11	(1985-10- 7)	1988-09-12	(1987-07-29)

ORIGINAL SIGNATORIES AND MEMBERS: the 12 states which made the Treaty and formed the Committee are CAPITALIZED; the *Treaty* dates given are those of the deposition of instruments of ratification, approval, or acceptance.

Consultative Parties of the Treaty: 26 states (**emboldened**), the 12 original signatories and 14 others which achieved this status after becoming actively involved in Antarctic research (with dates in brackets). A total of 42 states are currently adherents to the Treaty.

SCAR members are 25 Full and 5 Associate; the dates in brackets for some recent Full Members are those of admission as an Associate Member.

[1] The two German states unified on 3 October 1990.

[2] Succeeded to the Treaty after becoming independent of Australia.

[3] Formerly the Soviet Union, represented by Russia from December 1991.

[4] Succeeded to the Treaty as part of Czechoslovakia, which separated into two republics on 1 January 1993.

References

Documents of the Antarctic Treaty System

Collected documents

Handbook of the Antarctic Treaty System 1990. Edited by John Heap. Cambridge: Scott Polar Research Institute, Polar Publications. (Seventh Edition)
—— 1994. Edited by John Heap. Washington DC: US Department of State. (Eighth Edition)
Bush, W.M. 1982a. *Antarctica and International Law: A Collection of Inter-State and National Documents.* Vol. I. London: Oceana Publications Inc.
—— 1982b. *Antarctica and International Law: A Collection of Inter-State and National Documents.* Vol. II. London: Oceana Publications Inc.
—— 1988. *Antarctica and International Law: A Collection of Inter-State and National Documents.* Vol. III. London: Oceana Publications Inc.
—— 1992. *Antarctica and International Law: A Collection of Inter-State and National Documents.* Booklet AT91C (Issued November 1992). London: Oceana Publications Inc.
—— 1994a. *Antarctica and International Law: A Collection of Inter-State and National Documents.* Booklet AT91E (Issued February 1994). London: Oceana Publications Inc.
—— 1994b. *Antarctica and International Law: A Collection of Inter-State and National Documents.* Booklet AT91F (Issued February 1994). London: Oceana Publications Inc.

Antarctic Treaty documents

ATCM 1987. *Report and Recommendations of the Fourteenth Antarctic Treaty Consultative Meeting*, Rio de Janeiro, 15–16 October 1987.
—— 1989. *Final Report of the Fifteenth Antarctic Treaty Consultative Meeting*, Paris, 9–20 October 1989.
—— 1991a. *Final Report of the Sixteenth Antarctic Treaty Consultative Meeting*, Bonn, 7–18 October 1991.

References

—— 1991b. *Report to XVI ATCM*, submitted by ASOC. XVI ATCM/INFO 22. 8 October 1991: 1–3.

—— 1991c. *Draft, Initial Environmental Evaluation, Removal of World Park Base, Cape Evans, Ross Island, Antarctica 1991/1992*, submitted by ASOC. XVI ATCM/INFO 94: 1–36.

—— 1991d. *Report from the Scientific Committee on Antarctic Research (SCAR) to the XVIth Antarctic Treaty Consultative Meeting: A Framework for Antarctic Science into the XXIst Century: SCAR Perspective on Antarctic Research and Management.* In: *Final Report of the Sixteenth Antarctic Treaty Consultative Meeting*, Bonn, 7–18 October 1991: 230–45.

—— 1991e. *Antarctica Tour Operators Form Association.* XVI ATCM/INFO 20. 8 October 1991. (Submitted by the United Kingdom)

—— 1991f. *Report by the Depository of the Convention for the Conservation of Antarctic Seals to the Sixteenth Consultative Meeting.* XVI ATCM/INFO 13. 7 October 1991.

—— 1994a. *Final Report of the Eighteenth Antarctic Treaty Consultative Meeting.* Kyoto, 11–22 April 1994.

—— 1994b. *Liability Annex to the Protocol on Environmental Protection to the Antarctic Treaty.* XVIII ATCM/WP 2. 10 April 1994. Kyoto, 11–22 April 1994.

—— 1994c. *Recent Developments in Antarctic Tourism.* XVIII ATCM/INFO 35. 11 April 1994. (Submitted by the United Kingdom)

—— 1994d. *The Organizational Aspects of the Antarctic Treaty System.* XVIII ATCM/WP 16. (Submitted by Italy)

—— 1995a. *Draft Report of the Nineteenth Antarctic Treaty Consultative Meeting.* Seoul, 8–19 May 1995.

—— 1995b. *Liability Annex to the Protocol on Environmental Protection to the Antarctic Treaty.* XIX ATCM/INF 24. 11 May 1995. (Submitted by Germany)

—— 1995c. *Green Legislation for Antarctica.* XIX ATCM/INF 67. 11 May 1995. (Submitted by ASOC)

—— 1995d. *Tourism and Non-governmental Activities in the Antarctic Treaty Area.* XIX ATCM/WP 6. 11 May 1995. (Submitted by Argentina, Chile, New Zealand and the United Kingdom)

—— 1995e. *Establishment of an Antarctic Treaty Secretariat – Organizational Aspects.* XIX ATCM/WP 13. 8 May 1995. (Submitted by Australia, Italy and South Africa)

XI ATSCM 1990a. *Indian Proposal for Comprehensive Measures for the Protection of the Antarctic Environment and Dependent and Associated Ecosystems.* 26 November 1990.

—— 1990b. *Interim Report of the XI ATSCM*, Viña del Mar, 6 December 1990.

CCAMLR 1993. SC-CAMLR-XII/4. 12 August 1993. *Report of the Fifth Meeting of the Working Group on Krill.* 12 August 1993. Tokyo, 4–12 August 1993.

United Nations documents

UN Secretariat 1984. *Question of Antarctica: Study Requested Under General Assembly Resolution 38/77, Report of the Secretary General, Part Two (Views of States).* Doc. A/39/583, Part II, 9 November 1984: 82, 91–2, 95.

UN 1991. *Report of the United Nations Meeting of Experts on Self-government for Indigenous Peoples.* Doc. E/CN.4/1992/42. Nuuk, Greenland, 24–8 September 1991.

UNGA 1982. *United Nations General Assembly Records*, A/37/PV 10. 29 September 1982.

—— 1983. *United Nations General Assembly Records, 38th Session, 46th Meeting of the First Committee*, A/C1/38/PV 46. 30 November 1983.

—— 1984. *United Nations General Assembly Records, 39th Session, Study on the Question of Antarctica, Views of States*, A/35/583, Part II. 29 October 1984.

—— 1985. *United Nations General Assembly Records*, A40/C1/PV 22. 4 October 1985.

—— 1987. *United Nations General Assembly Records*, A42/C1/PV 46. 17 November 1987.

—— 1988a. *United Nations General Assembly Records*, A43/C1/PV 44. 21 November 1988.

—— 1988b. *United Nations General Assembly Records*, A43/C1/PV 45. 22 November 1988.

—— 1990a. *United Nations General Assembly Records*, A45/C1/PV 45. 21 November 1990.

—— 1990b. *United Nations General Assembly Records*, A45/C1/PV 40. 19 November 1990.

—— 1990c. *United Nations General Assembly Records*, A45/C1/PV 42. 20 November 1990.

Books and articles

Aagaard, K. 1993. "Contamination of the Arctic: Ocean Processes." Paper presented to the United States Interagency Arctic Policy Committee (IARPC) Workshop on Arctic Contamination, May 2–7, Anchorage, Alaska: 1–26.

Archer, C. (ed.) 1988. *The Soviet Union and Northern Waters*. London: Routledge.

Archer, C. and D. Scrivener (eds) 1986. *Northern Waters: Security and Resource Issues*. London: Croom Helm.

Agnew, J. and S. Corbridge 1988. "The New Geopolitics: The Dynamics of Geopolitical Disorder." In: Johnston, R.J. and P.J. Taylor (eds), *A World in Crisis? Geographical Perspectives*. Oxford: Basil Blackwell: 266–88.

—— 1995. *Mastering Space: Hegemony, Territory and International Political Economy*. London, New York: Routledge.

Agranat, G.A. 1991. "New Approaches to the North Global Aspects." *Polar Geography and Geology* 15(2): 116–31.

Agrawal, A. 1977. "Will Saudi Arabia drink Icebergs?" *New Scientist* (17 July).

Aidjex Bulletin 1971 (11).

Ambio, A Journal of the Human Environment 1989. XVIII(1). Special Issue on the Polar Regions.

Andersen, A.M. and J. Taagholt 1994. "Geopolitical Developments and their Significance for Greenland and the Circumpolar Arctic Area." In: Greiffenberg, T. (ed.), *Sustainability in the Arctic: Proceedings from Nordic Arctic Research Forum Symposium 1993*. Aalborg: Aalborg University Press: 241–52.

Arctic Research of the United States 1993 7 (Spring).

Arikaynen, A.L. 1991. "Sustainable Development of the Soviet Arctic: Some Possibilities and Constraints." *Polar Record* 27(160): 17–22.

Armstrong, T. 1965. *Russian Settlement in the North*. Cambridge: Cambridge University Press.

—— 1992. "Industrialization and its Consequences." In: Griffiths, F.G. (ed.), *Arctic Alternatives: Civility or Militarism in the Circumpolar North*. Science for Peace/ Samuel Stevens: Toronto: 125–35.

——, G. Rogers and G. Rowley 1978. *The Circumpolar North: A Political and Economic Geography of the Arctic and Sub-Arctic*. London: Methuen.

References

Ash, J.S. 1994. *Cold War Legacy: Radionuclide Contamination in the Barents and Kara Sea.* Global Security Programme, Occasional Papers No. 3. Cambridge.

Auburn, F.M. 1977. "Offshore Oil and Gas in Antarctica." *German Yearbook of International Law* 20: 139–73.

—— 1978. "United States Antarctic Policy." *Marine Technological Society Journal* 12(1): 31–6.

—— 1979. "Consultative Status Under the Antarctic Treaty." *International and Comparative Law Quarterly* 28: 514–22.

—— 1982. *Antarctic Law and Politics.* Bloomington: Indiana University Press.

Baker Jr, D.J. 1975. "The Southern Ocean: Currents, Fronts, and Bottom Water." *Oceanus* 18(4): 8–15.

Balchen, B. 1956. "Arctic Seen Key Area in Any Global Conflict." *The Polar Times* (June): 30.

Bankes, N. 1991. "Canadian–U.S. Relations in the Arctic Borderlands." Background paper prepared from a Canadian perspective for the Pearson–Dickey Conference, Whitehorse, May 1990. Canadian Arctic Resources Committee and the Canadian Institute of International Affairs.

Barnes, J.N. 1982. "The Emerging Convention on the Conservation of Antarctic Marine Living Resources, An Attempt to Meet New Realities of Resource Exploitation in the Southern Ocean." In: Charney, J.I. (ed.), *The New Nationalism and the Use of Common Space: Issues in Marine Pollution and the Exploitation of Antarctica.* (Published under the auspices of the American Society of International Law.) Allanheld: Osmun Publishers: 239–86.

Barnes, T. and J. Duncan (eds) 1992. *Writing Worlds: Discourse, Text and Metaphor in the Representation of Landscape.* London: Routledge.

Barnet, R.J. 1992. "A Balance Sheet: Lippmann, Kennan, and the Cold War." In: Hogan, M.J. (ed.), *The End of the Cold War: Its Meaning and Implications.* Cambridge: Cambridge University Press: 113–26.

Barthelmess, K. 1993. "A Century of German Interest in Modern Whaling 1860s–1960s". In: Basberg, B.L., J.E. Ringstad and E. Wexelsen (eds), *Whaling and History: Perspectives on the Evolution of the Industry.* Sandefjord: Kommandør Chr. Christensens Hvalfangstmuseum.

Bartelmus, P. 1994. *Environment, Growth and Development: The Concepts and Strategies of Sustainability.* London: Routledge.

Bassin, M. 1987a. "Race Contra Space: The Conflict Between German *Geopolitik* and National Socialism." *Political Geography Quarterly* 6(2): 115–34.

—— 1987b. "Friedrich Ratzel." *Geographers: Bibliographical Studies* 11: 123–32.

—— 1988. "Expansion and Colonialism on the Eastern Frontier: Views of Siberia and the Far East in Pre-Petrine Russia." *Journal of Historical Geography* 14(1): 3–21.

—— 1994. "Russian Geographers and the 'National Mission' in the Far East." In: Hooson, D. (ed.), *Geography and National Identity.* Oxford, UK, and Cambridge, USA: Blackwell: 112–33.

Bathhurst, R. 1994. "Where Cultures Cross: Old Russia in a New North." In: Stokke, O.S. and O. Tunander (eds), *The Barents Region: Cooperation in Arctic Europe.* London: Sage Publications.

Bauer, T.G. 1994. "The Future of Commercial Tourism in Antarctica." *Annals of Tourism Research* 21(2): 410–12.

Baughman, T.H. 1994. *Before the Heroes Came: Antarctica in the 1890s.* Lincoln, USA, and London: University of Nebraska Press.

Beach, H. 1994. "The Saami of Lapland." In: Minority Rights Group (ed.), *Polar Peoples: Self-determination and Development.* London: Minority Rights Publications: 147–207.

Beck, P.J. 1983. "British Antarctic Policy in the Early 20th Century." *Polar Record* 21(134): 475–83.

—— 1984. "Britain and Antarctica: The Historical Perspective." *FRAM: The Journal of Polar Studies* 1(1): 66–83.

—— 1986. *International Politics of Antarctica.* London: Croom Helm.

—— 1990a. "International Relations in Antarctica: Argentina, Chile and the Great Powers." In: Morris, M.A. (ed.), *Great Power Relations in Argentina, Chile and Antarctica.* London: Macmillan: 101–30.

—— 1990b. "Australia's New Course in Antarctica." In: *Australia's Maritime Interests – Views from Overseas.* Occasional Papers in Maritime Affairs 6. Canberra: Australian Centre for Maritime Studies Inc.: 106–15.

—— 1990c. "The Antarctic Question: A New Strategic Role for Antarctica." In: Maurice, P. and O. Gohin (eds), *Géopolitique et Géostrategie dans l'Hemisphère Sud.* Université de la Réunion, Faculté de Droit et des Sciences Economiques et Politiques.

—— 1992. "The 1991 UN Session: The Environmental Protocol Fails to Satisfy the Antarctic Treaty System's Critics." *Polar Record* 28(167): 307–14.

—— 1993. "The UN and Antarctica: Still Searching for that Elusive Convergence of View." *Polar Record* 29(171): 313–20.

—— 1994. "Managing Antarctic Tourism: A Front-burner Issue." *Annals of Tourism Research* 21(2): 375–86.

Behrendt, J.C. 1983. "Are There Petroleum Resources in Antarctica?" *Petroleum and Mineral Resources of Antarctica.* Geological Survey Circular 909 (US Department of the Interior): 10–21.

Beltramino, J.C.M. 1993. *The Structure and Dynamics of Antarctic Populations.* New York: Vantage Press.

Bennekom, S. van 1992. "A New Regime to Protect the Antarctic Environment." *Leiden Journal of International Law* 5(1): 33–51.

Berger, T. 1985a. *Village Journey: The Report of the Alaska Native Review Commission.* New York: Hill and Wang.

—— 1985b. "Village Journey." *Etudes Inuit Studies* 9(2): 39–41.

—— 1985c. "Behind the Façade: What the Alaska Native Claims Settlement Act Means to Village Alaska." *Northern Perspectives* 13(4): 1–10.

—— 1988. *Northern Frontier, Northern Homeland: The Report of the Mackenzie Valley Pipeline Inquiry.* Vancouver/Toronto: Douglas & McIntyre.

—— 1989. "The North as Frontier and Homeland." In: *The Arctic: Choices for Peace and Security.* The True North Strong & Free Inquiry Society. West Vancouver: Gordon Soules Book Publishers Ltd: 37–44.

Berkman, P.A. 1992. "The Antarctic Marine Ecosystem and Humankind." *Reviews in Aquatic Sciences* 6(3, 4): 295–333.

Bertrand, K.J. 1971. *Americans in Antarctica 1775–1948.* New York: American Geographical Society.

Bjorklund, I. 1990. "On the Integration of Ethnic Minorities in the North – The Norwegian Experience." In: Kotlyakov, V.M. and V.E. Sokolov (eds), *Arctic Research: Advances and Prospects*, Part 2. Proceedings of the Conference of Arctic and Nordic Countries on Coordination of Research in the Arctic. Leningrad, December 1988: 310–13.

Blangy, S. and M.E. Wood 1992. "Developing and Implementing Ecotourism Guidelines for Wild Lands & Neighbouring Communities." In: Kempf, C. and L. Girard (eds), *Tourism in Polar Areas.* Proceedings of the First International Symposium, 21–3 April 1992, Colmar, Alsace, France. Published by Conseil Général du Haut-Rhin.

Boczek, B.A. 1984. "The Soviet Union and the Antarctic Regime." *American Journal of International Law* 78: 839–40.

References

—— 1988. "The Legal Status of Visitors, Including Tourists, and Non-governmental Expeditions in Antarctica." In: Wolfrum, R. (ed.), *Antarctic Challenge III: Conflicting Interests, Cooperation, Environmental Protection, Economic Development*. Berlin: Duncker & Humblot: 455–90.

Bohlin, I. 1988. "The Motive Structure in Contemporary Polar Science." Paper presented at The Study of Science and Technology in the 1990s, Joint Conference of the Society for Social Studies of Science and the European Association for the Study of Science and Technology (EASST), Amsterdam, 16-19 November.

Bone, R.M. 1992. *The Geography of the Canadian North: Issues and Challenges*. Toronto: Oxford University Press.

Bonner, N. 1991. "Report on the XIth Antarctic Treaty Special Consultative Meeting by the SCAR Observer." *SCAR Report* (6): 12–17.

Booth, K. (ed.) 1991. *New Thinking about Strategy and International Security*. London: HarperCollins*Academic*.

Boulding, K. 1979. *Stable Peace*. Austin, Texas: University of Texas Press.

—— 1991. "The Nature and Causes of National and Military Self-images in Relation to War and Peace." In: Kliot, N. and S. Waterman (eds), *The Political Geography of Conflict and Peace*. London: Belhaven: 142–52.

Brantenberg, O.T. 1991. "Norway: Constructing Indigenous Self-government in a Nation State." In: Jull, P. and S. Roberts (eds), *The Challenge of Northern Regions*. Darwin: Australian National University Press and North Australian Research Unit: 66–127.

—— 1993."The End of 13 Years of Silence." *Newsletter IWGIA* 4: 26–40.

Brigham, L.W. 1993. "Views on the Opening of the Northern Sea Route and the Russian Maritime Arctic." In: Simonsen, H. (ed.), *Proceedings from the Northern Sea Route Expert Meeting, 13–14 October 1992, Tromsø, Norway*. Lysaker: Fridtjof Nansen Institute: 167–73.

Brinken, A.O. and V.A. Pyzhin 1993. "Some Ecological Problems in Developing the Arctic (the Foreign Experience)." *Polar Geography and Geology* 17(1): 72–8.

Brown, L.R. 1994. "Facing Food Scarcity." In: Brown, L.R. *et al.*, *State of the World 1994*. A Worldwatch Institute Report on Progress Toward a Sustainable Society. London: Earthscan Publications Ltd.: 177–97.

—— *et al.* 1994. *State of the World 1994*. A Worldwatch Institute Report on Progress Toward a Sustainable Society. London: Earthscan Publications Ltd.

Brown, S.G. 1963. "A Review of Antarctic Whaling." *Polar Record* 2(74): 555–6.

Brunn, S.D. and K.A. Mingst 1985. "Geopolitics." In Michael, P. (ed.), *Progress in Political Geography*. London: Croom Helm: 41–76.

Burch Jr, E.S. 1979. "Native Claims in Alaska: An Overview." *Etudes Inuit Studies* 3(1): 7–30.

Burger, J. 1987. *Report from the Frontier: The State of the World's Indigenous Peoples*. London: Zed Books; Cambridge, Massachusetts: Cultural Survival Inc.

Bush, W.M. 1990. "The Antarctic Treaty System: A Framework for Evolution and the Concept of a System." In: Herr, R.A. and M.G. Haward (eds), *Antarctica's Future: Continuity or Change?* Hobart, Tasmania: Australian Institute of International Affairs/Tasmanian Government Printing Office: 119–79.

Butler, E.W. 1990. "Joint Ventures and the Soviet Arctic." *Marine Policy* (March): 169–76.

Butler, J.R. 1992. "Tourism in the Canadian Arctic: Problems of Achieving Sustainability." In: Kempf, C. and L. Girard (eds), *Tourism in Polar Areas*. Proceedings of the First International Symposium, 21–3 April 1992, Colmar, Alsace, France. Published by Conseil Général du Haut-Rhin.

Butler, R.W. 1991. "Tourism, Environment and Sustainable Development." *Environmental Conservation* 18(3): 201–9.

Butler, S.O. 1977. "Owning Antarctica: Co-operation and Jurisdiction at the South Pole." *Journal of International Affairs* 31(1): 35–51.

Buzan, B. 1991. *People, States and Fear: An Agenda for International Security Studies in the Post Cold War Era.* Boulder, Colorado: Lynne Rienner.

CAFF-Report No. 1 1993. *Conservation of Arctic Flora and Fauna: The State of Habitat Protection in the Arctic.* Prepared by the Directorate for Nature Management, Norway. (Second Draft)

CAFF-Report No. 1 1994. *The State of Protected Areas in the Circumpolar Arctic.* Conservation of Arctic Flora and Fauna: Habitat Conservation Report No. 1. Trondheim, Norway.

Cameron, I. 1974. *Antarctica: The Last Continent.* London: Cassell.

Camilleri, J. and J. Falk 1992. *The End of Sovereignty.* London: Edward Elgar.

Canadian Government 1993a. "Diamonds and the Northwest Territories, Canada." Northwest Territories Department of Energy, Mines and Petroleum Resources. Minerals Division. Government of Northwest Territories.

—— 1993b. "Federal Policy for the Settlement of Native Claims." Ottawa: Department of Indian Affairs and Northern Development.

—— 1993c. "Agreement Between the Inuit of the Nunavut Settlement Area and Her Majesty the Queen in Right of Canada." Ottawa: Department of Indian Affairs and Northern Development.

—— 1993d. "The Evolution of Public Governments in the North and the Implications for Aboriginal Peoples." Ottawa: Department of Indian Affairs and Northern Development.

—— 1993e. "Umbrella Final Agreement Between the Government of Canada, the Council for Yukon Indians, and the Government of the Yukon." Ottawa: Department of Indian Affairs and Northern Development.

Canfield, J.L. 1993. "Recent Developments in Bering Sea Fisheries Conservation and Management." *Ocean Development and International Law* 24: 257–89.

Castberg, R., O.S. Stokke and W. Østreng 1994. "The Dynamics of the Barents Region." In: Stokke, O. and O. Tunander (eds), *The Barents Region: Cooperation in Arctic Europe.* London: Sage Publications: 71–84.

Caulfield, R.A. 1992. "Alaska's Subsistence Management Regimes." *Polar Record* 28(164): 23–32.

Chambers, E.J. 1914. *The Unexploited West: A Compilation of all the Authentic Information Available at the Present Time as to the Natural Resources of the Unexploited Regions of Northern Canada.* Ottawa: Printed by J. de L. Tache, Printer to the King's Most Excellent Majesty.

Chance, N.A. and E.N. Andreeva 1993. "Sustainability, Equity and Natural Resource Development in Northwest Siberia and Arctic Alaska." Paper presented at the Annual Meeting of the American Anthropological Association, November 1993.

Chaturvedi, S. 1983. "National Claims on Antarctica." *Social Sciences Research Journal* VIII(1–2): 108–48.

—— 1985a. "Antarctica and the Soviet Union." In: Sharma, R.C. (ed.), *Growing Focus on Antarctica.* New Delhi: Rajesh Publications: 221–33.

—— 1985b. "Geopolitics of Antarctic Resources." *Social Sciences Research Journal* X(1–2): 1–48.

—— 1986a. "Antarctica and the United Nations." *India Quarterly* XLII(1): 1–35.

—— 1986b. "India and the Antarctic Treaty System: Realities and Prospects." *India Quarterly* XLII(4): 1–38.

—— 1990. *Dawning of Antarctica: A Geopolitical Analysis.* New Delhi: Segment Books.

Cherkasov, A.I. 1993. "Nunavut: The Canadian Experiment in Territorial Self-determination for the Inuit." *Polar Geography and Geology* 17(1): 64–71.

References

Child, J. 1988. *Antarctica and South American Geopolitics: Frozen Lebensraum.* New York: Praeger.
—— 1990a. "Latin Lebensraum: The Geopolitics of Ibero-American Antarctica." *Applied Geography* 10(4): 287–305.
—— 1990b. "The Status of South American Geopolitical Thinking." In: Atkin, G.P. (ed.), *South America into the 1990s: Evolving International Relations in a New Era.* London: Westview Press: 53–85.
Chomsky, N. 1992. *Deterring Democracy.* London: Vintage.
—— 1994. *World Orders, Old and New.* London: Pluto Press.
Christie, E.W. Hunter 1951. *The Antarctic Problem: An Historical and Political Study.* London: George Allen & Unwin Ltd.
Churchill, R. and G. Ulfstein 1992. *Marine Management in Disputed Areas: The Case of the Barents Sea.* London: Routledge.
Cline, D. 1992. "Panel III – Conserving Arctic Biodiversity: Preserving Ecosystems with a Human Element." In: *Arctic Perspectives.* Proceedings, New Perspectives on the Arctic: The Changing Role of the United States in the Circumpolar North, a Conference on US Arctic Policy, 12–14 August 1992. Fairbanks, Alaska: 69–73.
Coates, K.S. and W.R. Morrison 1988. *Land of the Midnight Sun: A History of the Yukon.* Edmonton: Hurtig Publishers.
—— and J. Powell 1989. *The Modern North: People, Politics and Rejection of Colonialism.* London: James Lorimer & Company, Publishers.
Cohen, M. 1970–1. "The Arctic and the National Interest." *International Journal* XXVI (1): 52–80.
Cohen, S.B. 1994. "Geopolitics in the New World Era: A New Perspective on an Old Discipline." In: Demko, G.J. and W.B. Wood (eds), *Reordering the World: Geopolitical Perspectives on the 21st Century.* Boulder: Westview Press: 15–48.
Colin, M. 1992. "Ecotourism and Conservation Policies in Canada." In: Kempf, C. and L. Girard (eds), *Tourism in Polar Areas.* Proceedings of the First International Symposium, 21–3 April 1992, Colmar, Alsace, France. Published by Conseil Général du Haut-Rhin.
Conant, M.A. 1992. "Perspectives on Arctic Petroleum." In: Griffiths, F. (ed.), *Arctic Alternatives: Civility or Militarism in the Circumpolar North.* Toronto: Science for Peace/Samuel Stevens: 180–91.
Conference on Antarctica Documents 1959: Document 15. Scott Polar Research Institute Archives, Cambridge.
Conference on Antarctica/COM/SR/2 (Final) 1 November 1959. Scott Polar Research Institute Archives, Cambridge.
Cooley, R.A. 1969. "International Union for the Conservation of Nature and Natural Resources (IUCN): First Working Meeting of Polar Bear Scientists." *Polar Record* 14(91): 511–13.
Corbridge, S. and J. Agnew 1991. "The U.S. Trade and Budget Deficits in Global Perspective: An Essay in Geopolitical Economy." *Environment and Planning. D. Society and Space:* 71–90.
Cox, D. 1988. "Canada's Changing Defence Priorities: Comparing Notes with the Nordic States." In: Möttölä, K. (ed.), *The Arctic Challenge: Nordic and Canadian Approaches to Security and Cooperation in an Emerging International Region.* Boulder, Colorado and London: Westview Press.
—— 1992. "Ballistic Missile Defences, Cruise Missiles, Air Defences." In: Griffiths, F. (ed.), *Arctic Alternatives: Civility or Militarism in the Circumpolar North.* Toronto: Science for Peace/Samuel Stevens: 237–50.
Cramer, T. 1988. "Issues and Problems for the Swedish Sami 1988." *Nordic Journal of International Law* 57: 270–72.
—— 1993. "The Sami in Four Countries." *Newsletter IWGIA* 1: 45–8.

Creery, I. 1994. "The Inuit of Canada." In: Minority Rights Group (ed.), *Polar Peoples: Self-determination and Development*. London: Minority Rights Publications: 105–46.

Cumming, P. 1989. "Canada's North and Native Rights." In: Morse, B.W. (ed.), *Aboriginal Peoples and the Law: Indians, Metis and Inuit Rights in Canada*. Ottawa: Carleton University Press: 695–731.

Curry-Lindahl, K. 1975. "Conservation of Arctic Fauna and its Habitats." *Polar Record* 17(108): 237–47.

Dacks, G. 1990. "Political and Constitutional Development in the Yukon and Northwest Territories: The Influence of Devolution." *The Northern Review*, Summer 1990 (5): 103–30.

Dahl, J. 1988. "From Ethnic to Political Identity." *Nordic Journal of International Law* 57: 312–15.

—— 1989. "The Integrative and Cultural Role of Hunting and Subsistence in Greenland." *Etudes Inuit Studies* 13(1): 23–42.

—— 1990. *Indigenous Peoples of the Soviet North*. IWGIA Document No. 67. Copenhagen.

—— 1992. "Development of Indigenous and Circumpolar Peoples' Rights." In Lyck, L. (ed.), *Nordic Arctic Research on Contemporary Arctic Problems*. Proceedings from Nordic Arctic Research Forum Symposium 1992. Aalborg: Aalborg University Press: 185–92.

—— 1993. "Indigenous Peoples of the Arctic." In: *Arctic Challenges*. Report from the Nordic Council's Parliamentary Conference in Reykjavik, 16–17 August 1993: 103–30.

Dalby, S. 1988. "Geopolitical Discourse: The Soviet Union as Other." *Alternatives* XIII: 415–42.

—— 1990a. *Creating the Second Cold War: The Discourse of Politics*. London: Pinter Publishers.

—— 1990b. "American Security Discourse: The Persistence of Geopolitics." *Political Geography Quarterly* 9(2): 171–88.

—— 1991. "Critical Geopolitics: Discourse, Difference and Dissent." *Society and Space* 9(3): 261–83.

—— 1992a. "Ecopolitical Discourse: 'Environmental Security' and Political Geography." *Progress in Human Geography* 16(4): 503–22.

—— 1992b. "Security, Modernity, Ecology: The Dilemmas of Post Cold War Security Discourse." *Alternatives* XVII: 95–134.

Darnley, R. 1930. *Discovery Reports*, Volume I. Cambridge: Cambridge University Press.

Dawisha, K. and B. Parrott 1994. *Russia and the New States of Eurasia: The Politics of Upheaval*. Cambridge: Cambridge University Press.

De La Barra, Oscar Pinochet 1955. *Chilean Sovereignty in Antarctica*. Santiago: Editorial Del Pacifico SA.

Devine, M. 1992. "The Dene Nation: Coming Full Circle." *Arctic Circle* 2(5): 12–19.

Dey-Nuttall, A. 1994. *Origins, Development and Organization of National Antarctic Programmes, With Special Reference to the United Kingdom and India*. Unpublished Ph.D. dissertation, Scott Polar Research Institute, University of Cambridge.

Diamond, B. 1991. "The Development of the North: Confrontation and Conflict." In: Seyersted, P. (ed.), *The Arctic: Canada and the Nordic Countries*. The Nordic Association for Canadian Studies Text Series, Volume 6: 87–99.

Dickerson, M.O. 1992. *Whose North? Political Change, Political Development, and Self-government in Northwest Territories*. Vancouver: UBC Press and Arctic Institute of North America.

References

Dodds, K.J. 1993. "Geopolitics, Cartography and the State in South America." *Political Geography* 12(4): 361–81.

—— 1996. "To Photograph the Antarctic: British Polar Exploration and the Falkland Islands and Dependencies Aerial Survey Expedition (FIDASE)." *Ecumene* (forthcoming).

—— and J.D. Sidaway 1994. "Locating Critical Geopolitics." *Society and Space* 12(5): 515–24.

Doering, R. 1994. "Canada's Northern Foreign Policy: Issues and Principles." In: Lamb, J.M. (ed.), *Proceedings of a Conference on "A Northern Policy for Canada"*. Ottawa: Canadian Polar Commission and Canadian Centre for Global Security: 79–81.

Dosman, E. 1989. "The New Arctic Challenge." In: Dosman, E. (ed.), *Sovereignty and Security in the Arctic*. London: Routledge: 1–8.

Drewry, D.J. 1992. "The Future of Antarctic Science." In: Mudge, G. (ed.), *Antarctica: The Environment and the Future*. Geneva: International Academy of the Environment and International Peace Research Institute: 4–11.

—— 1993. "The Future of Antarctic Scientific Research." *Polar Record* 29(168): 37–44.

Dugger, J.A. 1978. "Exploiting Antarctic Mineral Resources – Technology, Economics and Environment." *University of Miami Law Review* 33: 315–39.

Duhaime, G. 1993. *The Governing of Nunavik: Who Pays for What?* Collection Travaux de Recherche, Numéro 17. Groupe d'Etudes Inuit et Circumpolaires, Faculté des Sciences Sociales, Université Laval.

Dunbar, M.J. 1950. "Greenland During and Since the Second World War." *International Journal* (Spring): 121–40.

—— 1992. "The Physical and Biological Environment." In: Griffiths, F. (ed.), *Arctic Alternatives: Civility or Militarism in the Circumpolar North*. Toronto: Science for Peace/Samuel Stevens: 103–24.

Dunn, R. 1989. "Australia to Seek Wilderness Park Status for Antarctica." *Financial Review* (23 May).

Durning, A.T. 1994. "Redesigning the Forest Economy." In: Brown, L.R. *et al.*, *State of the World 1994*. A Worldwatch Institute Report on Progress Toward a Sustainable Society. London: Earthscan: 22–40.

Eco. 1989. LXXIV(2): 1–2.

Ellingsen, E. 1988. "The Military Balance on the Northern Flank." In: Goldstein, W. (ed.), *Clash in the North: Polar Summitry and NATO's Northern Flank*. Washington: Pergamon–Brassey's: 161–90.

Elliott, D.W. 1989. "Aboriginal Title." In: Morse, B.W. (ed.), *Aboriginal Peoples and the Law: Indians, Metis and Inuit Rights in Canada*. Ottawa: Carleton University Press: 48–121.

Elliott, L.M. 1992. *The Politics of the Antarctic: A Case Study of the Environment in International Relations*. Unpublished Ph.D. dissertation, Department of Political Science, Australian National University, Canberra.

—— 1994. *International Environmental Politics: Protecting the Antarctic*. New York: St Martin's Press.

El-Sayed, S.Z. 1988. "The BIOMASS Programme." *Oceanus* 31(2): 75–9.

Elzinga, A. and I. Bohlin 1993. "The Politics of Science in Polar Regions." In: Elzinga, A. (ed.), *Changing Trends in Antarctic Research*. Dordrecht: Kluwer Academic Publishers: 7–30.

Enzenbacher, D.J. 1992. "Tourists in Antarctica: Numbers and Trends." *Polar Record* 28(164): 17–22.

—— 1993. "Antarctic Tourism: 1991/92 Season Activity." *Polar Record* 29(170): 240–2.

—— 1994. "Tourism at Faraday Station: An Antarctic Case Study." *Annals of Tourism Research* 21(2): 303–17.

Everson, I. 1978. "Antarctica Fisheries." *Polar Record* 19(120): 233–51.

Falk, R. 1986. "The United Nations and the Antarctic Treaty System." *Proceedings, Eightieth Annual Meeting, the American Society for International Law.* Washington: 283–5.

—— 1994. "Regionalism and World Order After the Cold War." Draft paper presented for WIDER/IPSA Workshop and Panel, Berlin, 20–3 August 1994.

Fanning, E. 1924. *Voyages and Discoveries in the South Seas 1792–1832.* Salem, Massachusetts: Marine Research Society.

Fenge, T. 1992. "Political Development and Environmental Management in Northern Canada: The Case of the Nunavut Agreement." *Etudes Inuit Studies* 16(1–2): 115–41.

—— 1993–94. "Environmental Clean-up and Sustainable Development in the Circumpolar Arctic." *Northern Perspectives* 21(4): 1–3.

—— 1994. "Toward an Arctic Sustainable Development Treaty." In: Lamb, J.M. (ed.), *Proceedings of a Conference on "A Northern Foreign Policy for Canada".* Ottawa: Canadian Polar Commission and Canadian Centre for Global Security: 87–9.

Fisher, R. 1977. *Contact and Conflict: Indian–European Relations in British Columbia, 1774–1890.* Vancouver: University of British Columbia Press.

Fogg, G.E. 1992. *A History of Antarctic Science.* Cambridge: Cambridge University Press.

—— and D. Smith 1990. *The Exploration of Antarctica: The Last Unspoilt Continent.* London: Cassell.

Forsyth, J. 1989. "The Indigenous Peoples of Siberia in the Twentieth Century." In: Wood, A. and R.A. French (eds), *The Development of Siberia: People and Resources.* London: Macmillan: 72–95.

—— 1992. *A History of the Peoples of Siberia: Russia's North Asian Colony 1581–1990.* Cambridge: Cambridge University Press.

Foster, T.D. 1984. "The Marine Environment." In Laws, R.M. (ed.), *Antarctic Ecology*, Volume Two. London: Academic Press: 345–71.

Fotinov, V. 1991. "United Northern Emirates: The Future of the Former Soviet North?" *Arctic Circle* 2(3): 10–11.

Francioni, F. 1993. "The Madrid Protocol on the Protection of the Antarctic Environment." *Texas International Law Journal* 28 (Winter): 47–72.

Franckx, E. 1992. "Environmental Protection: An Arctic–Antarctic Comparison." In: Verhoeven, J., P. Sands and M. Bruce (eds), *The Antarctic Environment and International Law.* London: Graham and Trotman: 109–19.

—— 1993. *Maritime Claims in the Arctic: Canadian and Russian Perspectives.* Dordrecht/Boston/London: Martinus Nijhoff Publishers.

Fraser, W. 1994. "Arctic Science, Technology and Traditional Knowledge: Enhancing Cooperation in the Circumpolar North." In: Lamb, J.M. (ed.), *Proceedings of a Conference on "A Northern Foreign Policy for Canada".* Ottawa: Canadian Polar Commission and Canadian Centre for Global Security: 122–3.

Friedrich, Christof 1980. *The Secret Nazi Polar Expeditions.* Toronto: Samizdat Publishers.

Gad, F. 1970. *The History of Greenland: Earliest Times to 1700*, Volume I. London: C. Hurst & Company.

Gaddis, J.L. 1992. "The Cold War, the Long Peace, and the Future." In: Hogan, M.J. (ed.), *The End of the Cold War: Its Meaning and Implications.* Cambridge: Cambridge University Press.

Gardiner, B. 1992. "The Ozone Hole and its Scientific Implications." In: Mudge, G. (ed.), *Antarctica: The Environment and the Future.* Geneva: International Academy of the Environment and International Peace Research Institute: 16–21.

References

Gizewski, P. 1993–4. "Military Activity and Environmental Security: The Case of Radioactivity in the Arctic." *Northern Perspectives* 21(4): 16–21.
Glassner, M.I. 1990. *Neptune's Domain: A Political Geography of the Sea*. Boston: Unwin Hyman.
—— 1993. *Political Geography*. New York: John Wiley & Sons.
Goertz, G. and P.F. Diehl 1992. *Territorial Changes and International Conflict*. London: Routledge.
Golovko, E.V. 1993. "Native Languages of Chukotka and Kamchatka; Situation and Perspectives." In: *Sibérie III Questions Sibériennes*. Paris: Institut d'Études Slaves: 159–70.
Granberg, A. 1993. "International Economic Cooperation Along the Northern Sea Route." In: Simonsen, H. (ed.), *Proceedings from the Northern Sea Route Expert Meeting, 13–14 October 1992, Tromsø, Norway*. Lysaker: Fridtjof Nansen Institute: 153–66.
Grant, B. 1992. "The Nivkhi of Sakhalin Island: History, Ecology and the Savage." *Questions Sibériennes* (2): 72–7.
Gray, A. 1991. *Between the Spice of Life and the Melting Pot: Biodiversity, Conservation and its Impact on Indigenous Peoples*. IWGIA Document No. 70. Copenhagen.
Gray, C.S. 1976. "Foreign Policy – There is No Choice." *Foreign Policy* 24: 114–27.
—— 1977. *The Geopolitics of the Nuclear Area: Heartlands, Rimlands, and the Technological Revolution*. New York: Crane, Russak & Company.
—— 1979. "Nuclear Strategy: The Case for a Theory of Victory." *International Security* 4(1): 54–87.
—— 1988. *The Geopolitics of Superpower*. Lexington: University of Kentucky Press.
Greenland Home Rule Authority 1992. *Statistical Yearbook*.
Greenpeace International 1985. *The Future of the Antarctic: Background for a Third UN Debate*. [25 November]
Greiffenberg, T. (ed.) 1994. *Sustainability in the Arctic*. Proceedings from Nordic Arctic Research Forum Symposium 1993. Aalborg: Aalborg University Press.
Griffiths, F. 1992a. "Civility in the Arctic." In: Griffiths, F. (ed.), *Arctic Alternatives: Civility or Militarism in the Circumpolar North*. Toronto: Science for Peace/ Samuel Stevens: 279–309.
—— (ed.) 1992b. *Arctic Alternatives: Civility or Militarism in the Circumpolar North*. Toronto: Science for Peace/Samuel Stevens.
—— and O. R. Young 1989. "Sustainable Development and the Arctic." *Working Group on Arctic International Relations. Reports and Papers* [Reports, impressions of co-chairmen on second session of Working Group held at Illulissat and Nuuk, Greenland, 20–4 April 1989]: 27p.
Grove, E. (ed.) 1989. *NATO's Defence of the North*. London: Brassey's.
Gunnarsson, G. 1988. "Icelandic Security and the Arctic." In: Möttölä, K. (ed.), *The Arctic Challenge: Nordic and Canadian Approaches to Security and Cooperation in an Emerging International Region*. Boulder, Colorado, and London: Westview Press: 75–86.
Hale, P.B. 1990. "Offshore Hard Minerals." In: Grantz, A. *et al.* (eds), *The Arctic Ocean Region*, Volume L. Boulder, Colorado: Geological Society of America: 551–66.
Hall, C.M. 1992. "Tourism in Antarctica: Activities, Impacts and Management." *Journal of Travel Research* 30(4): 2–9.
—— and M.E. Johnston (eds) 1995. *Polar Tourism: Tourism in the Arctic and Antarctic Regions*. Chichester: John Wiley & Sons.
—— and M. Wouters 1994. "Managing Nature Tourism in the Sub-Antarctic." *Annals of Tourism Research* 21(2): 355–7.

280

Hall, S. 1987. *The Fourth World: The Heritage of the Arctic and its Destruction.* London: Bodley Head.

Hamley, W. 1993. "Problems and Challenges in Canada's Northwest Territories." *Geography* 78(340): 267–80.

Hanessian, John 1960. "The Antarctic Treaty 1959." *International and Comparative Law Quarterly* 9: 437–80.

Hanevold, T. 1994. "Security Policy and Natural Resources." In: Dellenbrant, J.Å. and M.O. Olsson (eds), *The Barents Region: Security and Economic Development in the European North.* Umeå: CERUM: 228–36.

Hansson, R. 1993a. "The NSR: A Route to Destruction or Protection." In: Simonsen, H. (ed.), *Proceedings from the Northern Sea Route Expert Meeting, 13–14 October 1992, Tromsø, Norway.* Lysaker: Fridtjof Nansen Institute: 133–9.

—— 1993b. "The Northern Sea Route: Plain Sailing or Environmental Disaster." *WWF Arctic Bulletin* (3): 10–12.

Harris, C.M. and B. Stonehouse (eds) 1991. *Antarctica and Global Climate Change.* London: Belhaven Press.

Hart, P.D. 1988. "The Growth of Antarctic Tourism." *Oceanus* 31(2): 93–100.

Hausladen, G. 1990. "Settling the Far East: Russian Conquest and Consolidation." In: Rodgers, A. (ed.), *The Soviet Far East: Geographical Perspectives on Development.* London: Routledge: 5–35.

Hayashi, M. 1986. "The Antarctica Question in the United Nations." *Cornell International Law Journal* 19(2): 275–90.

Haysom, V. 1992. "The Struggle for Recognition: Labrador Inuit Negotiations for Land Rights and Self-government." *Etudes Inuit Studies* 16(1–2): 179–97.

Hayton, R.D. 1956. "American Antarctic." *American Journal of International Law* 50(3): 583–610.

—— 1960. "The Antarctic Settlement of 1959." *American Journal of International Law* 54(2): 349–71.

Hazell, S. and O. Zella 1991. "Achieving Sustainable Development in Canada's North." In: Seyersted, P. (ed.), *The Arctic: Canada and the Nordic Countries.* The Nordic Association for Canadian Studies Text Series, Lund, Sweden: Volume 6: 45–62.

Headland, R.K. 1989. *Chronological List of Antarctic Expeditions and Related Historical Events.* Cambridge: Cambridge University Press.

—— 1994. "Historical Development of Antarctic Tourism." *Annals of Tourism Research* 21(2): 269–80.

Heap, J. 1992. "The Treaty and the Protocol." In: Mudge, G. (ed.), *Antarctica: The Environment and the Future.* Geneva: International Academy of the Environment and International Peace Research Institute: 35–40.

Heffernan, M.J. 1994. "The Science of Empire: The French Geographical Movement and the Forms of French Imperialism, 1870–1920." In: Godlewska, A. and N. Smith (eds), *Geography and Empire.* Oxford: Blackwell Publishers: 92–114.

Heininen, L. 1994. "The Military and the Environment: An Arctic Case." In: Käkönen, J. (ed.), *Green Security or Militarized Environment.* Aldershot: Dartmouth: 155–68.

Heintzenberg, J. 1989. "Arctic Haze: Air Pollution in the Polar Regions." *Ambio, A Journal of the Human Environment* XVIII(1): 50–5.

Helander, E. 1994. "The Status of the Sámi People in the Inter-state Cooperation." Paper presented at the Calotte Academy 1994, Regionalism in the Barents Region/North Calotte, 26–9 May 1994. Inari/Finland, Sör-Varanger/Norway and Nikkel/Russia.

Henrikson, A.K. 1992. "Wings for Peace: Open Skies and Transpolar Civil Aviation." In: Käkönen, J. (ed.), *Vulnerable Arctic: Need for An Alternative*

Orientation. Tampere: Tampere Peace Research Institute Research Report No. 47: 107–43.

Hepple, L.W. 1986a. "The Revival of Geopolitics." *Political Geography Quarterly* 5(4): 21–36.

—— 1986b. "Geopolitics, Generals and the State in Brazil." *Political Geography Quarterly* 5(4) *Supplement*: 79–90.

—— 1992. "Metaphor, Geopolitical Discourse and the Military in South America." In T. Barnes and J. Duncan (eds), *Writing Worlds: Discourse, Text and Metaphor in the Representation of Landscape*. London: Routledge: 136–54.

Herr, R.A. and B.W. Davis 1992. *Antarctica and Non-state Actors: The Question of Legitimacy*. IARP Publications Series, No. 4. Lysaker: Fridtjof Nansen Institute.

Hill, D. 1967. *The Opening of the Canadian West*. London: Heinemann.

Hobbs, D. 1986. "New Military Technologies and Northern Waters." In: Archer, C. and D. Scrivener (eds), *Northern Waters: Security and Resource Issues*. London: Croom Helm: 85–96.

Hoel, A.H. 1993. "Arctic Development: Economic and Political Aspects." In: *Arctic Challenges*. Report from the Nordic Council's Parliamentary Conference in Reykjavik, 16–17 August 1993.

—— 1994. "The Barents Sea: Fisheries Resources for Europe and Russia." In: Stokke, O.S. and O. Tunander (eds), *The Barents Region: Cooperation in Arctic Europe*. London: Sage Publications: 115–19.

Hofman, R.J. 1993. "Convention for the Conservation of Antarctic Marine Living Resources." *Marine Policy* (November): 534–6.

Hogan, M.J. (ed.) 1992. *The End of the Cold War: Its Meaning and Implications*. Cambridge: Cambridge University Press.

Holdar, S. 1992. "Political Geographers of the Past IX: The Ideal State and the Power of Geography, the Life-work of Rudolf Kjellén." *Political Geography* 11(3): 307–23.

Holland, C. 1994. *Arctic Exploration and Development c. 500 B.C. to 1915: An Encyclopedia*. New York and London: Garland Publishing, Inc.

Holst, J.J. 1994. "The Barents Region: Institutions, Cooperation and Prospects." In: Stokke, O.S. and O. Tunander (eds), *The Barents Region: Cooperation in Arctic Europe*. London: Sage Publications: 11–24.

Horner, R. 1989. "Arctic Sea-ice Biota." In: Herman, Y. (ed.), *The Arctic Seas*. New York: Van Nostrand Reinhold Co.: 123–46.

House, J.D. 1993. "Knowledge-based Development in the North: New Approaches to Sustainable Development." In: Käkönen, J. (ed.), *Politics and Sustainable Growth in the Arctic*. Aldershot: Dartmouth: 81–92.

Huldt, B. 1988. "Swedish Security in the 1980s and 1990s – Between the Arctic and Europe." In: Möttölä, K. (ed.), *The Arctic Challenge: Nordic and Canadian Approaches to Security and Cooperation in an Emerging International Region*. Boulder, Colorado, and London: Westview Press: 317–29.

Hummel, M. 1994. "Diamonds in the Arctic." *WWF Arctic Bulletin* (4): 13.

Hurrell, A. 1995. "International Political Theory and the Global Environment." In: Booth, K. and S. Smith (eds), *International Relations Theory Today*. Oxford: Polity Press: 129–53.

IASC 1994. *Report from IASC Executive Meeting 18–19 January 1994*. Oslo: International Arctic Science Committee.

Imbert, B. 1992. *North Pole, South Pole: Journeys to the Ends of the Earth*. London: Thames & Hudson.

International Conciliation 1956. "Issues Before the Eleventh General Assembly." 510: 35–43.

Inuit Tapirisat of Canada 1979. *Political Developments in Nunavut*. A Report prepared for the Board of Directors of Inuit Tapirisat of Canada, to be discussed at the Annual General Meeting, 3–7 September 1979, Igloolik.

Issraelian, E. 1992. "Gorbachev's Murmansk Speech." In: Griffiths, F. (ed.), *Arctic Alternatives: Civility or Militarism in the Circumpolar North.* Toronto: Science for Peace/Samuel Stevens: 269–77.

IUCN 1991. *A Strategy for Antarctic Conservation.* IUCN – The World Conservation Union. Gland: Switzerland and Cambridge, UK.

IWGIA 1990. *Indigenous Peoples of the Soviet North.* IWGIA Document No. 67. Copenhagen.

Jalonen, O. 1988. "The Strategic Significance of the Arctic." In: Möttölä, K. (ed.), *The Arctic Challenge: Nordic and Canadian Approaches to Security and Co-operation in an Emerging International Region.* Boulder, Colorado, and London: Westview Press: 157–82.

Janelle, D.G. 1991. "Global Interdependence and its Consequence." In Brunn, S. D. and T. R. Leinbach (eds), *Collapsing Space & Time: Geographical Aspects of Communications & Information.* London: HarperCollins*Academic*: 49–81.

Jervell, S. 1994. "Euro-Arctic Barents Cooperation." Elements used for a lecture at the Conference on "Trans-border Regional Cooperation in the Barents Region", Kirkenes, 24 February 1994.

Jessup, P.C. and H.J. Taubenfeld 1959. *Control for Outer Space and the Antarctic Analogy.* New York: Columbia University Press.

Johansen, L.E. 1992. "Greenland and the European Community." *Etudes Inuit Studies* 16(1–2): 33–7.

Johansson, O. and H. Myrlund 1992. "The Political Force of the Sami People in Northern Sweden." In: Lyck, L. (ed.), *Nordic Arctic Research on Contemporary Arctic Problems.* Proceedings from Nordic Arctic Research Forum Symposium 1992. Aalborg: Aalborg University Press: 213–22.

Johnson, D.T. 1994. "United States Announces New Policy for the Arctic Region." *WWF Arctic Bulletin* (4): 6.

Johnson, S.P. 1993. *The Earth Summit: The United Nations Conference on Environment and Development.* London: Graham & Trotman/Martinus Nijhoff.

Johnston, M.E. 1995. "Patterns and Issues in Arctic and Sub-Arctic Tourism." In: Hall, C.M. and M.E. Johnston (eds), *Polar Tourism: Tourism in the Arctic and Antarctic Regions.* Chichester: John Wiley & Sons: 27–42.

Jonson, L. 1994. "Russian Doctrine and the Arctic." In: Dellenbrant, J.Å. and M.O. Olsson (eds), *The Barents Region: Security and Economic Development in the European North.* Umeå: CERUM: 164–82.

Jørgensen-Dahl, A. and W. Østreng (eds) 1991. *The Antarctic Treaty System in World Politics.* London: Macmillan.

Joyner, C.C. 1991. "A Comparison of Soviet Arctic and Antarctic Policies." In: Brigham, L.W. (ed.), *The Soviet Maritime Arctic.* London: Belhaven Press: 284–300.

—— 1992. *Antarctica and the Law of the Sea.* Dordrecht: Martinus Nijhoff Publishers.

—— and P.J. Lipperman 1986. "Conflicting Jurisdictions in the Southern Ocean: The Case of an Antarctic Minerals Regime." *Virginia Journal of International Law* 27: 1–38.

Jull, P. 1979. "Greenland: Lessons of Self-government and Development." *Northern Perspectives* VII (8): 1–8.

—— 1985. "The Aboriginal Option: A Radical Critique of European Values." *Northern Perspectives* 13(2): 10–12.

—— 1991. "Canada's Northwest Territories: Constitutional Development and Aboriginal Rights." In: Jull, P. and S. Roberts (eds), *The Challenge of Northern Regions.* Darwin: Australian National University Press and North Australian Research Unit: 43–65.

References

—— 1993. "Nunavut Abroad." *Northern Perspectives* 21(3): 15, 18.

Käkönen, J. 1992. "The Concept of Security – From Limited to Comprehensive." In: Käkönen, J. (ed.), *Perspectives on Environmental Conflict and International Relations*. London: Pinter.

—— 1993a. "Regionalization and Sustainable Development in the Northern Europe." Paper presented for the 3rd Nordic Arctic Research Forum Symposium, Hundested, Denmark, 16–18 January 1994.

—— (ed.) 1993b. *Politics and Sustainable Growth in the Arctic*. Aldershot: Dartmouth.

—— 1994. *Perspectives on Environment, State and Civil Society: The Arctic in Transition*. Research Report No. 5 from Environment Policy and Society (EPOS). Uppsala and Linköping.

Kasayulie, W. 1992. "The Self-determination Movement of the Yupiit in South West Alaska." *Etudes Inuit Studies* 16(1–2): 43–5.

Kaser, M. 1983. "The Soviet Gold-mining Industry." In: Jensen, A. *et al.* (ed.), *Soviet Natural Resources in the World Economy*. Chicago: University of Chicago Press: 556–77.

Kazantseva, N. and L. Westin 1994. "Missing Networks in 'the Missing Region' – the Challenge for Infrastructure Development." In: Dellenbrant, J.Å. and M.O. Olsson (eds), *The Barents Region: Security and Economic Development in the European North*. Umeå: CERUM: 105–24.

Keeping, J.M. 1989. *The Inuvialuit Final Agreement*. The University of Calgary: Canadian Institute of Resources Law.

Keith, R.F. 1994. "The Ecosystem Approach: Implications for the North." *Northern Perspectives* 22(1): 3–6.

Keller, J. 1994a. "Sources of Radioactive Contamination in the Russian Arctic Waters." *WWF Arctic Bulletin* (2): 16–18.

—— 1994b. "Oil Spill: How to Help Russia." *WWF Arctic Bulletin* (4): 12–13.

Kennedy, P. 1989. *The Rise and Fall of the Great Powers: Economic Change and Military Conflict from 1500 to 2000*. London: Fontana Press.

Keys, J.R. 1984. *Antarctic Marine Environments and Offshore Oil*. Wellington, New Zealand: Commission for the Environment.

Keyuan, Z. 1993. "China's Antarctic Policy and the Antarctic Treaty System." *Ocean Development and International Law* 24: 237–55.

Kiernan, V. 1993. "Antarctic Welcomes Careful Tourists." *New Scientist* (17 July): 7.

Kimball, L. 1988a. "The Role of the Non-Governmental Organizations in Antarctic Affairs". In Joyner, C.C. and S.K. Chopra (eds), *The Antarctic Legal Regime*. Dordrecht/Boston/London: Martinus Nijhoff Publishers: 33–63.

—— 1988b. "The Antarctic Treaty System." *Oceanus* 31(2): 14–19.

—— 1990. *Southern Exposure: Deciding Antarctica's Future*. Washington DC: World Resources Institute.

Kirton, J. 1984. "Beyond Bilateralism: United States–Canada Cooperation in the Arctic." In: Westermeyer, W.E. and K.M. Shusterich (eds), *United States Arctic Interests: The 1980s and 1990s*. New York: Springer-Verlag: 295–318.

Klein, J. 1985. "Reflections on Geopolitics: From Pangermanism to the Doctrines of Living Space and Moving Frontiers." In Zoppo, C. and C. Zorgbibe (eds), *On Geopolitics: Classical and Nuclear*. Dordrecht: Martinus Nijhoff: 45–76.

Klotz, F.G. 1990. *America on the Ice: Antarctic Policy Issues*. Washington DC: National Defense University Press.

Knox, P. and J. Agnew 1994. *The Geography of the World Economy*. London: Edward Arnold. (Second edition)

Kock, K.-H. 1992. *Antarctic Fish and Fisheries*. Cambridge: Cambridge University Press.

284

—— 1994. "Fishing and Conservation in Southern Waters." *Polar Record* 30(172): 3–22.

Korsmo, F.L. 1993. "Swedish Policy and Saami Rights." *The Northern Review* (11): 32–55.

—— 1994. "The Alaska Natives." In: Minority Rights Group (ed.), *Polar Peoples: Self-determination and Development*. London: Minority Rights Publications: 81–104.

Korten, D.C. 1984. "People-centred Development: Toward a Framework." In: Korten, D.C. and R. Klauss (eds), *People-centred Development: Contributions Toward Theory and Planning Frameworks*. West Hartford: Kumarian Press: 299–309.

—— and G. Carner 1984. "Planning Frameworks for People-centred Development." In: Korten, D.C. and R. Klauss (eds), *People-centred Development: Contributions Toward Theory and Planning Frameworks*. West Hartford: Kumarian Press: 201–9.

Kost, K. 1989. "The Conception of Politics in Political Geography and Geopolitics in Germany Until 1945." *Political Geography Quarterly* 8(4): 369–86.

Kozyrev, A. 1994. "Co-operation in the Barents Euro-Arctic Region: Promising Beginning." In: Stokke, O.S. and O. Tunander (eds), The *Barents Region: Co-operation in Arctic Europe*. London: Sage: 25–30.

Kristof, Ladis K.D. 1992. "Geopolitics as a Field of Study." *The Ford Foundation Lectures in International Relations Studies*. Department of Political Science, The Maharaja Sayajirao University of Baroda, India.

Kristoffersen, Y. 1990. "Eurasia Basin." In: Grantz, A. *et al.* (eds), *The Arctic Ocean Region*. Boulder: Geological Society of America: 305–36.

Krupnik, I. 1993. *Arctic Adaptations: Native Whalers and Reindeer Herders of Northern Eurasia*. Hanover and London: University Press of New England.

Kulski, W.W. 1951. "Soviet Comments on International Law." *American Journal of International Law* 45: 762–70.

Lacoste, Y. 1976. Editorial. *Hérodote* (1).

Langlais, R. 1995. *Reformulating Security: A Case Study from Arctic Canada*. Göteborg: Humanekologiska skrifter 13. (Ph.D. dissertation)

Lantzeff, G.V. and R.A. Pierce 1973. *Eastward to Empire: Exploration and Conquest on the Russian Open Frontier, to 1750*. Montreal: McGill–Queen's University Press.

Larminie, G. 1991. "The Mineral Resource Potential of Antarctica: The State of the Art." In: Jørgensen-Dahl, A. and W. Østreng (eds), *The Antarctic Treaty System in World Politics*. London: Macmillan: 79–93.

Larsen, D.L. 1989. "United States Interests in the Arctic Region." *Ocean Development and International Law* 20: 167–91.

Laws, R.M. (ed.) 1984. *Antarctic Ecology*. Volumes One and Two. London: Academic Press.

—— 1985. "The Ecology of the Southern Ocean." *American Scientist* 73 (January–February): 26–40.

Lee, N. de 1986. "Iceland: Unarmed Ally." In: Archer, C. and D. Scrivener (eds), *Northern Waters: Security and Resource Issues*. London: Routledge: 190–207.

Lenarcic, D. and R. Retford 1989. "Sovereignty Versus Defence: The Arctic in Canadian–American Relations." In: Dosman, E. (ed.), *Sovereignty and Security in the Arctic*. London: Routledge: 159–75.

Levere, T.H. 1993. *Science and the Canadian Arctic: A Century of Exploration 1818–1918*. Cambridge: Cambridge University Press.

Livingstone, D.N. 1992. *The Geographical Tradition: Episodes in the History of a Contested Enterprise*. Oxford, UK, and Cambridge, USA: Blackwell.

References

Ljungkvist, T. 1988. "The Swedish Saami Rights Committee." *Nordic Journal of International Law* 57: 247–50.

Lockhart, A. 1987. "Community-based Development and Conventional Economics in the Canadian North." In: Bennett, E.M. (ed.), *Social Intervention: Theory and Practice*. Lewiston and Queenston: Edwin Mellen Press: 393–414.

Luzin, G. 1993. "Mega Projects and the Environment: The Use of Natural Resources in the Arctic." In: Jussila, H., L. O. Persson and U. Wiberg (eds), *Shifts in Systems at the Top of Europe*. Forskningsgruppen för Regional Analysis (FORA): Stockholm: Sweden: 89–97.

Lyck, L. 1990a. "Sustainable Development in the Arctic." *Polar Record* 26(159): 309–12.

—— 1990b. "Prospects for Sustainable Development in the Arctic in the Light of International Political and Economic Changes." Paper presented at the Third Northern Regions Conference: Northern Regions Conference and Opportunity for our Future 19 September 1990.

—— 1993. "Military Strategy and its Socio-economic Consequences in the Arctic Since World War II." Paper presented at the Conference on Military Development and Socio-Cultural Change in the North, Centre for North Atlantic Studies, Aarhus University, 25–7 October 1993.

—— 1994. "Considerations on Sustainable Development in the Arctic." In: Greiffenberg, T. (ed.), *Sustainability in the Arctic*. Proceedings from Nordic Arctic Research Forum Symposium 1993. Aalborg: Aalborg University Press: 7–24.

Lynge, F. 1985. "Cultural Genocide of Tomorrow or: A Future for Us All?" *Etudes Inuit Studies* 9(2): 21–6.

—— 1992. *Arctic Wars, Animal Rights, Endangered Peoples*. Hanover and London: University Press of New England.

—— 1993. "Greenland. Its People and Society." International Court of Justice, *Maritime Delimitation in the Area Between Greenland and Jan Mayen (Denmark/Norway)*. Denmark Intervention No. 3, The Hague, January 1993: 1–37.

Lyons, D. 1993. "Environmental Impact Assessment in Antarctica under the Protocol on Environmental Protection." *Polar Record* 29(169): 111–20.

Marcus, A.R. 1992. *Out in the Cold: The Legacy of Canada's Inuit Relocation Experiment in the High Arctic*. IWGIA Document No. 71. Copenhagen.

Martens, G. 1992. "Scenarios for Home Rule in Greenland After Implementation of the Plan for Home Rule." In: Lyck, L. (ed.), *Nordic Arctic Research on Contemporary Arctic Problems*. Proceedings from Nordic Arctic Research Forum Symposium 1992. Aalborg: Aalborg University Press: 193–206.

Mathisen, T. 1954. *Svalbard in the Changing Arctic*. Oslo: Gyldendal Norsk Forlag.

Maxwell, B. and L.A. Barrie 1989. "Atmospheric and Climatic Change in the Arctic and Antarctic." *Ambio, A Journal of the Human Environment* XVIII(1): 42–9.

McNabb, S. 1992. "Native Claims in Alaska: A Twenty Year Review." *Etudes Inuit Studies* 16(1–2): 85–95.

McGwire, M. 1989. "Strategic Interests in the Arctic." In: Dosman, E. (ed.), *Sovereignty and Security in the Arctic*. London: Routledge: 24–40.

Merritt, J. 1993a. "Nunavut Inuit Organizations and the Challenges of Post-Land Claims World." *Northern Perspectives* 21(3): 12–14.

—— 1993b. "Marine Co-management in the Canadian Arctic: The Features and Implications of Nunavut." Paper presented at Pacem in Maribus Conference XXI, Takaoka, Japan, September 1993.

Miller, S.E. 1988. "The Maritime Strategy and Geopolitics in the High North." In: Archer, C. (ed.), *The Soviet Union and Northern Waters*. London: Routledge: 205–38.

—— 1992. "The Arctic as a Maritime Theatre." In: Griffiths, F. (ed.), *Arctic Alternatives: Civility or Militarism in the Circumpolar North*. Toronto: Science for Peace/Samuel Stevens: 211–36.

Minority Rights Group (ed.) 1994. *Polar Peoples: Self-determination and Development*. London: Minority Rights Publications.

Mironov, V. 1994. "Russia's National Security Military Doctrine and the Outlook for Russian–U.S. Cooperation in the Modern World." *Comparative Strategy* 13(1): 49–54.

Mische, P.M. 1989. "Ecological Security and the Need to Reconceptualize Sovereignty." *Alternatives* XIV: 389–427.

Mitchell, B. 1984. "The Antarctic Treaty: Victim of its Own Success." In: Alexander, L.M. and L.C. Hanson (eds), *Antarctic Politics and Marine Resources: Critical Choices for the 1980s*. Kingston, Rhode Island: Center for Ocean Management Studies: 13–21.

Moe, A. 1992. "The Energy Sector of the Barents Region." *International Challenges* 12(4): 57–68.

—— 1994. "Oil and Gas: Future Role of the Barents Region". In: Stokke, O.S. and O. Tunander (eds), *The Barents Region: Cooperation in Arctic Europe*. London: Sage Publications: 131–44.

Morel, P. 1992. "The Earth's Climate, Past and Future Changes." In: Mudge, G. (ed.), *Antarctica: The Environment and the Future*. Geneva: International Academy of the Environment and International Peace Research Institute: 12–15.

Morris, M.A. 1988. "South American Antarctic Policies." In: Borgese, E.M. *et al.* (eds), *Ocean Yearbook* 7: 356–71.

Morrison, W.R. 1985. *Showing the Flag: The Mounted Police and Canadian Sovereignty in the North, 1894–1925*. Vancouver: University of British Columbia Press.

Morse, B.W. 1989. "Aboriginal Peoples and the Law." In: Morse, B.W. (ed.), *Aboriginal Peoples and the Law: Indian, Metis and Inuit Rights in Canada*. Ottawa: Carleton University Press: 1–14.

Moss, W. 1989. "The Implementation of the James Bay and Northern Quebec Agreement." In: Morse, B.W. (ed.), *Aboriginal Peoples and the Law: Indian, Metis and Inuit Rights in Canada*. Ottawa: Carleton University Press: 684–94.

Müller-Wille, L. 1979. "The Sami Parliament in Finland: A Model for Ethnic Minority Management." *Etudes Inuit Studies* 3(2): 63–72.

Nakazawa, A., F. Mitchell and G. Goldman 1992. "The Regulation of Subsistence in Alaska: The State's Current Dilemma." *The Northern Review, A Multidisciplinary Journal of the Arts and Social Sciences of the North* (8/9): 115–28.

Naveen, R. 1991. "The Promise of Antarctic Tourism: On the Cutting Edge of Ecotourism, or a Blight on Earth's Last Pristine Wilderness?" *Antarctic Century* 7: 1–11.

Naveh, C. 1994. "Regionalism and Regional Powers in New World Order." Paper submitted at the XVIth World Congress of the International Political Science Association, 21–5 August 1994, Berlin.

Nikolayev, M. 1993. "The Northern Forum and the Arctic Regions' Future. Article Two." *Northern News* 11(58): 1–3.

Norgaard, R.B. 1994. *Development Betrayed: The End of Progress and a Coevolutionary Revisioning of the Future*. London: Routledge.

Northern Forum: International Journal of the North. 1994. 2(1).

Northern Perspectives. 1991. "Arctic Council: Canada Prepares for a New Era in Circumpolar Relations." 19(2): 2–22.

Nunatsiaq News. 28 January 1994.

Nuttall, M. 1992. *Arctic Homeland: Kinship, Community and Development in Northwest Greenland*. London: Belhaven Press.

—— 1994. "Greenland: Emergence of an Inuit Homeland." In: Minority Rights Group (ed.), *Polar Peoples: Self-determination and Development*. London: Minority Rights Publications: 1–28.

References

O'Loughlin, J. 1994. "New Geopolitics." In: O'Loughlin, J. (ed.), *Dictionary of Geopolitics*. Westport: Greenwood Press: 174–5.

—— and H. Heske. 1991. "Converting a Discipline of War into a Discipline for Peace." In Kliot, N. and S. Waterman (eds), *The Political Geography of Conflict and Peace*. London: Belhaven: 37–59.

—— and A. Luc 1993. "Geography of International Relations: Theory and Methods." In Ward, M.D. (ed.), *The New Geopolitics*. Philadelphia: Gordon and Breach: 39–76.

Orrego Vicuña, F. 1988. *Antarctic Mineral Exploitation: The Emerging Legal Framework*. Cambridge: Cambridge University Press.

—— 1991. "The Effectiveness of the Decision Making Machinery of CCAMLR: An Assessment." In: Jørgensen-Dahl, A. and W. Østreng (eds), *The Antarctic Treaty System in World Politics*, London: Macmillan: 25–42.

—— 1992. *The Protection of the Antarctic Environment*. IARP Publications Series, No. 5. Lysaker: Fridtjof Nansen Institute.

Osherenko, G. 1993. "Using Peripheral Vision in the Northern Sea Route: Assessing Impacts on Indigenous Peoples." In: Simonsen, H. (ed.), *Proceedings from the Northern Sea Route Expert Meeting, 13–14 October 1992, Tromsø, Norway*. Lysaker: Fridtjof Nansen Institute: 115–32.

—— and O.R. Young 1989. *The Age of the Arctic: Hot Conflicts and Cold Realities*. Cambridge: Cambridge University Press.

Østreng, W. 1977. *Politics in High Latitudes: The Svalbard Archipelago*. London: C. Hurst & Company.

—— 1982a. *The Soviet Union in Arctic Waters: Security Implications for the Northern Flank of NATO*. Lysaker: Fridtjof Nansen Institute.

—— 1982b. "Norway's Law of the Sea Policy in the 1970s." *Ocean Development and International Law* 11(1/2): 70–93.

—— 1991a. "The Conflict and Alignment Pattern of Antarctic Politics. Is a New Order Needed?" In: Jørgensen-Dahl, A. and W. Østreng (eds), *The Antarctic Treaty System in World Politics*. London: Macmillan: 433–50.

—— 1991b. "The Northern Sea Route: A New Era in Soviet Policy?" *Ocean Development and International Law* 22(3): 259–87.

—— 1992a. "Political-military Relations among the Ice States: The Conceptual Basis of State Behaviour." In: Griffiths, F. (ed.), *Arctic Alternatives: Civility or Militarism in the Circumpolar North*. Toronto: Science for Peace/Samuel Stevens: 26–45.

—— 1992b. "The Barents Region: A Contribution to European Security and Cooperation." *International Challenges* 12(4): 13–20.

—— 1994. "The Northern Sea Route and the Barents Region." In: Stokke, O. and O. Tunander (eds), *The Barents Region: Cooperation in Arctic Europe*. London: Sage Publications: 159–72.

Oswalt, W.H. 1990. *Bashful No Longer: An Alaskan Eskimo Ethnohistory, 1778–1988*. Norman and London: University of Oklahoma Press.

O'Tuathail, G. 1994a. "Second Cold War." In: O'Loughlin, J. (ed.), *Dictionary of Geopolitics*. Westport: Greenwood Press: 214–17.

—— 1994b. "(Dis)placing Geopolitics: Writing on the Maps of Global Politics." *Environment and Planning. D. Society and Space* 12(5): 525–46.

—— and J. Agnew 1992. "Geopolitics and Discourse: Practical Geopolitical Reasoning in American Foreign Policy." *Political Geography* 11(2): 190–204.

—— and S. Dalby 1994. "Critical Geopolitics: Unfolding Spaces for Thought in Geography and Global Politics." *Environment and Planning. D. Society and Space* 12(5): 513–15.

Paine, R. 1982. *Dam a River, Damn a People? Saami (Lap) Livelihood and the Alta/ Kautokeino Hydro-electric Project and the Norwegian Parliament*. IWGIA Document No. 45. Copenhagen.

—— 1989. "Ethnodrama and the 'Fourth World': The Saami Action Group in Norway, 1979–1981." In: Dyck, N. (ed.), *Indigenous Peoples and the Nation-State. Social and Economic Papers No. 14.* Newfoundland: Institute of Social and Economic Research, Memorial University of Newfoundland.

Pannatier, S. 1994. "Acquisition of Consultative Status under the Antarctic Treaty." *Polar Record* 30(173): 123–30.

Parker, G. 1985. *Western Geopolitical Thought in the Twentieth Century.* London: Croom Helm.

—— 1994. "Political Geography and Geopolitics." In: Groom, A.J.R. and M. Light (eds), *Contemporary International Relations: A Guide to Theory.* London: Pinter Publishers: 170–81.

Parker, W.H. 1982. *Mackinder: Geography as an Aid to Statecraft.* Oxford: Oxford University Press.

Parsons, Sir Anthony 1987. *Antarctica: The Next Decade.* Cambridge: Cambridge University Press.

Pearce, F. 1994. "Samis Fear Curse of Diamonds." *BBC Worldlife* 12(8): 59.

Pentikäinen, J. 1993. "Northern Ethnography: Exploring the Fourth World." Universitas Helsingiensis Research: 20–9.

Petersen, N. 1993. "Greenland and the Global Balance of Power, 1941–1993." Paper presented at the Conference on Military Development and Socio-cultural Change in the North Centre for North Atlantic Studies, Aarhus University, 25-7 October 1993.

Peterson, M.J. 1988. *Managing the Frozen South: The Creation and Evolution of the Antarctic Treaty System.* Berkeley: University of California Press.

Pharand, D. 1991. "Draft Arctic Treaty: An Arctic Region Council." *Northern Perspectives* 19(2): 20–3.

—— 1992. "The Case for an Arctic Region Council and a Treaty Proposal." *R.G.D.* 23: 163–95.

Pika, A. and B. Prokhorov 1989 "Soviet Union: The Big Problems of Small Ethnic Groups." Newsletter *IWGIA* 57: 132–53. (Translation from the Russian source: *Kommunist*, No. 16, November 1988: 76–83.)

Polar Record 1975. "Agreement on the Conservation of Polar Bears" 17(108): 327–30.

Poole, G.R. 1994. *The Development of Greenland's Shrimp Fishing and Processing Industry Since 1979: A Study in Applied Economics.* Unpublished Ph.D. dissertation, Scott Polar Research Institute, University of Cambridge.

——, M. Pretes and K. Sinding 1992. "Managing Greenland's Mineral Revenues: A Trust Fund Approach." *Resources Policy* (September): 191–204.

Pretes, M. 1993. "Financial Resources for Sustainable Development in the Arctic." In: Käkönen, J. (ed.), *Politics and Sustainable Growth in the Arctic.* Aldershot: Dartmouth: 93–106.

—— and M. Robinson 1989. "Beyond Boom and Bust: A Strategy for Sustainable Development." *Polar Record* 25(153): 115–20.

Prins, G. 1990. "Politics and the Environment." *International Affairs* 66(4): 711–30.

Prokosch, P. 1994a. "How Many Polar Bears?" *WWF Arctic Bulletin* (3): 13.

—— 1994b. "New CAFF Task: Protected Area Network Plan." *WWF Arctic Bulletin* (4): 4–5.

Purich, D. 1992. *The Inuit and Their Land: The Story of Nunavut.* Toronto: James Lorimer & Company, Publishers.

Purver, R.G. 1988. "Arctic Arms Control: Constraints and Opportunities." Occasional Papers: Canadian Institute for International Peace and Security. No. 3: 1–80.

Putilov, V.A. 1994. "The Information Infrastructure of the Russian North." In: Dellenbrant, J.Å. and M.O. Olsson (eds), *The Barents Region: Security and Economic Development in the European North.* Umeå: CERUM: 125–37.

References

Quigg, P. 1983. *A Pole Apart: The Emerging Issue of Antarctica.* New York: Mc-Graw Hill.

Rabbani, M.M. 1994. "Pakistan's Interest in Antarctica." In: Herr, R.A. and B.W. Davis (eds), *Asia in Antarctica.* Canberra: Centre for Resources and Environmental Studies, Australian National University with Antarctica Cooperative Research Centre: 119–22.

Rasmussen, R.O. 1994. "Implementation of Sustainable Development – Methodological and Conceptual Considerations Concerning the Measuring of Sustainability." In: Greiffenberg, T. (ed.), *Sustainability in the Arctic.* Proceedings from Nordic Arctic Research Forum Symposium 1993. Aalborg: Aalborg University Press: 25–74.

Redclift, M. 1992. "Sustainable Development and Popular Participation: A Framework for Analysis." In: Ghai, D. and J.M. Jessica (eds), *Grassroots Environmental Action: People's Participation in Sustainable Development.* London: Routledge: 23–49.

Rees, J. 1991. "Resources and the Environment: Scarcity and Sustainability." In: Bennett, R. and R. Estall (eds), *Global Change and Challenge: Geography for the 1990s.* London: Routledge: 5–26.

Reich, R.J. 1980. "The Development of Antarctic Tourism." *Polar Record* 20(126): 203–14.

Richardson, D. 1994. "Sustainable Development: Terminological Implications of Politics and Political Implications of Terminology." Paper presented to the British International Studies Association Annual Conference at the University of York, December 1994.

Ries, T. 1988. "Soviet Military Strategy and Northern Waters." In: Archer, C. (ed.), *The Soviet Union and Northern Waters.* London: Routledge: 90–133.

Riffenburgh, B. 1993. *The Myth of the Explorer.* Chichester: John Wiley & Sons.

Roan, S.L. 1990. *Ozone Crisis: The 15 Year Evolution of a Sudden Global Emergency.* New York: John Wiley & Sons.

Roginko, A.Yu. 1992. "Conflict Between Environment and Development in the Soviet Arctic." In: Käkönen, J. (ed.), *Vulnerable Arctic: Need for an Alternative Orientation.* Tampere Peace Research Institute Research Report No. 47: 144–54.

Roots, E.F. 1992. "Co-operation in Arctic Science." In: Griffiths, F. (ed.), *Arctic Alternatives: Civility or Militarism in the Circumpolar North.* Toronto: Science for Peace/Samuel Stevens: 136–55.

——, O. Rogne and J. Taagholt 1987. *International Communication and Coordination in Arctic Science: A Proposal for Action.* Prepared at the request of an informal consultative meeting held in Oslo, Norway, on 13 February 1987, attended by the representatives from Canada, Denmark, Finland, Iceland, Norway, Sweden, the Union of Soviet Socialist Republics and the United States of America, 17 November 1987.

Rosing, H. 1985. "Native Land Claims: Assessing the Alaskan Experience." In: Brøsted, J. *et al.* (eds), *Native Power: The Quest for Autonomy and Nationhood of Indigenous Peoples.* Bergen: Universitetsforlaget as.

Rothwell, D.R. 1988. *Maritime Boundaries and Resource Development: Options for the Beaufort Sea.* Calgary, Alberta: University of Calgary, Canadian Institute of Resources Law.

—— 1993. "The Canadian–U.S. Northwest Passage Dispute: A Reassessment." *Cornell International Law Journal* 26(2): 331–72.

—— 1994. "Polar Lessons for an Arctic Regime." *Cooperation and Conflict* 29(1): 55–76.

—— and S. Kaye 1994. "Law of the Sea and the Polar Regions: Reconsidering the Traditional Norms." *Marine Policy* 18(1): 41–58.

Rowland, J.R. 1988. "The Treaty Regime and the Politics of the Consultative Parties." In: Joyner, C.C. and S.K. Chopra (eds), *The Antarctic Legal Regime.* Dordrecht/Boston/London: Martinus Nijhoff Publishers: 11–30.

Ruhala, K. 1988. "Finland's Security Policy: The Arctic Dimension." In: Möttölä, K. (ed.), *The Arctic Challenge: Nordic and Canadian Approaches to Security and Cooperation in an Emerging International Region.* Boulder, Colorado, and London: Westview Press: 117–30.

Sack, R.D. 1986. *Human Territoriality: Its Theory and History.* Cambridge: Cambridge University Press.

Sagers, M.J. 1994. "Oil Spill in Russian Arctic." *Polar Geography and Geology* 18(2): 95–102.

—— and V. Kryukov 1993. "The Hydrocarbon Processing Industry in West Siberia." *Post-Soviet Geography* 34(2): 127–52.

Sahurie, E.J. 1992. *The International Law of Antarctica.* Dordrecht: Martinus Nijhoff Publishers; New Haven: New Haven Press.

Sallenave, J. 1994. "Giving Traditional Ecological Knowledge its Rightful Place in Environmental Impact Assessment." *Northern Perspectives* 22(1): 16–19.

Sambo, D. 1989. "Report on Critical Issues in the Arctic." In: Churchill, W. (ed.), *Critical Issues in Native North America.* IWGIA Document No. 62. Copenhagen.

Santa Cruz, F.Z. 1978. "Antarctica System and the Utilization of Resources." *University of Miami Law Review* 33(2): 426–73.

Schindler, D.L. 1992. "Russian Hegemony and Indigenous Rights in Chukotka." *Etudes Inuit Studies* 16(1–2): 51–74.

Schwerdtfeger, P. 1986. "Antarctic Icebergs as Potential Sources of Water and Energy." In: Wolfrum, R. (ed.), *Antarctic Challenge II.* Berlin: Duncker & Humblot: 377–89.

Scoging, H. 1991. "Desertification and its Management." In: Bennet, R. and R. Estall (eds), *Global Change and Challenge: Geography for the 1990s.* London: Routledge: 57–79.

Scrivener, D. 1992. "Resources and Environment in Norwegian–Soviet Relations in the Arctic." Paper presented to BISA Annual Conference, 14–16 December 1992.

Scully, R.T. 1991. "Protecting Antarctica: Progress in Chile." *The Antarctic Society* 1(4): 4–9.

Seager, H. 1977. *Alfred Thayer Mahan: The Man and His Letters.* Annapolis, Maryland: Naval Institute Press.

Shabad, T. 1987. "Economic Resources." In: Wood, A. (ed.), *Siberia: Problems and Prospects for Regional Development.* London: Croom Helm: 62–95.

Shapley, D. 1985. *The Seventh Continent: Antarctica in a Resource Age.* Washington, DC: Resources for the Future Inc.

Sharp, J.P. 1993. "Publishing American Identity: Popular Geopolitics, Myth and the Reader's Digest." *Political Geography* 12(6): 491–503.

Shnirelman, V.A. 1994. "Hostages of an Authoritarian Regime: The Fate of the 'Numerically-Small Peoples' of the Russian North under Soviet Rule." *Etudes Inuit Studies* 18(1–2): 201–23.

Simon, M. 1992. "Militarization and the Aboriginal Peoples." In: Griffiths, F. (ed.), *Arctic Alternatives: Civility or Militarism in the Circumpolar North.* Toronto: Science for Peace/Samuel Stevens: 55–67.

—— and C. Stephens 1993. "Human Affairs in the Polar Regions." A Keynote Address at the Conference on Britain's Role in Polar Research: New Frontiers and New Policies in Science. Robinson College, University of Cambridge.

Simonsen, H. (ed.) 1993. *Proceedings from the Northern Sea Route Expert Meeting, 13–14 October 1992, Tromsø, Norway.* Lysaker: Fridtjof Nansen Institute.

References

Singh, E.C. and A.A. Saguirian 1993 "The Svalbard Archipelago: The Role of Surrogate Negotiators." In: Young, O.R. and G. Osherenko (eds), *Polar Politics: Creating International Environmental Regimes*. Ithaca and London: Cornell University Press: 56–95.

Skogan, J.K. 1992. "Militarization and Confidence-building Measures in the Arctic." In: Griffiths, F. (ed.), *Arctic Alternatives: Civility or Militarism in the Circumpolar North*. Toronto: Science for Peace/Samuel Stevens: 251–68.

Sloan, G.R. 1988. *Geopolitics in United States Strategic Policy, 1890–1987*. Brighton: Wheatsheaf Books.

Smith, D. 1993. *The Seventh Fire: The Struggle for Aboriginal Government*. Toronto: Key Porter Books.

Smith, G.W. 1966. "Sovereignty in the North: The Canadian Aspect of an International Problem." In: Macdonald, R. St.J. (ed.), *The Arctic Frontier*. Toronto: University of Toronto Press: 194–255.

Smith, V.L. 1994. "A Sustainable Antarctic: Science and Tourism." *Annals of Tourism Research* 21(2): 221–30.

Smyth, S. 1993. "The Constitutional Context of Aboriginal and Colonial Government in the Yukon Territory." *Polar Record* 29(169): 121–6.

Sollie, F. 1984. "The Development of the Antarctic Treaty System – Trends and Issues." In: Wolfrum, R. (ed.), *Antarctic Challenge: Conflicting Interests, Cooperation, Environmental Protection, Economic Development*. Berlin: Duncker & Humblot: 17–37.

Spencer, A. 1978. *The Lapps*. New York: Crane, Russak & Company.

Splettstoesser, J. and M.C. Folks 1994. "Environmental Guidelines for Tourism in Antarctica." *Annals for Tourism Research* 21(2): 231–44.

Sreenivasan, T.P. 1994. "India's Antarctic Policy and Interests." In: Herr, R.A. and B.W. Davis (eds), *Asia in Antarctica*. Canberra: Centre for Resources and Environmental Studies, Australian National University with Antarctic Cooperative Research Centre.

Stagg, J. 1991. "Economic Development in the Canadian North." In: Seyersted, P. (ed.), *The Arctic: Canada and the Nordic Countries*. The Nordic Association for Canadian Studies Text Series, Lund, Sweden, Volume 6: 19–23.

Starr, H. 1993. "Joining Political and Geographic Perspectives: Geopolitics and International Relations." In: Ward, M.D. (ed.), *The New Geopolitics*. Philadelphia: Gordon and Breach: 1–10.

Steel, R. 1992. "The End and the Beginning." In: Hogan, M.J. (ed.), *The End of the Cold War: Its Meaning and Implications*. Cambridge: Cambridge University Press: 103–12.

Stokke, O.S. 1991. "The Relevance of the Antarctic Treaty System as a Model for International Cooperation." In: Jørgensen-Dahl, A. and W. Østreng (eds), *The Antarctic Treaty System in World Politics*. London: Macmillan: 357–71.

—— 1992. "Arctic Environmental Cooperation After Rovaniemi – What Now?" In: Lyck, L. (ed.), *Nordic Arctic Research on Contemporary Arctic Problems*. Proceedings from Nordic Arctic Research Forum Symposium 1992. Aalborg, Aalborg University Press.

Stokke, O.S. and O. Tunander (eds) 1994. *The Barents Region: Cooperation in Arctic Europe*. London: Sage Publications.

Stoltenberg, T. 1992. "The Barents Region: Reorganizing Northern Europe." *International Challenges* 12(4): 5–12.

Stonehouse, B. 1989. *Polar Ecology*. Glasgow and London: Blackie.

—— 1991. "Polar Ecosystems, Management and Climate Modelling." In: Harris, C.M. and B. Stonehouse (eds), *Antarctica and Global Climate Change*. London: Belhaven Press: 147–54.

—— 1992. "Monitoring Shipborne Visitors in Antarctica: A Preliminary Field Study." *Polar Record* 28(166): 213–18.

Sturges, W.T. (ed.) 1991. *Pollution of the Arctic Atmosphere.* London: Elsevier.

Sugden, D.E. 1959. "The International Geophysical Year." *International Conciliation* (521): 261–83.

—— 1982. *Arctic and Antarctic: A Modern Geographical Synthesis.* Oxford: Basil Blackwell.

Sullivan, W. 1957. *Quest for a Continent.* New York: Mc-Graw-Hill.

Swan, R.A. 1961. *Australia in the Antarctic: Interest, Activity and Endeavour.* Melbourne: Melbourne University Press.

Swithinbank, C. 1993. "Airborne Tourism in the Antarctic." *Polar Record* 29(169): 103–10.

Taagholt, J. 1980. "Greenland and the Future." *Environmental Conservation* 7(4): 295–9.

—— 1993. "Technological Development in the Arctic in the Post-war Period." Paper presented at the Conference on Military Development and Socio-cultural Change in the North, Centre for North Atlantic Studies, Aarhus University, 25–7 October 1993: 1–8.

Tamnes, R. 1991. *The United States and the Cold War in the High North.* Aldershot: Dartmouth.

Taracouzio, T.A. 1938. *Soviets in the Arctic: An Historical, Economic and Political Study of the Soviet Advance into the Arctic.* New York: The Macmillan Company.

Tauli-Corpuz, V. 1993. "An Indigenous People's Perspective on Environment and Development." *Newsletter IWGIA* 1: 3–17.

Taylor, P.J. 1989. *Political Geography: World Economy, Nation-State and Locality.* New York: Longman.

—— 1990. *Britain and the Cold War: 1945 as a Geopolitical Transition.* London: Pinter Publishers.

—— 1993. "Geopolitical World Orders." In: Taylor, P.J. (ed.), *Political Geography of the Twentieth Century: A Global Analysis.* London: Belhaven Press: 31–61.

—— 1993a. *Political Geography: World Economy, Nation-State and Locality.* London: Longman.

—— 1993b. "Full Circle, or New Meaning for the Global." In: Johnston, R.J. (ed.), *The Challenge for Geography: A Changing World: A Changing Discipline.* Oxford, UK, and Cambridge, USA: 181–97.

The Commission on Global Governance 1995. *Our Global Neighbourhood.* The Report of the Commission on Global Governance. Oxford: Oxford University Press.

The State of the Arctic Environment Reports 1991. Rovaniemi: Arctic Centre, University of Lapland.

The Northern Forum, International Journal of the North 1994. 2(2).

Thompson, W.R. 1973. "The Regional Subsystem: A Conceptual Explication and a Propositional Inventory." *International Studies Quarterly* 17(1): 89–117.

Timtchenko, L. 1994. "The Legal Status of the Northern Sea Route." *Polar Record* 30(174): 193–200.

Tol, R. 1988. "A Naval Force Comparison in Northern and Atlantic Waters." In: Archer, C. (ed.), *The Soviet Union and Northern Waters.* London: Routledge: 134–63.

Toma, P.A. 1956. "Soviet Attitude Towards the Acquisition of Territorial Sovereignty in Antarctica." *American Journal of International Law* 50(3): 611–26.

Traavik, K. and W. Østreng 1977 "Security and Ocean Law: Norway and the Soviet Union in the Barents Sea." *Ocean Development and International Law* 4(4): 343–67.

References

Triggs, G.D. 1986. *International Law and Australian Sovereignty in Antarctica.* Sydney: Legal Books Pvt. Ltd.
Tunander, O. 1989. *Cold War Politics: The Maritime Strategy and Geopolitics of the Northern Front.* London: Sage Publications.
—— 1994. "Inventing the Barents Region: Overcoming the East-West Divide." In: Stokke, O.S. and O. Tunander (eds), *The Barents Region: Cooperation in Arctic Europe.* London: Sage Publications: 31–44.
Tundra Times 6 April 1994.
US Department of State 1994. *Fact Sheet: U.S. Arctic Policy.* Bureau of Public Affairs, Office of Public Communication. 1 December 1994. Washington D.C.
US Government 1994. *Presidential Decision Directive: United States Policy on the Arctic and Antarctic Regions.* Washington D.C.
Usher, P.J. 1984. "Property Rights: The Basis of Wildlife Management." In: *National and Regional Interests in the North: Third National Workshop on People, Resources, and the Environment North of 60°.* Ottawa: Canadian Arctic Resources Committee: 389–416.
——, F.J. Tough and R.M. Galois 1992. "Reclaiming the Land: Aboriginal Title, Treaty Rights and Land Claims in Canada." *Applied Geography* 12: 109–32.
Uspensky, S.M. 1994. "A Russian View of the Polar Bear: What Does the Future Hold?" *WWF Arctic Bulletin* (3): 14.
Vakhtin, N. 1994. "Native Peoples of the Russian Far North." In: Minority Rights Group (ed.), *Polar Peoples: Self-determination and Development.* London: Minority Rights Publications: 29–80.
Vaughan, R. 1994. *The Arctic: A History.* Dover: Alan Sutton.
Verhoeven, J., P. Sands and M. Bruce (eds), 1992. *The Antarctic Environment and International Law.* London: Graham & Trotman.
Vidas, D. 1992. *Antarctic Tourism: A Challenge to the Legitimacy of the Antarctic Treaty System?* IARP Publications Series, No. 6. Lysaker: Fridtjof Nansen Institute.
Volkov, A.E. and J. de Korte 1994. "Protected Nature Areas in the Russian Arctic." *Polar Record* 30(175): 299–310.
Wace, N. 1990. "Antarctica: A New Tourist Destination." *Applied Geography* 10: 327–41.
Wadhams, P. 1990. "The Resource Potential of Antarctic Icebergs." In: *Mineral Resource Potential of Antarctica. Antarctic Research Series* (51): 203–15.
—— 1991. "Variations in Sea Ice Thickness in the Polar Regions". In: *International Conference on the Role of the Polar Regions in Global Change.* Proceedings of a Conference, June 11–15, 1990 at the University of Alaska Fairbanks (ed. G. Weller, C.L. Wilson, B.A.B. Severin). University of Alaska, Fairbanks: Geophysical Institute and Center for Global Change and Arctic Systems: 4–13.
Walker, R.B.J. and S. Mendlowitz (eds) 1990. *Contending Sovereignties: Redefining Political Community.* Boulder, Colorado: Lynne Rienner.
Walton, D.W.H. 1987. "Antarctic Terrestrial Ecosystems." *Environmental International* 13: 83–9.
Wassermann, U. 1978. "The Antarctic Treaty System and the Natural Resources." *Journal of Trade Law* 1(2): 174–99.
Watts, A. 1992. *International Law and the Antarctic Treaty System.* Cambridge: Grotius Publications Limited.
Weber, P. 1994. "Safeguarding Oceans." In: Brown, L.R. *et al., State of the World 1994.* A Worldwatch Institute Report on Progress Toward a Sustainable Society. London: Earthscan Publications Ltd: 41–60.
Weller, G.E. (ed.) 1989. *The Role of Antarctica in Global Change.* Cambridge: ICSU Press and SCAR.

—— (ed.) 1993. *The Role of the Antarctic in Global Change: An International Plan for a Regional Research Programme*. Cambridge: SCAR.

—— *et al.* (eds), 1991. Volumes I and II. *International Conference on the Role of the Polar Regions in Global Change*. Proceedings of a Conference, 11–15 June 1990. University of Alaska, Fairbanks: Geophysical Institute, and Centre for Global Change and Arctic System Research, University of Alaska.

Wenzel, G. 1991. *Animal Rights, Human Rights: Ecology, Economy and Ideology in the Canadian Arctic*. London: Belhaven.

Westermeyer, W. 1982. "Resource Allocation in Antarctica. A Review." *Marine Policy* 6: 303–25.

White, K. 1994. "Tourism and the Antarctic Economy." *Annals of Tourism Research* 21(2): 245–68.

Wiberg, U. 1994. "From Visions to Functional Relationships in the Barents Region." Paper presented at the Conference Trans-border Regional Co-operation in the Barents Region, Kirkenes, Norway, 24–6 February 1994.

Williams, P.J. 1989. *Pipelines & Permafrost: Science In a Cold Climate*. Ottawa: Carleton University Press.

Wilmer, F. 1993. *The Indigenous Voice in World Politics*. Newbury Park: Sage Publications.

Wilson, D. 1987. "The Siberian Oil and Gas Industry". In: Wood, A. (ed.), *Siberia: Problems and Prospects for Regional Development*. London: Croom Helm: 96–129.

—— 1989. "Exploration for Oil and Gas in Eastern Siberia." In: Wood, A. and A.R. French (eds), *The Development of Siberia: People and Resources*. London: Macmillan: 228–54.

Wolfrum, R. 1991. *The Convention on the Regulation of Antarctic Mineral Resource Activities*. Berlin: Springer-Verlag.

Wood, A. 1989. "Avvakum's Siberian Exile." In: Wood, A. and R.A. French (eds), *The Development of Siberia: People and Resources*. London: Macmillan: 11–35.

—— 1993/94. "Siberian Regionalism Resurgent?" *Sibirica, the Journal of Siberian Studies* 1(1): 71–86.

Woolcott, R. 1984. "The Future of the Antarctic Treaty System." In: Alexander, L.M. and L.C. Carter (eds), *Antarctic Politics and Marine Resources: Critical Choices for the 1980s*. Kingston, Rhode Island: Center for Ocean Management Studies: 225–31.

World Commission on Environment and Development. 1987. *Our Common Future*. Oxford: Oxford University Press.

WWF Arctic Bulletin 1994a. "Dramatic Reduction of Norwegian Wilderness." (2): 12.

—— 1994b. "Circumpolar System of Protected Ecosystems." (1): 16.

Yablokov, A.V. 1993. "Facts and Problems Related to Radioactive Waste Disposal in Seas Adjacent to the Territory of the Russian Federation." (Materials for a Report by the Government Commission on Matters Related to Radioactive Waste Disposal at Sea, created by Decree No. 613 of the Russian Federation President, 24 October 1992.) Published by the Office of the President of the Russian Federation, Moscow.

Young, C. 1989. "Ecology and Conservation of the Polar Regions." *Ambio, A Journal of the Human Environment* XVIII(1): 23–33.

Young, O.R. 1987. "Arctic Shipping: An American Perspective." In: Griffiths, F. (ed.), *Politics of the Northwest Passage*. Kingston and Montreal: McGill–Queen's University Press: 115–33.

—— 1992. *Arctic Politics: Conflict and Co-operation in the Circumpolar North*. Hanover: University Press of New England.

References

—— and A.J. Cherkasov 1992. "International Co-operation in the Arctic: Opportunities and Constraints." In: Griffiths, F. (ed.), *Arctic Alternatives: Civility or Militarism in the Circumpolar North.* Toronto: Science for Peace/Samuel Stevens: 9–25.

Yukon Government 1995. *Yukon Economic Review and Short-term Outlook 1994/95.* Department of Economic Development, Economic Research and Analysis. Draft 2 – 28 February 1995.

Zaslow, M. 1971. *The Opening of the Canadian North 1870–1914.* Toronto/Montreal: McClelland and Stewart Limited.

—— 1988. *The Northward Expansion of Canada 1914–1967.* Toronto/Montreal: McClelland and Stewart Limited.

Zhuravlyov, V. 1993. "Diamonds of Yakutia." *Northern News* 1(48): 1–2.

Zorgdrager, N. 1984. "The Sami People: Their History and Identity." In: Nooter, G.W. (ed.), *Life and Survival in the Arctic: Cultural Changes in the Polar Regions.* The Hague: Government Publishing Office.

Zumberge, J.H. 1979. "Mineral Resources and Geopolitics of Antarctica." *American Scientist* 67(1): 68–77.

ZumBrunnen, C. 1990. "Resources." In: Rodgers, A. (ed.), *The Soviet Far East: Geographical Perspectives on Development.* London: Routledge: 83–113.

Index